Islamic Thought and Movement in the Subcontinent

Islamic Heritage in Cross-Cultural Perspectives

1. Gandhi's Responses to Islam; by Sheila McDonough (ISBN 81-246-0035-X)
2. Fawā'id al-Fu'ād — Spiritual and Literary Discourses of Shaikh Niẕāmuddīn Awliyā; Originally Compiled by Amīr Ḥasan 'Alā' Sijzī Dehlawī; English Translation with Introduction and Historical Annotation by Ziya-ul-Hasan-Faruqi (ISBN 81-246-0042-2)
3. Change and Continuity in Indian Sūfism — A Naqshbandi-Mujaddidī Branch in the Hindu Environment; Thomas Dahnhardt (HB: ISBN 81-246-0170-4) (PB: ISBN 81-246-0405-3)
5. Sūfic Thought of Shaikh 'Abdu'l Qādir Jilānī — And its Impact on the Indian Subcontinent; by Manzoor Ahmad Bhat (ISBN: 81-246-0450-9)

Islamic Heritage in Cross-cultural Perspectives, no. 4

Islamic Thought and Movement in the Subcontinent

A Study of Sayyid Abu A'lā Mawdudi
and
Sayyid Abul Hasan Ali Nadwi

Sheikh Jameil Ali

D.K. Printworld (P) Ltd.
New Delhi

Cataloguing in Publication Data — DK
[Courtesy: D.K. Agencies (P) Ltd. <docinfo@dkagencies.com>]

Ali, Jameil, *Sheikh,* 1968-
Islamic thought and movement in the subcontinent : a study on Sayyid Abu A'la Mawdudi and Sayyid Abul Hasan Ali Nadwi / Sheikh Jameil Ali.
p. cm. — (Islamic Heritage in Cross-cultural Perspectives ; no. 4)
Syed Abul A'la Maudoodi, 1903–1979, founder of Jamaat-e Islami, religio-political party of Pakistan and Abul Hasan Ali Nadwi, 1913–1999, Islamic scholar.
Includes bibliographical references (p.).
ISBN13: 9788124604915 (Hb)
ISBN10: 8124604916 (Hb)

1. Islamic renewal — South Asia. 2. Philosophy, Islamic South Asia. 3. Islam and state — South Asia. 4. Maudoodi, Syed Abul A'la, 1903-1979. 5. Nadwi, Abul Hasan Ali, 1913-1999. I. Title. II. Series: (Islamic Heritage in Cross-cultural Perspectives ; no. 4).

DDC 297.095 4 22

ISBN13: 978-81-246-0491-5 (Hb)
ISBN10: 81-246-0491-6 (Hb)
First published in India in 2010

Published and printed by:
D.K.Printworld (P) Ltd.
Regd. Office: 'Sri Kunj', F-52, Bali Nagar
Ramesh Nagar Metro Station
New Delhi-110 015
Phones: (011) 2545 3975; 2546 6019; *Fax*: (011) 2546 5926
E-mail: indology@dkprintworld.com
Website: www.dkprintworld.com

Preface

A great deal of historical literature has been produced on the Muslim period of the subcontinent both by local (Muslim and non-Muslim) scholars and Orientalists, concentrating mostly on the monarchs and their policies. Strangely enough, very meagre works have been written with regard to the contribution of Muslims to the cultural heritage of the subcontinent; rather, it has often been deliberately misrepresented. Similarly there has been scanty literature on the evolution and development of Islamic thoughts in the subcontinent. As a result of the peculiar situation in the subcontinent, where Muslims had to face challenges, Islamic thought developed on a particular pattern. Especially after the collapse of Muslim power in the subcontinent, Muslim scholars had to respond to many issues of varied nature, which the *Ummah* had not faced so far. These scholars adopted different approaches and methods to tackle the situation. However, their differences were of techniques and not of objectives. There was a common underlying goal to resuscitate Muslim society. Whatever methods they adopted, their endeavours contributed to the development of Islamic thought.

In the present work an attempt has been made to trace the contribution and influence of some of the important personalities, especially Sayyid Abu A'lā Mawdudi and Sayyid Abul Hasan Ali Nadwi, on the thought pattern of Muslim community and their response to the contemporary issues confronted by the Muslims in the subcontinent.

This book was actually written as a Ph.D. thesis for the faculty of Social Science, Shah-I-Hamadan Institute of Islamic Studies, University of Kashmir. In the first chapter attention is focused on the dynamism of the Islamic thought, its different manifestations and evolution throughout the early stages of development. The second chapter traces the inception, movement and development of Islamic thought, emphasizing the revivalist and reformist endeavours throughout its history in the subcontinent. The third chapter attempts at the study of Sayyid Abu A'lā Mawdudi's thought formation and his response to the issues facing Islamic Ummah in general and in the subcontinent in particular. The fourth chapter discusses the role of Sayyid Abu A'lā Mawdudi and his Jama'at-i-Islami in Pakistan. The fifth chapter studies Sayyid Abul Hassan Ali Nadwi's thought and his response to the challenges faced by Muslims in general and specifically in India. The sixth chapter discusses the role of Sayyid Abul Hassan Ali Nadwi in elevating the conditions of Muslims in India after partition. In the seventh chapter an attempt has been made to compare the paradigms of thought of these two leading Islamic personalities of the subcontinent.

A standardized system of translation has been employed for proper names and technical terms in the principal Islamic languages — Arabic, Persian and Urdu. Some anomalies have, however, been inevitable. Dates have normally been given according to both the Islamic (*hijiri*) and Christian eras. It has been my constant aim to treat this subject fairly and objectively and an attempt has been made to seek out the facts from original sources. Yet conscious as I am of the inadequate treatment that has been given to many subjects, I earnestly solicit the ciriticism of readers who are in a better position to correct the deficiencies, which only patient and scholarly investigation can remove.

Sheikh Jameil Ali

Contents

Acknowledgement

I WOULD like to express my deep gratitude to institutions and persons who have helped me. My greatest debt is to my supervisors Prof. Muhammad Ishaq Khan, Department of History and Prof. Hamidullah Marazi, Shah-i-Hamadam Institute of Islamic Studies, University of Kashmir, without whose guidance, help and encouragement the execution of this research project would have been impossible.

I owe an enormous debt of gratitude to Shah-i-Hamadan Institute of Islamic Studies, University of Kashmir under whose auspices this research was conducted; especially my grateful thanks are due to its Prof. Sayyid Muhammad Yunus Gilani, Prof. Naseem Ahmad Shah, Dr Abdur Rashid Bhat and Dr Manzoor Ahmad Bhat for many helpful suggestions, encouragement and kindness. I am also thankful to the non-teaching and ministerial staff of Shah-i-Hamadan Institute of Islamic Studies, for placing at my disposal its recently acquired collection of documents, books, and necessary help.

I also owe a great debt of gratitude to Mawlana Sayyid Muhammad Rabey Nadwi, then acting Rector of Darul Uloom Nadwatul Ulama Lucknow, for allowing me to stay and for providing necessary requirements at darul Ulum Lucknow, Nadwa, for about one week. I am also thankful to Mawlana Nazr-ul-Hafeez Nadwi, who on the recommendation of Mawlana Sayyid Abul Hasan ali Nadwi provided important information and guidance about the wirtings and views of

Mawlana Sayyid Abul Hasan Ali Nadwi, who himself was not in a position to answer questions because of sickness. My thanks are also due to Muhammad Gufran Nadwi of Academy of Islamic Research and Publications, Nadwatul Ulama Lucknow and staff of the Allama Shibli Nomani Library of Nadwatul Ulama for providing and placing at my disposal collection of documents, pamphlets and books on related topics.

I would like to thank the library incharge and staff of Mstkszi Maktaba Islami Publishers, Abu fazl Enclave, Jamia Nagar, New Delhi for the invaluable help in locating important research material on Mawlana Mawdudi.

I am greatly obliged to Mr Mir Jamsheed Hussain, Mr Ajaz Hussain and Mr Abid Gulzar for their painstaking and invaluable help in preparing this thesis. I would like to thank my several colleagues and friends — particularly Showkat Ahmad Shah, S. Nazir Ahmad, Dr. M. Sultan Shah and Mu'id-uZafar for their subtle encouragement. In addition to these many friends have helped me with valuable suggestions at various stages in the preparation of the manuscript; the full list would become too lengthy. I am under a deep obligation to all of them.

And, of course, I am most indebted to my parents, my sister, brother Sheikh Tahir and Amjad Hussain for encouragement and moral support. Thanks are also due to my wife and son Khafid. I thank them all and pray to the Almighty for bestowing His blessing upon them.

I would like to take this opportunity to thank the publisher D.K. Printworld (P) Ltd., especially Mr Susheel K. Mittal, for their patience and co-operation.

Sheikh Jameil Ali

Introduction

In the subcontinent, Islam from its inception has seen many vicissitudes and has always provided an abundant incentive for reformation. The message of Islam had reached the Indian subcontinent long before the forced incursions of Muslim armies started in the north of India. It was in the south of India that Arab traders after embracing Islam, continued their trade relations with the Western coast of India (Malabar), and thereby were the first Muslims to arrive with the message of Islam. Islam is essentially a missionary religion and every Muslim, whatever their calling in life, acted as *Dai*, "missionaries of their faith." It should not, therefore, surprise us that Islam was introduced and disseminated peacefully in the Malabar coasts by Arab merchants and traders soon after its advent in Arabia. The process of proselytization and Islamizing of the subcontinent by peaceful means, using soft power (moral suasion) was under way long before AH 93/CE 711 (Muhammad bin Qasim's conquest of Sind) and AH 603/CE 1206 (establishment of Delhi Sultanate). Nevertheless, in the wake of establishment of Muslim rule, first under Delhi Sultanate and then during Mughal rule, an impressive Muslim culture developed in the subcontinent, influencing every walk of life. Practically Muslims enjoyed dominance over the whole of the Indian peninsula, but whatever lasting success to implant Islam in the subcontinent was achieved, it was mostly the result of the patient missionary endeavours of selfless preachers of

Islam, who continued their individualistic missionary activity and moral suasion, before and after the establishment of Muslim rule and quite independently, uninterrupted and independent of the political life of the country.

After the establishment of Muslim rule in the subcontinent, an influx of *Ulama* and Sūfi saints entered this country; set-up mystic centres at a number of places. Within a short span of time the entire subcontinent from Multan to Lakhnuti (Bengal) and from Panipat to Deogir, Sūfi saints built their centres of *tabligh* and started preaching Islam and provided guidance to the Muslims. As a matter of fact, the Sūfis played an important role in the development and helped to spread the faith of Islam and won enormous mass following. Consequently, Islamic thought in the subcontinent developed predominantly on Sūfi pattern. Indeed it brought Islam to the masses and masses to Islam. However, due to imperfect conversion to Islam and through "liberal Sufism" Muslims in the subcontinent were enabled to absorb many religious beliefs and practices that were non-Islamic in origin but deeply rooted in the culture of the people who were converted to Islam. Thus there has been a protracted endeavour by *Ulamā* and *mashā'ikh* to preserve Islam in its pristine purity and to protect it assiduously from any encroachment of alien customs and beliefs.

Islam possessed a tradition of revival (*tajdid*) and reform (*islah*) down from its earliest day. They are fundamental components of Islam's world view, rooted in the Qur'an and the *Sunnah* of the prophet. Muslim had been quick to respond to what was regarded as the compromising of faith and practice. In succeeding centuries, a rich revivalist tradition expressed itself in a variety of concepts and beliefs, in the lives and teachings of individual reformers and in the activities of a host of movements. Medieval period of Islam produced a number of scholars and thinkers, who contributed to the development of Islamic thought considerably by using their *ijtihadi* capabilities. There were traditional scholars as well as the scholars who had philosophical bent of mind and both of these groups responded to the critical situations of their times. The prominent among them are Imam al-Ghazzali (1058-1111/450-505) and Ibn Taymiyyah (1263-1329/661-728) both throughout their tenure, did their utmost to rebutt the challenges confronting Muslim society and thought, thereby setting out models for future preachers of Islam.

In the subcontinent despite the vicissitudes of Muslim political power, Islam continued to sustain and reform itself. Undaunted by the local difficulties and changing circumstances the reformists *Ulama* as well as *masha'ikh* endeavoured to vivify Islamic thought from time to time to face the challenges. The role of Shaykh Abdul Haqq Muhaddith of Delhi, Shaykh Ahmad Sirhind, Shah Waliullah, Shah Abdul-Aziz, Sayyid Ahmad Shaheed and Shah Ismail Shaheed is unparalleled and significant in the development of Islamic thought in the subcontinent. It is because of their relentless perseverance of *Shari'ah* and efforts to dispel "ignorance," pristine Islam became firmly rooted in the succeeding generations and continued to resist the heretic and deviationist tendencies. They sought to sweep away the theological and legal incrustations of the intervening centuries that had covered the true faith. The movement initiated and programme of reformation delineated by these above-mentioned *mujtahidun* for the resuscitation of Islamic thought and the social and moral upliftment of Muslim society in the subcontinent was incessantly followed in later ages. At least they succeeded in kindling the flame that lighted the way of many who came after them and worked in different as well as difficult circumstances of their times for the preservation of religious beliefs and the ideological entity of the Muslim community, which was in constant danger of being overwhelmed by an environment that could be described as an anathema to their cherished ideals. Mawlana Sayyid Abul A'Lā Mawdudi (1903-79) and Mawlana Sayyid Abul Hasan Ali Nadwi (1914-99) are the continuation of this perpetual movement of revival and reformation of Muslim society there-by making Islam applicable to the changing circumstances. The Islamic paradigm was reinterpreted and reapplied by these scholars as it had been realized by revivalists and reformers in the past.

In the twentieth-century Muslim community on the whole and particularly in the Indian subcontinent was at a critical crossroads. For the first time, the Muslim *ummah* was confronted by a decidedly destructive enemy which threatened its entire civilization, and much of the Muslim world had lost its political and cultural sovereignty to the West. Western imperialism precipitated a religious as well as political crisis, with the help of a group of secularists who advocated the adaptation of Western culture, the separation of religion and politics, and the establishment of modern nation states modelled on the West. A variety of responses emerged from Muslim self-criticism and reflection on the cause of the decline. The actions spanned the spectrum, from withdrawal and rejection to adoption and cultural synthesis. Owing to different cultural and historical reasons, the tussle here in India between the East and the West had developed in such a manner that it could be tackled only in two ways: by opting out unequivocally for Islamic way of life on grounds of faith and conviction or by choosing, once and for all, the Western way of life on grounds of material progress and prosperity only. Most of the *Ulama* advocated total withdrawal, non-co-operation, or rejection of the West or any borrowing from this cutlure. This movement of *Ulama* after the debacle of 1857, finally culminated in the establishment of Darul Ulum Deoband (1866). The main objective in founding the *madrassa* at Deoband and other places was preservation and perpetuation of religion and culture. In their opinion religious consciousness, religious education and religious sentiments could help the Muslims to reconstruct the world according to their likings. There emerged another group of reform-minded Muslims who sought to respond rather than react against the influences of Western civilization. They proclaimed the need for Islamic reform and sought to delineate an alternative to the Western secular adaptations on the one hand and religiously motivated rejectionism on the other. They persuaded for internal reform through a process of reinterpretation (*ijtihad*) and selective adaptation of the Western philosophy, science, and technology. Islamic modernism, what it is called, is a process of internal self-criticisms. Thus they asserted to redefine Islam to demonstrate its relevance to the new situation. In the subcontinent two leading men Sir Sayyid Ahmad Khan (1817-98) and Allama Muhammad Iqbal (1875-1938) dominated the Islamic modernist movement during the nineteenth and early twentieth century. During the late twentieth century Mawlana Mawdudi as well as Mawlana Nadwi offered Islamic responses to the modern challenges and thereby contributed to the revitalization of Islamic thought in their own perspectives. Understanding the background and context of revival and reform, they, and their interpretation of Islam is essential for an appreciation of Islam's dynamism and diversity.

While acknowledging the internal weakness of the community and the external threat of Westernization, their holistic approach viewed Islam as a comprehensive guide for private as well as public life, a potent force in both the response to internal decline and the counterbalance to Westernization. They combined a holistic interpretation of Islam with its call for a social order based not on modernist acculturation but on a self-sufficient Islamic alternative. To both, Mawlana Mawdudi and Mawlana Nadwi, the plight of the Muslim community culturally and physically constituted the problematical paradox that had to be explained and redressed. Hence, the task of reformism consisted in sharpening the Muslims' consciousness of the dynamic characteristics of their faith, and its ability to halt the temporary state of decline. In order to achieve such an end, fatalistic beliefs and traditional practices were combated for their flagrant violation of true Islam.

However, Mawlana Mawdudi focused on a systematic presentation of Islam (presenting Islam as a system). He attempted to provide a theoretical blueprint of the revival of Islam, or what he termed as the process of Islamic revolution aimed at changing the system itself according to Islamic guidelines. He called upon Muslims to restore Islam's primacy in their personal as well as their political lives. In his revivalist version, the exclusive sovereignty of Allah and the decisive factor in performing the act of submission entails not the mere belief in Allah's existence; rather it is the admission of His exclusive authority in determining the moral, political and economic aspects of all societies. Convinced that Islam is a comprehensive way of life, he considered ideology the engine of other developments in society. Thus, his idea of the oneness of Allah and of His exclusive transcendental sovereignty is meant to reinstate Islam as a political system. He wrote extensively on the nature and character of an Islamic state and through the Jamaat-i-Islami worked to implement socially as well as politically the Islamic ideal.

Mawlana Nadwi, following the *Ulama* who decided to remain in India after Partition, espoused the traditional and "Sufistic" approach to religion. Adopting a more literary and rhetoric mode, he insisted upon moral and character-building through proper Islamic education and "**dawat**" and "**tabligh**." Emphasizing reformist endeavours, he remained influential in interpreting the Islamic message for both the common and the elite Muslims in India. He remained less inclined to the political concerns; however, issues like Muslim identity, safeguarding the Muslim personal law, patronage to traditional education *vis-à-vis* the modern education/national educational policies of Indian administration were seriously touched upon by him in his writings besides exploring the various themes of *sirah* of Prophet Muhammad (SAAW) and the early Muslim history in new perspectives. His views on the Muslim identity, education and religious harmony and tolerance, and minority affairs are of great significance, and his writings and endeavours deal with such issues extensively.

Moreover, despite distinctive differences in their blueprints for society Mawlana Mawdudi and Mawlana Nadwi reflect the belief that rectification of the plight of modern Islam requires the recognition and reappropriation of Islam as a total way of life. They were similar in their desire to respond to internal decline and external encroachment both having common themes but a diversity of interpretations. While there is a unity in Islamic belief, there is also a variety of understanding both as to its implications and its implementation.

Existing Studies

There are good number of works on these personalities by famous scholars of the East as well as the West, who have discussed different aspects of their thought especially that of: Mawlana Mawdudi. Some important works are that of:

Charles J. Adams, *Mawlana and the Islamic State*, and *The Ideology of Mawlana Mawdudi*; Leonard Bider *Religion and Politics in Pakistan*. G.E. Von Crunebaum and Aziz Ahmad, "Abul A'Lā Mawdudi" in *Muslim Self Statement in India and Pakistan 1857-1968*; Aziz Ahmad, "Mawdudi: Orthodox Fundamentalism" in *Islamic Modernism in India and Pakistan 1857-1964*; Masudul Hasan, *Sayyid Abul A'Lā Mawdudi and His Thought*; Syed Asad Gilani, *Mawdudi Thought and Movement*; Sayed Riaz Ahmad, *Mawlana Mawdudi and the Islamic State*; Khurshid Ahmad and Zafar Ishaq Ansari's works on Mawdudi. Sayyid Vali Riza Nasr's more recent work, *The Vanguard of the Islamic Revolution: The Jamaat-i-Islami of Pakistan and Mawdudi and Making of Islamic Revivalism*. And also many works on Mawdudi in Urdu language. There are some works in Urdu on Mawlana Abul Hasan Ali Nadwi by Bilal Abdul Hai Hasni Nadwi, Muhammad Asjid Qasim Nadwi. Khwaja Iqbal A. Nadwi and Ibn Junaid Qasmi. All these scholars have discussed them separately. In contrast to the works of these scholars ours is an attempt to discuss the key points of their thought and to compare these two paradigms.

Herein, both the Islamic personalities of Indo-Pak subcontinent have been studied separately and in comparison to each other, with respect to different trends in their thought.

The first chapter, "Islamic Thought: A General Survey," deals with the basic sources of Islamic thought and its evolution and development throughout the early stages as well as throws light on the early reformative endeavours. The second chapter is a glance at the inception of Islamic thought, its movement and development in the subcontinent, emphasizing revivalist and reformist endeavours throughout its history in the subcontinent. The third and fourth chapters study Mawlana Mawdudi's thought formation and his response to the issues facing Islamic *ummah* in general and finally in Pakistan in particular. The fifth and sixth chapters study Mawlana Nadwi's thought and his response to the challenges faced by Muslims in India. The seventh chapter attempts at comparing the two paradigms of Islamic thought.

Since the study is basically a library work, following the historical methodology all related data on the subject has been consulted, including all the major works of both the outstanding thinkers of the modern Indo-Pak subcontinent. Besides, some interviews were also held which, though not reported in the study as such, have definitely helped to explore various dimensions and trends and their contemporary impact as well as in confirming some conclusions.

1

Islamic Thought
A General Survey

THOUGHT generally is the action or process of thinking, reflection, meditation, cogitation, mental action or activity, exercise of the mental faculty, power of reasoning or of conceiving ideas, formation and arrangement of ideas in the mind. As a function or attribute of a living being, thinking has a permanent characteristic or condition, the capacity of thinking; the product of mental action or effort, what one thinks, what is in the mind (sometimes as expressed in language); in a collective sense, the intellectual activity or mental product, or mode of thinking characteristics of the thinkers of a particular class or place, what is or has been thought by the philosopher or learned men of some specified country, etc.

As far as the Islamic thought is concerned, it is a general term and interpretations of it differ. However, in simple terms it is the combination of revelation and reason, or the role of the mind in appreciating, comprehending and interpreting revelation and guiding the mind by means of the revelations, objectives, its comprehensive and universal outlook and its living and civilizational values.

Qur'an (Divine Revelation) and its explication, elaboration, expansion and application by Prophet Muhammad (SAAS) termed as *sunnah,* forms the firm foundation, over which the whole edifice of Islamic thought developed. Allah's bestowed intellectual faculties, what Qur'an would name the mechanism of *sama'-basar-fuād*[1] (abilities to listen, to see and to think), played an important role in the development of all the human thoughts as well as Islamic thought. One can also say that Islamic thought emerges when *sama'-basar-fuād* is used to understand and interpret the Divine Revelation. In the very first stage and in a very special way, Prophet (SAW) used these faculties to understand and interpret Divine text, himself of course under Divine supervision and with Divine help, so that the Prophet's thought and action produced a model for coming generations. It is only in the *sunnah* of the Prophet, first and foremost authentic study, that the Qur'an finds its only infallible concretization.[2] Being the personification of the Qur'an he is the living image of how the Qur'an should be applied in everyday life. Therefore, Qur'an is the text to be studied. *Sama'-basar-fuād* is the instrument through which this study is conducted. And the *sunnah* is the Qur'an's first and most authentic study — one that is singularly free from error.

---

1. *Al-Qur'an*, 16: 78, 23: 78, 32: 9, 46: 25, 67: 23. As in *surah al-Nahl* 16, *Ayat* 78, "Allah brought you out of your mother's womb devoid of all knowledge, and gave you ears and eyes and hearts, so that you may give thanks." It is through these faculties we enhance our knowledge and understanding of things, through *sama* or hearing, in which case it is communicated to us from there. In case of *basar* "seeing" understanding or knowledge is gained through direct observations. *Fuād* or heart which includes the capacity to think and to intuit, reflecting, analysing, contemplating, reasoning and such other mental acts should also be attributed to *Fuad*. Thus are regarded as among the primary sources of thought and knowledge.
2. Irfan Ahmad Khan, "Authenticity and Development of Islamic Thought," *International Journal of Islamic and Arabic Studies* 4(2), 1987, pp. 31-32 and 42.

After Prophet, the *ummah*, which keeps this model before itself, continues the task of reading the Book and applying it to emerging situations. The best example of its spirit and its creative application is to be found during the times of the *khulafa*, a time when revelation (*wahy*) and *sunnah* of Prophet was taken as the source of guidance and direction, and when reason and *ijtihad* were used both as tools for understanding and interpreting revelation, as well as for dealing with events and developing responses and making policies.

Later generations also continued to adopt themselves to the changing environment by assimilating the growth of learning and incorporating that form of reasoning which was suited to the times and circumstances, with the result Islamic thought manifested itself through different offshoots, i.e. the science of jurisprudence, scholarism, rationalism, spiritual and other forms in response to the needs of time. The methodology of Islamic thought as we know it today is represented by the science of *usūl-al-fiqh* (jurisprudence source methodology). This science represents the most important component of the methodology used in the classical Islamic disciplines. It is represented in its general principles and axioms by the rational foundation and basic precepts of the Islamic mind. In early days of Islam, the broad principles and universaling of this methodology reflected the nature of Islamic thought and its correlation to the religion and mission of Islam. However, *usūl-al-fiqh*, as a discipline, was developed by scholars of the successor generations (*tābi'īn*) that came after the age of al *khulafā' al rāshidin*. Even in the age of *ijtihad* that followed *al khulafā al rāshidin*, when the first schism occurred between the *ummah*'s political and intellectual leadership, Muslim thinkers and scholars were still in close touch with the spirit of the message and method of the earliest age of Islam. As a result, they wrote and thought on the basis of the early methodology.

These brilliant scholars over the centuries performed *ijtihad* despite the long stagnation of the institution itself. Their brilliance can surely be traced to their exposure to political and social life, which enabled them to excel in the contemporary sciences, to understand the situation of the *ummah* as a whole, and to look objectively at problems as opposed to dealing with them from purely theoretical or lexical perspective. This progressive movement was mainly possible by the dynamic element of Islamic thought known as *ijtihad*. In spite of the fact the Qur'an and the *Hadith* remain unchanged, *ijtihad* proceeds to address the new situations and changing circumstances according to the teaching of the Qur'an and the *Sunnah* and to adopt its primacy, *ijtihad* played a vital role.

Summun bonum and the first source of Islam are the Qur'an and the *Sunnah*. The reflective and interpretive endeavour of man *vis-à-vis* these sources can ordinarily be described as Islamic thought. The basic principles upon which the historical science and methodology of Islamic thought (*usul al fiqh*) are based may be classified into two types — primary and secondary. The primary foundations are composed essentially of studies related to the Qur'an, the *sunnah ijma'* (the consensus of the learned), and *qiyas* (analogy). The secondary foundations consist of studies dealing with those sources of evidence on which the scholars differed as to how and under what conditions they are to be applied (*al adillah al mukhtalif fiha*), sources of which are used in the main as the basis for the process of the *ijtihad*. Among the most important of these secondary sources are: *istihasan* (the more reasonable analogy), *al masālih al musalah* (the obstruction of ostensibly legitimate means to illegitimate ends), *'Uruf* (custom and legal usage), the sayings of *sahabah*, and the practices of the people of Medina.

Qur'an

The book of Allah (*kitab al Allah*). Literal word of Allah (*Kalām-ul-Allāh*), divine message, revealed through Gabriel to Prophet Muhammad (SAAW) who communicated it to mankind.[3] "In being a guide to mankind admonishing the unjust and giving glad tidings to the righteous."[4] Qur'an the sacred book of Muslims, is a book of wisdom[5] and original source from which all the principles and ordinances of Islam are drawn. It is actually the real foundation on which the whole superstructure of Islamic thought rests, thus being the absolute and final authority in any discussion encompassing Islam. The fountain to which Muslims return and continue to refresh spiritual vision. From the historical angle, no doubt, it is to be regarded as the source from which all systems of subsequent Islamic ethics and theology were drawn.[6] Thus the Qur'an as the collection of the divine revelations, is a constitution of Muslims, dealing with every subject of human life directly and indirectly, such as social, ethical, philosophical, political, economical, etc. Qur'an states with clarity that sovereignty and authority is vested in God alone.[7] The Qur'an is composed of the following Islamic fundamentals which together form an interlocking whole: a primary system of belief in the unity of God, Prophet-hood and the Day of Reckoning, accompanied by a second

---

3. *Al-Qur'an*, (*al-Shuara*), pp. 192-95.
4. *Al-Qur'an*, Ibrahim (14)-I, "al-Maida" (5), 49, Al-Furqan (25) 1-2 al-Anam (6)-19, Al-Baqarah (2), 185, Al-Zumar (39), 27; Al-Isra (17), 9; Al-Ahqaf (46), 12.
5. Yunus (10), 1.
6. Hamilton A.R. Gibb, "Structure of Religius Thought in Islam," in *Studies on the Civilization of Islam*, Standford J. Shaw and William R. Polk, eds., Lahore, Islamic Book Service, 1987, p. 169.
7. *Al-Qur'an*, 'al, An'am (6), 57, Yusuf, (12), 40.

group of beliefs, namely, belief in tablet, the pen (which delineates the sequence of cosmic events), the rule of destiny and the decree (without implying pre-destination), the angles, the throne of the Creator and finally in the creation of the sky, the earth and everything between them.[8] The book of Allah is like an ocean. The less earned, like children, collect pebbles and shells from its shores. The scholars and thinkers, like pearl divers, bring out from it the highest philosophy, wisdom and rules of perfect way of living. Thus the Qur'an and its teachings are comprehensive, having wide range of meaning still to be explored. There are certain sciences related to Qur'an known as Qur'anic sciences, they are *qiraat-ul-Qur'ān* and science of *tafsir*. The *qirat-ul Qur'an* recitation of Qur'an or the (*tajwid*) chanting or cantillation of Qur'an that is the reading of Qur'an with proper pronunciation of words and reciting it clearly, which has been stressed by Qur'an itself.[9] This has developed into an art bound by precise rule and together with the memorization of the entire Qur'an (*hifz*), brings great prestige as well as merit. The knowledge or science of *tafsir* is the interpretation and commentaries on Qur'an, to make it easily understandable intended for teaching purposes. Qur'an has itself laid the rule of interpretation.[10] The interpretation

---

8. Allama Sayyid M.H. Tabataba'i, The *Qur'an in Islam*, 1987, 22.
9. *Al-Qur'an, 'al-Muzzamil'* (73), 4.
10. *Al-Qur'an*, "it is He Who has revealed the book to thee; some of its verses are decisive, they are the basis of Book and others are allegorical. Then those in whose hearts is perversity follow the part of it which is allegorical, seeking to mislead, and seeking to give it their own interpretation. And none knows its interpretation except Allah, and those firmly rooted in knowledge. They say, we believe in it. It is all from our lord. And none does mind except men of understanding", 3, 6.

of Qur'anic verses sought from within the Qur'an[11] and the exegesis and meaning given by Prophet Muhammad (SAAS)[12] to his companions. Then the companions (*sahabah*) and who followed them, tried to interpret and explain accordingly, known as *Al-tafsir bil māthūr* [exegesis *of Al-Qur'an* by means of tradition received from the prophet (SAAS) and his companions]. It was not until second and third centuries of *Al-Hijra* that there developed organized discipline of commentaries *(tafasir*) on it.[13] Later *tafasir*, interpretations and commentaries *Al-Tafsir bil-rai* (exegesis of *Al-Qur'an* by means of free exercise of mind), were written in every age in order to meet necessities of growing civilization with the expansion of Islamic world, and the consequent widening of the outlook of Islam. Hence whatever may be the differences of interpretation, the fundamentals of religion are not affected at all.

Sunnah

Sunnah and *Hadith* [practice and the sayings of prophet Muhammad (SAAS)] is the Second source of Islamic thought.[14] In fact, Prophet's life was fundamental and practical of Qur'an,

11. Explanation of one Qur'anic passage can be drawn from another passage of *Qur'an*, "that there is no disagreement between the various portions of the Book" *al-Qur'an*, 4, 82 and never should a passage be interpreted in such a manner that it may be at variance with another passage, but more especially with the basic principles laid down in the decisive verses.

12. *Al-Qur'an, al-Nahl*-44.

13. Louis Gardet, "Religion and Culture" in *Cambridge History of Islam*, ed. P.M. Holt, A.H.S. Lambton and Bernard lewis, Cambridge, Cambridge University Press 1970, vol. 2B, p. 574.

14. *Sunnah* literally means a way or rule or manner of acting or mode of life, and *Hadith*, a saying conveyed to man either through hearing or through revelation. In its original sense, *sunnah* indicates the doings and *Hadith*, the sayings of the prophet; but in →

Quranic principles and values were concretized and interpreted by the *Sunnah* of the Prophet, the normative model behaviour of Muhammad (SAAS). As Qur'an says "And we revealed to you [Muhammad (SAAS)] the reminder (Qur'an) so that you may make clear to men what has been revealed to them, and that they may give thoughts" (*Al-Nahl* 44). There are other Qur'anic verses which refer to the importance of the *Sunnah* as "obey God and obey the messenger. If you should quarrel over anything refer it to God and the messenger" [4: 59] and "In God's messenger you have a fine model for one whose hope is in God and the Last Day of Resurrection" [33: 21].[15] Thus the *Sunnah* or Tradition is *sine qua non* of Islam. During the lifetime of Prophet Muhammad (SAAS) and *sahabah* (companions), the sayings of the prophet were not generally written, and memory was the chief means of their preservation.[16] Whatever the companions of the Prophet (SAAS) saw or heard from Him, they preserved the same with utmost care and transmitted it to the succeeding generations. However, during the first century *Hijra* and a half, the process of *Hadith* gathering and recording was still developing. It was not until second century that formal and organized collection of *Hadith* began to be compiled and the study of *Hadith* emerged as an organized discipline and later, a comprehensive science of *Hadith* got developed.

→ real sense both cover the same ground and are applicable to his actions, practices and sayings. *Hadith* being the narration and record of *Sunnah* but containing in addition, various prophetical and historical elements. There are three kinds of *sunnah*. Saying of the prophet (*qaul*) an action or a practice of his (*fi'al*) or his silent approval of the action or a practice of another, *taqrir*.

15. Also see the Qur'anic verses *al-Nisa*, 65 and 80.

16. Raghib *al-Tabagh*, *Tarikh Afkar* wa *Aloomi-Islami* Urdu trans. by Iftikhar Ahmad Balkhi. Markazi Maktaba Islami, Delhi, 1983, pp. 411-14.

The sciences concerned with prophetic traditions (*Hadith*) are numerous and varied.[17] These are: *Riwāyah al Hadith* [The reporting of words, deeds, description, attitudes of the Prophet Muhammad (SAAS)]; *Dirāyah al-Hadith* [the studies pertaining to the validity of the reporting and of what is reported about the prophet (SAAS)]; *Rijāl al-Hadith* (a science which studies the reporters of *Hadith* insofar as they are reporters); *Al-Jarh wal Ta'dil* (a science which seeks to investigate the reporters of *Hadith* in order to establish their trustworthiness or untrustworthiness); *'Ilal al-Hadith* (a science which studies the qualities or circumstances which may vitiate a *Hadith); Mukhtalaf al-Hadith* science which studies the apparent discrepancies between the varying *ahadith* with a view to reconciling them); *Nāsikh al-Hadith wa Mansūkhuhu* (a science which studies those *ahadith,* whose contents have revoked the meanings of other *ahadith,* or were revoked by them);[18] *Mustalah al-Hadith,* a science which studies the methodology of *Hadith* criticism, and the compilation of authoritative compendia. *Asm'aur-rijal*[19] scholars by using these tools of science of *Hadith,* travelled throughout the muslim world, collected and compiled the traditions. Among the writings of

---

17. For detailed story Ibn Khaldun, the Muqaddimah, New York, 1958, trans. by Franz Rosenthal, vol. II, pp. 447, 57, Passim.

18. When two traditions are mutually exclusive, and it is difficult to reconcile between them. In such a case if it is known that one is earlier than the other, it is definite that the later abrogates it, Ibn Kaldun, *The Muqaddimah*, p. 448.

19. The evaluation of tradition focussed on the chain (*isnād*) of narrators and the subject matter, *matn*. Criteria were established for judging the trustworthiness of narrators, moral character, reputation for piety, intelligence and good memory. Then a link (*Sanad*) by link examination of each of the narrator was conducted to trace the continuity of a tradition back to the Prophet. The process required detailed biographical information about →

other scholars *Muwatta* of Imām Malik was most important book on traditions in the middle of second century, and the *Musnad* of Imam Ahmad ibn Hanbal (AH 164-241). Then the six reliable collections (*Sahāh Sittah*) in particular came to be accepted as authoritative: Those of Ismail al-Bukhari (d.870), Muslim *Ibn al-Hajjaj* (d.875), Abu Dawud (d.888), al-Nisai (d.915), al-Tirmidhi (d.892), and Ibn Maja (d.896). However, the collections (*sahih*) of al-Bukhari and Muslim have enjoyed an especially high status as authoritative sources.[20]

The object of these traditionists (*muhaddithūn*) in addition to edification of Religious Sciences was to expound and elucidate the teachings of Qur'an and *Sunnah*.[21] In order to solve the new exigencies, arising out of expansion of Islamic state and coming in contact with people of different lands, in

---

→ narrators — where and when they were born, where they lived and travelled, and so forth. Such information might support or refute the authenticity of a narrator. The second criterion is evaluation of the traditions, subject matter, entailed an examination to determine whether, for example, a tradition contradicted the *Qur'an*, an already verified tradition or reason, After tradition have been subjected to both external (narrators) and internal, subject matters examination, they were categorized according to the degree of their authenticity or strength as sound *(Sahih)* good or acceptable (*hasan*) weak (*daif*) and spurious in content or *sanad, mawdu*.

20. The Shia recognizes the following collections of *Hadith*, 1. The *kafi* by Abu Jafar Muhammad ibn Yaqub, AH 329, 2, *Manlaysastihdziru-hu-l Fiqh* by Sheikh Ali, AH 381, 3. The *Tahdihb* by Sheikh Abu Jafar Muhammad ibn Ali ibn Husain (AH 466); the Istibsar by the same author.

21. The true understanding of the *Qur'an* can only be made through *Sunnah*. The *Sunnah* was a major source of legislation as the details of the law were only hinted at or sometimes not explicitly mentioned in *Qur'an* and thus these constituted the only means of regulating the rules of conduct and safeguarding the Islamic character of the Muslim society.

accordance with *shari'ah,* in addition to *Sunnah* of the Prophet (SAAS) the Sunnis believe that the practice of the caliphs and the Shiite believe that those of imāms are just as valid as those of Muhammad (SAAS) himself and are regarded as *Sunnah.*[22]

During the lifetime of the Prophet Muhammad (SAW) religious guidance came through the revelation and its explanation (in the source of *Hadith*). Whenever people face any problem, they inquired about that from the prophet — the Prophet's answer to that, resolved the issue — the generation of the prophet was the generation of action then thought and reflection. It was however, after the departure of the prophet that the *sahabah* had to reflect on the issue faced by them in one way or the other. Moreover the issues emerged under the new circumstances on which the texts — The Qur'an and the *Sunnah* was silent and the *sahabah* had to resolve it by giving their own thought to it. Thus after Qur'an and *Sunnah* comes the *ijma* "consensus of the companions" and *qiyas* "Analogical Reasoning" as third and fourth source of Islamic thought.

Ijma (Consensus of Opinion)

According to Iqbal the most important legal notion in Islam,[23] the authority for consensus is derived from a saying of prophet, "My community will never agree on an error." Furthermore *ijma* has not been restricted to the companions of prophet and that of the Muslim jurists of a particular age, but the consensus of Muslim community and jurists (including *imām* according to Shiites) of any age. But the *ijma* of the companions of the prophet cannot be reversed by any later generation. They are

22. A. Ezzati, *The Revolutionary Islam and the Islamic Revolution*, Tehran, Ministry of Islamic Guidance, 1981, p. 21.
23. S.M. Iqbal, *Reconstruction of Religious Thought in Islam*, Delhi, p. 173.

AlIjmā'Al-Sarih. They clearly expressed consensus and *Al Ijmā 'Al Sukūtī,* the consensus established by the jurists not objecting to the derivation of a certain perescriptions from a given source. [24]

Al Qiyās

The fourth source *qiyas* "analogy" (logical deduction from Al-Qur'an and the Sunnah as source of Islamic law) has almost universal sanction and *aql* (human reason) according to Shiite school. It has been applied by *sahabah,*[25] thus when faced with new situations or problems they sought a similar situation in Qur'an and *Sunnah.* By dint of it explicit provision of Qur'an or *Sunnah* could be enlarged by argument extending the "intention" of the directive to parallel situations which it could be arguably understood to include, though failing specifically to state them.[26] *Qiyas* can be understood here as a mental activity bringing together or separating two terms, such as to like or to dislike, greater to less, less to greater. Thus there are four basic sources, Qur'an, *Sunnah, ijma* and *qiyas,* and by their interaction not only the whole structure of doctrine has been built-up but also the structure of the socio-religious institution and the religious thought itself.[27]

---

24. Abd al-Aziz al-Bukhari, *Kashf al-Asrar,* III, p. 262.

25. The Caliph Umars (RAA), instruction to his judges, "use your intelligence in matter that perplexes you, to which neither law nor practice seems to apply. Study the theory of analogy, then compare things and adopt the judgement, which is most pleasing to God and most in comformity with justice so far as you can see, *Journal of Royal Asiatic Society,* London for 191, p. 311. Sqq, cited in Tyabji, *Muhammadan Law,* 3rd edn., pp. 83-84.

26. Kenneth Cragg, *Counsels in Contemporary Islam,* Edinburg, University Press 1967, p. 73.

27. H.A. R. Gibb, *Modern Trends in Islam,* New York, Octagon Books, 1978, p. 12.

Ijtihad

The process of resolving the issues of diverse nature where no clear, explicit, revealed text or general consensus existed within the administrative affairs itself and outside it, i.e. on individual level was carried on extensively in the subsequent times by the successors of the *sahabah* and, the *imām* of the community, caliphs, judges, and finally jurists or legal scholars. The tool used is known as *ijtihad* (creative self-exertion to derive laws from the legitimate sources). The word literally means to exert, to strive or struggle intellectually. It comes from same root as *jihād* (literally to exert one's utmost to promote a cause, i.e. to strive or struggle in God's path), According to Alama Iqbal is "the principle of movement in the structure of Islam." As he writes, "In the terminology of Islamic law it means to exert with a view to forming an independent judgement on a legal question. The idea, I believe, has its origin in a well-known verse of the Qur'an — 'and to those who exert we show our path'."[28] The exercise of *ijtihad* was sanctioned by Prophet Muhammad (SAAS) in a tradition which is regarded as the basis of *ijtihad* in Islam. "On being appointed Governor of Yaman, *Mu'ādh* was asked by the Prophet as to the rule by which he would abide. He replied, by the law of Qur'an, but if you do not find any direction therein, asked the Prophet. Then I will act according to the practice (*Sunnah*) of the Prophet, was the reply. But if you don't find any direction therein, he was again asked. Then I will exercise my judgement (*ajtahidu*) and act on that; came the reply. The Prophet raised his hands and said: Praise be to Allah who guides the messenger of His Apostle as He

28. S.M. Iqbal, *Reconstruction of Religious Thought in Islam*, Delhi, New Taj Office, p. 148.

pleases."[29] *Ijtihad* is a formation of *ijma* and *qiyas. Ijma,* after all is only *ijtihad* on a wider basis, as we can say, it is the *ijtihad* (reasoning or exercise of judgement) of many, whether it may be of companions or later jurists. *Qiyas* (analogical reasoning) reasoning by analogy was a more restricted, systematic form of *ijtihad* which according to Shafia is only another name of *ijtihad* which, within the limits of the revealed texts is absolutely free.[30] In fact, the sphere of *ijtihad* is a very wide one, and has played a vital role in the history of development of Islamic thought, as a continuous movement of causes and effects. It has given the opportunity to utilize the potential as the viceregents of Allah and to fulfil responsibility as the servants of God, under the inspiration of Qur'an and the *Sunnah* which is to exert or strive to discover the true application of the teachings of Qur'an and the *Sunnah* to a particular situation, and it may not go against the plain sense of these teachings.

Early Major Trends in Muslim Thought

It is actually from Ummayyad period, when corrupt leadership affected integrity and solidity of Muslim community perniciously. A crisis on both intellectual and social level set in during this period and expanded on a large scale during the Abbasid rule. It was imperative, truly, at this juncture of Islamic history, to collect, systematize and make analogical deductions in consonance with the teachings of the Qur'an and the *Sunnah,* to answer all possible questions of a sacred or secular nature and to establish the principle that law, custom, and belief should rest upon the practice of the Prophet and

---

29. Abu Dawud-Sunnah, *Sunnah of Abu Dawud*, 23, 11.
30. Cited in M. Iqbal, *Reconstruction of Religious Thought in Islam*, p. 177.

his companions and followers. "And this is why *ijtihad* or analogical deduction of legal opinions under the inspiration of Qur'an and the *Sunnah* had become unavoidable to meet the new situations and necessities of the then expanding Islamic community."[31] *Fuqaha* (jurists) are of great importance for their intellectual endeavours to resolve the disintegrating process of Muslim society, by making use of *ijtihad* on a larger scale, "the endeavours of the jurists supplied a framework for manifestation of the Islamic ideals of ethical percepts in day-to-day affairs of the people and protected them from intellectual confusion and social anarchy, which has brought many nations to rack and ruin in their initial stages. The jurists founded the Islamic legal system on a firm ground and formulated its canons in such a way that it could always solve new problems confronting the *ummah* in future and provided a pattern of behaviour in consonance with the sprit of Islam."[32]

Fiqh literally means knowledge, intelligence and the true understanding of what is intended. The Qur'an uses this word as denoting the knowledge of religion in its general sense.[33] An example of this usage can be found in the Prophet Muhammad's (SAAS) statement: To whomsoever Allah wishes good, he gives the *fiqh* (true understanding) of the Religion.[34] Accordingly *tafaqquh* (lit. understanding) means the correct

---

31. Abul Hassan Ali Nawdi, *Saviours of Islamic Spirit*, Lucknow, India Islamic Research and Publication, p. 57.

32. Ibid., p. 66.

33. *Al-Qur'an, al-Tawbah*, 122.

34. Al-Bukharee, *Sahih Al-Bukhari*, Arabic — English, vol. 4, pp. 223-24, no. 346. Muslim, Abdul Hamid Siddiqi, *Shahi Muslim* (English trans), Beirut Dar al-Arabia, n.d, vol. 3, p. 1061, no. 4720, *al-Trimidhee* and others.

understanding of Islamic thought.[35] Technically, however, *fiqh* refers to the science of deducing Islamic laws from evidence found in the sources of Islamic law. By extension it also means the body of Islamic laws so deduced.

Fiqh developed through many stages in the Islamic history. The first stage of foundation of the development of *fiqh* covers the era of the Prophet's apostleship (CE 609-32) during which the only source of Islamic law was divine revelation in the form of either the Qur'an or the *Sunnah* [the sayings and action of the Prophet (SAAS)]. The Qur'an represented the blueprint for the Islamic way of life, and the prophet's application of the blueprint in his day-to-day life (i.e. the *sunnah*) acted as a detailed explanation of the general Principles outlined in the Qur'an as well as practical demonstration of their application[36] and it was during this period that the foundation for the science of deducing law from the Qur'an and the *Sunnah* were laid by the Prophet (SAAS). It might be said that in this period the first *madhab* (school of legal thought) took shape as the Prophet guided and trained the *sahabah* (companions) in *ijtihad*, thus this period marked the beginning of the evolution of *fiqh*. After Prophet's demise, the era of Righteous caliphs and major *sahabah* [companions of Prophet (SAAS)] extending from the Caliph Abu Bakr (632-34) to the death of the fourth Caliph Ali (CE 661) presents the stage of establishment of *fiqh*. During this period Islamic borders expanded rapidly and the contact with totally new systems, cultures and patterns of behaviour

35. Imam Ali said to his son Muhammad ibn al-Hanafiyyah: Become learned in religion for verily the *fuqaha* are heirs of Prophets. Bihar *al- anwar*, vol. 1, p. 216.

36. Muhammad Mustafa Shalabee. *Al-Madkhal fee' al-Ta'reef bil-fiqh al-Islamee*, Beirut Lebanon, Daar an-Nahdah al-Arabeeyah, 1969, pp. 50. Cited in Abu Ameenah Bilal Philips, the evolution of *Fiqh*, Tawheed Publications Riyad, 1990, p. 5.

for which specific provision was not to be found in the laws of *Shari'ah*. To deal with the numerous new problems, the righteous caliphs relied heavily on decisions by consensus (*ijma*) as well as *ijtihad* in which they had been trained by Prophet (SAAS) while they were with him after his migration to Medina. In the course of their extensive use of *ijma* and *qiyas* (*ijtihad*) these caliphs established procedures, which later became the basis for legislation in Islam. The outstanding characteristic of *fiqh* during the period of Righteous caliphs was its realism; this realistic form of *fiqh* was later referred to in Arabic as *al-Fiqh al-Waqiee* (realistic *fiqh*).[37]

In addition to formal meetings of the major *sahabah*, which were called by the caliph for decision-making, there arose many day-to-day situations where individual *sahbah* were asked to make rulings. In general, *sahabah* also followed decision-making procedures, which helped them to avoid hard and fast rulings. Although the *sahabah* debated and differed on various points of law, their differences rarely reached the level of disunity and factionalism, which characterized the later periods. Reliance on mutual consultation (*Shura*) and the combined approval of the Righteous caliphs and the *sahabah* in the matter of legal rulings tended to promote unity and to provide little or no occasion for factionalism within the Islamic nation. However, only one *madhab* existed during the period of the Righteous Caliphs. Although there were some differences of approach among the *sahabah* in the matter of the use of personal opinion in making legal rulings, the majority of the *sahabah* preferred to stick closely to the literal meanings of texts of the Qur'an and the *Sunnah*. As a general practice,

---

37. Abu Ameenah Bilal Philips *The Evaluation of Fiqh*, Tawheed Publication, Riyadh 1990, p. 41.

they avoided giving personal interpretations. Abdullah ibn Umar, one of the leading jurists among the *sahabah* who remained in *Medina* all his life, followed this practice. On the other hand, there were other *sahabah* who favoured the wide use of personal opinion in areas undefined by either the Qur'an or the *Sunnah*. Abdullah ibn Masud (who later settled in Iraq) represented this school of thought. However, the different practices of such *sahabah* as ibn Umar in Medina relying upon the literal meaning of Qur'an and *Sunnah* only and Abdullah ibn Masud in Kufah (Iraq) making the use of personal opinion also, could be seen as the beginning or the foreshadowing of a division among Islamic scholars into different *madhabs*.

Ummayyad period[38] covers the third significant stage of building in the history of *fiqh* and evolution of *madhabs*. During this period, there was a notable increase in the number of individual *ijtihads* by scholars; since *ijma*[39] became more and more difficult, following the dispersal of scholars to outlying areas of the caliphate, as they attempted to deal with the multiplicity of new customs and problems in their own areas, independent of caliph. Whenever an outstanding scholar of *fiqh* arose in an area, the students and scholars in that region would gather round him. Often even students and scholars from other regions would join them and in that way a number of schools of Islamic thought (*madhab*) evolved. During this

---

38. This period extending from the demise of the last of the Righteous caliphs (Alee ibn Abi Taalib) in 661 A.B., and the ascendancy of the founder of the Ummayyad dynasty, Amir Mu'aawiyah ibn Abei Sufyaan, until the last of the Ummayyad caliphs around the middle of the eight century CE. The period marked social unrest, dissension, converion of caliphate into kingship.

39. *Ijma* of consultative government were lost due to the scholars avoidance of the degenerated Ummayyad court.

stage Abu Haneefah and Sufyaan ath-thawree became prominent in Kufah, Maalik ibn Anas in Medina, al Awzaaee in Beirut and Al-layth ibn Sa'd, in Egypt, to mention a few.

It was during this period the scholars of *fiqh* followed two main trends in making their rulings. The first group avoided making legal rulings on an issue if not clearly defined in texts from *Hadith* or the Qur'an. Because of their position, the scholars of this school of thought were called *Ahl al-Hadith* (the people of *Hadith*), their centre was Medina (*Hijaaz*). The other group of scholars used their power of reasoning to arrive at possible solutions. They applied that law to other circumstances which had similar causes. Due to this group's support of reasons, they became known as *Ahlar-Rai* (reasoning people or the people of opinion) and their centre was Kufah in Iraq. It should be noted that these two trends were merely extensions of trends which first appeared among the *sahabah*. Furthermore, the different approaches of *Ahl-al-Hadith* and *Ahlar-Rai* scholars may be traced to certain political factors combined with the different socio-cultural backgrounds of the two areas in which their schools of thought flourished.[40] It was during the Ummayyad period, in order to preserve the earlier rulings and contributions of the *sahabah*, attempts for the completion of legal rulings (*fiqh*) were carried out. Early scholars of *Hijaaz* collected various *fatawā*s of Abdullah ibn Abbas, Abdullah ibn Umar and Hazrati Aa'eshah, and similarly

40. As the capital of Islamic state shifted to Iraq and then to Syria, *hijjaz* was spared much of the turbulence and influx of foreign cultures and ideas. Life in the *hijjaz* continued to be easy going and simple, due to its Isolation. Iraq was a new and strange land for Muslims, it became a virtual melting pot of various cultures and gave rise to a great number of situations and events new to Muslim scholars, with the result Iraq school of thought and its scholars predominantly adhered to their reason and logic.

the scholars of Iraq collected the ruling of Abdullah ibn Masud and those of Hazrat Ali ibn Abi Taalib. Unfortunately, none of these early collections have survived in their original forms. However, a large number of the rulings contained in the original collections have been preserved by way of narration in the books of *Hadith,* in history books, as well as in later books of *fiqh.*

The early Abbasid period[41] saw the end of the formative stage of *fiqh* and it was during this period that *fiqh* took on a definite shape as an independent Islamic science. Due to the active support of the caliph given to the Islamic scholarship, the debate and discussion on controversial issues furthered and became more wide-spread. The many *madhab*s which had appeared in the later part of the Ummayyad period flourished and centres of learning increased throughout and for the first time the *fiqh* of the various *madhab*s was successfully compiled on a large and systematic scale. By the end of the period, *fiqh* was clearly divided into two sections: fundamental principles (*Usul*) and secondary principles of scientific, philosophical and theological work (*furu*). The positions of major scholars of *fiqh* were recorded and the primary sources of Islamic law were identified and classified in order of their importance.[42]

The *madhab*s: schools of Islamic legal thought, from early two main, *Ahlar-Rai* and *Ahlal-Hadith,* with respect to *ijtihad,* evolved into a number of new *madhab*s. During the shift from caliphate to monarchy, the caliph/king was no longer the head

41. Extended approximately from CE 750 to 950 and covers the rise of the Abbasid Dynasty founded by Abul Abbas, reign 750-754, its consolidation and the beginning of its decline.

42. *Al-Madkhal*, pp. 128, 34. Muhammad Mustafa Shalabee, *al Madkhal fee al-Tareef bil-fiqh al-Islaam,* Beirut, Lebanon, Daar an-Nahdah al-Arabeeyah, 2nd edn., 1978.

of the *madhab* since scholars and their students were dispersed throughout the Muslim world, their personal *ijtihad* increased in order to solve local issues, with the result, a number of *madhabs* evolved rather, we can say that *fiqh* was privatized. The major *madhabs* were the Hanafee *madhab* (School of thought),[43] the Maalikee madhab,[44] the Shafiée madhab[45] the

43. Hanafee Madh-hab, founder Nu'maan ibn Thaabit Abu Haneefah (CE 703–67), born in Kufah, Iraq. He was considered among the minor *Taabi'oon* (student of *sahabah*) because he had met a few of the *sahabah* and had related some *Hadith* from them. His main students were Zufar ibn al-Hudhyal (732–774 CE), Abu Yoosuf Yaqoob ibn Ibraheem (735–795 CE), and Muhammad ibn al-Hassan ash-Shaybanee (CE 749–805).

44. Founder Imam Maalik, Maalikh ibn Anas ibn Aamir, (717–801 CE), born in Medina. Compiled a book containing *Hadith* of the Prophet, (SAAS) and Athars of the *Sahabah* and their successors which he named *al-Muwatta,* 'The Beaten Path.' His main students Abu Abdur Rehmaan ibn al-Qaasim (745–813 CE), wrote extensive book on *fiqh* called *al-Mudawanah* and Abu 'Abdillah ibn Wahhab (742–819).

45. Founder Muhammad ibn Idrees Ash-Shafiée. Popularly known as Imam Ash-Shafiée (769–820 CE), born in town Ghazzah on the Mediterranean coast of what was then known as Shaam travelled extensively, learned all the existing *madhabs*, combined the *fiqh* of *hijjaz,* (Malikes thought) with that of Iraq, (Hanafee thought) and created a new madhab which he dictated to his students in the book called, *al-Hujjah,* (The evidence), in Iraq in CE 810. In Egypt he absorbed the *fiqah* of Imam al-Layth Ibn sa'd and dictated to his students in the form of another book which he named *al-Umm* (the essence). Imam Ash-Shafie holds the distinction of being the first *imām* to systematize the fundamental principles of *fiqh* which he recorded in his book called *ar-Risalah*. His main students where Ismael ibn Yahya al-Muzane wrote a book *Mukhtasar al Muzane*, widely read *fiqh* book of the Shafie *madhab*. *Ar-Rabee 'Al-Marade* (CE 790-873), Yusuf ibn Yahya al-Buwaytee.

Hambalee madhab,[46] and the Zaydee madhab.[47] The most important of the minor *madhabs* were the Awzaa'ee madhab,[48] the Laythee madhab,[49] the Thawree madhab,[50] the Dhaahiree Madhhab[51] and the Jareeree madhab.[52] These went out of

46. Founder Ahmad ibn Hambal Ash-Shaybaanee, popularly known as Imman Ahmad (778–855), born in Baghdad. His collection known as *al-Musnad* contained 30,000 *Hadith*. His main students were his own two sons. Saalih, died in CE 873, and Abdullah died in CE 903. Imam Bukhari and Muslim great scholars of *Hadith* studied under Imam Ahmad.

47. Founder Imam Zayd (700–42). This *madhab* traces its origin to one of Ali ibn Abi Talibs great grandsons through his son al-Husayn. Imam Zayd's father, 'Ali Zain al-Abideen, was well known for his great legal knowledge and his narration of *Hadiths*. Born in al-Medina. Zayd ibn Ali's main students were, Abu Khalid, Amr ibn Khalid al-Waasitee (CE d. 889). He compiled Imam Zayd's teachings in two major works entitled *Majmoo 'al Hadith* and *Majmoo 'al-Fiqh*. Together they are called *al-Majmoo al-Kaibir Al-Hadi ela al-Haqq*, Yahyaa ibn al-Husayn (CE 860–911) and Al-Hassan ibn 'Ali al-Hussayne (CE 845–917), followers of this *madhab* are mostly in Yemen. This is the closest Shi'i School of thought to the Sunni Schools.

48. Founder, Imam alk Awzaa'ee, Abdur-Rahman ibn al Awzaa'ee (CE 708-74) who was born in Ba'labek Syria, spent most of his life in Beirut; His *madhab* remained the main school of thought in Syria until the tenth century CE. Finally disappeared when Shafi *madhab* occupied the place.

49. Founder: Imam al-Layth (CE 716-91). Al-Layth ibn Sa'd was born in Egypt of Persian parentage. He was contemporary of both Imam Abu Hanifah and Imam Malik.

50. Founder, Imam ath-Thawri or Imam Sufyan ath, Thawri (CE 719-777), born in Kufah.

51. Founder, Imam Dawood or Dawood ibn Ali (CE 815–83), born in Kufah. He took an independent path of reasoning based on the obvious and literal meanings (*dhahir*) of the text of the *Qur'an* and the *Sunnah*. Because of this approach, his *madhab* was called the *Dhahiri madhab* as he became known as Dawood adh-Dhahiri.

existence either because of political reasons or due to their students failing to record the rulings of its founders for posterity. The majority of the madhabs which flourished during the earlier periods disappeared and four remained popular. The principle sources of Islamic law agreed upon by all the major *madhab*s were the Qur'an, the *Sunnah*, *ijma* of the *sahabah* and *qiyas*. All of the major *madhab*s set conditions for the acceptance of the *Sunnah* as a primary source of Islamic law, e.g. the Hanfee madhab stipulated that the *Hadith* be widely known (*mashhoor*). The Maalikes madhab required that the *Hadith* not contradict the *ijma* of the Madinites. The Shaafiee madhab insisted that the *Hadith* be authentic (*saheeh*). The Hambalee madhab only required that the *Hadith* be attributed to the Prophet (SAAS) and not fabricated. Thus, *Hadith*s of doubtful authenticity were not considered a part of the *Sunnah*.[53] Some *imāms* evolved certain secondary legal principles and made rulings based on them, such as *istihasān* preference) and *urf* (local custom) used by Hanfee madhab, *istislah* (welfare) and *masalih mursalah urf* (custom) by Maalikee madhab, *istis-hab* (linking) by Shaafiee madhab. Thus we find variations in the interpretations and terminology given to the same principle. For example, the Maalikee madhab considered

---

52. Founder: Imam al-Tabari; his full name was Muhammad ibn Jarir ibn Yazid at Tabari (CE 839–923) born in the province of Tabaristan. His *madhab* differed less in the principle than in practice from the *Shafi madhab* and fell comparatively quickly into oblivion. Ibn Jarir was most noted for his outstanding Tafsir of the *Qur'an* which he called Jami al-Bayan, but which became known as Tafsir at-Tabari of equal importance and fame was his history of world called *Tarikh ar-Rusul wal-Mulook*, commonly known as *Tarikh at-Tabari*. Quoted from Muhammad al-Khidari Berk Tarik at Tashri al Islami (Cairo: *al-Maktabah al-Tijariyah al-Kubraa*, 1960), 181-83.

53. Abu Aminah Bilal Philips, *The Evolution of fiqh*, Tawheed Publications, Riyadh, 1990, p. 90.

the Hanafee principle of *istihsan* unacceptable yet applied the same principle under the name of *istislah* and *masalih-mursdah* while the Shaafiee madhab rejected both these terms and applied a similar principle calling *Al-Istishāb.*[54] It should be noted, however that during both the periods of the Ummayyads and that of the early Abbasids, students of *fiqh* freely and frequently changed teachers and exchanged legal opinions. Thus the *madhabs* under the guidance of their founders continued to experience a great deal of mutual exchange of ideas and flexibility. But during the later part of the Abbasid dynasty,[55] the students of second generation developed a trend towards rigidity and a breakdown of flexibility. The compilation of *fiqh* was further formalized and used to further *madhab* rivalry, and *ijtihad* beyond the structure of *madhab* was dropped and *ijtihad madhabi* took its place.[56] The state of stagnation and decline of *fiqh* and existence of *madhab* factionalism have continued until the present day.

---

54. Ibid., p. 62.

55. This covers the period between the year CE 950 and the sacking of Baghdad (CE 1258) and represents the decline of the Abbasid dynasty until it evently collapsed.

56. The difference between the *madhabs* became emphasized due to states preference for some *madhabs* over others and the rise of inter *madhab* rivalry promoted by court debates *(Munad Harat)*. In time the spirit of rivalry largely generated by these debates spread to the masses, and *madhab* factionalism became widespread. The structure and operation of the survived madhhabs became highly systematized and organized. Scholars within a *madhabs* were obliged to base their *ijtihads* solely on the fundamental principles [*usul*] of their particular *madhab*. Shalabi Muhammad Mustafa-al-Madkhal fi at-Tarif bil-*Fiqh* al-Islami, Beirut: Dar an-Nandal al-Arabiyah 1969, pp. 147, 57. Cited in Abu Aminah *Evolution of fiqh*, 102.

This above-mentioned historical development of *fiqh* and the *madhab*s (schools of Islamic legal thought) shows the Intellectual endeavours and use of *ijtihad* by *fuqaha* (jurists) to the relevant social and political context of the respective periods, in order to resolve arising challenges according to *shari'ah* (body of revealed laws found both in the Qur'an and in the *Sunnah*). Both *fiqh* (Islamic Law) and the *madhab*s were necessary additions complementing the divine revelations which define the basic principles governing man's rights and responsibilities in his relationship with Allah and his fellow men. "This was a matter of an intellectual application (*fiqh*) in which there was applied to the authoritative argument of the inviolable text, either the judgement based on opinion (*rai*) of the prudence, or a reasoning by analogy (*qiyas*)."[57] The early scholars discharged their duties to Islam and to their fellow men by using their God-given power of intellect to interpret Allah's purposes for man. Their codification of Islamic law (*shari'ah*) from Qur'anic doctrines, *Sunnah* of the prophet, *ijma* of the companions and *qiyas* provided a remedy to the existing Muslim situation. Herein lies the true importance of *fiqh* and the *madhab* in Islam, notwithstanding the fact that human reason always played an important role in the development of *fiqh* and *madhab*s through the medium of *ijtihad*. Furthermore, the *fiqh* and *madhab*s itself contributed to a large extent in the development of Islamic thought; therein became a separate branch of Islamic science. *Fuqaha* not only codified Islamic law but also reacted to *mutakalimun* controversies, thus *kalam* too,

---

57. Louis Gardet, *"Religion and Culture", in The Cambridge History of Islam* vol. 2, eds. P.M. Holt. K.S. Lambton, Bernard Lewis, Cambridge University Press, London, 1970, p. 575.

was covered by the term *fiqh* in the early stage.[58]

Kalam

Kalam (dialectical theology) here means discussion on Theology matters. *Kalam* or *Ilm al-Kalam* (the science of *kalam*) is a title of that branch of knowledge in Islam that is usually translated as "Speculative Theology." Literally, *kalam* means "speech," "discourse" or "talk"; *yatakallamfi* means to talk about or discuss a matter or topic.[59] It emerged as a reaction to specific debates or issues that grew out of early Islam's socio-political context. Its scope reflected the mixing of faith and politics, question of belief, sin, eschatology, and legitimate governance. Among the key theological issues were the relationships of faith to

---

58. It appears that *fiqh* embraced the theological problems as well as the legal issue till the time of al-Mamun (d. AH 218) second century of *Hijrah*. Among the earliest is that by Abu Hanifah (d. 150/767), who gave it the name *al-fiqh al-Akbar* and stated "*fiqh* in usul *al-dīn* is better than *fiqh* in *furual ahkam*. *Fiqh* is knowledge of the beliefs and practices which are permitted and which are obligatory in both. What relates to belief is called *al-fiqh al-Akbar* and what relates to practice is simply *al-fiqh*." As quoted in Mabdel Halim, "Early *Kalam*," in *History of Islamic Philosophy* part 1, Seyyed Hossein Nasr and Oliver Leaman, eds, Routeledge, London and New York, 1996, p. 75, and in Ahmad Hasan, *The Early Development of Islamic Jurisprudence* (Islamabad IRI) 1970, p. 3.

59. In an early usage of the word *kalam* in this sense, the prophet (S.A.A.S) is reported to have come out and found a group of Muslim Yatakallamuna *fil-qadar*, i.e. talking about or discussing, predestination. He also said, "Mantakallama fi al-din hi rayihi fa qad itta hamah," meaning "whoever discusses religion, relying [solely] on his own opinion, had doubted it." The word occurred in other traditions and continued to be used in the same sense even when discussion on theological matters had become more extensive and specialized. Quoted in Nasr, *Islamic Philosophy*, p. 71.

work, the nature of Allah and the Qur'an, predestination, and free will. Such discussions were called *kalam* before the science of *kalam* became independent and recorded in writing, and people who engaged in such discussions were called *mutakallimun*. When books were written about these issues, the science, which was written down, was given the title that has been applied earlier to such discussions.[60]

Thus there seems no justification in the contention of Western scholars that *kalam* has its origin in Greek rationalism directly or via syriac. It has originated independently of any foreign influence and continued to be fostered in the Islamic atmosphere. There are many titles given to this science as an independent subject, than *Ilm al-Kalam*, such as, *Ilm al-Fiqh al-Akbar, Ilm Usul al-Din, Ilm al-Aqaid, Ilm al-Tawhid*.[61]

Ilm al-Kalam passed through stages of development and the earliest stage of *kalam* in Islam is surely to be found in the Qur'an itself. *Kalam* in its technical sense involves providing rational proofs to establish the article of faith. *Qur'an* dealt with all the issues that were discussed in *kalam* as fully developed latter. Al-Razi (606/1209) a pre-eminent commentator on the Qur'an and *matakallim*, points out that discussion is widespread in the Qur'an on *tawhid*, Prophethood and the hereafter. Accordingly he states: "Qur'anic verses dealing with *al-ahkam al-shariyah* are fewer than six hundred while the rest explain questions of the unity of God, Prophethood and refutation of idol-worshippers and various other types of polytheists If you examine *Ilm al-kalam* you will find nothing in it other than discussion of these questions and

60. M. Abd al-Raziq, *Tamhid Litarikh al-falsafah al-Islamiyyah*, Cairo, 1996, p. 265. Quoted by Nasr, *Islamic Philosophy*, p. 70.

61. Ibid., pp. 74-75.

refutations of doubts and counter-arguments."[62] The *Qur'an* calls for *nazar* and *tafkir* (reflection and thought) making these an obligation in Islam. It also contains verses known as *muhkamat* (perspicubus, in precise language) and these the *Qur'an* calls "the essence of the Book" and others known as *mutashabihat* (intricate, unintelligible, ambiguous). The *ta'wil* (interpretation) of this latter category taken in isolation or understood in the light of former was one of the distinguishing factors between sects and schools. These were the factors of influence of *Qur'an* on *kalām* discussions.

Discussions on religious matters began very early in Islam at the time of Prophet,[63] continued during the times of the *sahabah* (companions of the prophet) and the *tabi'un* (those who followed them) what they refrained from was not the discussion of such issues as *qadar* (free will) the attributes of God, the nature of belief and unbelief, eschatology and the fate of sinners, but from going deep into them or forcing the issues[64] and did not encourage disputation over such matters. During the early years of Islam, theological discussions revolved around number of issues. Discussion of the question of *jabar* (pre-destination) and *qadar* (free-will) appeared at the time of Prophet and continued after the prophet. With the appearance of different sects, such as Shiah, Kharijites and Murjites, many theological issues arose primarily as a result of their understanding and interpretation of the text. The

---

62. *Al-Tafsir al-Kabir,* 15 vols, 2.1, (Beirut, 3rd ed. nd) pp. 88-90. as quoted in M. Abdul Haleem, "Early *Kalām,*" in *History of Islamic Philosophy*, Seyyed Hossein Nasr Oliver Leaman, ed., Routledge, London and New York 1996), pp. 76-77.

63. Nasr, *Islamic Philosophy*, op. cit., pp. 77-78.

64. Nasr, *Islamic Philosophy*, p. 78, and also see Muzaffarnddin Nadwi, *Muslim Thought and its Sources*, pp. 11-12.

relationship of faith to works was the first major issue of *kalam* confronting the early community. Kharijites insisted on total commitment and observance of God's will, took extreme view regarding the status and fate of *murtakib al-kabirah* "grave sinner," considering such a person as an "infidel" (*kafir*). Their world-view admitted only two categories; believers and unbelievers, interpreting in their own way Qur'anic verses that do not agree with this stand. At the another extreme, there were the Murjites who considered that sinners are still believers and that action is not part of the faith, to the extent that no sins would harm anyone who is a believer and no good would benefit an infidel. The Murjites position also provided a justification for Ummayyad legitimacy and rule. The caliphs had asserted that, whatever sins and injustices they may have committed, they remained Muslim and ruled by divine decree and that their rule was pre-determined by God. This belief gave impetus to the other theological issue of *jabr* (pre-destinarianism) and *qadr* (free-will).[65] The theological question was, "did an omnipotent and omniscient God pre-determine all acts and events and thus constitute the source of evil and injustice; or were human beings free to act and therefore responsible of sin?" The opposition to the

---

65. The debate on predestination and free will was there before the advent of Islam, and during the prophet's time the question of *qadar* (freewill) gave too much discussion as to whether people have free will or are under compulsion. This gave rise to two groups. The Qadarites held that people had *quadrah* (power) over their actions: some went to the extent of denying the pre-existent knowledge of God in order to remove any compulsion; saying that people perform all their actions without divine assistance. This former group includes Ma'bad al-Juhani (d. 80/699) and Ghaylan of Damascus (d. 150/767). At the opposite extreme of this argument there were the Jabriyyah, who affirmed the divine power and held that one is under compulsion to the extent that →

Ummayyads maintained that it was not God but human beings who committed injustices and thus were responsible for their acts.[66] These Qadarites schools, supporters of free will, developed into one of the most important philosophical school of Islamic thought, "Mutazilites." Wassil ibn Atta (d. 132) was a scholar who developed the views that led to the establishment of the theological school known as al-Mu'tazila which was to have a great influence in Islamic thoughts. They recognized the pre-existent divine knowledge, even though they affirmed people's freedom and responsibility for their actions. They gave special importance to being forthright in enjoying what is right and forbidding what is evil, *al-amar bil m'aroof wa al-nahi al-munkar*. Wassil considered this as one of the five basic principles of Islam.

In addition to the previously mentioned theological questions by the time of the early Abbasids, other questions came forth such as createdness or uncreatedness of *Qur'an*, the divine attributes of the God and other attributes in general as regard their existence and connection with the divine

---

→ God creates one's action, good or bad, and one is like a feather in the breeze without any power of one's own. Amongst this group al-Jahm ibn Safwan (d. 128/745) is the most important representative. Scholars of the *sahabah* and the *tabi'un* argued against both groups, conforming the pre-existent knowledge of God and negative compulsion at some time, attributing to man-power, will and action with an attitude which takes middle course between absolute *jabr* and absolute *qadr [tafwid]*.

66. According to Shibli the emergence of the issue of freedom of will and pre-destination owes its origin to politics, as in the Ummayyad period especially during the governorship of Hajjaj bin Yousuf. The people were coerced to declare, we believe that good and evil (is from God). Shibli Noamani, *Illmul-a-kalam*, Masood Publishing House, Karachi, 1964, pp. 228-41.

essence and its unity. In fact, by this time all essential themes which were to constitute *ilm al-kalam* had arisen. Thus from the above facts, it becomes obvious that *ilm al-kalam* originated completely and developed in Muslim environment. The foreign element came only later as a result of mixing with other nations and also as a result of the translation of Greek texts into Arabic during Abbassid period. The view that the sources of Muslim thought are the *Qur'an,* the *Hadith* and Greek philosophy[67] or that the M'utazillism owed its origin to Greek Philosophy[68] is unjustified. Muslims' Rationalism was born of the *Holy Qur'an,* which always appeals to reason, which treated theological issues supported by rational proofs and fostered in the Muslim atmosphere, independently of foreign influence.[69]

In early *kalam* both traditional and rational argument, were given due weight. We find at first people like Al-Hasan al-Basri, Jafar al-Sadiq, Abu Hanifah and Al-thawri relying on both, even though the traditional proof comes first for them.[70] As *Ilm al-Kalam* grew and the different sects and schools appeared, such as Mutazilites, Asharites and some *mutakallimun* began to adopt method of argument that are different in style from those of the *Qur'an.* Also some began to question whether it was lawful to engage in *kalam* discussion. Mutazilites who called themselves "people of (divine) unity and justice" (*ahl al-tawhid wal-Adl*), the defenders of divine

67. George C. Anawati, "Philosophy and Mysticism," in *The Legacy of Islam,* 2nd edn., Joseph Schacht and C.E Bosworth, eds., Oxford University Press, 1979, p. 359.

68. Muzaffar-ud-din Nadvi, *Muslim Thought and its Source,* Idarah-i-Adibayat-I, Delhi 1946, p. 35.

69. Ibid., pp. 34-35.

70. Nasr, *History of Islamic Philosophy,* p. 81.

unity (monotheism) and justice. Influenced by the influx of Greek philosophical and scientific thought during the Abbasid period with its emphasis on reason, logical argumentation, and study of laws of nature, they relied on reason and rational deduction and tools in Qur'anic interpretation and theological reflection. They raised the status of *aql* (reason) almost making it equal to *naql* (tradition as can be seen from statements of Wasil-bin-Ata, who said, "truth can be known from four sources: the *Qur'an,* agreed *Hadith,* rational arguments and *ijma."*[71] The rational tendency grew gradually until it grave *aql* status which is above *naql.* In the days of Abul Hassan al-Ashari (d. 935), the founder of the Asharite School of Theology, the Asharites began by taking a balanced view between *naql* and *'aql.* They stated that there were five ways to knowledge: *aql, Qur'an, Sunnah, ijma* and *qiyas.*[72] Al-Ashari used reason to provide a rational defence for that what which transcended, and at times seemed contrary to reason. Thus, while reason and logic might be used to explain and defend belief, revelation was not subordinate to the requirements of reason. *Sam* (*Qur'an* and *Sunnah*) and *aql,* where the two sources again recognized by Al-Maturidi, but the scale tended to favour *aql,* with the infiltration of the concept of *dawr* (circularity in argument): [Since *aql* is our first means of establishing the truthfulness of the Prophet and *Qur'an,* if one later puts *naql* above *aql* one is undermining the very means which led to the acceptance of *naql*][73] into the *kalam.* It was such development that led Ibn Taymiyyah to write his book, *al-Muwafaqah* (harmony) or *Dar ta'ārud al-'aql wa'l-naql* [Rejection of the conflicts between *aql* and *naql]* in which he criticized the

71. Ibid.

72. Ibid., p. 82.

73. Ibid.

method, of putting *aql* before *naql*.[74] It was chiefly their ways of understanding the *Qur'an* and the way their views related to the Qur'anic position that differentiated theological sects and schools. Throughout the Islamic era, the numerous scholars, of various schools, came to engage in theological discussion and thereby creating this very important science *al-kalam* of Islam. Although the *mutakallimun* schools fell into the complex controversies among themselves yet *Ilm al-Kalam* serve as a formative and progressive endeavour in the development of Islamic thought, for which theological colleges are now well-established in the main Sunni and Shi'i centres of learning.

These *mutakallimūn* under the influence of Greek philosophy and science paved the way for Muslim philosophers — A number of Muslim thinkers schooled in Greek philosophy, wished to be placed at the service of their faith the resources of reason and dreamed of reconciling Greek wisdom with revelation.[75] Because of the movement to translate classical texts into Arabic during Abbasides, Muslim thinkers were able to appropriate Aristotle, Plato, Platinus and the stoics, and rework these materials within their own context.

This encounter of Greek philosophy with Islam, was however, remarkable. "The Muslims accepted neither the language nor the humanistic values nor they thought the religion of the Greek; their borrowings came exclusively through translation and, more, were severely limited to a

---

74. IbId.

75. George C. Amawati- "Philosophy, theology and Mysticism," in *The Legacy of Islam*, Joseph Schacht and C.E. Bosworth, eds., Oxford University Press, Oxford, 1979, pp. 354-55.

technical and scientific Hellenism."[76] Islamic philosophy derives its principles, inspirations and many of the questions with which it had been concerned from the sources of Islamic revelation despite the claims of its opponents to the contrary. Muslim philosophers had their independent views and far from imitating Greek thought, freely criticized it and endeavoured to purge it of inconsistencies and contradictions.[77] Men like the Arabs, Abu Yaqub al-Kindi (d. 873) and al-Farabi (d. 950). The Persian ibn Sina (Avicenna d. 1037) and Spaniard ibn Rushd (Averros, d. 1198) were among the intellectual giants of their times. Their ideas challenged their Muslim contemporaries. Throughout history, many Islamic philosophers have identified *falsafah* and later *hikmah*, the two main terms used with somewhat different meaning for Islamic philosophy and regarded the *Qur'an* and *Hadith* as source and inspiration of Islamic philosophy, as Sayyed Hossein Nasr has observed:

> A deeper study of Islamic philosophy over its twelve hundred years history will reveal the role of the *Qur'an* and *Hadith* in the formulation, exposition and problematics of this major philosophical tradition. In the same way that all of the Islamic philosophers from al-Kindi onwards knew the *Qur'an* and, *Hadith* and lived with them, Islamic philosophy has manifested over the centuries its inner link with the revealed sources of Islam, a link which has become even more manifest as the centuries have unfolded, for Islamic philosophy is essentially a philosophical hermeneutics of the sacred text, while making use of the rich philosophical heritage of antiquity. That is why, far from being a transitory and foreign phase in the history of Islamic thought, Islamic philosophy has remained over the

---

76. F.E. Peters, "The Greek and Syriac background," in *History of Islamic Philosophy*, Hosein Nasr, pp. 41-42.
77. Muzaffar-ud-din Nadwi, *Muslim Thought and Its Sources*, p. 143.

> centuries and to this day, one of the major intellectual perspectives in Islamic civilization with its roots sunk deeply like everything else Islamic in the *Qur'an* and *Hadith*.[78]

As some of the Muslim scholars have accepted Islamic philosophy, there are many of the *'Ulama'* (scholars of tradition, law and theology alike) who have stood opposed to it and viewed philosophy as embodying the conflict between reason and revelation, which, took reason and not revelation as its starting point and method, a direct threat to faith. Al-Gazzali, the great theologian, legal scholar and mystic, mastered philosophy simply to refute it, fought sharply against philosophy. In *Tahafut al-falasifah* (the incoherence of the philosophers). The famous work directed properly against philosophy, Al-Gazzali intended to demonstrate that philosophers are unable to prove, from a theoretical point of view, the religious truths. In *al-Raddu, 'Alal-Mantiq* (the refutation of logic) Ibn-Taimiyah strongly criticized philosophers. Ibn Rushd countered with his ringing defence, in his *Tahāfut al-tahāfut* (the incoherence of the incoherence) and in his *fasal al-maqāl* concentrated his efforts on the defence of philosophy itself. Though not without some criticism of Ibn Sina.[79] He argued that the difference between philosophy and religion were only apparent, since both pursued the real, the former relying on the language of reason and science and the latter on the metaphorical language of revelation.

Despite the accomplishment of many great philosophers, not only in philosophy but also in medicine and the science

---

78. Seyyed Hussein Nar, *History of Islamic Philosophy*, p. 37.

79. Louis Gardet, "Religion and Culture," in *The Cambridge History of Islam*, P. M. Holt, Ann K. S. Lamton, and Bernard Lewis, eds., vol. 2, p. 599.

(for they were truly renaissance men) they met with criticism, more often then not they were viewed as rationalists and non-believers. Muslim philosophers produced an extraordinary contribution to Islamic civilization and had a major impact on the west. As observed by M.M. Sharif :–

> Although the Muslims did not originate philosophical thought as they originated scientific enquiry, some of their achievements in this field were most remarkable. They were acquainted with Hindu philosophy, were masters of Greek thought, and speculation was deep and extensive. Their problems were the same as philosophy has had to solve in all ages. Their solutions of these problems were as little final as those of any other people in any other age. Nevertheless, they satisfied their own times, the mediaeval ages, and paved the way for further speculation and opened the door for the European Renaissance."[80]

By transmitting Greek philosophy to medieval Europe, it influenced the curriculum of its universities and the work of such scholars as Albertus Magnus, Thomas Aquinas, Duns Scotus and Roger Bacon.

Islamic philosophy called *falsafah* and later *hikmah,* is an Islamic intellectual discipline in contention, debate, accord or opposition with other intellectual disciplines but in any case it was and remains a part and parcel of Islamic intellectual life despite the opposition of many jurists. Though met with criticism and strictures, it has developed as a separate discipline or branch of the Islamic thought, with its defenders, not only in the Shi'ite world but also in certain areas and schools of the Sunni world.

---

80. M.M. Sharif, *Muslim Thought. Its Origin and Achievements,* Institute of Islamic Culture, Lahore, 1980, p. 55.

Tasawwuf or Sufism

There developed, alongside the philosophical thought, one of the most arresting branch of Islamic thought known as *al-tasawwuf* or Sufism, often called "Islamic mysticism" though misleading.[81] There are many theories about the origin of this movement in Islam and considerable misunderstanding has been created to attribute its rise and growth to foreign influence on Islamic thought, such as Syrian monasticism, Neo-platonism, Persian Zoroastrianism, Indian Vedānta and Buddhistic thought.[82] It has, however, been shown that the hypothesis of more borrowings is untenable.[83] The fact is that

81. The use of the term mysticism *tasawwuf* is thoroughly misleading. There is nothing mysterious or mystical about it. The *Sūfi* path (*tariqah*) is as open and clear as any system could be; in fact it is just a continuation of the path of *Shari'ah*, the main difference being that the commands of the latter are obligatory while most of the practices pertaining to the former are supererogatory and are voluntarily followed only by those who are anxious to attain higher stages of moral and spiritual elevation. (S. Moinul Haq, *Islamic Thought and Movement*, Karachi, 1979, p. XXV. Furthermore, Muslim *Sūfi* is neither an ascetic nor a recluse, and therefore he is not mystic in the sense in which this term is understood in reference to other religious systems. "Islamic mysticism," understood in the sense is primarily a path of knowledge (*al-marifah, irfan*) to which the element of love attached in accordance with the structure of the Islamic revelation, but is very rearly the sentimental and individualistic mysticism found in many circles in the Christian climate.

82. George C. Anawati, "Philosophy, theology and Mysticism," in *Legacy of Islam*, Joseph Schacth and C. E. Borsworth, eds., p. 366.

83. For the theory that the growth of *tasawwuf* was the result of foreign influences on Islamic thought See, A. Schimmel, "The

→

tasawwuf is as old as Islam itself and has its origin in the teachings of and in the personality of Prophet Muhammad (SAAS). It is the esoteric dimension of Islam or spiritual discipline of mind and body whose goal was to directly experience the ultimate reality. So to say it is an attempt of individual Muslim to realize in their personal experience the living presence of Allah.

As far as the term *tasawwuf* or Sufism is concerned, it is a later development, contentious and has been derived variously, such as *ashabi-safa[sahaba* who lived in the mosque of Medina], *saff* (rank) Greek word *sophia* (wisdom) *sufiy* [wise, pious] *safa* (purity) *safi* (pure) and *suf* [wool] whatever may be the origin of this term, it became popular two hundred years after the demise of prophet (SAAS). In *Qur'an* and during the life of prophet (SAAS). The term *tasawwuf* or "Sufism" is not found as such. As far as the aim or essence of this term is concerned, it resembles with the terms as, *ihsān, tazkyah, dhikr, muttaqi, tawakkul, tahārah, tabattala, Taqwa,* etc. these terms are constantly used in *Qur'an* and *Hadith* and much importance has been given to them, so as to use a life of total purity and devotion to Allah. Men possessing such qualities are known in *Qur'an* by the terms *Muqarrabin* (friends of God), *Sabirin* (patient men), *Abrar* (virtuous men), *Zuhhad* (pious men), etc. Thus there may be doubt about the use of term *tasawwuf* or Sufism for this important dimensions of Islamic thought, but not the aim, which is based firmly upon the intuitive insights of *Qur'an* and *Sunnah.*

→ Origin of Early Development of *Sufism,*" in *Journal of the Pakistan Historical Society*, Karachi, vol. VII, pt. n, p. 55, et. seq. and R.A. Nichalson, "Historical Enquiry Concerning the Origin and Development of Sufism," in *JRAS*, 1906, pp. 303-486.

In the opinion of Sayyid Abul Hasan Ali Nadwi,

> It is more appropriate to name this *ilm* "knowledge"(of *tasawwuf*) which attempts at *tazkiyah* (purification of self). *Tahzyb-i-ikhlaq* (reformation of morals), endows the human self with bounties of the *Shari'ah* and purifies it from evils and blesses it with perfect belief, the stage of *ihsan* [lit "virtue" "excellence," "making beautiful" the state of the person where deeds achieve the perfect fulfilment of the commandments of Allah (SWT)] adherence to the prophet (SAAS) in both practical and spiritual matters and standing for its preaching, as *tazkiyah* or *ihsan* or at least *fiqh batin* [law of esoterics]. If this would have been treated on this very pattern, there would have hardly been difference and conflict surrounded this "tasawwuf" which is on the basis of semantics and terminology only.[84]

Tasawwuf or Sufism went through considerable development and modification as the Muslims came into contact with people of other races and cultures in the course of their history. The first, formative period, covers the first three centuries of Islam (seventh to ninth centuries) begins from the time of the Prophet and ends with the rise of the Abbasid dynasty. Including particularly the companions of Prophet, *kulafa-i-Rashidin* and *Ahl-us-suffa,* whose association with Prophet was long and continued, followed in his footsteps, so as to provide a complete example for humanity in all fields of endeavour and maintained the dignity of labour and simplicity of life. They had no heart in worldly riches, and did not allow themselves even innocent pleasures and ordinary comforts of life, although they wielded authority over extensive territories. In them,

84. Sayyid Abdul Hassan Al Nadwi, *Tazkiah Wa Ihsan Ya Tasawwuf Wa Salooq,* Majlis Tahkiqat wa Nasriyat Islamic, Lucknow, 1989, p. 16.

piety, spirituality *"zuhd"* and *"taqwa"* was prevalent, that is why many Sūfi orders trace their origin to Khalifah Abu Bakr (RAA)[85] Khalifah Umar (RAA)[86] and Khalifa Ali (RAA).[87] *Ashāb as-suffah* (lit. the people of the bench) were noted for their intense zeal and enthusiasm for the cause of Islam, for piety and the ascetic life they led. They were devoted to Islam and passed their time in reading the *Qur'an* and discussing matters of religion.

Towards the close of the period of *Kula fa-i-Rashid din*, a group of selfless, devoted people dissatisfied with Ummayyad rule, sought to check their extravagances and refocus the vision and goals of Muslim life. Among them who devoted themselves solely to a life of peace and piety typifying the ascetic reaction to what they regarded as the decadence of imperial Islam. Urwah b. Zubayr (d. 717) spent his time in prayers and the study of *Hadith.* An eloquent spokesman of this protest was Hasan al-Basri (643–728), an eminent scholar, widely respected for his learning, a pupil of Hazrat Ali. The first Muslim, however, who is generally recognized as Sūfi.[88] His influence on Sufism was very profound and through him several Sūfi *silsilah*s (confraternities) trace their link to Khalifa Ali and then to Prophet (SAAS) "His mystical and ascetic

85. Shaykh Ali, Al-Hujwari, *Kashfal al-Mahjub*, Lahore, Nicholson, Eng. tr., London 1936, p. 70.

86. Shah Wali Allah Dilhawi, *Izalat alkhafa 'a Khilāfat al-Khulfa*, Bareilly n.d., p. 142. et. seq.

87. Abu Nasar Siraj, Kitab al Lum'a (Urdu. trans. Asrar Bukhari), Delhi 1991, p. 218.

88. The term *Sūfi* was first adopted by Abu Hashim a Syrian Zahid (d. CE 780); in his time was built the first *takyah* (convent). But some say that the seed of Sufism; was sown in the time of Adam, germed in the time of Nuh, budded in the time of Ibrahim. Shahbuddin Suhrawardi, *The Awarif ul Maarif*, tr. Col. H. Wilberforce Clarke, Taj Company, New Delhi, 1984, p. 2.

doctrine is rooted in a feeling of contempt for the world. His rule of life is inspired not only by scrupulous abstention from all works questionable in the eyes of the religious law (*wara*) but also above all by ascetic detachment towards everything that is transient. Face-to-face with God, he recommends over and above this *wara*, awe of and attentive regard for the word."[89] This Sūfi movement spread throughout the Muslim world. Ibrahim b. Adham (d. 160/777), Shaqiq Balkhi (d. 194/810), Sufyan al Thawri of Kufa (d. 161/778), Dawud Tai (d. 165/781), Fudayl b. Iyad (d. 187/803) and Maruf Karkhi (d. 200/815) are some of the well-known figures of early Sufism. Their tendency of despising the world, arising out of love of Allah, accounts for several fundamental concepts of *Sūfi* system of thought as for instance, *faqr* (poverty), *tawakal* (trust in God) *zuhd piety, qanā'āt* (contentment), etc.

The most distinguished woman-*Sūfi* of the age, Rabiah al Basri (d. 801) who fused asceticism with all selfless devotional love of Allah, thereby permanently influenced the nature and future of Sufism. She is credited with the following. "The best thing that leads man on to God is that he must not care for anything of this world or of the next other than God. Engagement in the world is the abandonment of God. Everything bears fruit, and the fruit of knowledge is absorption in God."[90] Taking the lead from this ascetic detachment (worldly renunciation) and meditation of the early *sūfīes*, *Sūfi* thought developed independently throughout the ninth and tenth centuries CE in Arabia, Egypt, Syria and Iraq. *Sūfīs* like Al-Harith b. Asad al Muhasibi (165-243/781-857),

---

89. Georges C. Anawati, op. cit., pp. 368-69.

90. Syed Muzaffar-ud-din Nadwi, *Muslim Thoughts,* op. cit., pp. 92-93, quoted from *Nafahat-ul-uns,* Calcutta, 1858, of Jami; Abd al-Rahman Nur-al-din.

Dhu al-Nun al-Misri (246/860), Al-Junayd of Baghdad (d. 298/910) and the Persians, Abu Yazid (Bayazid) al-Bistami and Mansur al- Hallaj (d. 309/922) made major contributions to the formation of the *Sūfi* thought. The transition from simple asceticism to the complex theory of the mystical discipline, and thereafter to highly developed theosophy, and later to pantheism, took place during this period, probably under the foreign influence.[91]

The history of Sufism in the fourth and fifth century *Hijrah* is marked by a systematization of its creed and doctrines and there developed the close nexus between philosophy and mysticism. At once a *Sūfi* and philosopher, people like ibn Səb'īn and Shihab al-Din surhrawardi (d. AH 632) created major syntheses between *Sūfi* doctrine and philosophy in the history of Islamic thought.[92] In the *Muhiy* al-Din b. ibn al-Arabi, born at Murcia in southern Spain in 560/1165, the philosophical aspect of *Sūfi* thought reached its culminating point in the doctrine *of wahdat al-wajud,*[93] which remained a controversial doctrine and was equated with pantheism in Vedāntic and neo-Platonic philosophies. These doctrines threw open the

91. It is far from right to assert that Islamic mysticism is a product of the Greek or any other foreign culture. All that can fairly be said is that some doctrines of Sufism resemble the Neo-platonic or Vedanta theories but in the words of R.A. Nicolson A, *Literary History of the Arabs*, p. 384. "Such resemblance can prove little or nothing unless they are corroborated by evidence based on historical grounds," as mysticism in all ages and countries is fundamentally the same, Muzzafar-ud-din Nadwi, *Muslim Thought*, op. cit., p. 102.

92. Nasr, *Islamic Philosophy*, op. cit., p. 369.

93. Ibn al-Arabi is stated to have left behind a large number of books of various sizes. However the two most famous of his works are the *al-Futuhat al-Makkah*, "Meccan Revelations" and *Fusus al-Hikham*, "Bezels of Wisdom."

door to a number of ideas and practices which were destructive for the religious values of orthodox Islam.[94] Thereby, Sufism, representing the esoteric dimension (*tariqah*) gets separated from the real and straight path of Islam (*shari'ah*).

In the twelfth century, Sufism grew and became mass movement and its adherents organized themselves in *silsilah*s and *tariqah* or *dervish* orders. The four principal schools of Sufism named after their leaders, from which many sub-schools have emerged, are: Qadiriyyah (after Abdul Qadir Jilani, d. AH 552/ CE 1166), Naqshbandihyya (after Bahauddin Naqshband, d. AH 791), Chishtiyyah after Abu Ishaq Shami and Khwajah Moin-uddin Chishti, d. AH 663; CE 1265) and Suhrawardiyyah (after Shehab-uddin Suhrawardi, d. AH 632). On one side the *Sūfi* movement, at a time when the orthodox institution and *'Ulamā* had, partly because of its rigidity and partly because of co-option with secular authorities, lost much of its power to touch the hearts and wills of the ordinary Muslim, offered not only the warmth of personal participation in communal worship but also gave power and depth to Islamic teachings. Between the thirteenth and eighteenth centuries, the survival of official Islam as a religion was due to the nourishment, which it drew from the *Sūfi* brotherhoods.[95] On the other side, its degenerative effect began with the popularity of *tariqah* and as a separate system against the very foundation of the entire structure of Islamic way of life the *Shari'ah.* Which led the saints to constitute themselves into a separate body. The root cause of the deviations, exaggerations and weaknesses that became increasingly prominent in the new popular Sufism,

94. H.A. R. Gibb, *Studies on the Civilization of Islam*, Islamic Book Service Lahore, 1987, p. 213.

95. Ibid., p. 217.

was the revival of saint worship and their canonization as saints, whose blessed power (*barakah*) continued to be effective even after death.[96]

Amid the confusion, between the Sufism and *Ulama'*, in the eleventh and twelfth centuries, came Abu Hamid Muhammad b. Muhammad al-Gazali (1058-1111) known as *Hujjatul-Islam* (Proof of Islam) as a reconciler and revivalist. A Master of law, theology, and philosophy, for many years studied and practicsed Sufism. He systematized the study of the doctrines of Sufism and made them a regular branch of Islamic thought. He has exercised an influence on Sufistic and theological thinking. Despite continued differences of opinion between the *sūfīs* and many of the *Ulama*, Al-Ghazzali had secured a place for Sufism within the life of the community. He completed a reconciliation between orthodoxy and mysticism, which was early realized by Al-Harith b. Asad al-Muhasibi (d. 243/837) in a series of books most famous like *Al-Ri'āya li huquq Allah* (The Observance of God's rights) and the *Kitab al-nasā'ih* (Books of Counsels) claiming the *sūfīs* to be the truly orthodox and opening the door to reconciliation between theology and mysticism.[97] Al-Ghazzali's *magnum opus*, the *Ihya al-'Ulūm al-Dīn* (the Revivification of the Religious Sciences) proved to be the need of time, were intended for the edification of the general public and satisfying the demands of intellectualism. It remained relevant and panacean for all times scholars continued to bend fervently over the pages of Al-Ghazzali's great works for the reformation of Sufism and its reconciliation with *Shari'ah*.

96. Ibid., p. 215.

97. A.A.J. Arberry, *Mysticism in the Cambridge History of Islam*, pp. 608-09.

It is the contribution of these men of learning who came forward to reform "Sufism" and tried to reconcile it with theology and to purge it from heretic doctrines the corrupt influences and confusing deviations which penetrated it, throughout its history. Thereby saved "Sufism" from becoming an independent sect of Islam, a separatist movement such as those which had broken to fragments the legendary monolithic communion of the early years of the faith.[98] Thus "Sufism" is a legitimate spiritual manifestation and part and parcel of Islamic thought.

Reformism

The above-mentioned early major trends are in fact the manifestations of Islamic thought, throughout its history of development and response to the issues it encountered. There are certain personalities, whose contribution to its development is immense and un-paralleled.[99] Imam Al-Ghazzali was one of the greatest glories, renovator of the faith and contributor to the Islamic thought of the fifth–eleventh centuries Islam, which were particularly turbulent times in Muslim history. The universal caliphate had disintegrated into a system of decentralized and competing [states] sultanates whose only unity was the symbolic, though powerless, Abbasid caliph in Baghdad. Superstitious and fatalistic tendencies had infected much of popular Islamic belief and practice. The Isma'ili missionary propagandist, philosophers, deeply indebted to Hellenism and Neo-Platonism, and Sufism with strong emotional component and an electric propensity to accept superstitious practices were

98. Ibid., p. 614.

99. It has been foretold in the tradition that in the beginning of every century God brings forth a man who restores and reanimates the faith of the people.

actively undermining pristine Islam. Imam Ghazzali in his book, *Al-Munqidh Min al-Dalal* (Deliverance from Error) describes situations as:

> When I looked round, I found that faith of the people has been shaken owing to the influence of the philosophers, ignorance of the mystics, inertness of the religious doctors and the weak disheartened vindication of religion by the dialecticians. People were losing their conviction and, although some, overborne by philosophy, still fulfilled the religious obligations, they had hardly any conviction of faith left in their hearts.[100]

This was the period of Imam Al-Ghazzali. When he came forward, being well versed in the Muslim science, master of law, theology and philosophy and mysticism and his mind nourished on the purest marrow of the *Qur'an* and traditions and maintained an unshakable faith in the truth of Islam. As he writes:

> I realized that I could easily dispel their doubts. As a matter of fact, I found myself fully capable of exposing the hollowness and implausibility of their philosophic convictions because of the deep knowledge of speculative science. I, therefore, felt an ardent desire to take up this work, since it appeared to be the crying need of the time. I said to myself, How far does it befit thee to sit in seclusion? It is an epidemic that is spreading like wild fire and the learned have themselves fell a victim to the same disease. The bondsmen of God have reached the brink of destruction.[101]

Al-Ghazzali, accounted as the greatest Ish'ari theologian since

---

100. Abbreviated from *al-Munqid*, pp. 55-56, English translation from *al-Munqidh* by Claud Field.

101. Ibid., pp. 55-56.

Al-Ash'ari and the greatest *shafi* lawyer since Al-Shafi'i.[102] His contribution to Islamic thought to some extent can be estimated through books he authored, which have been counted among the best works written on the religion and philosophy of Islam, and has received a tribute of appreciation and praise from numerous scholars, both medieval and modern. Al-Ghazzali dedicated many works to refute and respond the challenges posed by the Isma'ili extremism, perhaps the important of which is the *Fadāih al-batinyyah wa fadā'il al-mustazhiriyyah* or *al-Mustazhiri* (the infamies of the Batinites and the excellences of the Mustazhirites) composed in 487-8/1094 and dedicated to the new caliph Al-Mustazhir.[103] He viewed Isma'ilism as a real danger for orthodox Islam, both politically and dogmatically. His effective answer to the challenge of Batinites made it a discredited sect ever after him.

Al-Ghazzali shows a certain reserve with regard to *'ilm al-kalam;* he wants to keep to essentials. He wrote his very last work, the *Iljam-ul-'Awam 'an-'Ilm il-kalam* (the restraining of

---

102. Abu Hamid Muhammad ibn Muhammad al-Ghazzali was born at Tus, a city in Khurasan, in Persia, in 450/1058. He received a good traditional education first at Jurjan and then Nishapur, provincial capital, where he attended the lessons of the most distinguished theologians of his times. The Asharite Imam al-Harāmayn Abul-Ma'ālial-Juwayni, under his guide, al-Ghazzali adopted the main principles of the Asharite *kalām*, to which he remained faithful until the end of his life. Nizamul Mulk Omnipotent vizier of Saljuk Sultan Malikshah appointed him teacher of Shafiite jurisprudence in the Madrasah Nizamiyyah of Baghdad, 484/1091.

103. Al-Ghazzali perhaps wrote three other treatises entitled *Hujjat-ul-Haq*, *Mufsalul-Khilaf* and *Qasim-ul-Batiniyah* and has mentioned the name of these books in his another book *Jawahir-ul-Qur'an*, p. 26. Two more books on the subject *Fadhayah al-Ibahiyah* and *Mawahim ul-Batiniyah* have been mentioned in the list of his writing.

the community from the science of *kalam*) to show how many and how great are the hazards of propagating science among people not prepared to receive it. He observes:

> The *Qur'anic* arguments are like food which provide nourishment to everyone while the logical system built-up by the dialecticians is similar to a medicine, which can be administered profitably to a few only, and may even have harmful effects for others not requiring it. . . . Since the time it was popularized, it has given rise to many evils which were not be found during the times of the Prophet's companions.[104]

In *Al-Iqtisad fi'l-i'tiqad* (the golden mean in belief)[105] al-Ghazzali stressed the importance of this science; as it allows us to know God, his attributes, the work of his messenger. But remarks that this interests only a certain number of persons, for *kalam* should not normally be used, save to dissipate the doubts of believers and try to convince intelligent infidels.[106]

Al-Ghazzali studied philosophy closely and it was through certain of his works on philosophy especially *Maqāsaid al-falāsifah* (the aims of philosophers) a reasoned and objective exposition of the main philosophical topic of his time; the west looked on him as *faylasuf* like *ibn sina* or *Ibn Rushd*. He did not consider himself a philosopher, nor liked to be considered as

---

104. *Iljam ul-Awamm*, p. 20, as quoted in Sayyed Abul Hassan Ali Nadwi, *Saviours of Islamic Spirit*, vol. I, p. 167.

105. Al-Ghazzali wrote only one treatise properly concerning *kalam*, namely *al-Iqtisad fil-itiqad*, composed the last time he stayed in Baghdad as a Professor in the Madrasah Nizamiyyah.

106. Georges C. Anawati, *Philosophy, Theology and Mysticism in Legacy of Islam*, Josep Schacht and C.E. Bosworth, eds., Oxford, 1979, p. 364.

such. Al-Ghazzali fought sharply against philosophy, trying to demonstrate its contradictions; argued that philosophy cannot assure the truth because it does not produce certainty. His famous work directed properly against philosophy, *Tahāfut al-falasifah* (the incoherence of the philosophy). Al-Ghazzali refuted those aspects of the philosophy of Avicenna (d. 1037) that he found unaccepted and argued dogmatically that philosophy is as dangerous as Ismailism, and in *Tahafut* Al-Ghazzali intended to demonstrate that philosophers are unable to prove, from a theoretical point of view, the religious truths. He argues that philosophers cannot demonstrate the creation of the world by God, or the spiritual substance of the human soul. Al-Ghazzali keeps religion and philosophy well separated, being aware of the essential irreducibility of the two positions. He maintained that while reason was most effective in mathematics and logic, its application to theological and metaphysical truths merely led to confusion and threatened the fabric of faith. He does not fight philosophers with the weapons of authority and divine revelations, but with the same techniques philosophy uses, and takes perhaps an even more rationalistic position.[107] It ought to be clear that Al-Ghazzali's attack on the philosophers, both the Greek and the Muslims was not aimed at philosophy as such, that is as *hikmah*, because *hikmah* as revealed in *Qur'an* is God's gift, the application of reason with wisdom, not only in religion but also in philosophy and science is commendable. It is significant to note that in the *Qur'an*, the major prophets were not only given the book that is *Al-kitāb*, but also the wisdom, that is *al-hikmah*, which explains accord between revelation and reason. What al-Ghazzali attacked was the metaphysical and religious

107. Massimo Companini, *Al-Ghazzali in History of Islamic Philosophy*, S.H. Nasr and Oliver Leaman, eds., London, 1996, pp. 261-62.

theories of the Greek philosophers, and their belief and the claim of the Muslim philosophers with regard to primacy of the intellect as the sole guide to the knowledge of the ultimate reality.

Al-Ghazzali at the peak of his power and fame, in 488/1095 owing to spiritual and psychological crisis, suddenly resigned from his chair of divinity in the Nizamiyya Academy in Baghdad and went into retirement. He left Baghdad and for two or three years, took up the life of a wandering *dervish*-lived in Syria and Palestine and made the pilgrimage to Mecca, dissatisfied with the speculative interest and legalistic approach to religion, studied and practised sufism. Later Al-Ghazzali reveals his conversion to Sufism in his moving spiritual autobiography *Al-Munqidah min al-Dalal* (Deliverance from Error) composed approximately between 501/1107 and 503/1109.

After an interval of self-discipline and meditation, Al-Ghazzali, more imbibed in Sufism than philosophy and scholastism, took up the task of reformation and revival of Muslim societies. He made a critical evaluation of the religious and moral state of the then Muslim society from an Islamic point of view, proposed measures to reform it and awakened the spirit of re-Islamization in the community. He pursued his reforming aim by composing what many regard as his great work, the revivification of the religious sciences *'Ihya' al-'Ulūm al-dīn* and an exhaustive abridgement of the major work, "that is the book of the forty principles of religion" *kitab al-arba'īn'* in *fi usul al-dīn,* as well as its Persian summary *kimiya-yi sa'ā dat* (the alchemy of happiness). *Ahya'ulum al-dīn* proved to be more than what its title claimed, and occupied a significant place among the few literary works which had an enduring effect in moulding the moral and spiritual life of the Islamic world and thereby a good contribution to Islamic thought itself.

After Al-Ghazzali, among the most distinguished figures of Islam, who took pains to reform and revitalize the Muslim societies on Islamic lines to purge them from corrupt ideas and practices — Ibn Taymiyyah is the most significant. His contribution to the Islamic thought was to reassert the supremacy of the *Qur'an* and *Sunnah,* and to demonstrate how, in the changed circumstances, the whole of the religious life and thought could be reconstructed on that basis. His full name, Ahmad Taqi ud-din Ibn Taymiyyah 1263-1329/AH 661-728; came of a reputed family of theologians belonging to Harran near Edessa (Roha) in northern Iraq. At the age of five he migrated with his father to Damascus, where he received a thorough education in the Hanbalite schools. As a result of his intellectual brilliance and wonderful memory, he completely assimilated all the knowledge of his time. The remarkable treasure house of lbn Taymiyya's mind enabled him to have at his finger tips the whole of the extant literature on exegesis, traditions, jurisprudence, dogmatic theology, scholastism history, biography, lexicography and syntax. He could always utilize this store house of knowledge in his thrilling career of intellectual and literary pursuits.[108]

Ibn Taymiyya's primary concern and literary endeavours, like Al-Ghazzali, which combined the dogma (tradition) with reason, was to clear away the cobweb spun by corrupt theologians and thought borrowed from un-Islamic sources. It was an age of Aristotelianism dominating the intellectual

---

108. Nadwi, *Saviours,* vol. II, op. cit., p. 61.

and literary scene.[109] Ibn Taymiyyah outstripped Al-Ghazzali in his assault on philosophy who had allowed for the right of reason to arbitrate in theological conflicts, and regarded logic as an instrument of thought. Ibn Taymiyyah advocating the empiricism and literalism; on his first small treatise entitled *Naqdh-ul-mantiq* and thereafter another detailed dissertation under the title of *Kitab ur Raddo 'al 'alal al-Mantaqin* (Refutation of the Logicians) criticized the philosophers because they brought so many foreign elements into theology from philosophy and other sources. He outrightly denounced all theological and philosophical methods of proof and called for the return of the way of *al-salaf al-salih* (pious ancestors). Ibn-Tayimiyya did not spare any of the philosophical sciences, including logic. In the words of Ibn Taymiyyah, the endeavour of the logicians amounted to mere "waste of time and energy, and unnecessary mental exercise and bragging which led people to useless disputation."[110] According to Ibn Taymiyyah, the Aristotelian theory of definition, which is one of the cornerstones of logic, is untenable, because of the difficulty of determining the infinite number of species and essential distinguishing traits, upon which definition actually depends. Another ill-effect of excessive logical ratiocination, according to him was that the theologicians too often become "incapable

109. It was because of the influence of great Muslim philosopher like Ibn Rushid, (d. AH 595) born after Abi Sina, but he shows for Aristotle the most unconditional reverence, going in this respect much further than his predecessors. When Ibn Taymiyyah came of age it was the influence of Nasir-ud-din Tusi (d. AH 672) and his two disciples Qutub-ud-din Shirazi and Qutub-ud-din Razi, regarding Aristotle as Agent Intellect whose findings were touchstone of reality, thereby giving a new lease of life to the Aristotelian thought in the east.

110. Ibn. Taymiyyah, Hafiz Ahmad Taqi ud-din, *Kitab-ur-Raddo'ala Mantiqiyin*, Bombay, 1368/1949, p. 31.

of expressing their ideas freely. It bridles their tongue and pen by restraining exercising their mind independently."[111] On the whole his attitude towards logic was not negative. He agreed that a part of it was not only correct and useful but even instinctive to a man endowed with reason. At the same time he contended that it also included fallacious arguments, which were not needed at all.[112]

Ibn Taymiyya's criticism was not confined to philosophy and its admirers alone; he did not spare even those dialecticians who strived to defend Islam but employed the philosophical doctrine and its terminology and syllogism to establish the facts of unseen and unknowable reality; for, the philosophical terms tended to impart a limited and incorrect exposition to the transcendental realities owing to their association with the philosophical traditions and percepts. In *Kitab-un-Nabowat* he says:

> the writings of these dialecticians affirming creation, resurrection, hereafter and the existence of the creator are neither rationally persuasive nor canonically reassuring, and this has been acknowledged by the dialecticians as well. They followed neither the path of the rationalists nor followed the teachings of the Prophet with the result that on the one hand; they deviated from their ingenious nature, and, on the other, were also deprived of the conviction imparted by the *Shari'ah.* Their rationalism led them only to uncertainty and unnecessary quibbling and hairsplitting of imaginary issues.[113]

---

111. Ibid., p. 194.
112. Ibid., p. 201.
113. Ibn Taymiyyah, *Kitab-un-Nabuwat*, Matb'a Muniriyah, Cairo, AH 1346, p. 148, as quoted in Sayyid Abud Hassan Ali Nadwi, Saviours of Islamic Spirit, vol. 2, p. 106.

According to Ibn Taymiyyah, the theory of the syllogism is not the only satisfactory method of reasoning, and is equally untenable because the ultimate validity of the syllogism dependant on self-evident propositions intuitively apprehended. Considering the diversity of human aptitudes, such apprehension will always remain dubious or questionable. Ibn Taymiyyah strongly pleaded that the arguments put forth by the *Qur'an* which are much more assuring and carry a deeper sense than proposition of the philosophers and dialecticians and do not suffer from paralogism, which is a common feature of logical disputation.[114]

Ibn Taymiyyah as an independent thinker, well-grounded in a wide range of religious and non-religious sciences, wrote enormously on many subjects, which he found are challenging the Islamic thought from within and without. His enormous work entitled *Al-jawab-ul-sahih liman baddala din-il Masih* (The Correct Answer to those Who have Changed the Religion of the Christ). As name indicates is a refutation, in particular of the work of a trans-Jordanian Melchite bishop named Peter who wrote at the end of the ninth century.[115] This incisive work of Ibn Taymiyyah adequately met all the objections raised against Islam, quoted the prophecies about the Prophethood of Muhammad (SAAS) contained in the Bible argued against the possibility of the incarnation of God in Christ by using Peter's own arguments against him traced the history of Christian church and its scholasticism and examined the varying interpretations of the Christian faith as expounded by church fathers from time to time.

Ibn Taymiyya's approach to Sufism was critical, he

114. *Kitab-ur-Raddo'alal Mantaqiyin*, op. cit., p. 150.

115. Jane I. Smith, "Islam and Christendom" in *The Oxford History of Islam*, John L. Esposito, ed., Oxford University Press, 1999, p. 332.

protested vehemently against pantheistic doctrines and all sorts of innovations (*bidat*) diffused by the *Sūfi* mystics; which threatened to contaminate the teachings of Islam, and had given birth to numerous heretical beliefs and customs. In the process of refutation of pernicious *Sūfi* ideas and practices, Ibn Taymiyyah left number of writings, which includes *ar-Radd-o-alal Baki, al-Tawassul wal-Wasilah* (Monograph on the Subject of Intercession), *Ziarat Qabboor wa-Istanjad bil-Qaboor,* which aims at rejecting everything resembling "Union with God" which many *sūfīs* believe as the highest aim of human life. Absorption into one or even contemplation of the greatest good,[116] supplicate to any departed soul, whether a prophet or a saint either by way of appeal or intercession. Similarly to prostrate before any being, living or dead, or to pay homage to anybody in a way prescribed for divine service and many prevalent *Sūfi* practice, which he felt to be at variance with *Shari'ah.* For him the highest aim was the worship or service of Allah (*Ibada*), whose basis was the observance of the prescriptions of the *Shari'ah.* And regarded all the later *Sūfi* developments as deviations or heresies *bida.*

Ibn Taymiyyah endeavoured to use his intellect and erudition to revitalize all branches of Islamic thought including jurisprudence. Islamic law, the product of an essential dynamic and creative process, after the tenth century tended to become fixed and institutionalized. Jurists were no longer to seek new solutions or produce new regulations, instead it was generally considered that Islamic law (Islamic way of life) has been satisfactorily and comprehensively delineated in its essential principles, and preserved in the regulations of the law books or legal manuals produced by the law schools. This attitude led many to conclude that individual, independent

116. W. Montgomery Watt, *Islamic Philosophy and Theology,* Edinburgh University Press, Edinburgh, 1962, p. 162.

interpretation (*ijtihad*) was no longer necessary or desirable, commonly referred to as the closing of the gate or door of *ijtihad,* thereby over emphasizing to simply follow or imitate (*taqlid*) the past. Ibn Taymiyyah originally a *Hambali,* but did not follow any particular school exclusively. In specific matters, he preferred the school, which more appealed to reason, or which he found upheld by a greater number of Prophet's companions and their successors.[117] And in few cases he drew up his statement of legal position disagreeing with all the four principle juristic schools, reviewed several issues with the fullness of a critical mind, which imparted a fresh dynamism to the legal system.[118] Therefore, breaking the stagnation and paving the way for *ijtihad*. His constant endeavour was to provide guidance for the changing needs in the light of the *Shari'ah,* and to bring in a closer conformity between the principles of legal system and the *Qur'an* and the *Sunnah.*[119]

Ibn Taymiyyah recognized only the *Qur'an* and the *Sunnah* as the two valid basis for the reconstruction of religious thought and followed none but the *salaf as-salihin* "the pious ancestors" in formulating his scheme of reform. He never compromised with any un-Islamic thought or practice pernicious to the oneness of God and the revelatory basis of creed and dogma, be it the popular belief of the misguided mystics and masses or the abuse of intellectual subtlety of philosophers and dialecticians or else the dogmatism of the

117. Abul Hassan Ali Nadwi, *Saviours of Islamic Spirit,* vol. II, ed. and trans. by Muhiuddin Ahmad, op. cit., 1947, p. 51.

118. Ibid., p. 51.

119. Ibid., p. 141, Ibn Taymiyyah's works on jurisprudence comprise, *Iqtidha-us-Sirat-il-Mustaqim,* smaller treatises like *Al-Qiyas* and *Minhaj-il-wasul ila-ilm-il-Usul* and voluminous collection of his juristic opinions under the title of *Fatawah Sheikhu-ul-Islam Ibn Taymiyyah.*

theologians and jurists.[120] Ibn Taymmiyya's contributions to the Islamic thought proved to be a milestone; with profound effect, set-up a trend; influence of his thought is still active in modern revivalist movements. His best known disciple Ibn Qayyim al-Jawziyya (1292–1350) did much to disseminate the ideas and perpetuate the influence of Ibn- Taymiyyah, both by transmitting the works of the master and through his own works.[121] The influence of Ibn-Taymiyya's teachings culminated in the eighteenth century in the rise of the "Wahhabi movements." The theological founder of this movement. Muhammad ibn Abd al-Wahhab (1703-92), born in Uyaynah studied at Mecca and Medina, travelled in Iraq and Iran; originally a Hanbali; incited by the teachings of Ibn Taymiyyah; led revivalist movement by making an "alliance" with local tribal chief of Diriyyah (in the Najd desert) Muhammad Ibn Saud (d. 1765).

The alliance of Abd-al-Wahhab, as religious or ideological head, with Ibn Saud as political and military chief, made it possible to launch a campaign to "purify" the Islamic faith and thereby control major parts of Arabia by "Wahhabis"[122] who preferred to call themselves *Muwahiddun* [unitrians, those who uphold and practice *tawhid* (monotheism)]. This rigid and confrontationist "Wahhabi movement" share with Ibn Taymiyyah and his school in addition to literalism, strict observance of the rituals, the condemnation of the cult of saints and "excesses" of the *Sūfi* orders, and its general insistence on a return to pristine Islam. "For the most part it is concerned

120. Nadwi, Saviours, vol. II, op. cit., p. 142.

121. Watt, *Islamic Philosophy*, op. cit., p. 164.

122. Wahhabism and Wahhabis are names, often used derogatorily by those outside its fold, given to the doctrine and followers of Muhammad Ibn Abdul-Wahhab, who annoyed by practice which he claimed were bordering on *kufr*.

largely with externals, like much of Islamic religious thought, it shows no interest in the methodology of Ibn-Taymiyyah, which he devised in order to escape from the rigidity of the scholastic methods and to make possible an adaptation of Islamic truth to contemporary conditions."[123] However the influences of Ibn Taymiyya's approach remains an important precursor in the formulation of Abdul-Wahhab's thought and his movement. Which (Wahhabism) has grown from its small localized beginnings to encroach into minds of many Muslim individuals and groups throughout Muslim world, its influence is undeniable.

The Salafiyyah movements started by Muhammad Abduh (1849–1905) and Rashid Rida (1865–1935) of Egypt also shows some signs of the influences of Ibn Taymiyyah. Actually a reformist movement owing much to the thought of Sayyid Jamul al-din al-Afghani (1838-97). Their journal called *al-Manar* ("The Beacon" or "Light-House") first published in 1898, principle vehicle for Abduh's and Rida's *salafi* reformism, remained infused with the influence of Ibn Taymiyya's thought.[124] More especially after the death of Abduh Rashid Rida adopted more radical approach and became an admirer of Ibn Taymiyyah and in particular of his methodology.[125]

The present day salafiyyah groups (the upholders of the traditions of the pious fathers of Islam). Sometimes known as "Neo Wahhabis" acknowledge the authority of Ibn Taymiyyah as the greatest medieval scholar and follow his pattern of interpretation of the Islamic thoughts. Thus the impact of Ibn Taymiyyah remains alive throughout, right from its inception and is continuing to bear fruit in present day Islam.

123. Watt, *Islamic Philosophy*, op. cit., p. 165.

124. H.A.R. Gibb, *Modern Trends in Islam*, Octagon Books, New York, 1978, pp. 34-35.

125. Watt, *Islamic Philosophy*, op. cit., p. 165.

2

Islamic Thought and Movements in the Subcontinent

THE message of Islam had reached the Indian subcontinent long before the forced incursions of Muslim armies started in the north of India. It was in the south of India that Arab traders after embracing Islam, continued their trade relations with the Western coast of India (Malabar),[1] and thereby were the first Muslims to arrive with the message of Islam. Islam is essentially a missionary religion and every Muslim, whatever their calling in life acted as *Da'i*, "missionaries of their faith." It should not, therefore, surprise us that Islam was introduced and disseminated peacefully, in the Malabar coasts by Arab merchants and traders soon after its advent in Arabia.[2] It is reported that Cheramān Permual Rājā of Malabar embraced Islam after being captivated by the report of Prophets miracle of lunar bisection and lucid exposition of the noble teachings

---

1. Malabar, Westernmost corner of India, Kerala of ancient times and the Malabar (Mali — mountain, bar — country) of the present day. (The old name, Kerala has now been restored to this region.) According to Arab geographers, Malabar was bound on the north by Gujarat and on the south by Kolam (Travancore). See Syed Sulaiman Nadwi, *Indo-Arab Relations* an English rendering of *Arab O' Hind ke ta'alluqat*, tr. Prof. M. Sallahudin (The Institute of Indo-Muslim East Cultural Studies, Hyderabad, India, 1962), p. 145.
2. Syed Sulaiman Nadwi, *Indo-Arab Relations*, p. 142.

of Islam preached by the visiting *dervishes*.[3] Another King, Rājā Zamorin, encouraged Muslim settlements in the Malabar Coast and allowed to build mosque. He was most partial to Muslims, and treated them with great consideration, most probably, in order to man the Arab ships on which he depended for his aggrandizement. Rājā Zamorin gave orders that in every family of fishermen (*makkuvans*) in his dominion, one or more of the male members should be brought up as Muslims.[4] Whatever may be the reason, the early Muslim traders and preachers found congenial environment in south India to preach and practice their religion; married with local women. They had entered into relationship with the people living round them, and from this intercourse of Arabs and locals a number of settlements of mixed descent had arisen, e.g. the Nawaits of Natia community in the Koṅkaṇ, the Mappilārs or Moplāhs of the Malabar coast, the Ravuttans and the Labbes[5] or Labia's on the east Tamil coast.

3. A company of pilgrims from Arabia were making a journey to visit Adam's footprints in Celone in a ship, which accidentally reached Kandanklur (Kandanganuur) a town on the Malabar Post, where they paid a visit to the Rājā Cheramān Perumal. After hearing from them *rājā* embraced Islam and when the pilgrims returned from their journey, he secretly accompanied them on their way back to Arabia, to visit the Prophet (SAAS). For full details see Zayn-ud-Din, *Tuhfah al-Mujahideen*, tr. Rowlandson, pp. 34-36 which is quoted by T.W. Arnold, The *Preaching of Islam*, Low Price Pub., Delhi 2nd edn., 1993, pp. 264-65 and also see, Tara Chand, *Influence of Islam on Indian Culture*, Indian Press (Pub) Private Ltd., Allahabad 1963, p. 34.

4. C.A. Innes, *Malabar and Anjengo Madras District Gazetter*, pp. 190 as quoted in Tara Chand, *Influence of Islam*, p. 36 also quoted by T.W. Arnold, *Preaching of Islam*, p. 264.

5. Tara Chand, *Influence of Islam*, p. 37; Murray Titus, *Indian Islam*, Oriental Books Reprint Corporation, New Delhi 2nd edn. 1979, p. 37 and "Muslim Colonies in India Before the Muslim Conquest" *Islamic Culture*, vol. VIII, p. 474, et seq., p. 600 et seq., vol. IX, p. 144 et seq.

The process of Proselytization and Islamizing of sub-continent by peaceful means, using soft power (moral suasion) was underway long before AH 93/CE 711 when an incident, seemingly minor forced the Muslim armies under the leadership of young and enterprising Imad-ud-din Muhammad bin Qasim, to undertake a regular campaign of reprisal against the Rājā Dāhir of Sind, who had refused to comply and expressed his inability to punish the perpetrators and return the property to Arab families[6] plundered near Sind by pirates on their route from cylone to Arabia.[7] Rājā Dāhir's connivance with pirates and the use of hard power (military muscle) by Hajjaj bin Yusuf governor of Basra, of the Ummayyad Kalifah Walid led by Muhammad bin Qasim resulted in the establishment and beginning of Muslim rule in Sind and its inclusion into the world of Islam. From that time onwards, Sind was never without Muslim influences. This episode marked an important chapter in the history of Islam in the subcontinent. A large section of population of Sind welcomed the victorious Muslim armies and looked at them as the liberator, from oppressive rule.[8]

Muhammad bin Qasim's rule in Sind though short-lived (AH 93/CE 712 – AH 96/CE 716) was hailed by the people of Sind. It served as a lodestar, a glorious precedent for

---

6. *Al-Baladhuri-Kitab Futuh-ul-Buldan,* tr. Elliot and Dawson, *History of India,* vol. I, p. 118.

7. For other causes cited for the invasion of Sind see C.K. Kareem, *What Happened in Indian History,* Paico Publishing House, Cochin, 11-1971, pp. 112-13.

8. *Al-Baladhuri-Futuh-ul-Buldan,* pp. 437-38 quoted by Syed Sulaiman Nadwi, *Indo-Arab Relations,* pp. 13-14 and also see Stanley Lanepole, *Medieval India under Muhammadan Rule [7102-1764],* Low Price Publications, Delhi, rpt. 1990, pp. 9-10.

subsequent Muslim rulers in India. Not a single instance of forced conversion to Islam occurred during this period. Religious tolerance was a reality and no temple was wilfully destroyed. The brāhmaṇas were treated with dignity and were entrusted with the offices of administration.[9] People of Sind enjoyed perfect freedom of worship and their religious practices were at no time interfered with the administration and financial affairs of the country were left almost entirely in the hands of conquered people.[10] The impact of Muslim rule under the leadership of Muhammad bin Qasim seems to be of immense benefit to the people of the region, as they accepted it wholeheartedly. When Muhammad bin Qasim was recalled, the people of the country bemoaned at the departure of so generous and just ruler. As a memorial they set-up a statue for him.[11] This phenomenal success of Muslim rule in Sind has been slurred over and deliberately ignored, by many for obvious reason of misrepresenting Muslim rule in India. The observation of Stanley Lane-poole that "The Arabs had conquered Sind, but the conquest was only an episode in the history of India and of Islam, a triumph without results"[12] seems jejune generalization. The fact is that it marks the commencement of Muslim rule in subcontinent even though, the campaign to conquer India militarily was not taken up after the establishment of Muslim rule in Sind and no further territorial gain was accomplished. But thenceforth, Sind never remained without Muslim influence; at least two independent Muslim states Mansura and Multan survived till the Ghaznavids storm erupted into northern India.

---

9. Iswari Prasad, *History of Muslim Rule*, p. 46.

10. C.K. Kareem, *What Happened in Indian History*, pp. 114-15.

11. *Al-Baladhuri-Futuh-ul-Buldan*, Beirut edn., 1958, p. 618; which is also quoted by S. Sulaiman Nadwi, *Indo-Arab Relations*, p. 10.

12. Stanley Lane-Poole, *Medieval India*, pp. 11-12.

In CE 1001 Ghaznavid's, after a interregnum of two and a half centuries of suspended military operations and abandonment of forceful conquest and expansion by Arabs from west of India via Markan into Sind started to storm India from north through Khyber Pass. This second wave of conquest was not led by Arabs but the Turks, the new enthusiastic entrants into the faith of Islam. Sultān Mahmud Ghaznavi (d. CE 1030) from CE 1001 to CE 1007 led almost seventeen incursions as far as Gujarat in west and Kannauj in the east of India, but contended himself with the annexation of the Punjab only. That with a governor at Lahore administering the outlying province as best he could. Punjab remained a political frontier of Muslim power in India and province of Ghaznavid Sultanate till it was disposed of by the Ghurids in 1186. It was century and a half after Mahmud Ghaznavi, Mu'izz al Din Muhammad bin Sam [Muhammad Ghori] (1030–1206) later assumed the title of the Sultan Shihab-ud-din[13] leading third series of campaigns, which finally culminated into the installation of Muslim government at Delhi in AH 582/CE 1192 after defeating Pṛthvīrāja at Tārain. Qutub-ud-din Aibak, a slave of Muhammad Ghori, was appointed viceroy of India, executing on behalf of Sultan at Ghazni. After the death of Muhammad Ghori in 603/1206,[14] Qutub-ud-din Aibak was enthroned as Sultan of Delhi, and thus India had a Muslim ruler of its own, ruling not from an outside capital but in India itself, which

13. Abdul Qadir Ibn-i, Muluk Shah [al Badaoni], *A History of India,* Muntakhabu-i-Tawarikh, tr. George S.A. Ranking, Atlantic Pub. & Distributors, New Delhi, 1990, pp. 64-65.

14. The days of his reign from the commencement of the rule of Ghaznin to the end of his life were thirty, two years and some months, and he left no heir save one daughter. He made expeditions to Hindustan nine times, twice was defeated and seven times victorious. Al-Badaoni, *A History of India,* p. 72.

ushered into existence the Sultanate that gradually brought the greater part of the subcontinent under its sway and established Muslim rule on a firm foundation, which was consolidated under numerous rulers and survived many tumults. From the enthronement of Sultan Qutub-ud-din Aibak CE 1206 to the catastrophe of Indian Mutiny CE 1857, there was always a Muslim ruler upon the throne of Delhi and the period can be divided into two phases — Delhi Sultanate and Mughal India. First phase comprises slave sultans, (CE 1206-90). They were all Turks. Next followed the Khaljis (CE 1290–1321) probably Turks in origin but essentially Afghans in association and character. The third was the Turkish house of Tughlaq (CE 1321-98). Finally routed by the Timur who marched upon Delhi in 801/1398; only to pave the way for Sayyid dynasty to hold power at Delhi which lasted till 1451. The Sayyid dynasty, though natives of India, claimed to be Arabian descent from the family of the Prophet Muhammad (SAAS).[15] Finally the Afghans Lodis (CE 1451–1526) seized the power, until defeated by the emperor Babur on the fatal field of Panipat in 1526.[16] Babur's assumption of power at Delhi marked the beginning of the second phase of Muslim rule in India, which lasted up to 1857; when the last Mughal ruler Bahadur Shah was deposed and exiled to Burma by Britishers.

Despite overwhelming military and political victories and more than six hundred years of Muslim rule, the total

---

15. I.H. Qureshi "Muslim India before the Mughals" in *The Cambridge History of Islam*, P.M. Holt, Ann K.S. Lambton and Bernard Lewis, eds Cambridge: Cambridge University Press, 1970, vol. 2, p. 5, Stanley Lane-Poole, *Medieval India*, p. 61.

16. The decisive battle was fought in 21 April 1526, on the plain of Panipat — the historic sites where the throne of India has been thrice won, ibid., pp. 200-01.

transformation of Indian subcontinent into a Muslim country was not achieved, save North-West Frontier Province, the Punjab and Bengal, where Muslims predominate. As compared to countries, Egypt, North Africa, Asia Minor, Persia, Central Asia, where Muslim armies and missionaries penetrated in the early centuries, complete victory of faith and power was accomplished in a short span of time and all the areas are now predominantly Muslim. The Muslim Empire in the subcontinent was sustained by comparatively a small Muslim population though numerous, as compared to many states but failed to translate its longevity to supplant and subsume the local population.[17] This cast light on the fact that the Muslim ruling class of subcontinent was interested not in the propagation of religion but the aggrandizement of their own rule, or if some of them were interested in religion but they did not use force to convert the people to their faith. After conquering Sind and Multan, Muhammad bin Qasim would have found no difficulty in forcing its people to accept Islam, if he had so desired, but the young Muslim leader scrupulously followed the teaching of Islam and avoided the use of force in matters pertaining to religion.[18] First of all, the fact that Islam never entertained the practice of forced conversion and an act of clear defiance against its teachings. The power of *Ulama'*, who exercised greater influence over the government, was an inhibiting factor and did not like any open violation of

---

17. L.S.S O'Malley, ed., *Modern Indian & West*, Oxford University Press, London 1968 pp. 5-7 — it gives some ideas about its failure, also see Monstuart Elphinstone, *The History of India*, 6th edn., London, 1874, p. 313.

18. S. Moinul Haq, *Islamic Thought and Movement in the Subcontinent (711-1947)*, Pakistan Historical Society Publication, No. 69, Karachi, 1979, p. 52.

Shar'iah.[19] Secondly, most of the rulers cared little for things spiritual and had indeed no time for the work of conversion, because of being continually engaged in wars.[20] It can also be judged from the fact that even in the centres of the Muṣlim power, such as Delhi and Agra, Muslims, after the decline of their power in the former district hardly exceeded one-tenth and in the later they did not form one-fourth of the population.[21] T.W. Arnold has mentioned some examples of astray cases of forced conversion, which proved futile and worthless, because fear occasionally dictated a timely acceptance, generally short-lived and ceased to be effective after the release of pressure[22] and he further says that "we undoubtedly find that Islam had gained its greatest and most lasting missionary triumphs in times and places in which its political power has been weakest, as in southern India and Eastern Bengal."[23]

Whatever, lasting success, to implant Islam in the sub-continent was achieved; it was mostly the result of the patient missionary endeavours of selfless preachers of Islam, who

---

19. Sikandar Lodi was once so carried away by his zeal that he wanted to destroy an old temple in Kurukṣetra and stop Hindu pilgrims from bathing in the water of a pond held sacred by them. Malik-ul-Ulamā' Abdullah Ajodhani Proclaimed boldly that the sultān could not do so under the law. This displeased the sultān, but he had to forego his intention — Abdullah, *Tarikh-i-Daudi* (British Museum Ms. Or. 97), F.19 as quoted in Ishtiaq Hussain Qureshi-*Ulamā' in Politics* Renaissance Pub., House Delhi, 1985, p. 25.
20. Sir Alfred C. Lyall, *Asiatic Studies,* London, 1882, p. 289; also quoted in T.W. Arnold Preaching, pp. 227-28.
21. Sir W.W Hunter, *The Religions of India* (Times, 25 February 1888), also quoted by ibid., p. 262.
22. Arnold, *Preaching in Islam,* pp. 256-63.
23. Ibid., p. 263.

continued their individualistic missionary activity and moral suasion, uninterrupted before and after the establishment of Muslim rule and quite independently of the political life of the country.[24] As mentioned above, missionary work was carried by traders and merchants in the south of the subcontinent. It has been on record that several companions of Prophet (SAAS) have visited the subcontinent in the time of the Khulafa-i-Rashidin[25] and it seems most probable that they must not have remained without indulgence in *Da'wah* work [Preaching of Islam], though lacking any records containing accounts of regular missionary activity in these days. Soon after the establishment of Muslim government in Sind, a large section of natives considering it a blessing and encouraging support by local population for its good governance created a favourable climate for missionary work. It also paved the way for large number of migration of *Ulama* and *mashā'ikh* armed with *zuhad* [asceticism], *taqwa* (piety) and religious zeal. Who, through their own personal interest in the spread of Islam and inspired with a Divine call,[26] dutifully, came to the subcontinent, unhindered by political anomaly. Little is known about the personalities of these early missionaries and their ideas and method of work.[27] A regular record of missionary work could be drawn from the *sūfīs*, who took over the *tabligh* (preaching of Islam) work, achieved prominence and are credited for the conversion of large section

24. Ibid., p. 255.

25. S. Moinul Haq, *Islamic Thought*, p. 51.

26. M.T. Titus, *Indian Islam*, pp. 41-42.

27. For some references to the activities of early missionaries please see Abdal-Hayy, *Mawlana Nuzhat al-Khawatir wa Bahjat al-Masamic wa'l Nawazir*, Hyderabad, Deccan, 1947; Shaykh Abd al-Haqq Dihlawi, *Akbar ul-Akhyar* (ed.), Mujtabai Press, Delhi, 1322 H and Nadwi Abu Zafar, *Tarikh-i-Sindh*, Azamgarh, 1947.

of population in the subcontinent, starts with Shaykh Ismail. He was the most famous of the Sayyids of Bukhara. He is said to have been the first Muslim to start *tabligh* in Lahore and settled there in 395/1005. After a long period of education and *tabligh* work he died in 448/1056.[28] Another *alim* and *Sūfi* Shaykh Hussayn Zanjani, is said to have come and settled in Lahore before and died on the arrival of Shaykh Ali Hujwiri,[29] the author of well-known work on Sufism and the *sūfīs*, *Kashf al-Mahjub*. He also settled at Lahore and died there sometime between CE 1072 and 1079. Ali Hujwiri popularly known as Data Ganj Bakhsh (lit. a giver of treasures), greatest and most important of the early *Ulama* and *sūfīs* of the subcontinent, left no *silsilah* of disciples behind him, but through his book he has exercised an extensive and lasting influence over the succeeding generations of Muslims in the subcontinent. *Kashf al-Mahjub* originally in Persian, is a compendium of *Sūfi* doctrines and practices of various *Sūfi* schools.[30]

Khwajah Shaykh Mu'in-ud-din Chishti established himself at Ajmer, probably a little before the decisive second battle of Tarāin between Shihabuddin Ghori and Pr̥thvīrājā. He was the most famous Muslim missionary and leading personality of the thirteenth century. His philanthropic, pious way of life and fame as a teacher attracted a number of devoted disciples around him and a large number of people embraced Islam

28. For details and dates see Sarwar Ghulam, *Khazinat al Asfiya*, Lahore, 1284 H, vol. II; also see Mawlawi Rahman Ali, *Tadhkirah-i-Ullema-i-Hind*, Urdu tr., Karachi, 1961, p. 111.

29. Shaykh Nizam al Din Awliya, *Fawaid al-Fu'ad*, Lucknow, 1849, p. 35.

30. For a brief account of the subject and topics discussed in the *Kashfal Mahjub*, see S.A. Rashid, *The Life and Teachings of Hazrat Data Ganj Bakhs*, Lahore, 1967, chapter III.

because of his *tabligh*. He died in Ajmer in CE 1236. Shaykh Baha'ud din Zakariya and Shaykh Jalal Tabrizi and many others, are only few leading names that came to the subcontinent to win peaceful spiritual battle.

In the wake of establishment of Muslim rule in the subcontinent, an influx of *Ulama* and *Sūfi* saints entered this country; set-up mystic centres at a number of places within a short span of time in the entire subcontinent from Multan to Lakhnuti [Bengal] and from Panipat to Deogīr, *Sūfi* saints built their centres of *tabligh*. Early in the fourteenth century a traveller informed Shihab-ud-din al-Umari at Damascus: "In Delhi and its neighbourhood are *khanqah*s, and hospices numbering two thousand."[31] These *Sūfi*-Shaykhs sent their trained disciples to different regions, where they settled and started the work of *tabligh* (preaching Islam) and provided guidance to the Muslims. Like the *madrasahs* of the *Ulama* network of *Sūfi*-centres or *khanqah*s spread over the entire subcontinent. While the former concentrated on teaching and popularizing education, the *Sūfi*-Shaykhs mostly devoted their energies to the spiritual and moral aspects of life and laid great emphasis on *Khidmat-i-khalq* (Service of Humanity).

By the thirteenth-century spiritual aspect of Islamic thought "Sufism" or *tasawwuf* had entered the last and most important phase of its historical development, the organization of *silsilah*.[32] It had become a movement and had pervaded Muslim religious thought. Indeed it brought Islam to the

31. *Masalik al-Absar fi mamlik al-Amsar*, English tr. O. Spies, p. 24. As quoted in Khaliq Ahmad Nizami, *State and Culture in Medieval India*, Adam Pub. and Distributors, New Delhi, 1985, p. 180.

32. Khaliq Ahmad Nizami, *Some Aspects of Religion and Politics in India During the Thirteenth Century*, Idrah-i-Adabiyat-i-Dehli-Delhi, 1961, p. 174.

masses and the masses towards Islam, especially in the subcontinent. It also supplemented the work of *Ulama* in building up springs of spiritual fervor that deepened religious consciousness and loyalty to Islam, however the vogue of Sufism opened the way to many abuses.[33] In the earlier stages the *Ulama* and *Sūfi*-Shaykhs. The two groups of religious leaders worked in harmony, and in a way their activities were complementary, but it appears that in course of time some of them began to criticize and even oppose one another. Political leadership became completely immersed in the administrative and allied problems. Literary classes remained confined to *madrasah*s, most of which were attached to mosques. They were started either by the scholars themselves or by philanthropic individuals who were interested in the growth of knowledge and were in a position to maintain educational institution; some of them were started and patronized by the rulers and had developed into famous centres of learning. The responsibility of preserving and maintaining the fundamental aspects of Islamic society became the concern of the *Ulama* who devoted their lives to the study of religious sciences and the dissemination of knowledge. The attitude of the *Sūfi*-Shaykhs [*masha'ik*] towards society and state was sharply in contrast to that of the Muslim governing classes and the orthodox section of the theologians.[34] They threw open the doors of their *khanqah*s to all sorts of people, concentrated their attention on moral and spiritual purity of life. They worked even among the Laity and lower section of society. The majority of people in the subcontinent embraced Islam after being induced by teaching and moral suasion of *Sūfi*-

---

33. I.H. Qureshi, *Ulama in Politics*, Renaissance Pub. House, Delhi, 1985, p. 26.
34. Khaliq Ahmad Nizami, *State & Culture*, p. 180.

Shaykhs. They exercised greate. influence on the people than any other, even the rulers and elite revered them, and their influence is still powerful and active in the subcontinent.

During the long period of Muslim rule in the subcontinent Islamic culture got nourished more on *Sūfi* path than following the *Shari'ah* rules befitting the local deep rooted system of mystical religious thought of the subcontinent. It took roots immediately in the life of the people and from the very beginning did not seem extraneous element.[35] The *Sūfi silsilah*s which thrived in the subcontinent, were the Chishti and the Suhrawardi simultaneously flourished with the foundation of sultanate of Delhi and Naqshbandi and Qadiri *silsilah*s during the Mughal period. Chistiyya *silsilah* was introduced in the subcontinent by Khwajah Muin al-din, it was first to enter the subcontinent and its leaders and workers spread themselves in much large number and vast areas came under their influence than those of other, *silsilah*s. The Suhrawardiyya *silsilah*, founded by Shaykh Abu al-Najib 'Abd al-Qadir Suhrawardi (490/1097-562/1168), uncle and spiritual guide of Shaykh Shuhab al-din Suhrawardi (d. 632/1234) was established in the subcontinent by the latter's *khalifah*, Shaykh Baha al-din Zakariya in the early decades of the thirteenth century. The origin of the Naqshbandiyya *silsilah*, which draws its name from Khwajah Baha'al- din Naqshbandi, the *shaykh*s of the Naqshbandi *silsilah* started coming to the subcontinent soon after the establishment of Mughal rule. It is however through Khwajah Baqi bi Allah (971 or 972/1563 or 1564 - 1012/1603) and his successors that the Naqshbandiyya *silsilah* was fully established in this region. The Qadiriyya *silsilah* which was established in the subcontinent much later than the Chishtis and the Surhrawardis drew its name from the great Shaykh

35. M. Mujeeb, *The Indian Muslims*, p. 117.

Muhyi al-Din 'Abd al-Qadir Gilani of Baghdad (471/1079-1166) who is regarded as one of the most distinguished *Sūfi-shaykhs*. In the subcontinent the chief centre of the early Qadiriyya Shaykhs was Uchh; it was set up by Shaykh Muhammad al-Hussyani al Gilani who died in 923/1517. He had left four sons who were all respected by the people, but none commanded wider influence than Sayyid 'Abd al-Qadir Thani; he was given this epithet because in saintliness (*wilayat*) he was true descendent of his great ancestor. Besides Sind and the Punjab, the Qadiriyya *silsilah* also spread into other regions of the subcontinent.

Early *Sūfi-shaykhs* and the establishment of their *silsilah* made substantial contribution to the growth and expansion of Islam, played most effective role in the evolution, development and stability of Islamic society. They laid great stress on the observance of *Shari'ah*. But the liberal attitude of many *Sūfīs* towards other modes of thoughts and behaviour, incompatible with the *Shari'ah*, brought derisive comments from the *Ulama* "orthodox theologians" and severed their relations. The early harmony of *Ulama* and *Sūfi-shaykhs* began to drift apart as corrupt and deviationistic ideas crept in some *sūfīs* by absorbing outside influence. Along with men of great attainments, it also bred many charlatans and pretenders, who opened the way to many abuses and created misunderstanding about the true mission and achievements of Sufism. The strong emotional component and an eclectic propensity to accept superstitious practices were causes, which led many *Ulama* to regard sufism as a distinct creed and its doctrines and practices as heretical, as an unwarranted deviation or innovation (*bidat*) from the orthodox Islam.

The orthodoxy in Muslim India from the time of establishment of Delhi Sultanate, came to mean *taqlid* (acceptance or pursuit) of the Sunni Hanafi *fiqh*,[36] which received official recognition and support, and constituted the *Shari'ah* of Islam,[37] and it was the duty of rulers to maintain and enforce through the qadis, the *muhtasib*s and the jurists. Sultan himself had no authority in matters of religion, and these official *Ulama* were unable to implement the same without the permission of Sultan.[38] This alliance and sometimes the complicity of official *Ulama* and rulers, was often criticized by independent *Ulama* and *sūfī*s, whenever there was anything contrary to *Shari'ah*. These *Ulama*, as government servants; were often seen as co-opted by power, tolerating and supporting the socio-political abuses and excesses of the government. The independent *Ulama* and *Sūfi*-Shaykhs kept themselves aloof from the establishment of power and confined their activities to social and religious reform only. Usually they preferred to live at a distance from the court, but at the same time they did not evade the responsibility of serving humanity as a whole and reforming the influential element of society. It was due to the reformative endeavours of these independent *Ulama* (religious thinkers) and genuine *Sūfi*-Shaykhs that dignity and preponderance of *Shari'ah* was maintained in the society.

Religious thought in the subcontinent from very beginning was torn between the orthodoxy and Sufism. Genuine religious thinkers (among *Ulama* as well as *mashaik*) persistently strived

---

36. The standard work on Hanafi *fiqh* being the *Hidayah* of Burhanuddin Abul Hassan Ali Marghinani, written in the twelfth century. The Hanafi Sunnis being a vast majority in India had dominated the Shiah Sects, existing in India from the ninth century and other *sunni* schools of thought smaller in number.

37. Ibid., p. 58.

38. *Fatawa-i-Alamgiri, Kitab al-Qadi,* Matba al-Kubra, in Egypt, 1310 AH, vol. I, p. 145 as quoted in ibid., p. 67.

to harmonize dogmatic beliefs with the spiritual qualities of Sufism and they continuously endeavoured to purge pernicious and negative aspects; indictment of the hypocrisy of the orthodox (official *Ulama*) and innovation and extravagance of Sufism. The religious thinkers, who struggled for the reformation and dissemination of religious thought, independently, during the period of Delhi Sultanate, provided us with scanty records of their assertiveness. Mawlana Nur Turk, prominent for his captivating eloquence, erudition, spirituality and audaciousness in criticizing the official *Ulama* on account of their materialistic pursuits himself led an austere life, refused to accept money gifted to him by Razia Sultana (1236-40). Undaunted by the life of penury he unrelentingly persuaded his mission.[39] Mawlana Shaykh Nizam-ud-din Abul Muwayyid was another very effective speaker of Medieval India, reputed for his personal piety, adherence to the laws of *Shari'ah* and punctuality in the performance of religious duties.[40] Mawlana Diya'uddin Sunami,[41] Mawlana A'Lā-ud-din Usuli,

39. His eloquent sermons elicited praise from a scholar and saint of Shaikh Farid Ganj-i-Shakar's eminence. But Minhajuddin Siraj, who was Sadr and Shaikh al-Islam at the time, has written adversely about him in *Tabaqat-i-Nasri*, pp. 189-90. English tr. by H.G. Raverty (Bibliotheca Indica, 1897). For brief notice K.A. Nizami, 13th century, op. cit., p. 157 and M. Mujeeb, *Indian Muslim*, p. 99.

40. *Fawaid-ul-Fuād*, p. 192 (Conversations of Shaikh Nizamuddin Auliya, compiled by Amir Hassan Al Sijzi, Newal Kishore Press, Lucknow, 1302 AH).

41. Mawlana Diyauddin Sunami was contemporary of Shaikh Nizamuddin Auliya and must have lived between 1225 and 1325. He was known for his integrity and piety critisised Nizamuddin Auliya for listening to songs and of dancing in ecstasy. He was very particular in the matters of the *Shari'ah* and wrote a book *The Nisab-i-Ihtisab* which is not extant Shaykh Abul Haq Muhadith, *Akhbar ul-Akhyar*, Mujtabai, Press, Delhi, AH 1309, p. 108.

Mawlana Kamaluddin Zahid and Shaykh Burhanuddin Nasafi[42] were also among the reputed religious scholars with rare spirit of independence; resisted co-option by the state, even when pined in penury. They stressed for the adherence to *Shari'ah* and imparted free education to students who gathered round them in large numbers, during the time of Delhi Sultanate Mir Sayyid Muhammad of Jaunpur[43] (1443–1523) reputed for his erudition and piety. His eloquence and effective preaching influenced a number of earnest minded men who gathered around him and culminated into a reformist movement known as the *mahdavis*.[44] "The first expression of religious thought was an active and assertive force in Indian Muslim society."[45] Because of Sayyid Muhammad's claim to be the *mahdi* and resultant confrontation with the orthodox *Ulama* and the government (the active and militant *mahdawis* took upon themselves the enforcement of the *Shari'ah* upon the populace. They not only preaced and admonished but also used force; this naturally brought them into conflict with the government, the enforcement of law was rightly considered to be whose monopoly) this originally a reformist movement demanding greater conformity with the *Shari'ah* was denounced as unorthodox therefore a heresy. That subdued its efficacy and could not serve long enough as leavening influence, resulting only into the creation of a small insignificant sect of Islam

42. For brief notices see *Fawaid-ul-Fuad*, pp. 165-66, *Akhbar ul-Akhyar*, pp. 76-77.

43. Abdul Qadir Badaoni, *A History of India* (*Muntakhabui-Tawarikh*, English trn. George S.A. Ranking, Atlantic Pub. & Distributors, New Delhi, 1990, p. 420.

44. For a history of the *mahdawi* movement, vide W.A. Erskine, *A History of India under the First Two Sovereigns of the House of Taimur*, V.II, London 1845, p. 475.

45. M. Mujeeb, op. cit., p. 101.

about which one does not hear much either in the religious or the political sphere.[46]

During the Delhi Sultanate and Early Mughal period, when Muslim rulers as well as established system of official *Ulama* was strong and claimed to be the sole representative of orthodox Islam. The reformist tendencies to address the serious morbid conditions of Muslim community were individualistic and localized, generally passive in their attitude and apprehensive to call for social action against state structure and policy; what they considered as negation of the *Shari'ah*. Therefore, they showed restrains and resorted only to admonition. This passive resistance of the independent religious thinkers was owing to the fact that they feared to incur the sin of creating dissension and conflict within the Muslim body politics which was still in the early stages of stabilizing the foundations of their social structure and thereby were apprehensive of not to jeopardize Muslim rule in the subcontinent by resorting to active resistance.

The unorthodox and heretic tendencies, which had crept in the religious ideas and practices of the Muslim community in the subcontinent finally culminated in the Akbar's folly[47] — *Dīn-i-Ilahi* (Divine Faith). It was a novel experiment in the domain of religion, made by a powerful sovereign with the assistance and co-operation of group courtiers. It could not spread beyond court circles and died with the monarch around whose personality it was made to grow around and revolve. Nevertheless, it left behind deep traces on the socio-religious life of some sections of the Muslims, particularly a growing

46. I.H. Qureshi, *Ulamā'*, p. 40.

47. Vincent Smith, *Akbar, The Great Mogul*, 2nd edn., Indian Prir.:, Delhi, 1958, pp. 159-60.

laxity in the observance of *Shari'ah* laws. This was natural because the main target of the attack of the promoters of *Dīn-i-Ilahi* was the supremacy of *Shari'ah* for which they used the term, *Islam-i-Majazi*. It was considered by them to be a great obstacle in the path of despotism.[48] Popularly as well as legally, Muslim Empire in the subcontinent had been a citadel of orthodoxy and were expected to be the protector of the purity of the faith. Instead it was being subverted by hostile elements at the instigation and with the active support of the head of the state.

This was fundamentally irresistible phenomenon; Akbar's persecution of orthodox Islam and the dissemination of heretic ideas and practices could not evade reaction. The first manifestation of discontent was the rebellion in Bengal, which was fomented and abetted by the Mulla Muhammad Yazdi's *fatawā* and the reports about Akbar's aberrations. Insurrections in the north-west as well as in Bengal were quelled by Akbar. As a preemptive policy to stop any rebellion the number of *Ulama* were uprooted from their homes and dismissed from their offices.[49] The leaders of orthodox *Ulama* at the court Makhdum al-Mulk Shaykh 'Abd al-Nabi and Shahbaz Khan Kanbu had gradually lost their influence and were subjected to disgrace. Their fall was a symbol of the defeat of orthodoxy at the court.

Independent *Ulama* and *Sūfi-shaykhs* were quick to realize the dangerous consequences of the growth of heretic tendencies, and therefore, endeavoured to restore the supermacy of *Shari'ah*. *Sūfi-shaykhs*, who usually remain aloof for spiritual elevation and confine themselves to moral reform;

48. S. Moinul Haq, *Islamic Thought*, p. 258.
49. I.H. Qureshi, *Ulama*, pp. 75-76.

took upon themselves the responsibility of safe-guarding the ascendancy of *Shari'ah*. The leading *Sūfi-shaykhs* and *Ulama* who fought against the forces of heterodoxy in the reign of Akbar and Jahangir, were Shaykh Abd-ul-Haqq Muhaddith of Delhi[50] and Shaykh Ahmad of Sirhind.

Shaykh Abd-ul-Haq (b. 1551) was born in a family noted for its piety and learning. Received his early education under his father Sayf al-Din who was both an eminent scholar and a devoted *Sūfi* of Qadiriyya *silsilah*, which he instilled into his son also. Shaykh Abd-ul-Haq being an assiduous student from his childhood went to Hejaz, where he became a pupil of the famous scholar, Shaykh Abd-ul-Wahhab Muttaqi;[51] whose influence on Abd-ul-Haq remained throughout. He taught him not only *Hadith* but, after he had acquired proficiency in it, Shaykh Muttaqi gave him books on *tasawwuf* to read and then prescribed suitable exercises[52] in order to equip him with the requirement, which suits a person who has to work in the subcontinent. In spite of Abd-ul-Haq's reluctance his teacher was firm and wanted him to return as expeditiously as possible to work as a reformer in the subcontinent, envisaging it a dire need. Abd-ul-Haq realized that the conditions in the subcontinent did invite such endeavour therefore, payed attention to his teacher's admonitions and finally obeyed and returned to the subcontinent in 1000/1591 after having spent three years under Abdul Wahhab's guidance.[53] In the subcontinent, Abd-ul-Haq obtained training in Naqshbandiyya *silsilah*, under Khwajah Baqi bi Allah, without loosing his ties

50. For his life and works see Khaliq Ahmad Nizami, *Hiyat-i-Shaikh Abdul-Haqq Muhaddith Dehlawi*, Delhi, 1953.

51 Ibid., p. 108.

52. Ibid., pp. 134, 136.

53. Ibid., p. 123.

with the Qadiriyya *silsilah*. Naqshbandis added a new dimension to his spiritual accomplishment because this *silsilah* was strongly tied to the basic teachings of *Shari'ah* and discouraged heretic ideas and practices, which had infiltrated in some extremist *Sūfī*s of other *silsilah*s. Shaykh Abd-ul-Haq acknowledged himself of having got benefited from Naqshbandi relation as they provided a better balance for the intellectual and mystic trends which suited Shaykh's mind.[54] Shaykh Abd-ul-Haq was a reputed *muhaddith* (an authority on *Hadith*) and a *Sūfi* of great attainments, a dichotomy well balanced in him.[55] This provided him an opportunity to bridge the gap between *Ulama* and *mashaikh* and harmonize their activities in the field of religious reform.[56]

Shaykh Abd-ul-Haq was a remarkable scholar of *Hadith; sirah, tafsir, fiqh* and *tasawwuf*; with his erudition, he made a substantial and lasting contribution to the reformative movement for the restoration of the supremacy of *Shari'ah*. His *modus operandi* included teaching and writing. He started teaching the exegesis of the *Qur'an* and *Hadith*, hitherto, there was more stress on the study of *fiqh*,[57] as is customary with the theological seminaries even today. He adopted a different

54. I.H. Qureshi, *Ulama*, pp. 82, 84.

55. Ibid., p. 82.

56. In the beginning there was no such distinction, but later it appeared as if the *Ulama* advocated the *Shari'ah* while the *sūfī*s clung to *tariqah* and that the two were different paths, the main cause of difference between them was that most of the persons who pretended to be *sūfī*s were ignorant and illiterate and majority of the *Ulama* had become worldly-minded. Both used their energies to criticize one other and thereby furthering the deterioration of Islamic society.

57. It was in vogue to lay emphasis on the study of jurisprudence because graduates of their seminaries were mostly employed as *qadi*s and *mufti*s and were required to be well grounded in *fiqh*. →

core, and felt it necessary to lay emphasis on fundamentals of religion (*aqidah*) in order to equip the students of religious sciences properly to eradicate and extricate Muslims of the subcontinent from the confusion and mess created by heretic ideas of heterodox *sūfīs*, *bhakti* saints and disastrous aberrations of Akbar.[58] Being a prolific writer Shaykh Abd-ul-Haq produced voluminous literature of high quality and varied in its scope. He wrote books and treatises on the importance of *Shari'ah* and study of *sirah, Hadith, fiqh* and *tasawwuf* and has thus made a lasting contribution to the development of Islamic studies in the subcontinent, which could not fail to produce significant results. His famous book on *sirah* (life of Prophet) is *Madarij al-Nubuwwat,* which is an authentic and comprehensive work and one of the earliest biographies of the Prophet written in the subcontinent. The aim of writing a book on the life of Prophet (SAAS) was to reiterate and explain the significance of his *Hadiths.* As he writes "due to the mischief of the present age, deviation (from the right path) has found a way into the disposition of some proud *darwishe*s of the day and owing to the opacity and narrowness of their understanding they are unable to assess the height and sublimity of the sacred position of Prophet Muhammad (SAAS) hence, being a Muslim it is my duty to write a book on the life and virtues of the leader of the Prophets, educator of all (*ustad-i-kull*), means of all proficiency and perfection and manifestation of goodness and beauty. Thereby make known

---

→ Furthermore the general populace was more concerned with problems of *fiqh* alike in the performance of religious rites and dealings with others. They, therefore, expected every person educated in the religious science to give them guidance in the field of *fiqh*., I.H. Qureshi, *Ulama,* p. 81.

58. I.H. Qureshi, *Ulama*, p. 81.

to these benighted people, the true facts and realities and wake up those who are indifferent and provide guidance to those who want to know the truth and intensify the ardour and desire of the lovers."[59] His another famous book *Akhbar-al-Akhyar* is an excellent and authentic work on the lives of the *Sūfi-shaykh*s of the subcontinent. Shaykh Abd-ul-Haq used his academic excellence for the reformation of Muslim society and also emphasized the need of complete accord in the various disciplines of Islamic learning. His efforts could not fail to produce significant results, besides important writings, he wrote letters to his friends, eminent scholars, *shaykh*s of the time and people of high rank and position, which are like short treatises (*risalah*) on important topics. Shaykh Abd-ul-Haq endeavoured through his letters to persuade leading figures of the period to emphasize on the observance of the laws of *Shari'ah*. Shaykh Abd-ul-Haq Muhaddith Dehlawi had a significant, scholarly role as a socio-religious reformer in the history of the subcontinent.

Shaykh Ahmad of Sirhind better known as Mujaddid-i-alf-i-Thani (renovator of the second millennium) (AH 971/CE 1564 – AH 1034/CE 1624) is among the most prominent of religious leaders of seventeenth-century subcontinent. In fact, his vigorous efforts to restore the supremacy of *Shari'ah* and reform lives of the people accordingly, overshadowed all other reformists of the period. Born in a family with a long scholarly tradition which traced its decent from the caliph Umar Farūq (RAA). He received his early education from his father, Shaykh Abd-ul-Ahad (927/1521 – 1007/1598) a reputed scholar and *Sūfi*. After memorizing *Qur'an* he learned logic, philosophy

---

59. Shaykh Abd al-Haqq, *Madaraji al, Nubuwwat,* Kanpur, 2nd ed., 1905, p. 3.

and theology from Mulla Kamal Kashmiri (d. 1017/1608-9) at Sailkot and then studied *Hadith* with Shaykh Yaqub Sarfi (d. 1003/1594) and read some advanced texts of *tafsir* and *Hadith* with Qazi Bahlul Badakhshani.[60] He was also trained first in Chishtiyya and later in the Qadiriyya and Kubrawiyya *silsilah* under his father's guidance and proved to be as proficient in Sufism as he did in formal theological learning.[61] In the 1008/ 1600 a year after the death of his father Shaykh Ahmad left his home in Sirhind for *hajj*. On his way to much cherished pilgrimage Shaykh Ahmad was introduced to Shaykh Abdul Baqi (Khwajah Baqi Billah) [971/1563 - 1012/1603], the first Naqshbandi saint deputed to India, who had attained high reputation as a *Sūfi* and a spiritual guide of great attainments. He established and propagated Naqshbandiyya *silsilah* in the subcontinent, prosperously. Like Shaykh Abd-ul-Haq, Shaykh Ahmad was so deeply impressed by him that he got himself enrolled as his disciple, subsequently he was invested with *khilāfat* and returned to Sirhind after fully imbibing the Naqshbandiyya doctrine.[62]

Shaykh Ahmad who was not new to *Sūfi* discipline after completing the probationary period with Khawja Baqi Billah, went on a retreat at his house in Sirhind for some period and soon reached the sublime heights of experience and beatific vision.[63] Then with the permission and the blessing of his guide Khawja Baqi Billah, he started propagation of the Naqshbandi

---

60. Muhammad Abdul Haq Ansari, *Sufism and Shari'ah*, Islamic Foundation, UK, 1986, p. 11.

61 I.H. Qureshi, *Ulama*, p. 85.

62. Abul Hassan Ali Nadwi, *Saviours of Islamic Spirit*, vol. III, Academy of Islamic Research and Pub. Lucknow, 1983, pp. 119-20.

63. Ibid., pp. 122-23.

tariqah and the purification of souls.[64] Shaykh Ahmad made it his mission to reform and revive Muslim life in the subcontinent and endeavoured to make it concurrent with the *Shari'ah* in every respect. He consecrated himself to purge un-Islamic practices, criticize unbelief, heresy, false doctrines and reform popular *Sūfi* practices and reaffirm faith in prophecy, revelation and the religion of the Prophet; to condemn evil, disobedience and innovation, and revive virtue, piety and adherence to the *Sunn..h*; to oppose anti-Islamic forces and power and restore Islamic institutions and laws.[65] Shaykh Ahmad and his movement gained tremendous popularity; people from different areas came to him and entered into his discipleship. It can be ascertained from Jahangir's (1014/1606 - 1037/1627) remarks in the *Tuzuk*, that "the disciples of the Shaykh have spread all over the cities and towns of India."[66] He had appointed disciples in different areas and cities to further the cause of reform. A section of *Ulama* and some persons at royal court being envious of Shaykh's popularity conspired against him and instigated Jahangir to summon Shaykh to appear in the court. Whereupon in 1028/1619 Jahangir as his remarks not being satisfied with Shaykh's answer, a very proud person and in order to chastise him and pacify public sentiments, he ordered his incarceration[67]

64. M. Abdul Haq Ansari, op. cit., p. 17.

65. Ibid., p. 17.

66. Jahangir, *Tuzuk-i-Jahangir*, ed. Sayed Ahmad Khan, Aligarh, 1281/1864, pp. 272-73.

67. Ibid.

However some sources mention that Jahangir was satisfied with Sirhind's answer, but since he did not prostrate in honour when he entered the court, Jahangir sent him to jail for some time. Badri-Din, *Hadrat i-Qudus*, pp. 116-17 cited by S.A. Ali Nadwi, *Saviours of Islamic Spirit*, vol. III, pp. 132-33.

in the fort of Gwalior where he remained for about a year. However Shaykh Ahmad being fortitude bore the suffering of his imprisonment with patience. He neither regretted his action nor made any effort to secure release. He thought that he would not have been imprisoned had God not allowed it. He took it as a way of lord to bring him closer to himself and it had done him some good, as it was a manifestation of the beloved's *jalal* (awe).[68] During his imprisonment, he not only devoted himself to prayers and meditation but also to preaching. After about a year Jahangir released him, called him to the court, honoured him with a robe and a thousand rupees for his expenses. He gave him the option to go home or stay with him in the camp.[69] Shaykh decided to remain with the camp because he found it more advantageous for leading a movement of reform and an opportunity to preach to the king and people around him, especially soldiers in the camp. The royal camp took the shape of a mystic cloister because of his presence.[70] The Shaykh remained with the army as long as his health permitted.

It is from the writings of Shaykh Ahmad Sirhindi through which he tried to reform the ideas of learned men and his role as a socio-religious reformist can be assessed. Like Shaykh Abd-ul-Haq he used his pen for the purification and renewal of Islam which had been sullied by heterodox *Sūfi* ideas and Akbar's policies of executing eclecticism and openly vilifying Islam. Shaykh himself claimed of not being merely a *Sūfi-shaykh*

---

68. Shaykh Ahmad Sirhind, *Maktubat*, ed. Nur Ahmad, Lahore, Jvur Company, 1384/1964, vol. III, Letter 5 & 6 pp. 1202-03.
69. Shaykh Mohammad Ikram, *Rawd Kawthar*, Taj Company, Delhi 1987, Urdu, pp. 272-73.
70. *Maktubat*, vol. III, letter No. 72, also cited by A.H. Ali Nadwi, *Saviours of Islamic Spirit*, p. 138.

directing the aspirants in spiritual pursuits, but a renovator (*mujadid*) of Islam.[71] According to him the sponsors of *Dīn-i-lahi* had objected and ignored the belief in prophecy and the *Shari'ah*. To counteract this trend he wrote *Ithat'l-Nubuwah* "Defense of Prophecy" which is a concise cogent and forceful work on the subject. He also wrote *Radd-i-Rawafid* against and in reply to those who vilified the companions of the Prophet. Among the several books and tracts, the most important work of Shaykh Ahmad is *Maktubat Imam Rabbani* (a compilation of 536 letters of Shaykh Ahmad divided into three volumes) which gives expression not only to his heart-felt affections, sentiments and thoughts but also his researches in the realm of spiritual realities.[72] In his letters, which he sent to many outstanding figures in different walks of life, he demonstrated the limitations of reason in matters of faith, defended the laws of the *Shari'ah* and established the necessity of prophecy.

The most important contribution of Shaykh Ahmad Sirhindi to Islamic thought is his work concerning *tasawwuf* and its relation with the Prophetic Islam. Islam in the sub-continent in particular was famishing for such reformative endeavour. As a number of ignorant and irresponsible *sūfīs*, who were unable to understand the real significance of the subtle ideas and concepts propounded and discussed by eminent *Sūfi* thinkers, had developed a wrong view of Sufism and of its relation with the *Shari'ah*, over emphasizing *tariqah* (*Sūfi* path) than *Shari'ah*, exalting *kashf* (intuition) over the *wahy* (Divine revelation) of the Prophet. Moreover the theosophy of Ibn-i-Arabi (560–638/1165–1240) regarded as *summum bonum* of most mystic experience, the realization of union with God,

71. *Maktubat*, vol. 1:30, pp. 90-1; 1:36, pp. 115-16. cited by M Abdul Haqq Ansari, *Sufism and Shari'ah*, p. 95.

72. Nadwi, *Saviours* vol. III, p. 337.

the feeling of *wahdat-al-wajud* (unity of being or monism) a prominent feature of *Sūfi* thought, was being explained and interpreted by the mediocre among the *Sūfi-shaykhs* in a manner which appeared to be contradictory to the dictates of *Shari'ah.* The propagation of contradictory ideas under the cover of Sufism had created grave misconceptions in the popular mind, who had already contracted various forms of *shirk* and *bidat* (innovation) under the influences of the polytheistic culture of the subcontinent. Shaykh Ahmad responded to these challenges in the following words:

> At this time there are many people who believe in this unity of existence [*wahdat-al-wajud*] and consider everything to be "from God" [*haq*] or "God." They release their necks from the noose of the obligation to follow the *Shari'ah* by means of this subterfuge, and are hypocritical towards the commandments of the *Shari'ah*, and are quite cheerful in their mind about their hypocrisy. Even if they acknowledge the commandments of the *Shari'ah*, they consider them only as means; the end they have in mind is something other than the *Shari'ah*; *tariqah* and *Shari'ah* are completely identical; they do not diverge even by a hair's breadth. The difference between them is only the difference between what is summarily indicated (*ijmal*) and what is elaborated in detail (*tafsil*), between what is reasoned out (*istidlal*) and what is revealed (*kasf*). Whatever is opposed to the *Shari'ah* deserves to be repudiated, and every (so-called) truth (*haqiqat*) which is inconsistent with the *Shari'ah* is heresy (*zandaqah*). It is unbecoming of (brave and upright) men to put the *Shari'ah* aside and look (else where) for the truth.[73]

In this and in many other letters Shaykh Ahmad clearly elaborated that the Prophet's experience and revelation

73. *Maktubat*, vol. I, Letter No: 43, cited by M. Mujeeb, *The Indian Muslim*, p. 246.

possessed the ultimate validity. The criterion of the soundness of any truth learned through mystic exaltation was mainly that it should not, in any way come into conflict with *Shari'ah*. Thus there should, indeed can, exist no conflict between *Shari'ah* and *tariqah*, between the exoteric and esoteric aspects of Islam.[74]

Shaykh Ahmad criticized *wahdat al-wajud* and declared that it was a lower stage in the progress of spiritual journey. He claimed on the basis of his personal experience of attaining this stage and leaving it behind. As he writes:

> At last, I was induced to renounce that doctrine [*wahdat al-wujud*]. I was shown that this was a lower stage, and was asked to move to the stage of *zilliyat* [i.e. the vision that things are the shadows of God and different from him.]
>
> I wished I had not moved again from that stage of *zilliyat* because it had an affinity with *wahadat 'al-wujud* which was still a symbol of perfection for me. But it happened that God by a pure act of grace and love carried me beyond that stage and brought me to the stage of *'abdiyat* (i.e. the vision that man is nothing more than a servant of God, that things are merely His creation and that He is absolutely other and different from the world. I regretted my earlier experience, turned to God and begged for his mercy. Had I not been guided in this manner and shown the greatness of one stage after the other, I would have remained at the stage of *tawhid* (*wujudi*) because in my view there was no stage higher than that. God alone established the truth and shows the way.[75]

Shaykh Ahmad expounded and laid stress on the theory of *wahdat al-shuhud* [unity of phenomena] which he considered

---

74. I.H. Qureshi, *Ulama*, pp. 88-89.

75. *Maktubat*, vol. 1:31, p. 102. cited by M.A. Haqq Ansari, *Sufism and Shari'ah*, p. 15 and also see A.H. Ali Nadwi, *Saviours*, vol. III, pp. 239-43.

higher and true than the *wahdat al-wujud* and claimed it on the basis of his own spiritual experience. The summation, which he drew, was that adherence to the *Shari'ah* and the fulfilment of its injunctions, if inspired by a supreme and unconditional devotion, was the means to the highest form of self-realization.[76] Hence the Prophet's experience and revelation possessed the ultimate validity. This was necessary not only to counter the influence of heresy but also to check irresponsible trends, which were growing among the ignorant *sūfīs* and their followers. Thereby Shaykh Ahmad made a substantial contribution to the perpetual movements of reformation and restoration of *Shari'ah* ascendancy in the subcontinent which finally culminated in the ascendancy of Muhiyi-ud-din Alamgir Aurangzeb (1659–1707) to the throne of Mughal Empire, a strong supporter of orthodoxy and supremacy of *Shari'ah*. Fifty years of his rule were spent in consolidation of empire and for the preponderance of orthodoxy.

Alamgir's death on 1707 marks the beginning of the downfall and disintegration of Muslim power in the sub-continent. Pernicious forces so far contained by the audacious endeavours of Alamgir, thrived after his death. None of his successors was able to retain previous glory and control vicious forces. The lack of proper leadership left the Muslims confused and ineffective. They had no sense of purpose or direction left. Now for the first time since the establishment of Muslim rule in the subcontinent, the Muslim community was facing threats on the external as well as internal front. Not only the disintegration of its political rule, challenged by external forces such as Marāṭhās, Jāṭs and Sikh uprising, but also internal

76. M. Mujeeb. *Ulama*, p. 246.

decay (spiritual and moral) and disunity of conflicting factions: *Sunni* and *Shi'iah*, *Hadith* and legal scholars, *Ulama* and *sūfīs*, precipitated crisis. Amid this confusing and pathetic situation of Muslims in the subcontinent Shah Waliullah of Delhi started his reformative endeavour and provided the foundation for revivalism in the subcontinent. His remarkable contribution to Islamic thought catered at a crucial conjuncture, when medieval period was ending and the modern era was dawning, he served as a permanent link between medieval and modern Islamic thought.

Shah Waliullah (1703-63) was born four years before the death of Aurangzeb Alamgir at Phulat in modern district of Muzaffarnagar in Uttar Pradesh, not very far from Delhi. Qutb al-din Ahmad his original name, the title *waliu'llah*, was given to him by his father, Shah Abd-ur-Rahim. Shah Waliullah got his early *Sūfi* training and education from his father, who was a great scholar and accomplished *Sūfi*; Founder of a college, the Madrasah-i-Rahimiyyah, and was its principal. Waliullah being a precocious child at a very early age of fifteen years completed his formal education. He mastered the different branches of learning *tafsir*, *Hadith*, *fiqh* and logic, and so great was his command over them that at the age of seventeen, he obtained his father's formal permission to teach at Madrasah-i-Rahimiyyah. He carried on this work quietly for about twelve years. As he later reveals "for twelve years, I could give my deep thought to every branch of learning. I used to get inspiration (*tawajjih* from the soul of my father) at his grave, and it was during these days that the nature and meaning of *tawhid* and significance of concentration and inclination towards *Sūfi* path (*suluk*) were revealed to me; the inspirational truths (*ulum-i-wijdaniyah*) dawned upon me in profusion (*fawj*

fawj nazil shudand).[77] Shah Waliullah later in the year AH 1143/ CE 1730 decided to proceed to Hijaz for further studies and pilgrimage. where he studied *Hadith* under the guidance of a distinguished scholar, Shaykh Abu Tahir Muhammad Ibrahim al-Kurdi al-Madani and then returned to the subcontinent in mid CE 1732. After arrival Shah Waliullah resumed principalship of Madrasah-i-Rahimiyya, which he had attained after his father's death before leaving for Hijaz.

Like many scholars and *sūfīs*, Shah Walliullah did not remain in isolation free from sense of responsibilities. He was quick to realize the seriousness of crisis. With his deep erudition and rare insight into the religious science combined with the vigour and dynamism of his thought, which could analyse complex social, political and economic issues in the light of religious principles, Shah Waliullah endeavoured to rescue the Muslims of the subcontinent from debacle. For him as with other revivalists and reformists of Islam, the evolution of Islamic society and stabilization of its foundation was within the framework of *Shari'ah* which encompassed all areas of life. He sought that nearly all sectors of Muslim society needed reform because of the yawning gap between the pattern of life as enunciated in the *Qur'an* and the *Sunnah* and the one, which the Muslims had devised for themselves. The gap between the social and political institutions, the framework of which had been supplied by Islam and the institutions the Muslim had developed and set up for themselves in the course

77. Shah Wali Allah/*Anfas, al-Arifin,* Delhi 1917, p. 203 et seq. In this and *Al-juz-ul-latif fi tarjumati abd-id-daif,* Delhi 18907. He gives the main events of his early life and education. Shah Waliullah, *Al Qawlul-jamil fi bayani Sawa-i'sabil,* Lahore, 1950, pp. 111-20 gives a full description of the *silsilah* into which he was initiated by his father.

of history, ought to be reduced.[78] His multi-dimensional approach to the reformation and restoration of Muslim society in the sub-continent did not permit him to ignore the political developments taking shape in the subcontinent. He called for the restoration and strengthening of Mughal authority. The keystone, which had to be saved and strengthened at all costs.[79] He wrote letters to Najib-ud-dawlah[80] and Ahmad Shah Abdali (Durrani)[81] (AH 1160-87/CE 1747-73) an Afghan chief and persuaded them to head off Jāṭ and Marāṭhā rising power from gaining ascendancy over the depleted Mughal empire and thereby dominating the subcontinent completely. It will be difficult to assess to what extent these letters instigated Ahmad Shah Abdali or he had a plan of his own, to launch campaign (1174/1761) against Marāṭhā.[82] However, Marāṭhās were defeated but this victory of Ahmad Shah Abdali failed to produce desired results of building a Muslim empire anew.

---

78. Abdul Hamid Siddiqi, *Renaissance in Indo-Pakistan,* Shah Walliullah Dihlwi in A *History of Muslim Philosophy,* vol. 2, ed. M.M. Sharif, Atlantic Pub. and Distributors, 1989, p. 1559.

79. Khaliq Ahmad Nizami, *Shah Waliullah Ke Seyasi Maktubat,* Aligarh, 1950, pp. 80-81, 84.

80. A collection of Shah Waliullah's letters is extant in manuscript, out of which Khaliq Ahmad Nizami has published letters of political importance. Several of these are addressed to Najib ud-Dawlah which show how Shah Waliullah encouraged him to fight against the Jāṭs and the Marāṭhās. Najib ul-Dawlah succeeded in suppressing the Jāṭ incursions. Ibid., pp. 24-25.

81. Shah Waliullah has written a long letter addressed to "a monarch." Its context clearly suggests that the addresse is Ahmad Shah Abdali, Ibid., pp. 51, 53. Ahmad Shah Abdali defeated and crushed Marāṭhās on 14 January 1761 in a fierce battle at Panipat. It took Marāṭhās at least ten years to reappear before Delhi.

82. A.A. Razivi, "The Breakdown of Traditional Society" in *The Cambridge History of Islam,* vol. 2, p. 72.

Shah Waliullah's immortality is because of his scholarship, originality of thought and reformative endeavour, on the whole his contribution to Islamic thought. The *holy Qur'an* and *Sunnah* formed the firm foundation on which he raised the edifice of his thought system. For him, purification and renewal of Islam were contingent on return to pristine *Shari'ah* (*Qur'an* and *Sunnah*). In order to disseminate the knowledge of the *Holy Qur'an*, among those who did not know Arabic, the overwhelming majority even in the educated classes, Shah Waliullah despite opposition, translated *Qur'an* into Persian bearing the title, *Fath-'ur-Rahman fi tarjumat-il-Qur'an*. The Persian was the language of culture, education and administration, thus it became possible even for the common man to learn the *Qur'an* and understand its meaning with the help of good translation. He also wrote *Al-fawz-ul-Kabir fi usul-i-tafsir* relating to the broad principles to be observed in the interpretation of *Qur'an*, emphasizing the universality of the application of the injunctions of the *Qur'an* and which are to be taken as absolute, applicable in all conditions and situations, limited only by their own sense or the context of other injunctions.[83]

Shah Waliullah endeavoured to popularize the study of *Hadith* by reviving its teachings and prepared commentaries on the subject. For him as with other revivalists the *Sunnah* of the Prophet preserved in numerous collections of *Ahadith* has always been the fountain of genuine Islamic thoughts as well as the passionate desire to reform and renovate the Muslim society. It has also been the inspirational force behind their fervid enthusiasm to invite the people back to the true faith and to fight every unsound norm and usage. Shah Waliullah opens his *magnum opus Hujjat Allah al-Baligah* with the words:

83. *Al-Fawzul Kabir fi usuli t-tafsir*, tr. by Muhammad Salim 'Abd-ullah, Karachi, 1960, pp. 192-93.

> The crown of all infallible knowledge and the source and foundation of religious branches of learning is the science of *Hadith* which gives us an account of the sayings and doings of the noble Prophet (SAAS) as well as tells us of his tacit approval of the things done in his presence. The *Ahādith* are like luminous torches in the surrounding darkness, the milestone of guidance or like the brilliant moon shedding light in a gloomy night. One who follows them finds guidance and is blessed with merit and those, who disregard them are misguided and ruined. For the life of the *Holy* Prophet (SAAS) is the infinite source of divine commandments and prohibitions, admonitions and glad tidings and instructions and God's remembrance, the *Ahadith* abound in all these matters like the *Qur'an* or even to a greater extent.[84]

This fascination with science of *Hadith* and witnessing less importance among the intellectual circles and educational institutions of the subcontinent towards its study, compelled Shah Waliullah after his return from Arab to engage whole-heartedly himself to the teaching, exposition and promotion of the study of *Hadith* in the country.[85] Before him, Shaikh Abdul Haq Muhaddith Dehlawi had strived laborious in diffusing the knowledge of *Hadith* in the subcontinent and to give it rightful place in the curricula of educational institution, but could not spark off the popular interest in *Hadith* for long. As observed by Sayyid Abdul Hasan Ali Nadwi "unfortunately, however, those who were shaping the new educational system had little intellectual contact with Makkah and Medina or those places which are known for the study,

84. *Introduction to Hujjat Allah, al-Baligah,* cited by A.H. Nadwi *Saviours*, vol. 4, p. 132.

85. Ibid., p. 135.

teaching and preaching of *Hadith*. They were chiefly influenced, as the evolution of *Dars-i-Nizami* and the literary and biographical works of its precursors show, by the intellectual sciences. Among the Islamic branches of learning their chief interest lay in jurisprudence."[86] Shah Waliullah's main contribution was the establishment of a school for the study of *Hadith*.[87] He wrote *Al-Musawwah min Ahadith al-Muwatta* (Arabic) and *Musaffa* (Persian). They were commentaries on the *Muwatta* of Imam Malik. He gave precedence to the *Muwatta* of Imam Malik among the authentic collections of *Hadith*, insisted[88] upon its study and took steps to popularize its study. He also categorized other books of *Hadith* in accordance with their authenticity and made it easier for students to utilize them with confidence.[89] Shah Waliullah's endeavours revived the study of *Hadith* in the subcontinent and made it recognized and essential part of curriculum of the religious schools.

Shah Waliullah on the basis of the *Qur'an* and *Ahadith* sought to restructure religious thought and juristic analysis, in consonance with the spirit of Islam and in the light of the exigencies of the situation. He earnestly strove to reconcile the areas of tension and conflict in the contemporary Muslim thought. In fact, the method of reconciliation was his genius and was essential for the evolution of a consolidated coherent and compact religious thought, which could express itself in the shape of a healthy moral order of society. He endeavoured

---

86. Ibid., p. 131.
87. Gulam Husain Jalbani, Shah *Waliullah Ki talim*, Hyderabad Pakistan 1963, p. 46.
88. Shah Waliullah, *Wasiyat Namah*, p. 11, cited Ibid., p. 23.
89. Shah Waliullah, *Hujjat-u'llah-i'l-balighah*, Urdu tr. Abd-ur-Rahim, Lahore 1953, V.I, pp. 308, 16.

to remove misunderstanding and conflicts by means of a synthesis (*tatbiq*) of the different points of view which he calls *Jama binul Mukhtalifat* (combining of opposites). From the tenth century, two opposing trends have developed among the scholars (*Ulama*) of the subcontinent. One emphasized strict and exclusive adherence to a particular school of law, and the other negating this method and instead stressed the rigorous following of the clear meaning of the *Sunnah* of the Prophet as found in the accepted compendia of *Hadith*. Shah Waliullah attempted to establish the rapport between the *hadith* and *fiqh*. In *Hujjat-Allah Al-Baligha*, He writes:

> The basis for juristic deduction, on the one hand, and following the *Hadith* literally, on the other, are both grounded in true religion and scholars have at all times acted in accordance with both these principles. It is only some who have attached a bit more importance to the deduction approach than to the literal adherence of the *Hadith* while others have taken a contrary course. It is not at all proper to ignore either of these principles to which commonality of both groups is accustomed. The right course in this matter lies in bringing about reconciliation between the two so that what is wanting in one is made up by the other.[90]

And at other place he writes, "the right procedure is to harmonize them and both these methods should be employed for raising the superstructure of Islamic jurisprudence. The edifice of the *Shari'ah* so erected would be sound and well-consolidated.[91]"

---

90. *Hujjal Allah al-Baligha*, op. cit., vol., p. 156.
91. Shah Waliullah, *al-Insaf fi Bayan-i Sabab al-Ikhtilaf*, Urdu tr. Sadr al-Din Ishlahi, Lahore, n.d., pp. 29, 80.

    Cited by M.M. Sharif, *Philosophy* op. cit., p. 1575.

Similarly Shah Waliullah adopted the moderate and balanced approach in regard to *ijtihad* (individual reasoning) and *taqlid* (unquestioning acceptance of the rulings of earlier jurists of one's own school). He emphasized the need of *ijtihad* as *sine qua non* for the health and vigour of the religious community (the *ummah*),[92] and essential for every age in order to meet the changing social needs of the time. He was of the view that *ijtihad* is duty *Fard-bil-Kifayah*[93] of Muslim scholars and *Ulama* of every age[94] and enunciates that right of new interpretation could not be taken away and therefore, in principle *ijtihad* could never be restricted nor could it come to an end.[95] This explains Shah Waliullah's rather emphatic stand on the question of importance of *ijtihad* in every age. He criticized the partisanship of jurists, which had hardened into a belief that their (*Imams*) interpretation or rulings were infallible and result in a rigid doctrine of blind imitation *taqlid*. He believes that the *ijtihad* of the old jurists, however high and exalted their status, is open to correction in the light of the *Qur'an* and the *Sunnah*. However in his *Iqd al-jid fi Ahkam al-Ijtihad wal-Taqlid*, he considered adherence to one of the four schools of *fiqh* at times prudent. As he says, "remember that there is great security in following the four juristic schools while a great risk is involved in rejecting them. There are

---

92. Shah Waliullah has dealt with the question of *ijtihad* in *Iqd-ūl-jid fi ahkam-il- Ijtıhād wāt-taqlid*, Delhi, AH 1310 also in *Al-insāf fi bayāni sababi ikhtilaf* Urdu trn., Sadr-al-Din Ishlahi as *Ikhtalafi masail men i'tidal kirah*, Lahore, n.d., et. seq.

93. A command which is imperative upon all Muslims, but if a sufficient number perform it the same will be supposed to be sufficient or equivalent to all having performed it.

94. Shah Waliullah, *Introduction* to *Al-Musaffa*, Matba Faruqi, Delhi, n.d., p. 11

95. Shah Waliullah, *Hujjat-ullah-il-balighah*, V.Is, p. 365.

several reasons for it,"[96] and then discusses the reasons. Shah Waliullah distinguishes between blind imitation, which was prohibited (*haram*), and more flexible *taqlid*, for those incapable of *ijtihad* and who does not possess the necessary qualifications. The best courses were *taqlid*. He approved of *taqlid* on the conditions that intention was seemly and proper and one was clear in his mind about emulating the Prophet and following the injunction of the *Qur'an* and the *Sunnah*.[97] He was aware of dangers inherent in the unrestricted *ijtihad*, which led into the rise of heretic sects in the past due to, what one could call, free license in religious thinking. Shah Waliullah held the view that every one was not qualified to undertake it, because it needed learning, wisdom and expertise.[98] Thus adopted the course of moderation between *ijtihad* and *taqlid*, which concurred, with the objectives of the *Shari'ah*, human psychology and the realities of life.

Shah Waliullah's emphasis on the *ijtihad* was also aimed to avoid the rigid particularistic following of one school of *fiqh*, clear of all extremes and without showing inclination or disfavour for other schools. He tried to bridge the gulfs that yawned between them by combining all the points of agreement in all the schools of *fiqh* and in matters of variance adhered to what is proved by the genuine *Hadith*.[99] According to him, all the prevalent systems of *fiqh* drew their inspiration from one single source, so that there could be no fundamental difference in them; there had been differences and there would

---

96. Shah Waliullah *Iqd al-Jid*, pp. 36-38 cited by A.H. Ali Nadwi, *Saviours*, vol. 4, pp. 149, 51.
97. Nadwi, *Saviour*, vol. 4, p. 150-51.
98. Shah Waliullah, *Fuyud-ul-haramain*, Bombay, n.d, Vision, p. 46.
99. Khaliq Ahmad Nizami, *State and Culture in Medieval India*, Adam Pub. & Distributors, New Delhi, 1985, p. 281.

be, but these were differences in interpretation only, not in principle.[100] He argued that small differences in interpretation are not of such tremendous importance as to cause serious dispute or divide Muslim society into hostile factions.[101] Mutual recriminations and difference between various sections and groups had played malignant role in tearing to pieces the solidarity of Muslim society and as well as destruction of its political power. Shah Waliullah deemed it necessary to remove all the inhibiting factors of disunity and stiff for revival of Muslim society and power; by first instilling into it a desire for self-preservation through the revival of unity of thought and action. *Sunni-Shi'ah* division resulted in as an impediment to the progress of Muslim thought and society all over, also had its pernicious effect on and played ruinous role in the destruction of Muslim solidarity and political power in the subcontinent.[102] Shah Waliullah was anxious to reduce the *Sunni-Shi'ah* difference to a minimum and made efforts to bring them closer together. Knowing that difference based in religious convictions could not be wiped off by simple appeals for unity, he made great efforts to reduce the difference to the level of academic and doctrinal disagreement and enlighten the people regarding the nature of these differences.[103]

---

100. M.M. Sharif, *A History of Muslim Philosophy*, vol. 2, Atlantic Pub & Dist, New Delhi, 1989, p. 1578.

101 Shah Waliullah in his *Al-Insaf fi bayan sabab il-ikhtilaf* has discussed the history and nature of differences among various schools of jurispurdance.

102. I.H. Qureshi, *Ulama*, p. 115.

103. For his views on Sunni-Shiah please see Shah Waliullah, *Izalat-ul-Khifa 'an khilāfat-I'l-Khulafa*, Urdu tr. Abd -u'sh-shakur and Inshā' a'llah, Karachi n.d., V. II, p. 487, F.F. Shah Waliullah, *Fuyūd-u'l-haramain.*, Vision, 6, 33 and also Shah Waliullah, *Al-aqidat-ul-Hasanan*, Agra, AH 1304 p. 9.

Shah Waliullah, also resolved the contradictions between the *Sūfi* doctrines ontological monism of Ibn al-Arabi's "unity of being" *wahdat al-wujud* and Sirhindi's "unity of experience" *wahdat al-shuhud*. He tried to show that they were not doctrines in conflict with each other, but were different ways of speaking about the same underlying reality. They were stages on the road to spiritual knowledge, *wahdat-al-wujud* being an earlier and *wahdah al shudud* a later and more advanced stage. He held the view that there was not any substantial difference between the two; instead, the problem had been one of semantics.[104] Shah Waliullah was himself a *Sūfi*, in fact a practising *Sūfi*, which is clear from his references to their ideas and practices in his works; he has written several treatises in which he has discussed various aspects of *tasawwuf*.[105] Like Sirhindi, he sought to reform Sufism, which had degenerated and deviated, particularly because of those ignorant *sūfī*s whose ideas and actions were not in conformity with the precepts and injections of *Shari'ah*. He wrote a short treatise *al-Balagh al-Mubin* in which he restated the aims and objectives of the spiritual movements and urged to shake off all its un-Islamic trappings. Shah Waliullah not only restored balance between *Shariat* and *tariqat* but established that any idea of conflict between the two was basically wrong, as *tariqat* was not the negation but elaboration of *Shari'ah*. Through his works on *tasawwuf* and allied problems, Shah Waliullah tried to bridge the gulf between the *Ulama* and the *sūfi*s, therefore, to create an atmosphere so that they could work in harmony.

Shah Waliullah's reformative endeavour was not confined to the exposition of the doctrinal or religious matters and to

104. Shah Waliullah, *Faisalat al wahdat-al-wujud wa wahdat al-shuhud*, Delhi AH 1304, p. 6.

105. For instance, *Fuyd al-Haramyan*, *Qawl al-Jamil*, *Asfas al-Arifin*, *Altaf al-Quds* and *Tafhimat*, etc.

remove the cause of mutual differences between various sections and groups only. But certainly more important objective of his efforts was to reform the moral life of the people by making them realize their responsibilities as individuals and also as members of the community in the light of the teachings of the *Qur'an* and *Sunnah* of the Prophet. His *magnum opus Hujjat Allah al-Baligah* and *al Badur al-Bezighah* in addition to various religious themes, deals at length with social, political and economic aspects of life and were aimed at, to bring about a reorientation and rescuing of the Muslim society; which had lost its bearings to an extent that they were plunged into a moral crisis of grave dimensions. He analysed with his characteristic insight the sociological and economic bases of society and has also spotlighted those factors that create fissures in human society and set one class against another.[106] Shah Waliullah has raised the structure of a social philosophy on the basis of a moral system and deals with some of the basic aspects of a social system as a dynamic process. In *Hujjat Allah al-Baligah*, he discusses the problem of human relations social as well as spiritual and divides human society into grades according to the stages of civilization under the headings of *irtifaqat*.[107] Including primitive societies of man; organized

106. *Hujjat ullah al-Baligah*, Lahore, AH 1323, Urdu tr. Maulvi Khalil Ahmad Matba-i-Islam, Lahore, vol. I, pp. 79-80. vol. II, 375, 408, *Budur-ul-Bazigah* XI.

107. *Irtifāq* is form root *rafaq* which means being benevolent, tender, gracious kind for easy. *Ratfaq* means use, utility, serviceability. Whatever man needs in the world is present but these forces are to be tamed and tutored to be brought under control and used. K.A. Nizmi, *State and Culture in Medieval India*, p. 289. Waliullah's use of it is somewhat in the sense of making the things soft and gentle to solve the growing needs of an individual *vis-a-vis* his environment. *Irtifaq* term used by Shah Waliullah has been also translated as "stages and forces in the progress of civilization," "social device" or "social institution."

society of men living in towns and cities and developed stages of society under which he discusses in some detail problems connected with family life; livelihood, professions, trade general affairs and dealings of individuals and lastly government and administration.[108] In dealing with each of these "social institution" *irtifaqat,* he looks at problems from all angles — psychological, spiritual, moral, social and economic. His genesis of society takes into account all its stages of growth. As society grows, larger human needs multiply and man seeks the formation of larger groups, villages, towns, cities and ultimately reaches the international community.[109] He calls human individual *insani-sagir* (small man) and humanity as a whole *insani-kabir* (big man) and works out his ideas of the unity and oneness of mankind which he considered to be the sole objective of religion. Islam therefore, seldom deals with the individual as an individual; it always envisages him as a member of a family or a community. He says "Allah wants that world should have a system of administration, marked by peace, goodwill and cooperation. Humanity should be like a body, in which various parts and joints are combined together to create an organism."[110]

In order to maintain equilibrium (*tawazun*) in the interest of the health of the society, Shah Waliullah laid great stress on *adalat*[111] (lit. being equitable) which is *sine qua non* for creating a just and balanced social organization (*al nizam al-adil*). *Adalat* and *tawazun* therefore are needed at every step and in all ventures, which alone can sustain any social or political fabric.

---

108. *Hujjat Allah il-Baligah,* Bareilly, AH 1286, pp. 38-48.

109. Ibid., V.I pp. 82-100.

110. Ibid., p. 260.

111. *Hujjat-ullah-il-balighah* (Urdu tr.), pp. 82-83.

It is intrinsic for stability and reformation and its manifestation may be numerous. When it expresses itself in social behaviour, dress, manners and mores it is called *adab* (etiquette). In matters relating to income and expenditure, it is called economy (*kifayat*) and in the affairs for the government and administration of state, it is named politics.[112]

Shah Waliullah considered morality (personal as well as social) an essential factor for dispensing *adl* (justice, equitability). It is for this reason he considered moral reformation necessary for curing the ills of diseased society and maintained that no morality is higher and efficacious in rejuvenating Muslim society than the morality of Islam, which together with spiritual fervour could change set of beliefs and moral code into a pleasure and a joy.[113]

Shah Waliullah explained all these concepts and other topics pertaining to social behaviour and human conduct in private as well as collective life in rationalistic style but within the framework of the fundamentals of Islam, which in fact is his main objective. This kind of work had been accomplished by Imam Ghazzali also but Shah Waliullah has clearly far surpassed him, the comprehensive and logical approach made by Shah Waliullah in presenting Islam as a great system of life is unique and unparalleled in the whole history of Islam. Intrinsically, he was a thinker and his contribution to Islamic thought and sociology is remarkable and of a lasting nature. He was a man of encyclopaedic learning, a versatile genius and his orginality of thought encompassed almost every branch of Muslim sciences. He has not confined his expositions to basic concepts only, but has also discussed even minor problems

112. *Hujjah-Allah al-Baligah,* Barielly. AH 1286, p. 261.

113. I.H. Qureshi, *Ulama*, p. 125.

and questions of *Shari'ah* law in the context of daily routine of life. Equally surprising is the fact that he has not deviated from the path of orthodoxy rather has tried to establish that in his writings.

Although, Shah Waliullah did not succeed on all fronts, but he did succeed remarkably in providing the foundation for the reconstruction of Muslim religious thought, revival of Muslim religious sciences and the social and moral edification of Muslim society. His successors Shah Abdul Aziz, Shah Abdul Qadir, Shah Rafiuddin, Sayyid Ahmad Barelwi, Shah Ismail Shaheed and others worked zealously on the guidelines delineated by their master to bring about an intellactual Renaissance of the Muslims of the subcontinent. He was undoubtedly the greatest Muslim thinker of the subcontinent, a formative influence on modern Muslim thought; his philosophy provides a connecting link between medieval Islamic thought and trends of modern interpretation of the fundamental teachings of Islam. His impact was felt in the religious, social and political spheres. Most of the institutions of religious learning in subcontinent owe its existence, directly or indirectly to Shah Waliullah. He is as much a source of inspiration and guidance for the *Ulama* and *mashaikh* as for modern Muslim thinkers like Sayyid Ahmad Khan, Shibli and Muhammad Iqbal to neo-revivalists like Mawlana Abdul A'Lā Mawdudi and Sayyid Abdul Hassan Ali Nadwi and many others.

After the death of Shah Waliullah, mission was carried on by a band of pupils and disciples, which he had left behind, including his own sons, who were fully charged with the spirit of his movement. Shah Abd al-Aziz (1746–1824/1159–1239). The eldest of Shah Waliullah's four sons was able to succeed his father at a very young age of seventeen as the head of their ancestral college (Madrasah Rahimiyyah). Like his father he was not only an eminent scholar, engaged in teaching, writing and training his pupils but was also anxious to reform his people. His younger brother Shah Rafi-al Din (d. 1817) Shah 'Abd al-Qadir (d. 1814) and Abd al Ghani, co-operated with him in resuscitating and strengthening the cause of Islam. Shah Waliullah's successors did not content themselves with the placid mission of popularizing religious knowledge among the masses and imparting mystic insight to a chosen few. Nevertheless, they did their best to keep alive the idea that the system of *Shari'ah* law was and should be the main foundation of Muslim society. They turned to the study of *Qur'an*, popularization of religious knowledge, the creation of a new aspiration to study, understand and live according to the doctrines of the *Shari''ah*. In order to disseminate and popularize the teachings of *Qur'an* among the less educated sectors of Muslim society, like Shah Waliullah, who translated *Qur'an* into Persian and his son's Rafi al-Din and Shah Abd al-Qadir translated the same into Urdu.[114]

Shah Abdul Aziz vigorously followed the traditions of his father. However, the circumstances in which Shah Waliullah had carried on his movement had changed considerably. The

114. In Shah Waliullah's times Persian was widely understood, and this was why he had translated the *Qur'an* into this language and also used it for some of his works. A generation later, Urdu seems to have become more popular; Shah Rafi al-Din and Shah Abd al-Qadir, both preferred to render it into Urdu. Shah Rafi al-Din's translation is literal while that of Shah Abd al Qadir is in idiomatic Urdu and is accompanied by a short commentary in the form of marginal glosses, called *Mudih al-Qur'an*. The latter is still considered to be one of the best and most authentic translations in Urdu. Shah Abdul Aziz's son-in-law produced a handy dictionary of the vocabulary of the *Qur'an*, which helped beginners to understand the book more easily.

evils against which his efforts were directed became more firmly rooted in the succeeding generations. The rapid political disintegration and social degeneration of the Mughal empire, taking the advantage of weakness of the central authority and disunity among the ranks of Muslim chiefs, Marāṭhās, Jāṭs, Rājpūts and Sikhs in the north-western regions carved out independent potentates and dominated the scene. Besides, a new threat to Muslim society was posed by the expanding power of the East India Company. No doubt emperor Shah Alam who had come under the influences of the Company authorities had now freed himself from their "custody" and returned to Delhi early in 1772; but in the last quarter of the eighteenth century they were able to strengthen and consolidate their hold on the extensive territories of Bengal and Bihar in the north and parts of the Deccan in the south. Under Wellesley (1798-1805), British imperialism became a vital force in the political life of subcontinent.

Haidar Ali of Mysore and after him Tipu Sultan, symbol of resistance against British imperialism and zealous fighter in the cause of freedom, was defeated and killed in 1799. Then in the first decade of the nineteenth century, the successive victories of the British over the Sindhia enabled them to establish their influence at the imperial court in Delhi. In 1803 General Lake, who commanded the British Army defeated Sindhia and offered to undertake the responsibility of protecting the emperor who was at that time under his influence (Marāṭhās who had previously exercised control over the emperor) and thus managed to enter the Mughal capital. It was soon realized by the emperor that he had been tricked, but it was now too late. After that almost everyday witnessed a diminution of his power and dignity. In lieu of the crown lands, which were taken over by the Company, he received an annual stipend, or pension[115] (*pishkash*). In the course of time Shah Alam and his successors were so completely demoralized that the Mughal court was soon reduced to a mere shadow of its former glory.

This cataclysmic loss of Mughal power enervated the Muslims of the subcontinent. Early efforts by Shah Waliullah to instigate Muslim rulers of the subcontinent as well as neighbouring rulers to make a concerted attempt to regain the control failed to produce desired results. Now the establishment of British authority was sure to kill the chances of the restoration of Muslim ascendancy, which Shah Waliullah had been trying to make effective through an extensive programme of political and socio-religious reform. The emasculate throne of Delhi had been reduced to a mere legal myth but "still considered the fountain of honour by Hindus and Muslims, and a patent of nobility under the imperial seal was as highly prized in the remotest provinces of Deccan as it had been in the days of Aurangzeb."[116] Notwithstanding, Shah Alam and his successors Akbar Shah II (1806-37) and Bahadur Shah II (1837-57), completely demoralized, and in state of penury and helplessness, were inept to lead and give direction. Realizing the lack of political authority, the Muslim populace were confused about the legal position. Shah Abdul Aziz with his penetrating judgement and keen sense of observation, removed the ambivalence about legal myth of Mughal sovereignty by issuing *fatawā* that the subcontinent was no longer *dar-ul-Islam*, a land where the Islam enjoyed sovereign authority and political power. He declared that they were now in a land of warfare, *dar al-harb*. Owing to the fact, that

115. Marsh John Clark, *Abridgement of the History of India*, Serampore, 1873, pp. 267-68.

116. Ibid., p. 268.

the emperor (*imam al-Muslimin*) at Delhi wields no authority and is utterly helpless and the real power was in the hands of the British. If certain areas had been left in native hands for administration, it was only because the British found it politic to do so. There are, indeed, certain Islamic rituals, e.g. Friday and Id prayers, *adhan* and cow-slaughter, with which they do not interfere. But that is of no account. They did not interfere with the observance of Muslim rites and practices because they did not want to, but they had the power to do so, if they desired.[117] By declaring subcontinent *dar-ul harb* a land were Islam was not free,[118] Shah Abdul Aziz cleared the perplexity, gave a clear direction for future action by bringing it to the notice of the Muslim population that they have been subjugated by Britishers. Implying that it was the duty of every Muslim to make all effort to restore former status of *dar-ul-Islam*. In no case should Muslim co-operate with the British in propagating false beliefs and un-Islamic practices and it was a mortal sin to help them to destroy Muslim lives or further subvert Muslim authority.[119]

This *fatawā* declaring the entire territory held by the British to be a *dar al-harb* was significant proclamation in the history of Islam in the subcontinent. For the first time Muslims were facing such situation, a complete paradigm shift. After being for centuries, the only full citizens of the state, Muslims discovered that they were now an unpopular and vulnerable minority. This *fatawā* by Shah Abdul Aziz was in a way remarkable development in the Islamic thought itself. It removed the perplexity and gave a clear direction to the

117. Shah Abdul Aziz, *Fatawa-i-Azizi*, *Mataba-e-Mujtabai*, Delhi, AH 1311, vol. 1, pp. 16-17.

118. Idem.

119. Ibid., p. 186.

Muslims of the subcontinent for future action which according to Shah Abdul Aziz, is Islamically appropriate response, what is to be understood from the *Hadiths*, and in accordance with the principle of following the lives and actions of the venerable companions and great *khalifahs*.[120] This *fatawā* against the British imperialism transpired into *jihād* movement led by his pupil and disciple Sayyid Ahmad Shaheed and nephew Ismail Shaheed.

Sayyid Ahmad (1201-46/1786–1831) was born at Rae-Bareli, lost his father Sayyid Muhammad Irfan, very early when he was only of thirteen years. He showed little interest in reading and writing, spent considerable portion of his youth in sports and physical exercise. Early death of his father made it necessary for him to earn a living. At the age of eighteen, accompanied by a party of seven other young men related to him, went to Lucknow in search of a suitable employment. After three or four months of fruitless effort he left for Delhi with the intention of getting enrolled as a disciple of Shah Abd-ul Aziz, who received him kindly and entrusted him under the care of his brother Shah Abdul Qadir for receiving education. Where he studied elementary works on Arabic grammar and *Hadith*. The Sayyid did not distinguish himself as a scholar; but he had a power and cultivated intellect as his later discourses and letters show.[121] Shah Abdul Aziz in 1804 himself gave him spiritual training and guided on the path of the "Chishtiyya", "Qadiriyya", and "Naqshbandiyya" orders. In this spiritual field Sayyid Ahmad made remarkable progress; excelled within a short span of time and developed into a "mystic" of great eminence.[122]

120. Ibid., p. 17.

121 Mohiuddin Ahmad, *Sayyid Ahmad Shahid: His Life and Mission*, Academy of Islamic Research and Publication, Lucknow, 1975, p. 36.

122. Sayyid Abul Husan Ali Nadwi, *Sirat Sayyid Ahmad Shahid* (Urdu), Majalis Tahkeekat wa Nashriyat Islamic, Lucknow 1986, p. 128.

After completing the course of *Sūfi* training and discipline he left Delhi and returned to Rae-Bareli. He did not stay here for long, ultimately in CE 1810 decided to join the forces of the Paṭhān leader Amir Khan in central India, and obtained considerable training and experience in guerilla warfare. It is not easy to determine his motive, which promoted Sayyid Ahmad to join Amir Khan's service where he spent more than seven years and participated in real fighting. However, the thought of joining Amir Khan's camp came to Sayyid Ahmad after his spiritual training had come to a satisfactory level under Shah Abdul Aziz. And one does not find the burning desire for *jihād* in the future leader of the movement before his attachment to Shah Abdul Aziz.[123] It seems plausible that Sayyid Ahmad intended to give practical shape to the *fatwā* of Shah Abdul Aziz and organize *jihād* movement against imperialists. It was the independent position and army of 8000 men of Amir Khan, which drew Sayyid Ahmad to join him.[124] If it had been simply earning a livelihood, Sayyid Ahmad would not have abandoned the service of Amir Khan soon after he surrendered and made peace with British. At the time of his departure from Amir Khan's camp, he informed Shah Abdul Aziz that no useful purpose would be served by his further attachment to Amir Khan[125] and made a beeline to Delhi to have rendezvous with Shah Abdul Aziz. Whatever may be the reason of his joining Amir Khan's service, it certainly whetted his appetite for launching movement of *jihād* on his own.

---

123. I.H. Qureshi, *Ulama*, p. 143.

124. M. Mujeeb, *The Indian Muslims*, p. 395.

125. Gulam Rasul Mhir, *Sayyid Ahmad Shaheed*, Kitab Manzil, Lahore, 1952, vol. I, p. 109 also quoted by I.H. Qureshi, *Ulama*, p. 142.

Sayyid Ahmad reached Delhi on May or June 1818. By that time he possessed the necessary competence and experience as a soldier and had achieved beatification and reputation as an experienced mystic.[126] Shah Abdul Aziz gave him warm welcome and found in him necessary qualities to lead movement and execute the plan, which he had envisaged for the reassertion of Muslim faith and power in the subcontinent.[127] In order to further the leadership of his protégé, Shah Abdul Aziz directed everyone, who approached him with the request for spiritual guidance to take an oath of fealty at the hands of the Sayyid Ahmad.[128] First it was Mawlana Muhammad Yusuf of Phulat, who was grandson of Shah Waliullah's elder brother, Shah Ahl-ullah. After he reported that Sayyid Ahmad was a competent preceptor, Mawlana Abd-ul-Hayy, son-in-law of Shah Abdul Aziz and Shah Ismail, son of Shah Abdul Ghani entered Sayyid's discipleship. Evidently their enrolment as his disciples augmented considerably the position and prestige of Sayyid Ahmad, and had tremendous impact upon the people. Furthermore, it was necessary to associate with him men, who were among the foremost religious scholars of the subcontinent, commanding considerable respect for their erudition and would constantly offer him counsel.[129]

Sayyid Ahmad accompanied by his disciples seeking permission from his spiritual mentor Shah Abdul Aziz, who accordingly robed the Sayyid in his own apparel (white gown and black turban) set out on his first missionary tour.[130] Like a

126. Mohiuddin Ahmad, op. cit., p. 59.

127. I.H. Qureshi, *Ulama*, pp. 143-44.

128. Mohiuddin Ahmad, op. cit., p. 62.

129. I.H. Qureshi, op. cit., p. 145; also see Mihr, p. 123.

130. Sayyid Ahmad Hassan Ali Nadwi, *Sirat-i-Sayyid*, vol. I, p. 160 and Mohiuddin Ahmad (English), op. cit., p. 63.

roving missionary, he visited a number of towns in modern Uttar Pradesh, Bihar and Bengal (northern India)[131] and exhorted the people to live according to the *Shari'ah*. According to his analysis of the situation the main cause of the degeneration of the Muslims laid in their getting away from the path of the real teachings of Islam. This in its turn was the result of the adoption by the Muslims of un-Islamic ideas and customs, borrowed from the Hindus and highly exaggerated, almost unbalanced, notions of some of the *Sūfi* doctrines and practices. Thus he went forth to preach against the abuses that had crept into the faith and practice of the Muslims of the subcontinent. His social and religious reformist movement received overwhelming response of the Muslims. Wherever he went, people turned out in hundreds to receive him, listened his sermons; magnetized by his charismatic personality, acknowledged him their spiritual guide by performing *bayat* (took oath of fealty or allegiance). Thus number of people became his disciples throughout north of India. Sayyid Ahmad's missionary endeavour of reformism produced encouraging results. It brought release from superstitious idiotic or economically ruinous practices, the number of which had been increasing; it promoted a rational way of looking at the affairs of life. In the field of religious observance, it swept away the objections to the performance of the pilgrimage. In social life, it initiated the struggle against the sentimental objection to widow remarriage, which had almost acquired the force of law, and it was a courageous and stimulating re-affirmation of the Islamic doctrine of equality. It began, in fact, a movement of reform, whose momentum lasted for generation.[132]

---

131. For details see Sayyid Abdul Hassan Ali Nadwi, *Sirat-i-Sayyid*, vol. I, p. 160 ff.

132. M. Mujeeb, op. cit., p. 397, also see Sayyid Abdul Hassan Ali Nadwi, *Sirat-i-Sayyid*, vol. I, p. 239ff. and also see Mohiuddin Ahmad, op. cit., pp. 64, 77.

Sayyid Ahmad on 30 July 1821 set-off for *hajj* accompanied by a large party including a number of women. He made this journey much publicized, invited his disciples from several places and opted to go via rather longer route of Calcutta. For the first time in the history of Muslim India, *hajj* was performed with such a splendour and enthusiasm, with an intention to remove misconceptions crept into the people's mind by some misguided people under Hindu influence about this obligatory practices (*hajj*) which in India had long passed into desuetude.[133] Soon after his return in 1824 he started his preparations for *jihād* against imperialists in the subcontinent. Finally in 1826 Sayyid Ahmad along with his disciples left for North West Frontier (now in Pakistan) to establish military base for launching campaign. Mawlana Mawdudi remarks that this seems strategically appropriate, and there could had been no politically as well as geographically better starting point.[134] They took on Sikh kingdom of Punjab first who have been widening their controls over the area; were extremely oppressive and had persecuted and vilified the Muslims of

---

133. Nadwi, *Sirat-i-Sayyid*, pp. 261-62.

The anarchy and pillage which marked the sea voyage in those days gradually reduced the number of pilgrims going for *haj*, and to ease their conscience came forward the self-seeking ecclesiastics with their juristic opinions allowing the *haj* to be deferred in case of danger to life and property. One such juristic opinion or *fatawā* was referred to Mawlana Abdul Hai and Shah Ismail, both of whom denounced the ruling as erroneous. Shah Abdul Aziz to whom both the sets of rulings were sent for review, agreed with Mawlana Abdul Hai and Shah Ismail and severely criticized those who sought to create a dangerous precedent by relinquishing the obligatory religious duties on different pretexts. Mohiuddin Ahmad, op. cit., pp. 80-81.

134. Sayyid Abul A'Lā Mawdudi, *A Short History of the Revivalist Movement in Islam*, Markazi Maktaba Islami, Delhi 6, p. 89.

the region. Sayyid Ahmad's *jihād* movement obtained considerable success in early skirmishes against the Sikhs. They tried to reform the society on the *Shari'ah* lines, and proclaimed the Islamic caliphate in the area under their influence. But apathy towards the implementation of *Shari'ah* rules; tribal jealousy and covetousness of the local leaders, on whose support *mujahideen* were rather supposed to relay, sapped the vitality of *mujahideen* forces. With the result *mujahideen* forces had to suffer many losses. Sayyid Ahmad disgusted by the machination and perfidy of tribe's men of North West Frontier, decided to shift his base to Kashmir and Hazara. Finally *jihād* movement, after five years of long and assiduous struggle in May 1831 culminated in the martyrdom of Sayyid Ahmad and Shah Ismail along with hundreds of disciples at Balakot. According to Mawlana Mawdudi "History bears evidence that the soil of the subcontinent had not witnessed the real Islamic *jihād* before them."[135]

The *jihād* movement of Sayyid Ahmad Shaheed and his disciples directed initially against the Sikhs (usurpers of power and perpetrators of excesses against Muslims in Punjab and surroundings) but intended, ultimately, to be converted into war against the British imperialists in the subcontinent. The military campaign of the movement of Sayyid Ahmad Shaheed, however, apparently failed to attain their larger objective but it triumphed in keeping alive the smouldering embers of hatred against foreign rule. In Bengal Mir Nithar Ali commonly known as Titu Mir, a well-known Calcutta wrestler led similar resistance movement. The landlords imposed a tax, which was quite heavy for a poor peasant, on each of them, which came to be known as the Beard tax, for all of them wore beards. Titu Mir, who is reportedly to have come under the influence

135. Ibid., p 90.

of Sayyid Ahmad Shaheed, led the campaign, which gave rise to a number of minor riots. Ultimately Titu Mir fell fighting against a British military contingent sent to crush his uprising. Then after that *jihād* against the British occupation was carried on intermittently for long even after the 1857-58. The movement of ideas initiated by them can still be seen at work in the subcontinent.

This movement was to become a thorn in the side of India's British rulers, who labelled it Wahhabi. To inhibit people from joining *mujahideen* forces; to create confusion and split because Abdul Wahhab and his followers had incurred opprobrium in the Muslim world including India which is predominantly Hanafi.[136] Almost every European historian especially W.W. Hunter in his book *Indian Musalmans* had dubbed "militant reformist movement" of Sayyid Ahmad as Wahhabi and Wahabism as synonymous with rebellion against the British government. They held the view that while performing *hajj*, Sayyid Ahmad Shaheed fell in with the teachers of the "Wahhabi" sect and was deeply impressed by the doctrine preached by Muhammad ibn Abdul Wahhab.[137] Sayyid Ahmad made pilgrimage to Mecca in 1822-23 ten years after Muhammad Ali of Egypt had conquered and petered out the so-called "Wahhabis" and suppressed their ideas. Anybody subscribed to "Wahhabis" was severely punished.[138] Although some of his ideas are strikingly similar to the "wahhabi" doctrines, In fact, both the movements seek to reform Muslim society in their respective lands. Sayyid Ahmad's movement

136. I.H. Qureshi, op. cit., p. 171. For detailed discussion on the topic please see Mohiuddin Ahmad, op. cit., pp. 98ff. and also Masood Alam Nadwi, *Hindustan Ki Pehli Islami Tahrik*, Urdu, Markazi Maktabat Islami, Delhi, 1977.

137. W.W. Hunter, *The India Musalmans*, London, 1876, pp. 60-61.

138. Masood Alam Nadwi, op. cit., p. 17.

was based on Shah Waliullah's ideas, but in different circumstances and with a greater emphasis on the "purification" of Islam from un-Islamic beliefs and practices, especially those borrowed from the Hindu society. Further more Sayyid *malfuzat* (utterance) edited by Mawlana Abd al-Hayy and Shah Ismail, and his own work *Taqwiat-al-Iman*, which are our main authorities on his teachings had already been complied before he left for *hijaz*. The two reformists movements of Arabia and India differed on some important issues, which cannot be overlooked by any historian. While the former movement totally rejected mysticism, denouncing it as a later accretion, the Indian revivalist movement represented by Shah Waliullah and Sayyid Ahmad Shaheed was nourished by rich traditions of *tassawwuf*. The followers of Sheikh Muhammad Ibn Abdul Wahhab were almost Hambalites, while as those of Indian reformers belonged to the Hanafite school as well as accepted the principle of the primacy of the *Hadith* over the rulings of all the four juristic schools of Islam. Thus the views expressed by some writers, notably William Hunter, that he took inspiration from "Wahhabi" is not tenable. However, reformist movements from Sayyid Ahmad onwards, Faraidi's as well as Karamat Ali's movements in India are loosely spoken of as Wahhabi. But this is without warrant. None of them was organically connected with the movement started in Arabia by Muhammad Ibn Abdul Wahhab (1703-87), which sought its inspiration from Imam Ibn Tayyimah of the Hanbali school of thought, was literalist and puritanical in tendency, many of the Indian movements followed the Hanafi and the Shafii school and expressly disclaimed or even criticized or attacked the "Wahhabi" rejection of *tasawwuf* or orthodox *Sūfi* philosophy, though they sympathized with the reform which seeks the abolition of extraneous customs and forms and rites.

The significance of the political aspect Sayyid Ahmad

Shahids movement (i.e. *jihād*) in its historical perspective has completely overshadowed the importance of his efforts to introduce socio-religious reform. It was however only in the last five or six years of his life that he devoted his exclusive attention to organizing the campaign against the Sikhs and that too under the urgency to stop their persecution of Muslims. Intrinsically, a reform movement culminated into *jihād* movement under given circumstances. A careful examination of Sayyid Ahmad's *malfuzat* compiled and published under the title, *Sirat-al-Mustaqim*, edited by Mawlana Abd al-Hayy and Shah Ismail, leaves no doubt that he was a *Sūfi-shaykh* both by belief and practice.[139] Sir Syed Ahmad Khan who wrote his *Athar-al-Sanadid* only fifteen or sixteen years after his death, includes him in the list of the leading *mashaikhs* of his time. According to Sayyid Ahmad Shaheed's analysis of the situation, like Shah Waliullah, the main cause of the degeneration of the Muslims lay in their getting away from the path of the real teachings of Islam. As a result of adoption by the Muslim of un-Islamic ideas and customs borrowed from the Hindus and highly exaggerated, almost unbalanced, notions of some of the *Sūfi* doctrines, practices and ideas spread by irresponsible pretenders who are referred to as "polytheists behaving like *sūfīs*."[140] Thus according to him, the resuscitation of Muslim society in all its phases could be achieved only through a campaign of socio-religious reform.

Among many other topics *malfuzat* contains a good discussion on their spiritual mode of Islamic thoughts, *tassawwuf*, believed to be permeable to heretic and pernicious

---

139. Sayed Ahmad Khan, *Athar al-Sanadid*, ed. Moinul Haq, Karachi, 1966.

140. Sayyid Ahmad Shaheed, *Sirat-al-Mustaqim*, Delhi edn., n.d., p. 46.

ideas, and responsible for the ruin of Muslim society. Therefore, its reformation is indispensable. In the first chapter of this book the author elaborates the distinctive features of the two paths. *Tariq-i-nubuwwat* (way of the *nabi*) and *tariq-i-wilayat* (way of the *wali*). And the follower of the path of *tariq-i-wilayat* which is also referred as *hubb-i-ishqi* dissociates himself from everything except his "beloved." He shows the lack of interest in mundane things (worldly affairs). His excessive devotion to his *murshid* (guide) not because he was his guide and source of Allah's grace on him but because it was the demand of love.[141] Reference is also made to the fruits (Samrat) of the *hubb-i-ishqi* of which the most significant is the attainment of the state of *fana* when a person feels bound to have a faith in the doctrine of *wahdat al-wujud*.[142]

Tariq-i-nubuwwat, according to him, arises from the consciousness of the fact that for the fulfilment of his needs and requirements man depends entirely on the grace of Allah, The Real Giver. Thus while concentrating on the study of His Word, which enlightens his intelligence and consciousness and purges them from evil ideas and desires to commit sins. With further contemplation, he feels ashamed and the intensity of his love and respect for Him grows. This intense love, tempered by extreme respect overwhelms the body and heart of the *mumin*, which is also refereed as *hubb-i-imani*.[143] In this case the lover is so strong that his sole concentration is on obedience to His will[144] and has complete trust in God "*tawakkul*." His exposition of "*tawakkul*" is that, it does not mean giving up worldly means entirely but it signifies, not placing one's trust

141. Ibid.
142. Ibid., pp. 8, 13.
143. Ibid., pp. 18, 20.
144. Ibid., p. 24.

on them.[145] In conclusion, it has been emphatically stated, that the two systems *tariq-i-nubuwwat* and *tariq-i-wilayat* are not incompatible with one another in fact the *hubb-i-imani* is like a royal paced horse moving forward on the accepted path while the *hubb-i-ishqi* is like its various stages. In case of some persons *hubb-i-ishqi* being stronger attracts them to the path of *wilayat* and becomes the manifestation of their *hubb-i-imani* also, while in others the latter reappears when the excitement of the former abates. However, some ignorant and idiot persons ignore the *hubb-i-imani* and pay stress on *hubb-i-ishqi* only. Thus in order to improve and set right the morbid conditions born out of their misconceptions it becomes inevitable to lead them towards the directives (*ahkam*) of the *Qur'an* and *Sunnah* in its letter and spirit.[146] Thereby giving preference to the *tariq-i-nubuwwat* and *hub-i-imani* but at the same time having liberal attitude towards the *tariq-i-wilayat* or *hubb-i-ishqi* as its distinctive features. The demand of situation as perceived by Sayyid Ahmad Shahid and his disciples to opt for resistance against external enemy side by side with internal reformation ultimately failed to succeed because of his martyrdom at Balakot in 1831. He did not get enough time to implement his projects of reform which were only possible in an independent state. Nevertheless, his successors continued the work for some time and it cannot be denied that the movement left deep traces on the socio-cultural history of the Muslims of the subcontinent in the decades preceding the Revolution of 1857.

There were other reform movements found to have originated in different circumstances, to have fostered by men of very different characters, and to have left their mark in

145. Ibid.

146. Ibid., pp. 29-40.

quite different degrees on the Islamic thought in India. They were Haji Shariat-ullah (1781-1840). The founder of Faraidi movement of eastern Bengal and the Maulvi Karamat Ali of Jaunpur (d. 1873).

Haji Shariat-ullah was born in the village of Bahadurpur, in the district of Faridpur, Bengal[147] and when eighteen years of age he went on a pilgrimage to Mecca. Here he stayed for twenty years as a disciple of Shaykh Tahir as-Sunbal al-Makki, who at that time was the head of the Shafi sect at Mecca. On his return to Bengal he began to preach purity of faith and conduct and obtained a large following. He sought to rid his followers of un-Islamic practices and superstitions (*bidat*) and concentrate on performing the *fara'id* (obligatory duties). It was for this reason that this movement came to be called Faraidis. Shariat-ullah denounced a number of *Sūfi* practices, like the offering of *fatihah* for the souls of the dead, veneration of the *shaykh* (*Sūfi*) and visits to their tombs. Like a true missionary, lived in the midst of common people like one of them. Exemplary selflessness and self-effacement is evident by his discontinuing the use of terms *pīr* (priest) and *murīd*, and substituting in their place the title *ustād* (teacher) and *Shāgird* (pupil). The age long practice of *bayat* was given up and *tawbah* (repentance) was insisted upon in its place. It is for this reason of concordance of views on certain issues with those of Wahhabi ideas, he is regarded as having been imbued with the spirit of Wahhabi reform during his stay at Mecca. However, it is certain that he adhered to the Hanafi School of *fiqh*.

Like Shah Abdul Aziz he declared the subcontinent to be

147. For details please see Muinuddin Ahmad Khan, *History of the Faraidi Movement* (Karachi, 1965), and also for account of his life and work, as given by M. Hidayat Husain, *The Encyclopaedia of Islam*, II, 57ff.

a *dar ul-harb*, therefore, he argued, Friday congregational prayers and the celebrations of the two Id festivals were not to be held in *dar ul-harb*,[148] and Muslims should exert themselves to bring about normal conditions in which they could exercise their important rites of their religion. He did not, however, preach *jihād* against the British, perhaps because he considered such an undertaking outside the capabilities of his followers.

The establishment of British influence over Bengal proved to be a signal for revolutionary changes not only in the political situation in the region but also in the socio-economic and religious life of its people. British had a clear policy of depriving Muslims of their leading position they previously held. Many of the finer and more skilled industrial arts of India had been in the hands of Muslims, and they were ruined by the fiscal policy of the East India Company. The higher posts in pre British India, in the army, in the administration, and in the learned professions, had been in Muslim hands. Many of the higher and middle classes of Indian Muslims were reduced to beggary. The permanent settlement introduced in 1793 completely upset life in rural areas by investing ownership of the land in the *zamīndāras*, who thus became landlords instead of mere agents of the state as they had been under the Muslim government. Soon it became evident that the British policy in Bengal was based on the principle of placating the Hindus by enabling them to strengthen and stabilize their position particularly in the economic and administrative fields. With an improvement in their economic life, Hindus who had previously been in the employ of Muslim rural gentry or had earned wealth as bankers and moneylenders had started purchasing land on a large scale. This change of hands in the possession of *zamīndārī* lands had a far-reaching effect on the

148. S. Moinul Haq., op. cit., pp. 450-51.

relations of the cultivators and new owners of land. Now the tenantry of eastern Bengal were mostly Muslims, whom the exactions of their Hindu landlords had reduced to great poverty.

Haji Shariat-ullah took up cudgels on behalf of poor people against the landlords and told his followers to stop paying undue cases and taxes. It gave this purely religious movement an agrarian touch. This movement was furthered by his son and successor Mushin al-Din, popularly known as Dudu Main (1819-62), who after 1838 led the movement started by his father. He had a genius for organization and by making his headquarters at Bahadurpur, he divided eastern Bengal into circles (*halqah*) appointing *khalifa* (deputy) to each. He took a determined stand against the levying of illegal cases by landlords and indigo planters. The cultivators and village artisans responded enthusiastically to his preaching. He was too realistic like his father to advocate an armed struggle and tried to avoid a head-on clash with landlords.[149] But they implicated him in a number of criminal suits; he served several terms of imprisonment and died on 24 September 1862. The sect continued for some time to exist and stuck to its beliefs.

The movement led by Maulavi Karamat Ali had a wholly, peaceful and religious aim. Through his works and preaching he made attempts to prevent reformist tendencies from becoming extremist and insisted upon to abandon the extreme doctrines by which they were being led into dangerous path of the political irredentism.[150] He taught that on account of the prevalence of complete religious liberty India was not a *dar ul-harb*, and the celebration of the Friday congregational

149. I.H. Qureshi, op. cit., p. 180.

150. M. Mujeeb, op. cit., pp. 446-47.

prayer and of the two Id festival was not only lawful but obligatory. Thus he was antithesis of Shah Abdul Aziz's and Haji Shariat Ullah's thought and movement. However Karamat Ali insisted upon the reformation of Muslim society by purging Hindu customs and superstitions that had been adopted by the Muslims of Eastern Bengal.

1857[151] marked the end of Mughal rule in the subcontinent and the beginning of a new historical phase. However, for more than a hundred years, after the death of Aurangzeb in 1707, the last of the powerful Mughals, disintegration had been going on, not only in Muslim political power, but in Muslim life and culture as well, owing to the lack of a strong central government and leadership. The Muslim, though in a minority, had been the rulers of the land, and it is not surprising that their reaction to British policies was sharper and more determined than that of the Hindus. "In that part of British India where Muslims were influential and also where their religion and culture had become strong rooted the mutiny took on the definite character of *jihād*."[152] *Ulama* not only supported it but actually fought in it. Indeed they were the main organizers of the Revolution of 1857. After the collapse of the movement, therefore, they had to pay a heavy price. The post-1857 policy of the British government was decidedly anti-Muslim. The tragedy of the great revolt marked the death of old orders, and brought political, economic and cultural disaster to the Muslims of the subcontinent. For many years

---

151. For detailed discussion on the subject see Syed Moinul Haq, *The Great Revolution of 1857*, Karachi 1968, pp. 551ff. and Kayes and Malleson, *History of Indian Mutiny*, London, 1898, vol. V, p. 339 et. seq.

152. Fazlur Rahman, *Islam*, 2nd edn., Chicago and London, 1979, p. 204.

afterwards the Muslims steadily lost ground in education, in the public services and in general leadership in India. The Muslim community stood defeated, powerless, and demoralized. As the resilient and protracted resistance failed to resuscitate the Muslims in the subcontinent and the enormous loss of worthy energy in these attempts, enervated Muslims and instilled in them the idea prescribed by some that the prosecution of a *jihād* was as an impracticable and counter-productive part of the revivalist programme. On the other side, the influence of Western civilization which was already, slowly but surely creeping closer and closer to Muslim mind in India and elsewhere and had been the dominant factor in moulding only the higher life of Muslims in the subcontinent. After 1857, with the removal of the last vestige of Mughal imperial authority and dejected Muslim morale, we find scarily any department of life, which has not been affected by Western influences.

At this juncture of Muslim history in the subcontinent, mainly two types of responses were offered, one by the orthodox *Ulama* and another by Muslim modernists. Majority among the former (religious leaders) advocated a policy of cultural isolation and non-cooperation. They equated any form of political accommodation of Western culture with betrayal and surrender. They determined to boycott the Western institutions, which were rapidly taking root and flourishing everywhere. This prohibition had a particular reference to Western education, which included the teaching of English and modern science in the government and Mission schools, springing up everywhere. With vehement language they inveighed against the institutions of foreigners, Western (Christian) ideas and values. Looking at them as dangerous as their governments and armies, therefore withdrawal, non-cooperation, or rejection of the West is indispensable, in order to preserve the Islamic culture and heritage under non-Muslim rule. After the failure of 1857 revolution some of the *Ulama* turned to more peaceful method. They decided to establish a *madrasah* on the lines of Madrasah-i-Rahimiyyah.[153] Mawlana Muhammad Qasim Nanawtawi[154] with other *Ulama* drew up the scheme and established famous Dar al-'ulum, a seminary of traditional Islamic learning at Deoband which became the main centre of orthodox Muslim thought in the subcontinent. In its own field, Deoband has established a high reputation in the Muslim world.

Another Muslim school of modernist thought sought to delineate an alternative to Western, secular adaptation on the one hand and religiously motivated rejections on the other. They sought to respond to, rather than react against, the challenges of Western imperialism. They stressed the dynamism, flexibility and adaptability that had characterized the early development of Islam, notable for its achievements in law, education and the sciences. They pressed for internal reform through a process of reinterpretation (*ijtihad*) and selective adaptation (Islamization) of Western idea and technology. Islamic modernism, what it is called, is a process of internal self-criticism, a struggle to redefine Islam to

---

153. Madrasah-i-Rahimiyya had been developed under the guidance of Shah Waliullah and Shah Abdul Aziz. It had held the torch of piety and spiritual fervour aloft in a society that had succumbed to the enervating influences of idle pleasure and moral decay and had inspired a burning for recapturing the former glory of Islam. It had ceased to exist after the destruction of its buildings by the British when they reoccupied Delhi in 1858. It was situated where Edward Park is located now. I.H. Qureshi, *Ulama*, p. 221.

154. For a short biography see Muhammad Yaqub-i-Nanawati, *Sawanih Umri*, Deoband, n.d.

demonstrate its relevance to the new situations that Muslims found themselves in as their societies modernized.

In the aftermath of 1857 in the subcontinent, Muslim sullenness, their aloofness and suppressed hatred for the new order became more marked than ever. As a result of this policy of isolation and self-sufficiency, for many decades Muslims in the subcontinent lost ground in education, in the public service, and in general leadership in India. And on the other side they fell farther and farther behind their Hindu compatriots in the matter of education. For the latter were not at all slow to avail themselves of the new educational facilities, and to adapt themselves to the changing circumstances and the requirements of the new government.[155] Many Muslim leaders realized the gravity of situation. For them the key to the whole situation was adaptation to the new environment, use of the new forces that had come into play, acceptance of new instrument of progress that had been created through English education.[156] Sporadic efforts were made in this direction in many places, but the concentrated efforts that won the field culminated in the person, was undoubtedly Sir Sayyid Ahmad Khan (1817-98) leading Muslim modernist of the subcontinent. He was convinced that the survival of the Muslim community necessitated a bold reinterpretation of Islam and the acceptance, not rejection, of the best in Western thought.

---

155. Titus, op. cit., p. 193.

156. S.A.A Rizvi, "The Breakdown of Traditional Society" in *The Cambridge History of Islam*, vol. 2, op. cit., pp. 81-82.

In fact, a beginning towards reform had already been made by the Muslims of Bengal under the leadership of Nawab Abd al-Latif Khan, who had founded the "Muhammadan Literary Association" in 1863, and in his effort he was later joined by Mawlana Karamat Ali Jaunpuri (d. 1873) to only name the few.

Sayyid Ahmad Khan, born of a noble Delhi family, received the usual orthodox education. He was a pupil of the famous erudite scholar Mawlana Mamluk Ali, who was entirely a product of the Wali-ullahi school and traditions.[157] Sayyid Ahmad Khan's active career is marked by three clear cut phases; the pre-revolution period, 1838-57, efforts for educational and social reform, 1858-85; full-fledged leadership of the Muslim community, 1886-98. In the first period he was a conservative Muslim and his ideas and pursuits do not appear to be different from those of other Muslims. He had received the influence of Shah Waliullah's thought in his early carrier of life through his teacher, especially his revivalist tradition. In his first theological work, *Rah-i-Sunnat wa Radd-i-Bidat*, this influence is recognizable. It was later when he turned to more rationalistic interpretation of Islam. He qualified for a subordinate position in the British government for the post of *munsif*, the lowest judicial officer, and he rose steadily in rank and esteem. "His loyal and fearless service to the cause of British in 1857 had won him their favour."[158] During that period he wrote *Athar al-Sanadid*, on the monuments and leading personalities of Delhi, first published in 1847, and also edited the well-known *A'in-i-Akbari* of Abdul Fadl in 1856.

In the second phase, the upheaval of 1857-58, which brought ruin on the Muslims of Delhi and the united provinces, was the turning point in Sir Sayyid's life. He felt a strong urge to lead and guide a regular movement to bring about a drastic

---

157. See, Mansoor Ali Akhta Hashmi, *Muslim Response to Western Education*, Commonwealth Pub., N. Delhi, 1989, pp. 37-39. and I.H. Qureshi, op. cit., pp. 220-26, Mawlana Mamluk Ali was also the teacher of Mawlana Qasim Nanawtavi and Mawlana Rashid Ahmad Gangohi, the founders of the Darul Ulum Deoband.

158. S.A.A Rizvi, op. cit., p. 82.

change in the political, social and religious outlook of the Muslims. His treatise *Asbab-i-Baghawat-i-Hind* (the cause of the Indian Mutiny) published in 1858, in which he criticized the uncommendable activities of the Christian missionaries, and tells the government that they were the main cause of disaffection among the people. At the same time the failure of revolution had convinced him of the need of new attitude towards life, which alone would save community from complete destruction. He arrived at the conclusion that in popularizing scientific and modern education lay the solution of the main problems facing the community. His programme of work was based on two fundamental concepts namely, educational and social reform and reconstruction of Islamic religious thought in the context of modern trends in civilization. To create a favourable atmosphere for the implementation of his projects co-operation with British government was absolutely necessary. Therefore, he insisted that there must be a change of political outlook. Instead of regarding the subcontinent under British rule as *dar ul-harb*, he insisted that, even though it was not under Muslim rule, it was to be regarded as *dar ul-Islam*, because Muslims were perfectly free to exercise all the essential rites and ceremonies of their religion. Despite serious opposition, he plunged into the task of removing misunderstanding between the British and the Muslims.

To promote education and understanding of Western thought, he started schools at Muradabad[159] and Ghazipur and tried to bring English works within the reach of his fellow countrymen through translation into Urdu. The establishment of scientific society in 1864 and two years later the publication

159. Ibid.

of a bi-weekly, Aligrah Institute were vital steps taken by him to give a practical shape to his ideas. He also urged patronage of vernacular education and strove for the establishment of a vernacular department in Calcutta University. In 1869-70 he visited England, during his stay he compiled *Al Khutbat al-Ahmaddiyah fi al-Arab wa al-sirat al-Muhammadiyah* (essays on the life of Muhammad SAAS) with a view to refute the charges made against Islam and Prophet by Western orientalists, particularly by Sir William Muir in his book, *Life of Muhammad.* He studied the educational system of the West and was deeply impressed by its cultural and material progress. On his return to the subcontinent he started Urdu journal entitled *Tahdhib al-Akhlaq* (Reform of Morals) to disseminate modernist ideas. Through it he and his co-workers conveyed their ideas on political, social and religious problems to the Muslims. It was not long before it became the chief organ of what has rightly been called the Aligrah movements.

The Aligarh movement is so-called after the college. Muhammadan Anglo-Oriental College at Aligrah, which he started in the form of a school in 1875, the foundation stone was laid by Lord Lytton in 1877, and it started functioning in 1879 on the lines of the College of Cambridge.[160] It forms a landmark in the history of Indian Muslim education. The Aligrah movement is usually looked upon as an educational movement, but it was much more than that. It was a comprehensive reform movement which attracted to its orbit some of the most brilliant contemporary Muslims of northern India. Prominent among them were Khawja Altaf Husain Hali of Panipat (1837-1914) the novelist, lecturer, legist and educationalist Maulavi Nazir Ahmad of Bijnor (1836–1912),

160. Ibid., 84.

and the professor intrepid traveller, and researcher Mawlana Shibli Numani of Azamgarh (1857-1914) a young man who for sixteen years (1882-98) taught at the college. They all desired to make modern knowledge a living force among Muslims, as it was in their palmy days. The Aligrah school aimed at the practical and fruitful method of making Muslim mind eager for the best modern knowledge in science and art, and to dispel the false notion that it was in any way inconsistent with the Islamic religion.

The work done by Mawlana Shibli Numani in making the results of modern research available to the Muslim public in their vernacular calls for special mention, and after his death it continued under the competent leadership of Sayyid Sulaiman Nadwi in the institution, Dar-ul-Musannifin, which he founded in his native place Azamgarh in 1883. Since then the institute contributed a lot. The foundation of Dar al-Musaunifin was laid on a rather moderate scale, but in course of time it became one of the leading centres of Islamic research in the subcontinent. Their research into the past history of Islam was not merely for the abstract acquisition of knowledge. They wished to spread knowledge in order to remove prevailing ignorance and make contemporary life more intelligent, fuller and richer. They aimed at teaching the teachers, especially the religious teachers, whose shortcomings and narrowness were a scandal that leapt to the eye in Muslim subcontinent. Later Shibli fell apart from Sayyid Ahmad Khan, because he did not agree with his interpretation of some of the fundamental doctrines of Islam. His only accord with his patron (Sir Sayyid) was the fact that the Muslims could not make much progress without modern education and not with his modern interpretation of Islamic thought. Shibli adopted a middle course between the views of the conservative section of Muslims, who sometimes went to the extent of superstition and those who could be called extreme rationalists. Shibli is essentially a historian and his contribution to modern Islamic thought is mainly based on the critical study of some of the most prominent figures in the history of Islam.

However, despite the admiration of some aspects of Western thought and civilization, Sir Sayyid Ahmad Khan was the first Muslim writer who started refuting the charges levelled against Islam and the prophet by Western orientalists like W.W. Hunter and William Muir. In that course Shibli, Chirag Ali and Amir Ali followed him. As far as the religious thought of Sir Sayyid Ahmad Khan is concerned, he far-exceeded the limits in presenting a modernized picture of Islam. On number of fundamental issues pertaining to Islamic belief and practice, he held views basically different from the orthodox interpretation. In his liberal interpretations of doctrines of Islam, he often would not accept even the rationalistic explanation put forward by medieval Muslim thinkers and philosophers. The reason was that he wanted to establish the principle of complete uniformity between the nineteenth century naturalism and Islam because of the influence of nineteenth-century European rationalism and natural philosophy on him and his belief that Islam was the religion of reason and nature. His main argument was that *Qur'an* was the word of God and nature was the work of God; disparity between the two was unthinkable.[161] In the naturalistic conception of existence there was no room for God as the creator of Universe, but Sayyid Ahmad Khan tried to present a theistic interpretation of nature. He attempted to prove the theory that "Islam is Nature and Nature is Islam,"

161. *Majmua*, I, 213-14, as quoted in J.M.S. Balijon, *The Reforms and Religious Ideas of Sir Sayyid Ahmad Khan*, Lahore, Pakistan, Sh. Muhammad Ashraf, 1964, p. 78.

which was too vague to be accepted even by the most liberal-minded among the Muslims. His compulsion was to prove Islam was in total harmony with the laws of nature and therefore compatible with modern scientific thought. These premises, reason and the laws of nature, governed Sir Sayyid's interpretation of the *Qur'an* and *Sunnah* and his treatment of such questions as evolution, miracles, and the existence of angles; which includes his multi-volume commentary on the *Qur'an*. This cannot be discussed here because of lack of space.[162] There was a widespread opposition to Sayyid's religious thought. Sayyid Jamal al-din al Afghani (1839-97) wrote in 1881 "the truth about the *Neicheri sect and an explanation of the Neicheris,*" but later more widely distributed in Arabic translation under the title *Refutation of the Materialist*. Its main target, though it does not mention him by name, was clearly Sayyid Ahmad Khan, whose followers were known to their opponents as "Neicheris" and whom Jamal-al-din attacked more directly in a series of articles published during his stay in India. He poured scorn on Sir Sayyid both for his attempt at rational interpretation of the *Qur'an* and for his loyalty and promotion of British education among Indian Muslims. Sayyid Akbar Hussain of Allahabad (1846–1921), eminent poet, had been a caustic critic, whose satires on Western civilization constitute a remarkable chapter in the history of Urdu poetry. He was not opposed to Western education as such, but was to guard the Muslim youth against the temptations of accepting and adopting Western ways of life and ignoring the traditions of their own culture. Among Sir Sayyid's colleagues who to some extent followed him or made some contribution to the

162. For discussion of the religious ideas of Sir Sayyid Ahmad Khan please see B.A. Dar, *The Religious Thought of Sayyid Ahmad Khan*, Lahore, 1957; and Aziz Ahmad, *Islamic Modernism in India and Pakistan*, London, 1961, Chap II as well as ibid.

development of modern Islamic thought only Muhsin al-Mulk (1837-1901), Mawlana Altaf Husayn Hali and Chiragh Ali have been mentioned. Their contribution to religious thought was not of a positive character; in fact education and politics were the main fields of their activity.

Sir Sayyid Ahmad Khan's real greatness lay in the breath of his vision. He was absolutely convinced of the truth of what he was preaching, but he never tried to force his views on others, nor did he lay the foundation of a new sect. In the M.A.O. College, which he had established and which in course of time became the greatest educational institute of the Muslims in the subcontinent, his religious ideas were never preached or propagated. He is therefore praised and respected by the Muslims not as a religious thinker, but as a reformer and a political leader, and there is no doubt that in these fields his contribution constitutes one of the most important chapters in the history of the subcontinent. Sir Sayyid Ahmad Khan laid the foundation of modernism among the Muslims of the subcontinent.

Sheikh Muhammad Iqbal (1876–1938), poet philosopher, political thinker, most eminent and honoured international figure, represented the next phase in modern Islam in the subcontinent. The situation in the subcontinent had changed a lot from that of Sir Sayyid's age, who endeavoured to promote Western education and thereby helped to create the class of Westernized Muslim intellectuals against the conservative Muslims *madrasah* production, resultant wide gap between the two reflected the cultural tensions of the period. The debacle of military and political power in 1857 instigated the invasion of ideas; hardly any department of life, which has not been affected by Western influences, could be found. It was however in the person of Iqbal that Muslims of the subcontinent found a thinker who had made a deep study both of Western philosophy and Islamic thought and thus presented Islamic thought in a modern and scientific perspective and thus made a lasting contribution to its evolution.

Dr. Iqbal had a deep, all consuming love for his community, an intense faith in Islam and profound reverence for Islamic traditions.[163] From the time he returned from his doctoral studies in Europe, he devoted himself to the revival of Islam in the subcontinent. He did this both as a poet-philosopher, using poetry vehicle for his thought, and more reluctantly, as a politician. Muslim religious and political survival and reform was his life long concern. He placed himself within the revivalist tradition of Shah Waliullah and Jamal al-Afghani, while addressing the question of Islamic modernism.

While admiring the accomplishment of the West — its dynamic spirit, intellectual tradition, and technology — Iqbal condemned the political domination of the West "imperialism" as well as the ever-growing onslaughts of Western culture, which were gradually destroying the very roots of the spirit of Islamic civilization. He was critical of its excesses, such as European imperialism and colonialism. The economic exploitation of capitalism, the atheism of Marxism, and the moral bankruptcy of secularism. For him Western civilization was bad, fraudulent, chaotic, unjust and greedy. He looks upon political and economic stability, peace and justice as essential elements in religions, but he thinks the Europe has deserted them. As he says

---

163. M. Mujeeb, op. cit., p. 452 and see also A.H. Ali Nadwi, *Western Civilization: Islam and Muslims*, Academy of Islamic Research and Pub. Lucknow, 1969, pp. 73, 81.

> The glitter of modern civilization dazzles the sight;
> But it is only a clever piercing together of false gems.
> The wisdom or science in which the wise ones of the West took such pride.
> Is but a warring sound in the bloody hand of greed and ambition.

His criticism of Western civilization is expressed in many scathing lines and passages in his poetry, both Persian and Urdu as the boasted power of the West is nothing but imperialism to oppress the weak and the league of nations is a mere society of robbers to parcel out the graves of those they have killed. The Western freedom of women is not real freedom. Modern civilization is a godless civilization and can lead to nothing but self-destruction.

Iqbal fully realized the dangerous consequences of the growing influence of Western civilization on educated sections of his people. He therefore emphatically condemned the superficialities of the materialistic culture of the West and advised the Easterners, particularly the Muslims, to take from the West only those things which were basically sound. Drawing on his Islamic heritage and influenced by his study of Western philosophy, he developed his own synthesis and interpretation of Islam in response to the socio-historical conditions and events of his time. While their secular counterparts looked to West rather uncritically and traditionalists shunned the West rather obstinately, Iqbal like other Islamic modernists attempted to establish a continuity between their Islamic heritage and modern change. Like Jamal al-Afghani, for him, the rubric was the reclaiming of a progressive, creative past whose political and cultural florescence demonstrated that the very qualities that were associated with the power of West were already present in Islam and accounted for its past triumphs and accomplishments. Thus, the belief that Muslims already possessed an Islamic rationale and the means for the assimilation of modern science and technology was strengthened. For them the key was to convince their co-religionists that stagnation and decline were caused by blind imitation of the past and that continued survival and revitalization of the Islamic community, which intrinsically was dynamic and creative, requires once again reassertion of *ijtihad,* to interpret and reapply Islam to changing social conditions.

At the heart of Iqbal's vision of Islam is the unity of God (*Tawhid*). The oneness of God applies not only to the nature of God but also to his relationship to the world. As God is the one creator, sustainer, and judge of the universe, so too his will or law governs every aspect of his creation and is to be realized in every area of life. The individual, the basic unit of Muslim society, is *Qur'an*ically (2: 30) charged as God's vicegerent with the mission of carrying out God's will on earth. Utilizing the *Qur'an,* Iqbal, developed a dynamic Islamic *Weltanschauung* in his theory of selfhood that embraced all reality, individual self, society and God. Thus Iqbal views the Muslim society as a religio-political State with the supremacy of Islamic law. For him "All that is secular is therefore sacred in the root of its being"[164] there is no bifurcation of the spiritual and the temporal. Church and state are not two sides of the same coin, for Islam is a single, unanalysable reality.[165]

Like Shah Waliullah, Sayyid Ahmad Shaheed and Jamal al-Afghani, Iqbal reasserted the *Shari'ah's* role as the

---

164. Muhammad Iqbal, *The Reconstruction of Religious Thought in Islam,* rev. edn., Lahore, Pakistan, Sh. Muhammad Ashraf 1968, p. 155.

165. Ibid., p. 154.

comprehensive guideline for a society of believers and the need for it to be reintroduced into Muslim societies. Their holistic approach, which viewed Islam as a comprehensive guide for private as well as public life, became part of the modern understanding or interpretation of Islam. Sir Sayyid Ahmad Khan had been the traditionally educated Muslim, who sought to make modern Western liberal thought Islamically acceptable. Muhammad Iqbal was the modern, Western educated Muslim who like other Islamic modernists reinterpreted Islam in conjunction with Western thought to demonstrate its relevance as viable and only alternative to Western ideologies. This thought was retritrated and further propounded by modern Islamic movements or neo-rivalists and in the subcontinent by Mawlana Sayyid Abu A'Lā Mawdudi and others, which will be discussed separately.

3

Sayyid Abul A'Lā Mawdudi and His Thought

ASSIDUOUS attempts by Shah Waliullah, Shah Abdul Aziz, Sayyid Ahmad Shaheed, Allama Iqbal and others to resuscitate and vivify Islamic faith and power in the subcontinent 'did not fully materialize to overcome challenges faced by the Muslims on the internal (decadence and deviation) and external (political as well as ideological) fronts. But their sustained and relentless perseverance to uphold *Shari'ah* (pristine Islam) and efforts to dispel ignorance and perpetual resistance against the heretic and deviations tendencies set out model for future revivalists to carry on the struggle, keeping in view the experiences of the past and the changing circumstances. Sayyid Abul A'Lā Mawdudi is a continuation of this movement, aimed at to rescue community to slide into abyss of frightful dark age. While the pre-modern revivalist movement in the subcontinent, such as of Shaykh Abdul Haq Muhaddith of Delhi, Shaykh Ahmad Sirhindi and up to the time of Shah Waliullah were primarily internally motivated. Islamic revivalist Sayyid Ahmad Shaheed and Islamic modernists Sir Sayyid Ahmad Khan and Allama Iqbal was a response both to the continued internal weaknesses and to the external political and religio-cultural threat of colonialism in their own perspectives. By the nineteenth and early twentieth centuries British increasingly dominated the subcontinent with the result the internal breakdown of Muslim society was exacerbated by the growing threat of their presence and imperialist designs, which precipitated a religious as well as a political crises.

A variety of response emerged from Muslims. Some Westernized (Western educated Muslims or secularists) adversaries of Islamic thought espoused that it has lost its vitality and is now outmoded. They advocated the separation of religion and politics, and the establishment of modern nation-states modelled on the West. Islam should be restricted to personal life and public life should be modelled on modern, that is, Western ideas and technology in the government, military, education, and law. Some orthodox Muslim leaders advocated total withdrawal, non-cooperation, or rejection of the West. A group of reform-minded Muslims sought to respond to, rather than react against, influence of Western civilization. They proclaimed the need for Islamic reform and sought to delineate an alternative to Western, secular adaptationism on the one hand and religiously motivated rejectionism on the other. Though, the record of Islamic modernism is mixed, most of them viewed Islam as a comprehensive guide for private as well as public and stressed the dynamism, flexibility and adaptability that had characterized the early development of Islam, notable for its achievements in law, education, and the science. Thus they struggled to redefine Islam to demonstrate its relevance to the new situations, which they are able to prescribe, but proved less successful in implementation. The ever-increasing domination of west and diminishing resistance on the part of Muslims further precipitated crisis, with the result, under the leadership of secular elites, Western theories and institutions were regarded as models to be emulated. In general, they continued to look Western models in their developmental effort. This whole phenomenon aroused a deep concern about the effect of a Western secular form of modernization upon Islamic life and values. In this void stepped in Mawlana Abu A'lā Mawdudi (1903-79), who in communion with previous Islamic revivalist (*tajdid*) movements, attributed the ills of society to its departure from Islamic ideal as found in early Islam — during the time of the Prophet Muhammad (SAAS) and his companions. Therefore, he too advocated a return to Islamic sources — the *Qur'an* and the example or practice of the Prophet. It is important to note that he did not reject modernization and technology but rather the Westernization and secularization of Muslim society. He reaffirmed the political nature of Islam and the need for political action to realize or re-establish a proper state based upon Islam in order to assure an Islamic society, governed by Islamic law and belief. He not only preached his message of social and political reform but also tried to implement it through the establishment of party.

Formative years of Mawlana Mawdudi's Life and Thought

Mawlana Sayyid Abul A'Lā Mawdudi was born on Rajab 3, AH 1321/25 September 1903 in the famous city of Aurangabad (founded and named after Aurangzeb Alamgir). The then princely state of Hyderabad (Deccan), presently Andra Pradesh, India. He was born into a respectable and religious family, having the honour of being Sayyid (descendents of Prophet Muhammad SAAS) through Imam Hussain (RA). One of his ancestors Khwajah Qutb al-Din Mawdudi (d. AH 527) a renowned leader of the Chisti *Sūfi* order, whose teachings were latter introduced by Khwaja Moin-ud-Din Chisti (d. 633/ 1236) in the subcontinent, Qutb-al-Din Mawdudi's family had migrated to Afghanistan and settled at Chist near Herat. It is after him his descendents came to be known as Mawdudi's.[1] It was during the reign of Sikander Lodi that Abul A'Lā Mawdudi (d. AH 935), ancestor and name sake of Mawlana Mawdudi and 25th descendant of Khwaja Qutb-ud-Din Mawdudi came to India from Chist and settled in a district Baras near Karnal. In the time of Shah Alam, this family then settled permanently in Delhi.[2]

Mawlana Mawdudi's father Maulvi Sayyid Ahmad Hasan, was born in Delhi, two years before the mutiny of 1857, who later shifted to Aurangabad from Delhi. He was among the first students to attend the Madrasatul Ulum, Aligarh, established by Sir Syed Ahmad Khan, who was related to Ahmad Hasan from maternal side and on his insistence was allowed to pursue education at Aligarh. However, he was recalled home by his father (Mawlana Mawdudi's grandfather) on being informed by his friend that his son Ahmad Hasan is wearing on English dress and playing English game cricket. In those days, hatred for Western education and culture was extreme amongst the Muslims and that too a boy from religious family following Western culture was disgusting and unthinkable. Ahmad Hasan was then admitted to law school at Allahabad, from where he passed the lawyer's course. He practised law for many years in Meerut, Ghaziabad and Bulandshahr and then in Aurangabad. Until that time, the influence of Western ideas and culture was present in him. By the time Mawlana Mawdudi was born, the Western influence

1. *Maktubat-i-Mawdudi*, vol. 1, Islamic Publication. It is the compilation of some of the Mawdudi's letters.

2. Mawlana Mawdudi, *Khud Nawisht*, an autobiographical article reproduced in Muhammad Yusif, ed.; Mawlana Mawdudi, *Apni aur Dusron Ki Naẓar Main* (Urdu), Markazi Maktaba Islami Delhi, 1998, pp. 25, 39, and also see *Mawlana Mawdudi Introduces Himself*, Radiance, 4-10 June 1989, p. 49.

of his father gradually diminished and Islamic ideas and culture recurred in him fully. Three years before Mawlana Mawdudi's birth, a holy man had met his father and prophesied the birth of another son, who would make a name for himself in the service of Islam and advised him to name child (in the family) Abul A'Lā. Soon after, a great change came over Ahmad Hasan and then under the influence of Mawlvi Mohy-ud-Din his preceptor and spiritual guide, Ahmad Hasan took to intense religious activity, meditation and worship. He even abandoned his legal practice, discarded the worldly life, went to Delhi and spent his time in religious meditation, staying near the shrine of Hazrat Nizam-ud-Din Auliya. After three years, Mawlvi Mohy-ud-Din his preceptor, not approving this course, recalled him to Aurangabad and brought home to him that worship did not mean renunciation and that he should earn his livelihood through *halal* means. Then afterwards he restarted his practice but never took a false case. He would first investigate the client's case to ascertain his innocence and then would agree to take up his case.[3]

Thus Mawlana Mawdudi was born and brought up in complete Islamic environment, even his upbringing and early education was taken care of by his father himself. His primary education was arranged at home, which proved more fruitful then education in a school. His father had first decided to make Mawdudi a Mawlvi. Hence he was educated accordingly; he was taught Urdu, Persian, Arabic, *fiqh* and *Hadith*. English modern subjects or ideas were kept away from him. His father took special pains to train Mawdudi on the right lines, inculcate right habits, personally taught him basic aspects of Islam and endeavoured to make him religious-minded. He was particular about the purity of his language

3. Ibid., pp. 26, 29.

and taught him to speak in standard idiomatic Urdu, dialect of Delhi without any admixture of the Deccan dialect. He kept Mawdudi in his company most of the time.[4] Thus Mawdudi's moral uprightness, his profound regard for propriety and righteouness largely reflect the religious environs which his parents provided and their concern for his proper moral upbringing.

After acquiring early education at home Mawlana Mawdudi at the age of 11, was admitted to Std. VIII (8th class) of High School Madrassa Furqania, Aurangabad which attempted to combine the modern Western with the traditional Islamic education. Here he took "Mawlvi matriculation" in religious knowledge in 1916. Later, his father's deteriorating health took the family to Hyderabad, where Mawdudi was admitted to the Mawlvi Alim class in the Dar al-Ulum Hyderabad.[5] This, however, he could not continue for more than six months, because of his father's illness and then death. Hereafter, when he was of a tender age, the struggle for survival started.[6] This did not deter Mawdudi from continuing his studies, having natural aptitude for writing, his studious habits and encouragement received from elders during his childhood whetted his appetite for writing. Thereupon Mawdudi decided to use pen to earn his living. His natural tendency and needs of journalism made him to do self-study. In addition to Urdu, Persian and Arabic in which he was

---

4. For biographical information about Mawdudi see, ibid., and also Misbahul Islam Faruqi, *Introducing Mawdudi*, Karachi, 1968; Abul Afaq, *Sayyid Abul A'Lā Mawdudi, Sawanih, Afkar, Tarik*, Lahore, 1971; Naim Siddiqi, *Mawlana Mawdudi, Ek Taaruf*, Lahore, 1963; Masudul Hasan, *Sayyid Abul Aala Mawdudi and His Thoughts*, Islamic Publication, Pvt. Ltd., Lahore, 1984, p.1 ff.
5. *Khud Nawisht*, p. 31
6. Ibid., p. 34.

already proficient, he concentrated on English language, so as to study books in English on history, philosophy, politics, economics, religion, and sociology and to understand them.[7] Thus, most of what Mawlana Mawdudi learned was self-acquired, though for short spells of time, he was able to receive systematic instruction or guidance from some competent scholars. The overall assessment of his early life suggests that he was a self-made man.

The influence and training of Mawlana Mawdudi's father played vital role in moulding and developing personality and mindset of Mawlana Mawdudi. As he himself recalls:

> My father related to me stories of the prophets, events and heroes of Islam and Indian history. I can, till today, feel the beneficial effects of that. These stories created in me great love for Islam. These stories with their morals laid down the foundation of my moral conduct.[8]

With his father he often used to visit the mausoleum of Aurangzeb in Aurangabad and came to regard Aurangzeb as the symbol of the renaissance of Islam. The young Mawdudi felt in himself the urge to carry forward the mission of Aurangzeb.[9] Among other things which influenced Mawlana Mawdudi at early age were the writings of Altaf Hussain Hali and Abul Kalam Azad. *Mad-o-Jazar-i-Islam* (the Ebb and Flow of Islam) written in 1886, popularly known as the *Musaddas* (six line stanzas) by poet Altaf Hussain Hali to recall the post-glory and achievements of the Muslims and call to follow Islam

7. Ibid., pp. 33-34.
8. Idem., and also see *Mawlana Mawdudi Introduces Himself*, Radiance, 4-10 June 1089, p. 49 and Interview published in the Mawdudi Number of Sayyara, 1980, also quoted by Masadul Hasan, *Mawdudi*, pp. 11-12.
9. Masudul Hasan, Mawdudi, p. 12.

to recapture their lost greatness. Likewise Mawlana Abul Kalam Azad's well-known daily paper *al-Hilal* aimed at inviting the Muslims to straight path of Islam and to inspire them to seek guidance and give serious consideration to the holy *Qur'an* and *Sunnah;* the only solution to their problems whether it is social, educational or political. Young Mawdudi enamoured of most of the poems of Mawlana Hali, including famous *Mussaddas* and had opportunity to study *al-Hilal*. Being acquainted with their writings Mawlana Mawdudi must have taken inspirations from them.[10]

Adapting Journalism as Career

After the death of his father Mawlana Mawdudi had to stand on his own feet. He had no inclination or interest in government service. However, the passion of writing made him to earn living through pen and thus he joined his elder brother Abul Khair in 1918 who was already working as the editor of the newspaper *Medina* at Bijnore. Mawlana Mawdudi worked with him in the editorial staff. This was his first step in the field of journalism, which lasted not more than two months and thereafter both shifted to Delhi.[11] Henceforth, Mawlana Mawdudi's career in journalism accelerated. In (CE) 1919, he along with his brother assumed the editorship of weekly paper *Taj*[12] from Jabalpur for few months, the paper could not continue because of prevailing difficulties of the time. Later

10. Ibid., p. 17, and also see Dr Sayeed Riaz Ahmad, *Mawlana Mawdudi and the Islamic State*, Peoples Publishing House, Lahore 1976, pp. 27, 31.

11. *Khud Nawisht*, p. 32.

12. The owner of this newspaper *Taj* was Tajuddin of Jabalpur a city in the province now called Madhya Pradesh. He was a very active member of the Majlis-i-Ia'nat-i-Nazar Bandan-i-Islam, society of the sympathizers of the prisoners in the path of Islam, and also was pro-Congress activist.

in 1920 the publication of *Taj* was resumed, with Mawlana Mawdudi as its independent editor as his brother had left journalism for good. Mawlana Mawdudi was successful in transforming it into a daily paper within a short span of time. However *Taj* was soon closed when one of Mawdudi's article was found politically objectionable by the government. He escaped persecution because the paper carried the name of Tajuddin as editor and publisher. This brought Mawdudi back to Delhi, where in 1921, he became acquainted with the senior leaders of Jam'iyatul *'Ulama'*-i-Hind, Mawlana Mufti Kifayatullah and Mawlana Ahmad Said. They recognized Mawdudi's talents and invited him to edit the Jam'iyats official newspaper "Muslim"[13] and later its successor Al-Jami'at, which from 1925 up to 1928 was published under his sole responsibility.[14] After his resignation from Al-Jam'iyat in 1928, Mawlana Mawdudi moved to Hyderabad, his home-town, and devoted himself to research and writing. It was in this connection that he took over the editorship of monthly *Tarjuman-ul-Qur'an* in 1932 from Mawlana Abu Muhammad Muslih, who had been his predecessor for seven months. Since then *Tarjuman-ul-Qur'an* became his cherished journal and the forum to express his views on different topics especially concerning Islam. These years in journalism were also utilized by Mawlana Mawdudi for removing the deficiencies in his education and were a period of learning and intellectual growth

---

13. Mawlana Mawdudi remained editor of *Muslim* till CE 1923 when publication ceased. After that Mawlana remained at Bhopal, concentrated on studies, then returned to Delhi in CE 1924 Thereupon after his return to Delhi, came into contact with Mawlana Muhammad Ali, who offered him the editorship of his newspaper the *Hamdard*. But Mawlana Mawdudi preferred *al-Jamaat* another paper of Jami'at-ul-Ulama'-i-Hind which came in place of paper *Muslim*.

14. *Khud Nawisht*, p., 35

for him. He learned English and became acquainted with Western works. His association with the Jam'iyat also encouraged him to acquire formal religious education. He studied Arabic literature, *tafsir, hadith, fiqh,* logic and philosophy from different teachers.[15]

In addition to writing Mawlana Mawdudi took some interest in politics of the country. As he says "Because of independence of nature, assiduous learning, family tradition and some impact of environment, we were at the outset bitter against the British culture and domination, and thus we were inherently inclined to support every movement that was launched to liberate the country which doubled with the religious aspirations."[16] Thus it was quite natural for him to participate and collaborate with political movements like *Majlis Ianat-i-Nazar Bandan-i-Islam* (society of the sympathisers of the prisoners in the path of Islam), Khilāfat Movement led by Muhammad Ali, Gandhi's movement of passive resistance (*satyāgraha*). He also wrote a book on the life of Gandhi, which was confiscated by police before its publication. His interest were then nativistic and focused solely on the issue of nationalism.[17] His acquaintance with the *Ulamā'* of Jamiyat-i-

15. Abul-Afaq, *Mawlana Abul A'Lā Mawdudi,* Lahore, 1971, p. 48, and also *Khud Nawisht*, p. 36.

16. *Khud Nawisht*, p. 32 also quoted by Masudul Hasan, op. cit., p. 23.

17. His interests were the secular and focused solely on the issue of nationalism 1918 and 1919 he wrote essays in praise of Hindu Congress leaders, notably Gandhi and Madan Mohan Malaviya. And at Delhi Mawdudi was exposed to variety of intellectual currents in the Muslim community. He became acquainted with modernist writings as well as the activities of the Independence movement. In Jabalpur he worked for the pro-Congress weekly *Taj*. There he became fully active in the *khilāfat* movement and in mobilizing Muslims in support of the Congress party. Sayyid Vali Reza Nasr, op. cit., p. 72.

Ulama-i-Hind and the responsibility of editorship of first in *Muslim* and then *al-Jamiat* stimulated Mawlana Mawdudi to concentrate more on the study of Islamic theology. There he developed a more acute awareness of Muslim political consciousness and became more actively involved in the affairs of Islam and Muslims.

Therefore, Mawlana Mawdudi's twelve years in journalism proved to be the formative years of his life, and played vital role in shaping his world-view in later years. During these years he was exposed to the variety of intellectual currents in the Muslim community and as well as outside influences. He went through a process of intellectual experience, his faith in Islam was temporarily shaken until restored by zealous self-study of the *Qur'an* and *Hadith*— as result of which he has shown the zeal and vitality of a convert. As he himself writes:

> I can say that as far as I was concerned, there was no attraction for me in Islam as practised in the overall Muslim society. The first thing I did after developing a sense of criticism and research was to throw off that soul less religion I had inherited from the past. If Islam were really the religion that was being practised by Muslims, I would have perhaps joined the ranks of irreligious free thinkers and atheists, for I do not cherish in the core of my heart the slightest inclination towards the "nazi philosophy" that, simply for the sake of national interest and existence, I should have remained entangled in the meshes of ancestral worship. But the thing that warded me off from plodding the path of atheism, or any other social cult, and converted me again to Islam was the (self) study of the *al-Qur'an* and the life of the Hazrat Muhammad (SAAS). This revealed to me the real value of humanism. This acquainted me with the conception of 'freedom' which is beyond the imagination of even the greatest liberal and the revolutionary. This presented to me

> glorious plan of individual conduct and social justice the like of which I have never seen. I found in it the scheme of life, balanced *par excellence*, as seen in the order of entire nature from the tiniest structure of an atom to the physical laws of the celestial system . . . I am thus a converted Muslim. . . . Convinced in my soul and mind that there is no other way for progress and prosperity of mankind.[18]

Thus the erudition of *Qur'an* and *Hadith* not only delivered Mawlana Mawdudi from the clouds of darkness[19] but also imbued him with a sense of mission. The deteriorating conditions of Muslims in general and that of the subcontinent in particular and earnest desire to address the problems augmented his resolve to devote all his energy to expound the teachings of Islam. With the failure of *Tahrik-i-Hijrat*[20] and collapse of the khilāfat movement in 1924, he became disenchanted with the political movements especially the Muslim leadership who accordingly failed to understand the situation and lacked proper planning and programme. Swāmī Śraddhānan's Śuddhi movement launched in 1925 to convert the Muslims to Hinduism[21] followed by communal disturbances

---

18. Muhammad Yusuf, "While Green in Age, Mawlana Mawdudis Childhood," in *The Universal Message*, Karachi, September 1980, pp. 5-6 also quoted by Maryam Jameelah, *Modern Ideals and Concepts in the World of Mawlana Sayyid Abul A'Lā Mawdudi in Islamic Studies*, 42: 2 (2003), p. 348.

19. Abu Tariq, ed., *Mawlana Mawdudi Ka Interview* (Urdu), Markazi Maktaba Islami, Delhi 6, 1994, p. 12.

20. *Tarikh-i-Hijrat*, was a movement in opposition to British rule over India and urged the Muslims of India to migrate *en masse* to nearest dar-al-Islam, Afghanistan. Mawlana Abdul Bari issued a *fatawa* recommending such *hijrah*. See Qadi Abdul Ghaffar, *Hayāt-i-Ajmal*, Anjuman Taraqqi Urdu, Aligarh, 1950, p. 221.

21. Masudul Hasan, op. cit., p. 33.

for which Hindu Congress leaders as a rule laid the blame for the riots on the Muslims, and projected the Hindus as an aggrieved party. He became suspicious of the Congress party's manipulation of nationalist sentiments to serve Hindu interests. All these factors together with the deep study of Islamic sources Mawlana Mawdudi developed repugnance against the nationalism and nationalist movement. Thereafter he abandoned *al-Jami'at* in 1928 and decided to part ways with his Deobandi mentors, who had chosen to support the Congress party in the interests of ridding India of British rule.

Moreover, Mawlana Mawdudi's retreat to Hyderabad in 1928 came after being disgusted with Indian journalism especially Urdu journalism and his urge for serious research studies and writing books,[22] for which he could not get the material for research in subjects of his interest, in Delhi. In Hyderabad he devoted himself to research, writing and translation of books. Although Mawlana Mawdudi embarked on his literary career at the tender age of thirteen with his translation from Arabic into Urdu Qasim Amin Bey's book (Cairo 1900) *al-Marah al-Jadidah* (The New Women).[23] He even translated three English books: *The State of the Christians in*

22. *Khud Nawisht*, p. 36.

23. Ibid., p. 38.

al-Marah al-Jadidah was a feminist classic, which vehemently rejected *purdah* in favour of Western style women's emancipation. Although they could only frown on the contents, Mawlana Mawdudi's father and Arabic tutors most enthusiastically praised his translation. Precisely why the youthful Mawdudi chose, The New Women for his maiden literary efforts remain shrouded in Mystery. In view of his later staunch upholding of *purdah* and conservative views concerning women, naturally no effort was made to preserve the manuscript, Maryam Jameelah, *Islamic Studies*, op. cit., p. 349.

Turkey; Tyrannis of the Greeks in Smyra; and *The Problem of Khilāfat* into Urdu during his early age.[24] It was his classical work produced during the period of 1916-28, *Al-Jihad fil Islam* a masterly treatise on the Islamic Law, War and Peace published in 1928, when Mawlana Mawdudi was only 24 years of age which brought him fame and recognition. It received warm accolades from the Muslim community especially Allama Iqbal and Muhammad Ali Jawhar (d. 1931) and confirmed Mawdudi's place among the Muslim Literati.[25] This was also a significant turning point for Mawdudi, because it was his first serious full scale attempt to write about an Islamic issue, and the effort of composing them apparently brought an insight of great vividness and intensity into the nature of Islam. This was a decisive factor in bringing him to a full understanding

24. Three books were published in 1922 by Darul Ishaat Siyasat Mashriqia, Delhi, but the books no longer exist. Khurshid Ahmad, *Adbiyat-i-Mawdudi, Markazi Maktab Islami*, Delhi, 1980, p. 16.

25. In 1925 a young Muslim activist assassinated Swāmī Śraddhānanda, leader of the *Śuddhi*, an extremist Hindu revivalist movement, who had advocated reconverting low caste converts to Islam back to Hinduism, had publicly slighted Muslim beliefs, the assassination led to widespread critism of Islam as a religion of violence by the Indian press. Even Mahatma Gandhi expressed strongly on this issue and had said "Islam has shown itself as a movement of which the decisive force has been the sword and is the sword." Mawdudi, *al-Jihad fil Islam*, Markazi Maktaba Islami, Delhi, 4th edn., 1985, p. 118. Angered by this response and summoned to action by Muhammad Ali's sermon at Delhi's Jama Mosque encouraging Muslims to defend their faith, Mawdudi took upon himself to clarify to critics Islami's position on the use of violence, the result was his famous treatise on war and peace, violence and *jihād* in Islam, *Al-Jihad fil Islam, jihād* in Islam. It was first serialized in the columns of *Al-Jamiyat* and three articles, which he wrote were later collected and were formally published in 1930 as a book.

of the Islamic way of life.[26] Mawdudi himself acknowledges that in *al-Jihad fil Islam*:

> Beyond other considerations this book has been of the great benefit to me personally. When I undertook the writing of the book I was prompted by national rather than religious considerations. During the course of research when I had the opportunity to study the injections and commandments of Islam in greater detail, I developed an understanding of the Islamic *Shari'ah,* and faith in Islam was fortified. That motivated me to work for the renaissance of Islam. I also hit upon the plan as to how this should be done. I decided that if in the future I overtook to journalism that would only be to promote the cause of Islam.[27]

From this time on, Mawlana Mawdudi devoted himself to a deeper study of Islamic theology. Thus the writing of *al-Jihad fil Islam* was the first step towards the fulfilment of his mission and it whetted his appetite to devote all his energy and power to expounding the teachings of Islam. The period in Hyderabad witnessed the efflorescence of Mawdudi's earnest urge. Despite the reputation of independent mindedness and of being something of iconoclast in his youth, throughout Mawdudi's life religion was the strong foundation upon which all else were to rest. Since then in Hyderabad he had consciously tried to live Islam and to live for Islam and it became clear to him that he had a religious mission to fulfil among India's Muslims. He chose the pen to be an instrument for the mission of his life and immersed himself in writing about Islam and major political and cultural issues confronting Muslims in India

---

26. Charles J. Adams, "Mawdudi and the Islamic State," in *Voices of Resurgent Islam*, John L. Esposite, ed., New York, Oxford University Press, 1983, p. 101.
27. Khud Nawisht, also quoted in Masudul Hasan, op. cit., p. 64.

at that time and tried to examine them from Islamic perspective rather than merely from the viewpoint of short-term political and economic interests.[28]

Mawlana Mawdudi's ten-year stay in Hyderabad from 1928 to 1938 began with the literary activities such as translation projects and historical works. He translated that part of history of *Ibn Khallikan* which dealt with the history of the *Fatimid Caliphs* and the translation of Mulla Shirazi's classical work *al-Hikmat ul Mutalia fil Sofaril* Aqlia known as *Asfar-i-Araba* a book on philosophy in Arabic. He also wrote two works on history, one was the history of the Seljuks and the other was the History of Deccan.[29] Most important book of this early period in Hyderabad was his seminal introduction to Islam *Risalah-yi-diniyat* (later translated as *'Towards Understanding Islam'*). Writen in 1932 at the behest of the government of H.E.H. the Nizam of Hyderabad, prescribed as a textbook for students in schools. The idea of writing this book struck Mawlana Mawdudi after hearing the lectures of Allama Iqbal during his visit to Hyderabad in January 1929 on the reconstruction of religious thought in Islam. These lectures of Allama Iqbal were too scholarly and subtle to be understood by the common man. Mawlana Mawdudi felt that if Islam was to be taken to the heart beats of the common man, it was necessary that the message of Islam should be conveyed in simple language that the common man could understand.[30] In his preface to second edition of *Towards Understanding Islam*, Mawdudi writes:

---

28. Khurshid Ahmad and Zafar Ishaq Ansari, ed., *Islamic Perspectives, Studies in Honour of Mawlana Sayyid Abul A'Lā Mawdudi*, Markazi Maktab Islami, Delhi, 1987, p. 362.

29. *Khud Nawisht*, 36 and also see Masudul Hasan, op. cit., pp. 74-75.

30. Masudul Hasan, op. cit., p. 68.

> My objective in writing this book has been to provide all those Muslims and non-Muslims alike — who have no access to the original sources with a brief treatise, giving a lucid, comprehensive and all-embracing view of Islam. I have avoided minute details and endeavoured to portray Islam as a whole in a single perspective. Apart from standing what we Muslims believe in and stand for, I have also tried to explain the rational bases of our beliefs. Similarly, in presenting the Islamic modes of worship and the outlines of the Islamic way of life, I have also tried to unveil the wisdom behind them.[31]

Furthermore, it seems that this seminal introduction to Islam by Mawdudi was a reaction to the lectures of Allama Iqbal on *Reconstruction of Religious Thought in Islam*. As such, while naming the book *Towards Understanding Islam*, Mawdudi appears to be of the view that Islam was complete and perfect in itself, therefore, the question of reconstructing any religious thought does not arise; the only question was of discovering, understanding and at the most reinterpreting Islam.[32] However, as a result of this book and earlier *al-Jihad fil Islam*, Mawdudi gained a wide reputation and sprang into prominence as one of the leading theologians in India.

In 1932 Mawlana Mawdudi assumed the editorship of *Tarjuman-ul-Qur'an*, the organ of the institution *Alamgir Tahrik-e-Qur'an*, already run in Hyderabad by Mawlana Abu Muhammad Muslih of Sasaram, Bihar. Subsequently the ownership of the monthly paper had been transferred in 1933 to Mawlana Mawdudi. Since then it became his sole responsibility and remained the main tool for the expression

---

31. Author's Preface to 2nd edn. of *Towards Understanding Islam*, English translation of *Risalah Diniyat*.
32. Masudul Hasan, op. cit., p. 89.

and dissemination of his thought and ideas and had been regularly published from that time with only occasional and brief interruption. Mawlana Mawdudi continued to guide and educate the Muslims of subcontinent through *Tarjuman-ul-Qur'an* from Dar-us-Salam[33] (Jamalpur, a small village in Paṭhānkoṭ tehsil of Gurdaspur district, Punjab) where he migrated in the second week of March 1938 after the persuasion by Chaudhri Niaz Ali and Allama Iqbal and from Lahore (before Partition) where he stayed for four years from

33. Dar-us-Salam Chaudhri Niaz Ali a retired S.D.O. of the Irrigation Department had an estate in the Paṭhānkoṭ teshil of Gurdāspur district. He created a *waqf* of his estate and constructed some buildings for setting up a religious institution to be utilized for promoting the purpose of Islam. He sought Mawlana Mawdudi's advice for setting up institution. Mawlana Mawdudi sent him outlines of the project, which suggested that a model settlement of the Muslims should be set up on the estate, which should be living demonstrations of the Islamic way of life. The plan was approved by Allama Iqbal and advised Chaudhri Niaz Ali to invite Mawlana Mawdudi to Punjab to take up Dar-us-Salam project to which Mawdudi finally acquiesced. It was a three-men affair, the three men being Allama Iqbal, Chaudhri Niaz Ali, and Mawlana Mawdudi. The project received a big blow at its very inception in the death of Allama Iqbal. In spite of the set-back, Mawdudi persevered, envisaging Dar-us-Salam as a pilot project in Islamic community life; invited people. The project invoked curiosity but did not produce any tangible results. The response to this project was not encouraging. That set Mawlana Mawdudi thinking. By October, 1938, he launched a movement to be known as Dar-us-Islam movement and to set-up an institution for the renaissance of Islam. The goal remained the same as before; there was to be a change in strategy. To this idea of launching a movement Niaz Ali did not agree and advised Mawdudi that he should concentrate on research, and not to indulge in running any movement, or criticizing the Muslim League in any way. At this point in December 1938 after nine months stay at Dar-us-Salam Mawdudi broke the camp and shifted to Lahore.

1938 to June 1942, during that period in 26 August 1941 Jamaat-i-Islami was founded. *Tarjuman-ul-Qur'an* served the purpose of organ of Jamaat-i-Islami, since its inception in 1941 and continued to be published from Dar-ul-Islam (Punjab) where Mawdudi shifted in June 1942 along with the central office of Jamaat-i-Islami, till the final migration to Pakistan (after Partition) on 29 August 1947. Thenceforth from Pakistan regularly.

The assumption of editorship of *Tarjuman-ul-Qur'an* was a watershed in the Mawdudi's life. It provided him an opportunity to express his thought now mature and consummate at much wider scale. It served the purpose he was pondering since long and marked the beginning of the movement, which culminated nine years later in 1941 in the establishment of Jamaat-i-Islami. Mawdudi expressed the message of the *Tarjuman-ul-Qur'an* in the following words:

> The sole purpose of the journal is to proclaim the word of God and to invite men to supreme effort in the way of Allah. Its special scope is to comment from the point of view of *Qur'an* upon the thought, the idea and the principles of the culture and civilization that are spreading in the world to explain the principles advanced by the *Qur'an* and the *Sunnah* in the context of contemporary philosophy, science, politics, economics, culture and sociology and to formulate to the application of the principles of the *Qur'an* and the *Sunnah* to the conditions of the present age. This journal invites Muslims to a new life.[34]

Visualizing, great flood about to sweep away the Muslims into oblivion, Mawdudi took up his pen to warn them against

---

34. *Tarjuman ul-Qur'an* (1st issue) also quoted by Masudul Hasan, op. cit., 91 and I.H. Qureshi, *Ulama*, p. 332.

this danger. He began to perceive that a mission had been laid upon him, to invite the Muslims especially Indian Muslims to a renewed and purified commitment to Islam and thereby to save them from destruction by the malevolent forces sweeping over their society. In the words of Mawlana Mawdudi:

> The paper served as an instrument of *tanqid* (criticism), *tablig* (preaching), and *talqin* (exhortation).[35]

It aimed at to expose the nature of *jahilliyyah* and all the evil that it contains especially in its modern Western form and to present the Islamic way of life in a reasoned, argued, demonstrated and systematic fashion. The series of articles published in *Tarjuman-ul-Qur'an* on different topics which have later been published as books of considerable merit. Such as *tanqihat, talimat, haquq-uz-zaujain, sood* and *purdah,* etc.[36] From 1937 to 1941 he published in *Tarjuman-ul-Qur'an* a series of essays dealing with the political matters and their implications for the Muslims. The essays were later printed in book form in the three volumes entitled *Musalman Aur Mawjudāh Siyāsi Kaśmakaś* and in the volume called *Maslah-i-Qawmiyat*. Through these series of articles in *Tarjuman-ul-Qur'an* some of which were published as books and other lectures and books which Were written on different issues and problems at different times, Mawlana Mawdudi gave expression to his thought

35. Abul A'Lā Mawdudi, Jamaat-i-Islami, *Us ka Maqsad, Tarikh aur Laihi aml*, Lahore, Markazi Maktaba Jamaat-i-Islami, 4th printing, 1953, p. 22 in a footnote. English trns., *Jammat-i-Islami: Objectives, History and Plan of Action.*

36. These books have been translated into English. *Tanqihat*, Eng. tr. *West Versus Islam*, Markazi Maktaba Islami, Delhi, 2000. *Talimat* as the *Education, Haquq-uz-Zawjain* as the *Rights and Duties of Spouses*, etc.

which he propounded and articulated after a long experience and deep study of sources of Islamic thought.

Holistic Vision of Islam

One of the most significant aspects, of Mawlana Mawdudi's thought, which he reiterated and delineated through prolific writings and speeches, was the holistic nature of Islam; a comprehensive system of life. He was always emphatic in asserting that Islam is not merely a body of metaphysical doctrines, nor merely a bundle of rituals, nor even merely a set of rules of individual conduct. It is indeed complete code of life, the bases of which is rooted in Divine Revelations; a way of life which permeated with God consciousness and is oriented to doing God's Will and actualizing good and righteousness in human life.[37] Most of Mawlana Mawdudi's writings which he wrote before as well as after the Partition of India heightened this idea of exclusive nature of Islam and regarded it as the all embracing ideology. Take any of his works — *The Rights of Spouses* (*Huqooquz-Zaujain*); *The Concept of Jihad in Islam; The Problem of Nationality; Muslims and the Present Political Struggle; Islamic Jurisprudence; Islamic State; Caliphate and Kingship; Interest; Islamic Economics,*[38] etc, he discusses same themes and they cannot be classified into political and apolitical or religious and worldly. Each of his works brings under discussion the focal point — to whom should we owe allegiance, whose commandments should be enforced in our personal and collective life, who has bestowed rights on us, who is the provider. Through these writings, not only

37. Khurshid Ahmad in his introduction to Sayyid Abul A'Lā Mawdudi's Towards Understanding Islam, Markazi Maktaba Islami, Delhi, 2002, p. 14.

38. These books are originally written in Urdu and the most of them are translated into English and other languages.

expounded the teachings of Islam to be transformed into practical realities, he tried to explain that Islam provides guidance and prescribes directives for individuals as well as collective life. These directives touch varied subjects as religious rituals, personal character, moral habits, family relationship, social and economic affairs, administrations, rights and duties of citizens, the judicial system, and law of war and peace and international relations.[39]

Mawlana Mawdudi presented Islam as "the system" and the all-embracing ideology. The union of religion and society, the relationship of Islam to all aspects of life, followed from the doctrine of *tawhid* (God's unity) and His sovereignty over all the creations as embodied in the comprehensive nature of the *Shari'ah*. He explains it as:

> Among the fundamentals of Islam, the most important is belief in one God — not just the conviction that He exists or that He is one — but that He alone is Creator, Master, Ruler and Administrator of all that exists. The universe exists because God wills it to exist, it functions because God wills it to function and God provides that sustenance and the energy which everything of the universe requires for its existence. All the attributes of sovereignty reside in God alone, and no one else has a share in them in the slightest degree. He alone possesses all the attributes of Divinity, and no other than God possess any of the attributes. He views the whole universe, and all that it contains, in a single instantaneous glance. He has direct knowledge of the universe, and all that is there in the universe. This omnipresence and omniscience is an attribute of God alone and of no other. . . . He is man's single Diety. . . . Not to ask of

39. Mawlana Mawdudi, *Islamic Law and Constitution*, ed., Khurshid Ahmad, Karachi, 1955, p. 26.

> Him is senseless arrogance, and to turn to others is sheer ignorance. To seek of Him and also of others, is to associate equals with Him.[40]

In his book *Qur'an ki Char Bunyadi Istalahat* (The Four Basic Qur'anic Terms) written in 1941 Mawlana Mawdudi seeks to prove that although the four Qur'anic terms, *llah* (God, master or law-giver), *rabb* (lord), *ibādat* (worship) and *dīn* (faith) were well understood by the Arabs to whom the *Qur'an* was first revealed, their original meanings gradually lost force and comprehensiveness to later generations. With the result more than three fourth rather instrinsic essence of the teachings of *Qur'an* eclipsed and that is why, even after accepting Islam the faith and practices of most Muslims remained flawed.[41] Basing himself on an analysis of two words used for God in the *Qur'an*, *illah* (Master and Sovereign) and *rabb* (Lord), according to Mawlana Mawdudi the conception of the Unity of God is not a mere religious creed but the whole system of social life which is based on the conception that man is an independent being or that sovereignty belongs to any other being, animate or inanimate, is uprooted from foundation and a new superstructure rise on a different basis with belief in the oneness and sovereignty of God. It summons to give exclusive obedience to God. It should be brought home, to man that in the whole of this universe there is only one sovereign, master and ruler. Nothing can be left out of His Lordship, not even the tiniest territory in life, in heart or in behaviour. He is worshipped with everything, heart as well

40. S.A.A. Mawdudi, *The Message of Islam*, Markazi Maktaba Islamic Publishers, Delhi, 1996, p. 5-6.

41. Mawdudi, *Qur'an Ki Char Bunyadi Istalahen* (Urdu), Maktaba Islami, Delhi, 1972, pp. 5-10. Also see Mawdudi, *Political Theory of Islam*, Markazi Maktaba Islami, Delhi, 1081, pp. 8ff.

as body. He rules everywhere, in homes as in hearts, in manners as in minds, in public life as in private; He is the sovereign over soul as well as society.[42] Mawdudi further elaborates the point under discussion and argues that there is no one here besides Him, who can rightly claim to control and regulate the affairs of humanity, none who can administer justice in his own right, none who can answer the prayer of man and from whom man can expect help or succour in his distress; there is none besides Him, who possesses the key of authority and there is nobody else, who can claim absolute and unconditional allegiance for human beings. Thus there is no legislator here and no law-giver, for the only law deserving obedience is the law of God.[43] Mawlana Mawdudi stresses that sovereignty of God in Islam is not just a supernatural phenomenon. It is all encompassing sovereignty and nothing is outside his jurisdiction or shared by anyone. Thus all aspects of political and legal sovereignty remain only His purgative because He alone is the Creator, Sustainer and Ruler of the universe. In God alone vests the rightful authority to exercise power on this earth, and over those whom God has created in it. No monarch; no royal family, no elite class, no leader of any religious group. No democracy established on the basis of the sovereignty of the people, can participate in God's sovereignty. Whoever claims such a position is a rebel, as are those who leave God and turn to other people in obedience. Similarly, any institution or individual attempting to assume political and legal sovereignty and restrict the jurisdiction of God to sphere a personal law or religious duties, is really a usurper and a rebel; is equivalent to idolatry. The truth is that no one can claim to be law-giver on God's earth and no one

42. Ibid., pp. 20ff.

43. Ibid., p. 28.

can challenge the supreme authority of God Almighty in any sphere.[44]

Mawlana Mawdudi argued that Islam was a complete national system. In his book *Towards Understanding Islam,* he explained that everything in universe obeys laws ordained by the Creator; such as:

> Ours is a law-governed universe and everything in it is following the course that has been ordained for it . . . this powerful, all-pervasive law, which governs all that comprises the universe, from the tiniest specks of dust to the munificent galaxies of the heavens, is the law of God, the Creator and Ruler of the Universe. As the whole of creation obeys the law of God, the whole universe, therefore, literally follows the religion of Islam — for Islam signifies nothing but obedience and submission to Allah, the Lord of the Universe. The sun, the moon, the earth and all other heavenly bodies are thus Muslim. So are the air, water, heat, stones, trees and animals. Everything in the universe is Muslim for it obeys God by submission to His laws. Even a man who refuses to believe in God, or offers his worship to someone other than Allah, has necessarily to be a Muslim as far as his existence is concerned.[45]

According to Mawlana Mawdudi's interpretation everything in the universe obeys laws ordained by the Creator, even the unbeliever, bodily considered, may be said to be Muslim, for his organs are under law. However, with the exception of human beings who are endowed with free will. He explains:

> Man is so constituted that there are two distinct spheres of his activity. One is the sphere in which he finds himself

44. Ibid., pp. 28-29 and also Mawdudi, *Message*, p. 6.
45. M. Mawdudi, *Towards Understanding Islam*, p. 20.

> totally regulated by the Divine law. Like other creatures, he is completely caught in the grip of the physical laws of nature and is bound to follow them. But there is another sphere of his activity. He has been endowed with reason and intellect. He has the power to think and form judgements, to choose and reject, to approve and spurn. He is free to adopt whatever course of life he chooses. He can embrace any faith and live by any ideology he likes. He may prepare his own code of conduct or accept one formulated by others. In short, man has been bestowed with free will. Both these aspects coexist side by side in man's life.[46]

Thus it is the use of second free will — volitional faculty, which divides mankind into two groups; believers and non-believers.[47] An individual, who chooses to acknowledge his Creator, accepts Him or His real Master, honestly and scrupulously submits to His laws and injections and follows the code, perfectly revealed through the *Holy* Book of God *Qur'an* and the Prophet (SAAS), (*Shari'ah*) which is Islam as well as moral obedience of rational will.[48] Accordingly for Mawdudi, Muslim adherence is both natural and rational. To obey, to live in accordance with His Will and His Law or (to put it more precisely) to be Muslim is ingrained in the nature of things. Because "the whole of his existence is an embodiment of truth for, in all spheres of life, he voluntarily as well as involuntarily obeys the laws of one God — the lord of the universe. Now he is at peace with the whole universe for he worships Him whom the whole universe worships. Such a man is God's vicegerent on earth. The whole world is for him and he is for God."[49] And those, although born Muslims and

46. Ibid., p. 21.
47. Idem.
48. Idem.
49. Ibid., p. 22.

unconsciously remaining one throughout life, who misuse their freedom of choice and do not exercise faculties of reason, intellect and intuition to recognize lord and creator instead deny Him are unbelievers, *kafir* (concealer)[50] "because he conceals by his disbelief what is inherent in his nature and embalmed in his own soul for his nature is instinctively imbued with Islam."[51] Thus all life that observes the plain commandments of the law is Islam or submission to God, and all that does not is *jahilliyyah* (Ignorance).

Mawlana Mawdudi concludes "this universal and eternal religion is Islam"[52] which is a world-view and an outlook on life, based on the recognition of oneness of the Creator and of our submission to His will in all aspects of life, individual and collective. Thus, according to Mawdudi, the departmentalization of life into different water-tight compartments, religious and secular, sacred and profane, spiritual and material, is ruled out. There is unity of life and unity of the source of guidance. Each aspect of life is inseparable from the other. Religion and secular are not two autonomous categories, they represent two sides of the same coin. Complete submission; entails complete obedience to the Divine guidance in all areas of life and rejection of all kinds of

---

50. Idem.

51. Idem.

52. Ibid., p. 144, *Islam is Arabic word*. It is derived from two root words, one *salm*, meaning peace and the other *silm*, meaning submission. Islam stands for "a commitment to surrender one's will to the will of God" and thus to be at peace with the Creator and with all that has been created by Him. It is through submission to the will of God that peace is brought about. Harmonization of man's will with will of God leads to the harmonization of different spheres of life under an all-embracing ideal.

artificial division of life spiritual and life mundane.[53] Mawdudi argues that,

> [when] God is the Creator of the world and He alone has complete and direct knowledge of the reality of man and of the world. only He can guide man through the complicated course of life and instruct him regarding good and evil. Since God alone is the Creator and the Master he has exclusive authority over the Universe and man. It is an act of blasphemy for man to become independent or claim authority over other men. For men to become his own law-giver, to accept the authority of any other individual or institution as such is equally blasphemous. The ultimate law-giver and master of His creation on this earth is no other than God, and His law has the status of the supreme law, man can legislate subject to His supreme law beyond that he has no legislative authority.[54]

He further contended that God has endowed man with the capacity of cognition, reflection and understanding, with the ability to distinguish between good and evil, with the freedom of choice and volition and with the power to exercise his latent potentialities to perform his role of vicegerency.[55] Hence it is his duty to use all the power with which he is invested and all the means placed at his disposal in this world, in accordance with the Divine will. He should utilize to the fullest extent all the faculties and potentialities bestowed upon him for seeking

---

53. Sayyid Abul A'Lā Mawdudi, *Islamic Way of Life*, tr. by Khurshid Ahmad, IIFSO, Kuwait, Salmiyah 1983, and also see *Qur'an ki Char Buniyadi Istilahen*, p. 28 and p. 74.
54. Mawdudi, *The Message of Islam*, pp. 6-7.
55. Sayyid Abul A'Lā Mawdudi, *Towards Understanding Qur'an*, English version of *Tafhim al-Qur'an*, translated and edited by Zafar Ishaq Ansari, Kiicester, The Islamic Foundation, 1988, vol. I, p. 9.

the approbation of God. In brief, all his efforts of this world in the manner in wh'ch God wants them to be regulated.[56]

This will of God is revealed, Himself, through *Qur'an* and its explanation, elaboration, expansion, realization and applications by Prophet Muhammad (SAAS) termed as *Sunnah*.[57] Mawdudi writes:

> Through His Grace and Benevolence, He raised for mankind men from among themselves to whom He imparted the true knowledge of His attributes, revealed to them His law and Right code of living, gave them the knowledge of the meaning and purpose of life and of life after death and thus showed them the way by which man can achieve success and eternal bliss.[58]

Mawlana Mawdudi dwells at length upon prophethood and considered it God's response to man's perennial need for guidance. Because of the perenniality of this need, prophethood began with the beginning of human life on earth. The first man was also the first Prophet. He further explains that the *Sunnah* of the Prophet is an unerring guide to man in

---

56. Mawdudi, *Islamic Way of Life*, p. 86.

57. The Sunnah of Mohammad is, in fact, an exposistion of the purpose of the *Qur'an*, and this exposition too was conveyed to the Prophet by God, Himself as the author of the *Qur'an*. The Prophet's explanation of the *Qur'an* enjoys divine sanction and no one else can interpret *Qur'an*, which may be in conflict with or repugnant to the explanation given by the Prophet. God declared the life of Muhammad (SAAS) as a model life. No one can be true believer unless he accepts the decision of the Prophet. Muslims don't have an independent position in a matter determined by the Prophet. Before deciding any matter, Muslims must first ascertain whether any analogous matter was decided earlier by God and His prophet, and if a precedent exists they must follow it — Mawdudi, *The Message of Islam*, pp. 8-9.

58. Mawdudi, *Towards Understanding Islam*, p. 36.

all respects. Without this belief in the prophet, belief in God would become a mere theoretical proposition, what Islam envisages is orthodoxy (correct doctrine or belief) as well as orthopaxy (correct action). It is the example of practical leadership, and the ideological guidance provided by the Prophet which transforms belief of God into a culture and civilization and enables man to evolve a way of life. We get through the Prophet not only rules of guidance, but a complete scheme of values and a practical code of conduct.[59]

Therefore, Mawlana Mawdudi reasoned, basing himself on the verses of *Qur'an* as well as his own observations, that Divine will have laid down a law (*Shari'ah*) for human conduct just it has ordained a law for everything else. The law that God has prescribed for men to follow is set forth in the Book of the God, the *Qur'an*, and in the lives of those through whom God has revealed His book, the Prophets; but especially in the practice of the last Prophet Muhammad (SAAS). Prophecy is the means chosen by the divine to give concrete expression and exemplification to its will[60] which he explains as

> No one can claim to be a believer without believing in the Prophet. He who obeys the Prophet, in fact, obeys God. God has not designated any prophet, except to be obeyed according to His will. The path of the Prophet is the path of Divine guidance. Whatever the Prophet ordains must be accepted and whatever he instructs to avoid, must be avoided. The *Sunnah* of Mohammad (SAAS) is, in fact, an exposition of the purpose of the *Qur'an*, and this exposition too was conveyed to the prophet by God, Himself, as the author of the *Qur'an*. The Prophet's explanation of the *Qur'an*

---

59. Mawdudi, *The Message of Islam*, p. 7.

60. Charles J. Adams, "Mawdudi and the Islamic State," in John L. Esposito, *Voices of Resurgent Islam*, Oxford University Press, New York, Oxford, 1983, p. 112.

> enjoys divine sanction, and no one else can interpret *Qur'an* which may be in conflict with or repugnant to the explanation given by the Prophet. No one can be true believer unless he accepts the decision of the prophet.[61]

Furthermore regarding the primacy of *Shari'ah* Mawlana Mawdudi reiterates that

> Muslims have not an independent position in a matter determined by the Prophet. Before deciding any matter Muslims must first ascertain whether any analogous matter was decided earlier by God and His prophet and if a precedent exists they must follow it.[62]

These two, the *Qur'an* and the *Sunnah* of the Prophet, therefore, are the ultimate authorities for all true Muslims in every question that may concern either individual or their collective lives. When the *Qur'an* and the Prophet speak on an issue, there is no higher court of appeal for to displace or impugn them would be an offence against the majesty of God, to commit the unpardonable sin of associating others with the purgatives that are exclusively His. There is one true and unimpeachable source of law, one rightful law-giver and only one, who has chosen to make his *Shari'ah* known through the agencies of revelation and prophecy. Everything that men enact or observe as law in their societies is to be measured against the dictates and the spirit of the ultimate law (*Shari'ah*) found in the two major sources of *Qur'an* and *Sunnah*.

According to Mawlana Mawdudi, the mission of the Prophet was not only to prescribe a moral code, enunciate the principles of culture and civilization, lay down the mode of worship, establish a framework of belief, and define the moral imperatives, which must govern our life. He determined the

61. Mawdudi, *The Message of Islam*, p. 8.

62. Ibid., pp. 8-9.

rules which form the basis of social and cultural relationship, economic, judicial and political dealing, matters of war and peace and international affairs. "it is a fact of history that Muhammad (SAAS) succeeded in establishing the kingdom of God on earth, as it is in the heavens."[63] The Prophet of Islam and his companions developed and established a complete model of Islam on this earth for mankind to follow.[64] Now, the *Shari'ah* in both its broad objectives and its specific provisions envisages more than the fostering of good and avoidance of evil in the lives of individuals. "It is a complete scheme of life and all-embracing social order where nothing is superfluous and nothing lacking."[65] Mawdudi describes that Islam of Prophet was not mere "religion" in a sense normally identified in popular parlance as mere contemplation or code of rituals or abstract doctrines. He brought with him a whole system of thought and action, which is called *Al-Dīn* in Islamic terminology.[66] In his book *Qur'an ki Char Bunyadi Istilahat,*

63. Ibid., p. 4.

64. As far as form of the state, Mawdudi of course took the government of Mohammed and the first four caliphs as his model.

65. Mawlana Mawdudi, *Islamic Law and Constitution*, ed. Khursheed Ahmad, Lahore, Islamic Publication, 1967, p. 53.

66. Mawdudi, *The Message of Islam*, p. 4. In Arabic the word "din" is used to convey meanings. It means (a) Power, suzerainty and control (b) Obediance and submission, (c) Compensation and atonement; and (d) Way of life, rule of conduct and ideology. And in the verse of the *Qur'an* in view, the term is used in the fourth sense. That is "*din*" implies that way of life or attitude of mind and thought, and mode of behaviour and action which is pursued or followed by an individual or a society. But it should be noted that the *Qur'an* says *al-dīn* and not merely "*din*". . . The claim of the *Qur'an* is not that in the eyes of God Islam is away of life, but that Islam is the only true way of life, the correct attitude of thought and behaviour, *the ideology of life*. Mawdudi, *The Religion of truth*, Markazi Maktaba Islami, Delhi, 06, 4th edn. 1984, p. 5.

Mawdudi dilated upon the word *"al-din"* defined the broadest sense and connotations of the term used in *Qur'an*. He derived the same conclusion that it is comprehensive style of thought and living, a plan of life following from the exclusive sovereignty (*hakimiyya*) of God, which encompasses the entire human life individual and collective existence as well as, the entire gamut of the society[67] (of all human beings of all ages). The word *al-dīn*, as it occurs in the *Qur'an*, is not used in any restricted sense, it is not limited to some particular aspect of phase of life but it encompasses the entire human life with all its fullness. And has not been used in the sense of "religion" (as the word nowadays understood in Western terminology) but is more or less synonymous with state, and cultural system"[68] To Mawdudi, the fundamental of the doctrine of Islam and tenets of its laws are one single whole; the later is a practical translation of the former. The mere recognition of God's existence entails the belief in His sovereignty and rulership. There is, al Mawdudi asserts, no separation between faith in God and adherence to His social, political and economic injections. Only an insane person would venture to think otherwise. He writes ". . . If it is a *dīn* of our lives as an individual, it should also be *dīn* of our social relationship, our home and household affairs, the training and education of our children. It should be the *dīn* of our schools, our business, our vocational pursuits, our national conduct and behaviour, our cultural pursuits, our socio-political affairs, our art and literature, and our state."[69]

---

67. Mawdudi, *Qur'an ki Char Bunyadi Istilahen*, pp. 108-09.
68. Ibid., p. 104.
69. Mawdudi, *The Religion of Truth*, p. 37.

Therefore, according to Mawdudi the conception of the unity of God (*tawhid*) is not a mere religious creed, but whole system of life (*al-Dīn*) follows from it.[70] He is not merely the Creator but a Guide too. For everything created, He has made provision for light and guidance that was most appropriate and suitable for its particular needs and requirements. The proper course for man, therefore, is to forsake his own arrogance and conceit and submit to Him, and live according to the complete and comprehensive system of life *al-dīn*, which He in His infinite mercy has bestowed upon mankind through His prophets.[71] Furthermore, in his book, *Shahadat Haq* (Eng. tr. *Witnesses Unto Mankind*) Mawlana Mawdudi asserts that as soon as we acknowledge Allah as our only lord and His guidance *dīn* as our only way of life, we take upon ourselves certain unavoidable obligations and duties. Among all these duties, there is one which is most important and one must always remain conscious of: that our lives bear witness to the truth that we have been given by God before all mankind — the truth which we believe to be true.[72] This is a testimony that will make the authenticity and truthfulness of Divine guidance self-evident, for all to see, and a witness that will make it clear and indisputable for all the people. Prophets were sent to the world for this very purpose and obligatory duty. And now the Muslim *ummah*, as the successor to the last Prophet Muhammad (SAAS) is charged with this very mission and has been made accountable for, just as he was charged

---

70. Mawdudi, *Process of Islamic Revolution*, Markazi Maktaba Islami, Delhi, 1959, p. 29.

71. Mawdudi, *Religion of Truth*, pp. 29-30.

72. Mawdudi, *Shahadat Haq* (Urdu) ed. and trans. as *Witnesses Unto Mankind, The Purpose and Duty of the Muslim Ummah*, by Khurram Murad, Markazi Maktaba Islamic, Delhi, 2000, pp. 26-27.

with it during his lifetime.[73] According to Mawdudi this witnessing to the truth demands manifestation both by words and deeds, which he calls witness by words, or the word-witness. The other, witness by acts and deeds, or the act-witness.[74] He explains: "the guidance that Islam gives to humanity in thought and belief, in morality and behaviour, in culture and civilization, in economic and business, in jurisprudence and judiciary, in politics and civil administration, that is, in all aspects of inter-human relations — we should clearly and fully expound before mankind. By rational discourse and convincing evidence, we should establish its truth and soundness. And for the purpose of acts and deeds witness to the truth, the guidance that we hold to be true must be put into practice. Our action should demonstrate the principles we profess to believe in."[75] Mawdudi emphasized that this witness to the truth must be demonstrated individually and collectively and our lives should become a living embodiment of Islam.[76] Therefore, the establishment of state on the guidelines envisaged by (*al-dīn*) Islam becomes *sine qua non.* He writes: "this witness of ours would not be complete unless we establish a state based on the principles and teachings of Islam. By translating its ideals and practices, its norms and values, its rules and laws, into public policies and programmes, such a state would demonstrate how the Divine guidance leads to equity and justice."[77]

Islamic State

Furthermore, the *Qur'an*, Mawdudi explains, clearly indicated the real position of those persons, who set out to enforce God's

73. Ibid., p. 28.
74. Ibid., pp. 30-31.
75. Ibid., p. 31.
76. Ibid., p. 32.
77. Idem.

law on earth as being God's representatives on earth (*khalifah*).[78] This vicegerency (*khilāfat*) delegated by God for the sole purpose of executing His injections or that of *ummah* to witness Islam unto mankind which is the *raison d'être* of the Muslim *ummah*, cannot be performed, according to Mawdudi, unless Islam is established in all its totality. Thus every activity of life, individual and collective is related to this universal mission of the *ummah* to perform the vicegerency of Allah as a trust. The Islamic state for Mawdudi, therefore, is part of a broad integrated theology whose cardinal principle is the sovereignty of nature's creative lord[79] and is essentially related to his comprehensive vision of Islam.

Accordingly in Mawdudi's understanding, Islam makes all life God-centred. To accept the reality of the Creator is to accept Him as the only lord, the only source of guidance. Accepting that and being under His rule brings all life. That is to say, the edifice of a complete Islamic life can only be built on a belief in God's unity (*tawhid*) that permeates a man's entire personal and social life and which is so strong that he considers himself and all that he possesses as belonging to God; he accepts Him as the sole rightful owner, object of

78. Allah hath promised such of you as believe and do good works that, He will surely make them to succeed (the present rulers) in the earth as His vicegerents even as, He caused those who were before them to succeed (others) Al-Qurāñ XXIV, *Khilāfat*. According to the Arabic lexicon, it means representative man. According to Islam, is the 'representative' of God on earth, His vicegerent, that is to say by virtue of the power delegated to him by God, he is required to exercise his god-given authority in this world within the limits prescribed by God, Mawdudi, *Islamic Way of life*, Markazi Maktaba Islami, Delhi, 1986, pp. 30-31.

79. Charles J. Adams, "Mawdudi and the Islamic State" in *Voices of Resurgent Islam*, ed., John L. Esposit, Oxford University Press, 1983, pp. 111-12.

worship, receiver of obedience and law-giver for himself as well as the rest of the world; he considers Him the fountainhead of guidance.[80] Therefore, law is nothing other than the will of the Creator, which has been laid down as *Shari'ah* for human conduct, just as it has ordained a law for everything else in universe. Thus, no life can be God's without bringing all of them under God. Nor can anyone claim or exercise power, or demand obedience, independent of God without becoming a god. Neither effort nor power is there save with God, the Most High and Great. A state or some other institution that will exercise political power is the necessary consequence of this conception of a universal divinely ordained pattern for the life of men in the world. Not only the realization of the objective of the *Shari'ah* to foster good and interdict evil in society be impossible without the agency of the state and the power it commands, but the *Shari'ah,* according to Mawdudi, itself specifically prescribes the creation of a state as witnessed in certain verses of the *Qur'an* but above all in the examples of the Prophet, who himself laid the foundation of Islamic state and afterwards furthered by the Rightly guided caliphs.[81]

The state, as we see it today, is a recent invention, but state power has always been there. Wherever it exercises its authority, independent of God, it becomes god. Such powers and institutions nurtured in a Godless culture always have the propensity to become gods. Whereas, distinguishing feature of the Islamic state is that the basic conception underlying all its outward manifestation according to

80. Mawdudi, *The Islamic Movement Dynamics of Values, Power and Change,* ed. tr. by Khurram Murad, Markazi Maktaba Islami, Delhi, 2001, p. 113.

81. Mawdudi, *Islamic Law and Constitution,* p. 175.

Mawdudi's writings, is the idea of Divine sovereignty. Its fundamental theory is that the earth and all that it contains belongs to God, who alone is its sovereign. No individual, family, class or nation and not even the whole humanity can lay claim to sovereignty, either partially or wholly, God alone has the right to legislate and give commands.[82] Therefore, as God is one (*tawhid*) so all of his creation has an underlying unity and is subject to His rule. In this connection, Mawlana Mawdudi also identified the intimate relationship between *tawhid* and state. So nothing can be left out of His Lordship, not even the tiniest territory in life, in heart or in behaviour. For, to that extent, God's worship will be incomplete, less than total, and life less Islamic. How then can power, politics and state be allowed to remain outside His kingship? Thus God as sovereign ruler, and man, as His vicegerent, must implement His rule on earth. As he writes, "the state, according to Islam is nothing more than a combination of men working together as servants of God to carry out His will and purpose."[83] Mawlana Mawdudi called this state governed by *Shari'ah*, as ideological state, as it is exclusively built on principles.[84] He writes, "From the dawn of history down to modern days, Islam is the only creed in the world which seeks to organize the state on the basis on ideology free from all traces of nationalism and invites mankind to form a non-national state by accepting its ideological system."[85] *Tawhid* according to Mawdudi, requires the establishment of the

82. Mawdudi, *Process of Islamic Revolution*, p. 9. Also for the purpose and structure of the Islamic State please see. Mawdudi, *Political Theory of Islam and his Islamic Law and Constitution*, ed. Khurshid Ahmad and also see Charles J. Adams, *Mawdudi and Islamic State in Voices of Resurgent Islam*, ed. John. L. Esposito.

83. Ibid., p. 9.

84. Ibid., p. 4

85. Ibid., p. 5.

Islamic state or system in its entirety because then alone could the provisions of Islamic law (*Shari'ah*) be properly implemented. Like a refrain, he wrote repeatedly over and over again that Islamic *Shari'ah* does not recognize any division between religion and other aspects of life, and most specifically between religion and the state are two sides of single coin in Islam.

Mawlana Mawdudi asserted that "the concept of state envisaged by Islam is built on the foundation of *tawhid* (unity of God), *risalat* (prophethood) and *khilāfat* (vicegerency)[86] and its aim and purpose *Qur'an* clearly states is the establishment, maintenance and development of those virtues, which the creator of the universe wishes human life to be enriched by and the prevention and eradication of those evils which are abhorrent to God."[87] So that, kingdom of God may really be established on earth where law of God becomes the law by which people lead their lives. The establishment of Islamic state is therefore, incumbent upon every Muslim society in every age and in any environment and is the ultimate purpose of Islam.[88] Therefore, according to Mawdudi, political power cannot be ignored and left to remain outside; in the hands of those, who have turned away from God. He argues that power and leadership in society are crucial because these are the decisive factors in human affairs; human civilization travels along in the direction determined by the people, who control the centres of power.[89] A society in the hands of those, who

86. For a detailed study of all these and other relevant concepts of Mawlana Mawdudi, see *Islamic Law and Constitution*, Ch. 4, see IV and V; Ch. 5 see III, V and VI; Ch. 6, see IV.

87. Mawdudi, *Islamic Way of Life*, p. 32.

88. Ibid., p. 32 and also see Mawdudi, *Dynamics of Values*, pp. 79-80.

89. Mawdudi, *Dynamics of Values*, pp. 77-78.

have turned away from God . . . drifts towards rebellion against God.[90] To maintain the sovereignty of God on earth power and leadership must remain in the hands of true believers. He writes "those who profess faith in this religion cannot fulfil their duty merely by trying to pattern their lives on outward appearances. The nature of their faith requires them to concentrate all their efforts upon wresting leadership from unbelieving and corrupt men in order to entrust it to the righteous, and upon establishing and maintaining the way of life that has been ordained for the conduct of the world according to the will of God."[91] Thus Mawdudi asserted that only when power in society is in the hands of believers and the righteous, can the objectives of Islam be realized in its entirety[92] and it was the goal towards which he strove and established Jamaat-i-Islami. For him "the importance of securing power for the righteous is so fundamental that, neglecting this struggle, one has no means left to please God."[93] He further argues, the very nature of the *al-dīn* demands that it must prevail, and every one who professes to be the upholder of truth must make use of down all the energies to subdue the forces of evil and make *al-dīn* truth and righteousness dominant in this world. A believer of *al-dīn* cannot rest unless he endeavours his best to bring the entire environment under its sway. Contrary to that, if one feels no restlessness, the pain, and the compelling urge to wipe out wrong and establish the right, it is an indication that his soul is dead.[94]

90. Idem.

91. Ibid, p. 80.

92. Ibid., p. 79.

93. Idem.

94. Mawdudi, *The Religion of Truth*, p. 38.

Mawlana Mawdudi described Islamic morality in the same context of total submission to God (*tawhid*) and the establishment of Islam in its entirety. Embracing not only generally accepted but much more; faith, fundamental values deep inside man as well as their articulation in his conduct and society, his entire individual and societal behaviour, his ceaseless pursuit of ideals laid down by God. According to the *Qur'an* and the *Hadith*, Mawdudi says, "what we characterize as Islamic morality contains four aspects or grades; *imān* (faith in God), *Islam* (Surrender to God), *taqwa* (God-consciousness), *ihsan* (Godliness).[95] *Imān* is the foundation of this edifice. Upon it is built the structure of *Islam* and then *taqwa* and *ihsan*. Without *imān*, none of other three can exist. . . . And a limited *imān* means limited *Islam*, *taqwa* and *ihsan* . . . the first priority in the development of Islamic morals is, therefore, a firm and deeply-rooted *Imān*."[96] Real *imān*, according to him, is not mere verbal profession accepting God to some extent or only in a religious sense. It is complete and total submission to His will without any reservation, to live doing His will, seeking nothing but His pleasure and countenance. It implies for asking loyalties and obedience to every object other than God, unless that it be in accordance with His will.[97]

Furthermore, it is obvious from the *Qur'an*, Mawdudi argues, that the inner conviction of faith and the practice of Islam are essentially interdependent. One cannot fail to notice in numerous Qur'anic verses. The striking feature that both *imān* (faith) and *amal salih* (righteous conduct) are almost always mentioned together. Significantly, whereas at places it has been

95. Mawdudi, *Dynamics of Values*, op. cit., p. 111.

96. Idem.

97. Ibid., p. 113.

made clear that without true *imān* good conduct may not be of much avail (see al-Nisa 4: 124, al-Nahl, 16: 97, al-Isra 17: 19). The relations between the two is the same as that between seed and plant. *Imān* is the seed and Islam represents its fruition. In fact, Islam is the practical demonstration of *imān*.[98] Hence, where there is deficiency in submission to God, where one's desires differ from God's Will, where loyalty to others co-exist with loyalty to God, where attention is being devoted to activities other than the struggle for the establishment God's guidance, where efforts are being made for causes other than the cause of God, *imān* does necessarily suffer from flaws and blemishes.[99] Therefore, according to Mawdudi *taqwa* and *ihsan* cannot be built on defective *imān* no matter how much effort is made to acquire the outward appearance and as long as misconceptions persist, one can never expect to complete the full course of Islamic morality. The mere appearance without reality is a sham. Narrow the concept of God, the narrow will be the application of Islamic principles in man's life and narrow will be the base of his morality.[100] One can feign of being *muttaqin* (the God-conscious) and behave as *muhsinin* (the godly who attains excellence in doing good deeds) but these highest stages of Islamic morality can never be reached unless the foundation of *imān* is firm and the proof of its strength is provided by a life lived completely according to Islam. He passionately inveighed against any less than total commitment and loyalty to God, whether it be by dividing life into compartments and living in compromise with *kufr* or by hoisting an outward religiosity devoid of "real *imān*." Therefore, it is both a state of total being, and a process of

98. Ibid, p. 115.

99. Ibid., p. 116.

100. Ibid., pp. 111, 114.

total life. More one attains to this ideal more should one struggle to subdue all powers to God's Will.[101]

Mawlana Mawdudi, presents the broad foundational principles of the Islamic system — social, political educational, economic and moral. He made it abundantly clear that these sub-systems are correlated with each other since Islam is not a disjointed and fragmented ideology and does not divide life into compartments. Islam implies the complete submission of man to God in all aspects of his life, individual and collective. Complete submission entails complete obedience to the Divine guidance in all areas of life and rejection of all kinds of artificial division of life — life spiritual and life mundane.

Reformist Thought

MAWLANA MAWDUDI ON *TAJDID* (REVIVALISM) AND *ISLAH* (REFORMATION) IN ISLAM

Tajdid and *islah* are two important terms in Islamic science. The former is derived from a *Hadith* while later has been used in the *Qur'an*:

> Allah will raise at the head of century such people, who will revive His religion.[102]

And as to those who hold fast to the Book (i.e. act on its teachings) and perform *as-slat*, certainly we shall never waste the reward of those who reform (morals of people).(*al-Araf*).

Tajdid means "renewal" "revival" and *islah* means "reform." Technically they connote the renewal or revival of (religion) at the various stages of history. Sometimes, scholars have used almost both the terms interchangeably. Among them

---

101. Ibid., p. 116.

102. Abu Huraira, *Abu Dawud*.

included are Fazlur Rehman, John O. Voll, John L. Esposito and Ibrahim Abu Rabi. This operates due to the eternal values and principles of *dīn*, serving as a model to revitalize it in the changing times. New times require new interpretation (*ijtihad*) of Islam, which is its renewal and continuity. It is an effort to define Islam solely in relation to its authentic sources (i.e. the *Qur'an* and the *Sunnah* of the Prophet) and on the other hand, an attempt to work towards a situation in which the lives of Muslims, in personal and social terms, really would confirm to the norms and values of that religion. It is a permanent feature in the religious and cultural history of Islam. In the modern times an ample discourse took place on the Islam's concept of *tajdid*.

Although Mawlana Mawdudi has touched upon this subject comprehensively in most of his writings yet his *Tajdid-i-Ihya-i-Din* (Eng. tr. *A Short History of Revivalist Movement in Islam*) is exclusively devoted to this theme. It discusses the concept of *tajdid* critically and marks some departure with the views of the other modern scholars including Muslims and orientalists.

Mawlana Mawdudi discusses *tajdid* (revivalism) of Islam in a wide historical and epistemological perspective. He finds every system of life rooted in metaphysics. As he says:

> All the existing and the past systems of life have had to adopt some basic metaphysical philosophy and some basic moral theory. It is these basic concepts, which distinguish one system of life from the other, not only in major principles but also in the minutest details.[103]

Mawlana holds that every system of life whether past or present is characterized by one of the four metaphysical

103. Mawdudi, *A Short History of the Revivalist Movement in Islam*, Markazi Maktaba Islami, Delhi, 1997, p. 15.

outlooks, viz., atheism, polytheism, asceticism and monotheism. While he categorizes the former three systems under the general title of *jahilliyyah* (ignorance) which according to Mawlana Mawdudi has been the antithesis of Islam. So these four systems are in fact only two, as he emphasizes that these are two basically different, in fact mutually opposed, attitudes to life: one, of accepting God as the sovereign and law-giver and as such responding to Him as His slave and servant; the other, of defiance and rebellion against God, and arrogation to oneself or to others than the one true God of the authority to command.[104]

The doctrine of atheism, according to Mawdudi, is based on the theory that the whole universe has come into existence by mere accident, and that there is no wisdom and purpose behind it, and also it has no master. This theory has given rise to materialism devoid of any morality. Policies are based on the Machiavellian principles of politics. Stronger gets encouraged to suppress the weak. This has led to the rise of nationalism, imperialism, colonial opportunism and the greed to grab the weaker nations.[105]

According to the doctrine of polytheism, the universe has more than one masters. The number of gods go on changing from time to time at the sweet wish of the people. Rulers and religious functionaries are made gods in this system, which results in the creation of a separate class, and gradually, the idea of the superiority of one family over the other and of one class over the other gets established. Weaker classes get exploited by higher classes.[106]

---

104. Mawdudi, *Islam and Ignorance*, Lahore, 1976, Passim.

105. Mawdudi, *Revivalist Movement in Islam*, pp. 15, 18.

106. Ibid., pp. 18, 21.

Under asceticism, bodily pleasures are to be sacrificed for the upliftment of the soul. Salvation is sought by renouncing the world. The good and pious people withdraw from the world and the affairs of the world come in the hands of evil and wicked people. They corrupt the earth and oppress the weak.[107] The fourth metaphysical doctrine is Islam, which is the one presented by the prophets of God. According to this system, Mawdudi holds, the whole universe including human beings is the kingdom of God, who is the master and the sole Ruler. Man on the earth is His vicegerent, and is responsible to Him; and he does not have the right to choose a way of life for himself. Rather he has to follow the guidance from the Supreme Ruler (Allah) revealed to the prophets. Man has also been endowed with reasoning faculty by which he can distinguish between right and wrong; has been given freedom to choose any course of action, a trial till death. He is not being punished for any wrong thing here, nor is he rewarded for anything good. The real assessment of and judgement on his actions will be conducted hereafter.[108]

The aim of all the prophet's missions in the world, according to Mawlana Mawdudi, has been to establish the kingdom of God on the earth and to enforce the system of life received from Him. Prophet Muhammad (SAAS) was the last in this category of prophets; he succeeded in the establishment of the kingdom of God on the earth.[109] This order was maintained by the rightly guided caliphs. But soon, with the expansion of the Islamic state, the evils of the *jahilliyyah* found their way into the Islamic social order. The evil systems of atheism, polytheism and asceticism began fast spreading their

107. Ibid., pp. 21, 24.

108. Ibid., pp. 24, 26.

109. Ibid., pp. 29, 30.

influence in the Islamic community.[110] Now Islam began to feel the onslaught of *jahilliyyah* in the garb of Islam. The caliphate gave way to monarchy; the title of God's reflection on the earth was invented for the kings; the meanings of the verses of the *Qur'an* and the traditions of the prophet (SAAS) were distorted by the world seeking *Ulama*, thus paving way for saint worship. Under the influence of asceticism, Muslims fell a prey to Greek philosophy, monastic morality and a pessimistic attitude towards life. This on the one hand perverted Islamic literature and sciences, and incapacitated the thinking element of the society, and on the other hand it reinforced monarchy, retarded the progress of Islamic arts and sciences by growing narrow-mindedness and reduced religion to few special rituals.[111]

To purge Islam of the above evils says Mawlana, and to present it in its original form, was the heavy task for the *mujaddids*. But at the same time, Mawlana Mawdudi makes this point very much clear that it is wrong to assume that Islam, at any time during the course of history, was completely overpowered by the forces of "ignorance." The fact of the matter is that Islam imprints upon its followers with some degree of its reformative message, and the effect of the same has been displayed by the people throughout history. It is "on this very account the Muslim people all over the world has been morally superior to the non-Muslim communities."[112] Yet it was not enough on the part of the Muslim community for the accomplishment of the real task of the prophetic mission. As Mawlana says,

---

110. Ibid., p. 32.

111. Ibid., pp. 33, 34.

112. Ibid., p. 34.

> Obviously, Islam being a force of secondary importance only could not prosper, when the real power was in the impious hands. Nor could a few scattered individuals, who practised Islam in the restricted sphere of their personal lives only and who felt little concerned about the various admixture of Islam and un-Islam in the wide sphere of social life around them, bring about a noticeable change in the prevailing social conditions.[113]

So, according to Mawdudi, for the revival and reformation of Islam it needs in every age strong men, groups and organizations, which could change the course of the time and bring the world round to bow before the authority of the one, Almighty.[114]

Mawlana Mawdudi also touches upon the *Hadith* generally quoted by scholars to illustrate the concept and validity of *tajdid*. He says that the *Hadith* has been narrated by Abu Hurairah and quoted by Abu Dawud. Unlike from other exegetes Mawlana Mawdudi says that *rasin* does not mean only the end of each century but also the beginning of the century at which the *mujaddid* will be raised from the *ummah*. He further says that it does not mean only a single *mujaddid* but may even mean several persons or a group of persons who will perform this work of revivalism. What the Prophet (SAAS) actually meant, says Mawdudi, "no century will remain devoid of such persons, who will rise in the face of ignorance and try their best to purge Islam from the impurities and will enforce its system in the world in its original form and spirit. At the same time it is not necessary that such person or persons will be attributed with the title of *mujaddid* and, as a matter of

---

113. Ibid., p. 35.

114. Idem.

fact, such title is acquired by those only, who would have made great and distinguished achievements in the field."[115]

While elaborating the concept of *tajdid,* Mawlana makes an interesting analysis of the nature of *tajdid.* He distinguishes it from modernization (*tajdid*). To him, it is just to re-shape the material condition of the community or society at the time of decline. It implies compromise and adoption of the values of "the ignorants." On the other hand *tajdid* or revivalizing means shifting the elements of *jahilliyyah* and the promotion of pure and pristine values of Islam to its utmost. Unlike the former, here we do not have mixture of the two but the clear-cut difference of the two.[116]

On the nature of the work of a *mujaddid,* Mawlana enumerates the following points:

(1) That the *mujaddid*'s work is to make the diagnosis of the current situation. It means he has to assess his predicament circumstances and identify the position of this *jahilliyyah* and that of Islam.

(2) A *mujaddid* has to device a scheme of reformation. This becomes possible, when he first makes the assessment of the situation of the age and his scheme is to overcome the anti-Islamic, non-Islamic *jahilliyyah* and pave the way for Islam.

(3) That the *mujaddid* is well aware about his resources and limitations. He examines what kind of resources he has to use for his purpose and what are his limitations in it that makes him to plan properly and get proper results.

---

115. Ibid., p. 36.

116. Ibid., p. 37.

(4) Since *tajdid* work is a fundamental change and transformation in the society, a *mujaddid* works for the intellectual change initially. The *aqaid* (beliefs) and thoughts of the people are changed, educational system becomes the means of reviving Islamic sciences and Islamic thought. This inculcates Islamic attitudes among the people.

(5) A *mujaddid* brings even radical change in the society and this comprises the adherence to *Shari'ah* among its equal and generating leadership qualities in men. The change ultimately culminates in the formation of a good and righteous society.

(6) Exercising of *ijtihad* is also the work of a *mujaddid*. This is required to develop Islamic civilization in the new set-up and make Islam a leading system.

(7) A *mujaddid* also safeguards Islamic power and authority so that Islam can become a living force and reality. It will at the same time overcome the false system of polity and leadership.

(8) The *mujaddid* brings all embracing revival of Islamic system of life.

(9) The revival change can be brought at the global level by a *mujaddid*. This makes the spread of Islamic *Dawa* in other places and nations and vindicates the truth and efficacy of Islamic ethical and civilizations principles. Islam emerges as a universal movement.[117]

According to Mawlana Mawdudi, one who undertakes first four jobs of revival is a *mujaddid* and one who undertakes all these items of revival works is a perfect *mujaddid*.[118]

---

117. Ibid., pp. 34, 40.

118. Ibid., p. 40.

Response to Nationalism and Freedom Struggle of India

Mawlana Mawdudi joined the political arena of the subcontinent by associating himself with the leaders of the *khilāfat* movement at very young age of sixteen years. Muslims in India had staked everything for the preservation of the *khilāfat* and the protection of the holy places of Islam. Hindus led by Gandhiji also joined the *khilāfat* movement. At the same time, Jallianwala Bagh incident ignited among Indians the passion to free the country from foreign dominion. Indian Muslims and Hindus were united — the former were primarily interested in promoting the purposes of the *khilāfat* movement and the latter with the aim of attaining *svarāja*.

But soon after joining the *khilāfat* movement, it dawned upon Mawdudi (after making an extensive study on the subject of caliphate) that Turkish leadership was based on Turkish nationalism ingrained with the elements of secularism, which the Westernized young Turks had imported from the West. The enemies of Islam, Mawdudi holds, instigated the feelings of Arab nationalism among Arabs in response to that of Turkish nationalism. With the result the Turkish and Arab Muslims took to different camps in the First World War.

Mawlana Mawdudi laments both the nationalist Turks and the nationalist Arabs for their becoming the easy preys of the colonial conspiracies. He says,

> Unwise were the Turkish leaders, who held fast to *khilāfat* based on Islam on the one hand, and on the other hand fostered secularism. It was a great mistake on their part to run their state on the basis of Turkish nationalism while the country comprised of Arabs, Kurds and other non-Turkish people as well, who could be loyal to the Islamic caliphate, but who could not be faithful to Turkish nationalism. . . . On

> the other hand, foolish were the Arab leaders, who were befooled by the Christians and the Jews, and suffered their lands to be occupied by them.[119]

This was going to have far-reaching consequences so far as Indian Muslims were concerned, who were bent upon saving the Turkish Islamic caliphate, come what may an issue far off and far beyond their control. Mawdudi describes their situation:

> When this bitter reality came to my notice, I felt anguished that the *khilāfat* for which the Muslims of India had staked everything had really no roots, our entire community favoured a foreign cause, which was beyond our control. I wondered that if the West-oriented secular Turks did away with the *khilāfat* on their own account what would be the fate of the *khilfat* movement, which the Indian Muslims had launched.[120]

With these doubts in mind, Mawdudi continued to work for the *khilāfat* movement as he did not want to question the audacity of the great leaders of his community. This was the time when the Hindus and the Muslims enjoyed good relationship and both the communities were working together. This relationship proved short-lived and the duo fell apart. Mawlana was studying the developments with keen eye. Giving a detailed account of the Hindu-Muslim problem and the policies of the Congress, Mawdudi says:

> I studied the history of the Congress, and informed myself of its objective and purpose. I studied how democratic institutions has developed in the country, and how the

---

119. Mawdudi, *The Khud Nawisht*. Also quoted by Masudul Hasan, *Mawlana Mawdudi and His Thought*, p. 31.

120. Idem.

> Congress wanted to run them. As a result of this study it was revealed to me that the British considered that as the people living in Britain formed one nation, so that people living in India formed one nation. The various democratic institutions, that were set up in the country were based on the assumption that the people of India formed one nation. For the Hindus that was an agreeable proposition for they were in a majority, and felt that whatever democratic order was set up assuming the people to be a nation would be to their advantage, and the Muslims being in a minority would occupy a secondary position. Having reached this conclusion I felt very much concerned as to why the Muslim leaders were throwing the Muslims in the lap of the Congress. I wondered how in India an independent democratic government could be set up on the assumption that all the people formed one nation, and that all that the Muslims needed were a few safeguards.[121]

Mawlana Mawdudi could not convince himself about this theory that the Hindus and the Muslims together constitute one nation. And he wondered what constitutional safeguards could be provided to the Muslims, when they were to be a part of the Indian nation. About the latter, Mawlana says:

> About the constitutional safeguards my view was that as long as the British were there, these safeguards could be implemented but when the British left and all power came to vest in the Hindus because of their majority, the safeguards would command no value. The Hindus on the basis of their majority would enforce such order as they might deem expedient and the Muslims would have no power to enforce their claims.[122]

121. *Khud Nawisht*, quoted in Msudul Hasan, op. cit., pp. 31, 32.

122. Ibid., p. 32.

Despite these doubts in mind Mawlana continued to work under senior Muslim leaders. The doubt which Mawlana Mawdudi feared had soon to take the practical form. In the words of Mawlana himself:

> In 1924 all my apprehensions materialized. These developments shook my confidence in the leadership of my community. In 1924, the rulers of Turkey themselves did away with the *khilāfat*, for which the Muslims of the Indian had staked everything and had won the ill–will of the British. The result of this development was that the back of the Muslim community in India was broken. During the same year the Hindu-Muslim unity also came to an abrupt end. Hindu-Muslim riots broke out throughout the length and breadth of the country. During these riots the Hindu Congress leaders as a rule laid the blame for the riots on the Muslims, and projected the Hindus as an aggrieved party. This made the Muslims realize that they had been heretofore living in fools paradise, and that in the circumstances of India, Hindu' Muslim unity could never be a practical proposition.[123]

Yet another moment of alarm for the Muslims for India dawned with the launching of *Śuddhi* movement by the Hindu fanatics led by Swāmi Śraddhānanda in 1925. The *Śuddhi* movement was aimed at the conversion of Muslims to Hinduism. Mawlana Mawdudi studied the problem while thinking what had gone wrong with the Muslims, who in the past had spread the message of Islam throughout the world, are now at such a state where efforts are being made to convert them to Hinduism. Mawlana's study led him to the conclusion that Muslims are not a nation in the normal sense of the term. They constitute a missionary community with a definite mission. And that Islam had not spread through professional missionaries. Every

123. Ibid., pp. 32-33.

Muslim is a missionary in himself. He ought not only to be a practising true Muslim, but should also preach by word and deed, by his character and conduct, to all others the religion of Islam. So long as the entire Muslim community remained a missionary nation, it conquered nation after nation without the use of any force. Indonesia, Malaysia, Eastern and Western Africa among several others, fell into this process of Islamization. Even the several crores of Indian Muslims are not all the descendants of the foreign Muslims who settled here. Most of them were converted to Islam through preaching."[124]

"Now if Hindus have risen to convert Muslims to their fold" says Mawdudi, "it is simply because the Muslims have forsaken their missionary activities,"[125] which according to Mawdudi was the fountain of Muslim's strength.[126] A Muslim is a Muslim only in the name and in practice, he has ceased to be a Muslim, and there is little difference between him and a non-Muslim.[127]

Mawlana Mawdudi was convinced beyond doubt that Islam was not revealed upon mankind just to survive under the patronage of un-Islam. On the contrary, its purpose was the supremacy of Islam with non-Muslims as its subjects. Like the Muslim community, Mawlana held, Islamic government was also a missionary government, which by its justice, honesty, welfare activities and good conduct bears witness to the truthfulness of Islam. Its judiciary, police, army; its foreign

---

124. Ibid., pp. 33-34.

125. Ibid.

126. The series of articles written by M. Mawdudi, during this period in *al-Jamiat* on the missionary aspect of Islam were later published in a booklet entitled *Islam ka Sarchasma-i-Quwwat,* meaning of the sources of Islam's strength.

127. Ibid.

relations, and everything related to it should project the difference between Islam and *kufr*. In short, an Islamic state was a missionary state aiming at the supremacy of the faith. The purpose of *jihād* was that Islam should dominate over unbelief.[128]

It was after the *khilāfat* tragedy of 1924 that Muslim in India, according to Mawdudi, were passing through a very grave situation. There was great disunity among them and were falling victims of Western culture and thought. There was an open sermonizing of irreligiousity and atheism among the Muslims. The two types of educational systems in vogue in the country, one secular which made Muslims strangers to Islam, and the traditional which made them misfit in the modern world, created a rift between them. Mawlana Mawdudi felt that the crisis through which the Muslims were passing could not be overcome unless the gap between these two educational systems was bridged.[129]

The situation was even more deplorable on the political front. Mawlana describes the helplessness of the Muslim during this period in the following words:

> Till 1928 the general impression in India was that no movement for Independence could make any headway unless the Muslims joined it. The Muslims were also under the impression that the Congress could not afford to lose their cooperation. Towards 1929, Gandhi became cognizant of the helplessness of the Muslims. The Muslims had no organization and no leadership, and Gandhi felt that under the circumstances, he could wage the struggle for Independence with the help of the Hindus alone. Gandhi

---

128. See Mawlana Mawdudi's presidential address, Jamaat-i-Islami, August, 1970.

129. Idem.

> plainly told the Muslims that he would wage the struggle with the Muslims if they chose to follow him, and in spite of them in case they did not choose to follow him.
>
> At that time it dawned on me that the future for the Muslims in India was indeed very dark. Gandhi was actually in the position to fight against the British with the help of the Hindus, and the Muslims were so disorganized that they could not stand in the way of the Hindus. The Muslims were forced to the position that they should unconditionally accept the leadership of the Congress, and acquiesce in the establishment of Hindu Raj, or they should watch developments as mute spectators only.[130]

Under these circumstances, Mawlana Mawdudi shifted from Delhi to Hyderabad where after some time, in 1932, he took up the editorship of the monthly *Tarjuman al-Qur'an* for the propagation of his views. "At that time," says Mawlana, "my scheme was to break the bonds of Western thought and civilization, which had captivated the minds of Muslim intellectuals. I tried to bring home to them the fact that Islam had its own way of life, its distinct civilization, political, educational and economic systems, which were by far-superior to the Western civilization. I also tried to expose the weak aspects in the Western thought and culture. Side-by-side I also endeavoured to project Islam in its proper perspective so that Muslims realize that their salvation lay in holding fast to Islam."[131]

Mawlana Mawdudi continued to write in the *Tarjuman al-Qur'an* on the above referred to subjects up to 1937. He kept himself away from the political engagements and

---

130. Idem.

131. Mawdudi, *Khud Nawisht*.

controversies. From 1937, Mawlana began to concern himself with the political problems of Indian Muslims. The cause of this concern was the Government of India Act, 1935, and the provincial elections of 1937 which resulted in the massive majorities for the Congress. Mawlana, during his visit to Delhi, in this period, had seen clear signs of defeatism among the Muslims. Later on, when he went again to Hyderabad, he wrote a series of articles which were later published under the title *The Muslims and the Present Political Struggle.*

In 1938, the Congress started the Muslim Mass Contact Movement aimed at taking into its fold every individual Muslim. According to Mawdudi; this was the policy of the Congress to absorb Muslims at individual levels without making any negotiations with any political organizations of the Muslims. For this purpose, Jawaharlal Nehru had employed Muslim communists. In his presidential address to All Indian National Convention, Nehru had declared that "it had been a mistake to waste time in negotiations with communal leaders and that future efforts should be concentrated upon the common people. There is no room for the old idea of two communities, in the present age, which should be discarded as outdated. Common economic interests are the basis of all present-day political activities."[132]

Mawlana Mawdudi has quoted profusely from the writings of Jawaharlal Nehru and says that the latter regards all the people inhabiting India to be a nation. According to Nehru, the Muslims could not be a nation for that tentamounts to setting up a nation within a nation.[133]

---

132. Mawdudi, *Tarikh-i-Azadi-i-Hind Awr Musalman*, Lahore, 1981, vol. I., p. 218.

133. Ibid., p. 200.

The second point in the philosophy of Jawaharlal Nehru was his belief in the Marx's concept of history according to which economic interest is the force which shapes the political thinking of various classes.[134]

Mawlana Mawdudi argued against both these points of Nehru. He said that if all the people formed a nation and if there were no differences among its peoples except by way of economic considerations, then why there were differences between the Hindus and the Muslims, who were different religious communities.[135] Jawaharlal Nehru also ascribed the Hindu-Muslim differences to the British rulers and he also held that India suffered on account of the British, the religion and the vested interests. He deplored all the three and wished to do away with them.[136] For this purpose, he had the vision of the establishment of the socialist system, first within the state and then in the whole world. And such a system according to Nehru cannot be discarded merely on the pretext that it is being opposed by few people. If any political or cultural institution (more precisely a religious institution) comes as an impediment in this change, it shall be destroyed.[137] Mawlana Mawdudi observed that Nehru's programme was based on four phases. The first phase of which was the submergence of communal identities in the Indian nation. The second phase was the replacement of religious ties by economic interests. The third stage was the use of force against those minorities, who would not shun their religious loyalties in favour of the new economic order. And the fourth phase was

---

134. Ibid., p. 201.
135. Ibid, p. 202.
136. Ibid., p. 206.
137. Ibid., p. 207.

that on the basis of the principles of third international, a worldwide campaign would be launched in favour of the communism.[138]

Pt. Nehru realized that Muslims stood for equality and at the same time were poor also. As a matter of fact he expected the ideology of communism to spread among them. But he was fully aware that it was not easy to assimilate the Muslims first in composite nationhood and then in communism. The first obstacle in the way was the presence of the bond of Islamic solidarity, which prevented the Muslims from being absorbed into one nation side-by-side with non-Muslims. Second was the Islamic culture and civilizations, which the Muslims considered dearer and superior to other cultures and civilizations. The third and the most important impediment in its way was the social system of Islam which extended over all aspects of a Muslim's life, and over which he may not like any other social system.[139]

After understanding these problems Congress devised its own strategy to handle this issue. Mawlana observed that the strategy of the Congress was that all the people should consider themselves as one nation. In order to achieve this object, their first strategy was that the Muslims should be made to feel that they were not a separate nation but were merely a part and parcel of the Indian nation. Their second strategy was to attack the Islamic culture so that the Muslims might give it up and adopt the Indian culture. The third strategy was to wean the Muslims from Islam by spreading socialist views among them.[140]

---

138. Ibid., p. 209.

139. Ibid., p. 210.

140. Masudul Hassan, p. 187.

Mawlana Mawdudi also pointed out that the Indian National Congress was not a communist organization; it neither wanted to do away with capitalists and capitalism nor was it in favour of that social (cultural) revolution often referred to by Jawaharlal Nehru and Subhash Chandra Bose.[141] It was very much against the infiltration of communists among its ranks, but encouraged them to work among the Muslims.[142] The natural corollary of it according to Mawdudi would be the disintegration of the Muslim masses into mere individuals and "when they (Muslims) begin progressively to discard their culture and cut themselves off from the Muslim middle classes to join the non-Muslims of their own class, the process of their *śuddhi* would have started and they would be assimilated into Hindu society as a lump of salt is slowly dissolved if placed in water."[143]

Mawlana Mawdudi strongly opposed the Western concept of nationalism. He spoke against the divisive nature of this creed which "divides man from man on the basis of nationality."[144] Under this ideology, a nationalist has to give preference to his nationality over all other nationalities and "even if he were not an aggressive nationalist, nationalism, at least, demands that culturally, economically, politically and legally he should differentiate between national and non-national; secure the maximum of advantage for his nation; build-up barriers of economic preferences for national profit; protect with tenacity the historical traditions and the traditional prejudices, which have come down to wake his

141. Mawdudi, *Tarikhi-i-Azadi-i Hind Awr Musalman*, vol. I., p. 245.

142. Ibid., p. 246.

143. I.H. Qureshi, *Ulama in Politics*, p. 336.

144. Mawdudi, *Nationalism and India*, p. 14.

nationality and breed in him the sentiments of national pride."[145] And if a nationalist finds a chance of his nation obtaining more advantages as against the other, his heart would be sealed against all sentiments of justice and propriety.[146]

Nationalism as an ideology, according to Mawdudi, is a new concept, which grew in peculiar conditions of Europe. After the break-up of the religious and political unity of the Christian West in the aftermath of the movement of reformation initiated by Martin Luther, the European nations separated from one another and began to establish their own national states. The language and literature of each nation carved out a separate line of progress for itself. The economic interests of each nation were demarcated from others. The result of which was the new conception of nationality based on political, economic and cultural foundations. Then commenced mutual conflict, instigation and competition between nations. Wars were raged; one nation snatched the rights of another nation; worst demonstrations of tyranny and cruelty were made, which gradually raised the bitterness of national sentiments to such high pitch that the consciousness of nationality was converted into nationalism.[147] Born out of competition and conflict with neighbouring nations, this nationalism, according to Mawlana Mawdudi has four essential ingredients in its nature.

(i) The sentiment of national pride . . . which compels a nation to exalt itself over all other nations in every respect.;

145. Ibid.

146. Ibid.

147. Ibid., p. 18.

(ii) The sentiment of national consciousness, which keeping aside the question of truth and justice, obliges a man to support his nation whether it stands for right or wrong;

(iii) The sentiment of national self-preservation, which, to protect its actual and visionary interests, compels every nation to adopt tactics, which commences with self-defence and end in invasion; and

(iv) The sentiment of national prestige and national aggrandisement, which produces in every progressive and powerful nation the assertion that it should dominate and rule over the nations of the earth.[148]

Mawlana Mawdudi makes this point clear that the nationalism, which he abhors is not the natural sentiment by which a man loves his nation and wishes it to be free. "If it were so," he holds, "it would be a noble sentiment."[149] He rejects the modern ideology of nationalism, which according to him is "generated and nurtured by the sentiments of hostility, hatred and revenge rather than those of love."[150] Mawlana holds that "apparently it rises to redress the injustices inflicted or supposed to have been inflicted on the nation by another nation or nations, but since it is not guided and regulated by any moral code, by any spiritual teachings, by any God-made law, it exceeds its limits and assumes the forms of imperialism, economic nationalism, racial hatred, war and international anarchy."[151]

Mawlana Mawdudi speaks of Islam as the only alternative to the menace of nationalism. "Islam" Mawlana says "deals with

148. Ibid., pp. 18-19.

149. Ibid., p. 20

150. Ibid.

151. Ibid.

man as man."[152] He further says that "those who accept the principles of Islam are not divided by any distinction of nationality or race or class or country."[153] The ultimate goal of Islam, according to Mawdudi is a world state in which the chains of racial and national prejudices would be dismantled.[154] Islam's appeal to mankind is general and humanitarian rather than national and parochial. He says, "whatever the principle of human good Islam defines, and whatever the scheme of life it prescribes, it would appeal to mankind in general only when they would free themselves of all ignorant prejudices and dissociate themselves altogether from their national traditions, with their sentiments of racial pride, and with their love of *sanguinary* and material affinities, and be prepared, as mere human beings to inquire what is truth, where lies righteousness, justice and honesty, and what is the path that leads to the well-being of not a class or a nation or a country, but of humanity as a whole."[155]

Islam and nationalism, Mawlana Mawdudi held were diametrically opposed to each other. "Islam," he said "can-not flourish in the lap of nationalism, and nationalism too cannot find a place in the fold of Islam."[156] "The progress of nationalism would starve Islam to death and the progress of Islam would spell the death-knell to nationalism."[157] And to Mawdudi any person who wants to be loyal to both nationalism and Islam "only betrays a confusion of mind and a looseness of thinking."[158]

152. Ibid., p. 13.
153. Ibid.
154. Ibid.
155. Ibid., p. 14.
156. Ibid., p. 15.
157. Idem.
158. Idem.

The conceptions and principles, which have been responsible for the development of nationalism in Europe, according to Mawdudi, are just the reverse of humanity; "they have degraded man to the level of beasts"[159] and "have filled God's earth with evils, tyrannies and bloodshed, and thwarted the peaceful evolution of human civilization."[160] These principles have also "blighted the sacred ideals for which the messengers of God have endeavoured since the earliest times."[161] These have stood as formidable obstacles against the moral and spiritual teachings embodied in the heavenly books, and against the law of God and also make man narrow-minded.[162]

In quite contrast to it is the law of God (the *Shari'ah*), which according to Mawlana Mawdudi has always aimed at bringing together mankind into one moral and spiritual framework and make them mutually assistant to one another on a universal scale.[163] Islam provides the greatest opportunities of free contact between man and man because on it depends the progress of human civilization and culture.[164] Islam wants that every individual or group "should obtain full opportunities of developing its natural characteristics and its inherent potentialities so that it may be able to subscribe its due share to the collective progress of mankind.[165] Islam recognizes the rights of man which "are based on moral code and not on

159. Ibid., p. 25.
160. Idem.
161. Idem.
162. Idem.
163. Idem.
164. Idem.
165. Ibid., p. 27.

force."[166] Islam is also not opposed to individual self-preservation or national self-preservation. It rather encourages it because "the collective progress of humanity is dependent on the fact that each nation should progress within its own sphere."[167] Islam "encourages a national self-love, which should extend to humanity at large its sympathy, cooperation and well-wishing."[168]

Mawlana Mawdudi is quite aware of the popularity of the doctrine of nationalism througout the world as the "only tried method of achieving freedom, progress, prestige and honour."[169] The reason why the nations are falling to nationalism, according to Mawlana, is that they do not possess a national moral teaching, which may regulate individual and social wants, keep within legal limits desires and ambitions and give right directions to the power of action and motivity.[170] It is this lack of guidance that even in India Hindus, Sikhs and Pārsīs are adopting the nationalistic ideas of the West.[171] The cure of the calamity of nationalism, Mawdudi says, lies only in the *Shari'ah*s of God; the custodians of which are the Muslims alone.[172] Thus it was the duty of the Muslims to fight against the evils of nationalism; who "should have told the nations of the earth that for them not only the path of freedom, progress, honour and prestige but also that of safety, peace and real happiness is that defined and demarcated by the *rasool*s

166. Idem.
167. Idem.
168. Ibid., p. 28.
169. Ibid., p. 40.
170. Idem.
171. Idem.
172. Idem.

of God."[173] Mawlana Mawdudi laments at the affairs of the Muslims of his time who according to him, failed in performing their duties. He calls it the "greatest and most grievous tragedy of modern times" because the Muslims according to him were the only party "appointed by God to spread the mission of *rasools* on this earth."[174] This community has declined its fundamental responsibility, and "instead of guiding the misguided world with the torch of truth, is itself eager to follow those going into wilderness."[175]

According to Mawlana Mawdudi, there exist two kinds of nationalities; political nationality and cultural nationality. Political nationality, according to Mawlana, could bread nationalism nowhere in the world and even common desire for freedom could not generate nationalism.[176] Nationalism according to Mawdudi can take birth only from cultural nationality.[177] It is on this premises that Mawlana held that nationalism cannot have success in India, because though it has political nationality, it is devoid of cultural nationality. Here the difference between various nations (Hindu, Muslim, etc.) are more deep-rooted than those found between the different cultural nationalities in Europe.[178] He further says that in India "one creed differs from another as much as the East from the West; the principles of one culture are entirely different from those of another; there are wide gulfs between the sources of tradition; emotions and sentiments are mutually

173. Idem.

174. Ibid., p. 41.

175. Idem.

176. Ibid., p. 45.

177. Idem.

178. Ibid., p. 51.

repulsive and antagonistic and the national type of one bears hardly anything common to that of another in general appearance.[179]

So under these circumstances, Mawlana calls it foolish on the part of those who, aping the Western nations, consider nationalism the only successful tool of freeing the country from the foreign yoke. Suggesting federal principles over unitary principles for the solution of India, Mawdudi, says:

> In a country where different cultural nationalities exist, to try to mould them into one would not only be unnecessary and wrong in principle, but considering the consequences, it would be harmful instead of being of any use. In such circumstances not unitary principles but only federal principles can work. The permanent status and individuality of every nation should be recognized; everyone of them should be allowed autonomous and sovereign control over its national subjects, and the different nations should agree upon a joint action only in so far as the common interests of the country were concerned. Therefore, this is the only way, which can guarantee safety and preservation to the individuality of all the parties in the country; and this is the only thing which can bring on to one front all the forces in the country which are struggling for political supremacy.[180]

---

179. Idem.
180. Ibid., pp. 54-55.

4

Sayyid Abul A'lā Mawdudi's Formation of Jamaat-i-Islami and its Role in Rebuilding Islamic State in Pakistan

Formation of Jamaat-i-Islami

THE formation of the Jamaat-i-Islami by Mawlana Mawdudi in 1941 was not a chance occurrence. It was not the result of any spontaneous thought occurring. It was, in fact, Mawdudi's deep study and thought coupled with his two decades' observation of the political atmosphere of Indian sub-continent, which resulted in the establishment of the party. Speaking about the dilemma and uncertainty of Indian Muslims, Mawlana says,

> From 1924 to 1937 the circumstances were very distressing for the Muslims. The *khilāfat* movement ended in failure, and thereafter the Hindu-Muslim riots began. There were divisions in the ranks of the Muslims, and they had no leader, who could command the confidence of all the people. The Muslims had no ideal before them, and they quarrelled among themselves on petty matters. The Hindus took advantage of this situation and their real intentions *vis-a-vis* the Muslims became manifest. Gandhiji led the Hindus and safeguarded their interests. Some Muslims also depended on him though he was of no use to them. Instead

> of being an asset for the Muslims, he proved to be a liability. It was apparent that Gandhiji's intentions were different from what he expressed. In the Hindu-Muslims riots, he always sided with the Hindus and blamed the Muslims. Even where the Hindus were the aggressors, Gandhiji supported them. As a consequence most Muslims lost faith in him . . . . All the leaders that we had, failed in delivering the goods, and they had no plan or programme to satisfy the people. We did not know what to do. During this period, the Muslims fell victims to numerous social and intellectual perversities. After the *khilāfat* movement there were riots for four or five years, and thereafter the Muslims came under the influence of alien thoughts which led to atheism. Even religious institutions were affected, and the persons who graduated from these institutions did not have much faith in Islam. At that time I felt that unless some organized effort was made to save Islam, its survival would be at stake. At that time, I felt that some work should be done at the intellectual level to make the people understand Islam. During that period, I tried to project Islam in the proper perspective, and to point out the deficiencies in other thoughts.[1]

From 1939 the movement for Pakistan gained momentum under the leadership of Mohammed Ali Jinnah, who led Muslim League. The Lahore resolution was passed on the 23 March 1940, demanding a separate homeland for the Muslims on the ground of being a nation by all the definitions of the term. This development made Mawlana Mawdudi partly happy as he felt that now Muslims were not going to lose their national identity by being assimilated with a non-Muslim nation. As he says,

---

1. *Chiragh-i-Rah, Tehrik-i-Islami,* 1963.

> I felt sure that the national awakening among the Muslims had reached such a high pitch that no Gandhi or Nehru could integrate them with the Indian nation.[2]

Mawlana Mawdudi was not in favour of creation of a separate nation state for Muslims on secular lines. This was the reason of his strong criticism of Muslim League leaders whom he considered ill-equipped to lead Muslims on Islamic lines which the Muslim masses aspired. So Mawdudi deemed it his duty to emphasize upon Indian Muslims that their aim shall not be confined to the formation of a Muslim nation state rather they must inculcate in them such characters as would go in the making of an Islamic state.[3]

Mawlana Mawdudi found himself and the Indian Muslims at the crossroads. His apprehensions at this time were if the British leave India after handing over power to the Hindu majority, what would be the position of Muslims in a united India. And if the Muslim League succeeds in carving out Pakistan of its conception, what would be the fate of the crores of Muslims who would be left in India. And also what would be the fate of Islam in Pakistan. Seeing the lifestyle, educational background and ideas of the people leading the Pakistan movement, Mawlana Mawdudi was more than certain that these persons might succeed in establishing a separate Muslim nation state but it was illogical to expect of them that they could establish an Islamic state.[4] Thus there were three issues, which haunted Mawlana Mawdudi and these were:

---

2. Mawlana Mawdudi's address at the annual session of Jamaat-i-Islami, August 1970.
3. Ibid.
4. Ibid.

(1) If the subcontinent remains a single country, what should be done to save Muslims as a distinct community;

(2) If the country is partitioned, what should be done of the Muslims staying in India;

(3) Thirdly, if Pakistan is established, what should be done to make it an Islamic state.[5]

With these issues in mind, Mawlana Mawdudi thought of founding the Jamaat-i-Islami. He gave the call for the establishment of the party of righteous persons in an editorial in the *Tarjuman ul-Qur'an* of April 1941. In his appeal Mawlana invited only those for his party, who were dedicated to the cause of Islam and were having a burning desire in their hearts to work for Islam.[6]

Against this call, 75 persons from all over India attended the first conference of the Jamaat, at Lahore on 26 August 1941. The gathering was simple, and the persons who attended were men of ordinary means. Most of them had not seen Mawlana Mawdudi before and they knew him only through his writings in the *Tarjuman ul-Qur'an*.[7]

The meeting was presided over by Mawlana Mawdudi himself, who after thanking the visitors for responding to his call, delivered a long speech setting forth the objectives of the Jamaat-i-Islami. Speaking about the distinctive features of the proposed organization, Mawlana observed that while other movements took up a part of Islam or some worldly aim of the Muslims, the Jamaat had entire Islam as the object of its

---

5. Ibid.
6. Ibid.
7. Proceeding of Jamaat-i-Islami, part I.

movement. The second thing that Mawlana maintained was that he would adopt the same form of organization for his party as was adopted by the Holy Prophet for his organization. The third distinctive feature of the party would be that unlike other Muslim organizations, who admitted to their membership such persons as are Muslims in name only, the Jamaat shall admit only devout Muslims, who are ready to undergo sacrifices in the cause of Islam. Lastly, the activities of the Jamaat wouldn't confine to India alone rather its message was going to be extended to whole Muslim world and also to all non-Muslims.

Role of Jamaat-i-Islami in Rebuilding Islamic State in Pakistan

As mentioned earlier, Mawlana Mawdudi had established his party, the Jamaat-i-Islami, with the sole purpose of serving Islam and the Muslims of the subcontinent and to face the challenges posed to the Muslim community of India after the withdrawal of the British, with or without Partition.

As a result, when the withdrawal of the British and the Partition of the country seemed imminent, Mawlana Mawdudi made preparation for his party accordingly. Speaking at the last gathering of the Jamaat in undivided India at Paṭhānkoṭ in May 1947, Mawlana Mawdudi declared:

> It is almost settled now that our country will be divided and partitioned. A portion of it will be handed over to Muslim majority, and the other will be dominated by a non-Muslim majority. In the first region we will try to awaken and guide the popular will to base the foundations of our state on the law and constitution, which we Muslims consider to be divine. Our non-Muslim brethren should, instead of opposing this idea of ours, allow us the opportunity to work it and see for themselves how far in contradiction to a secular,

> irreligious, national democracy, this God-worshipping democratic caliphate, founded on the guidance vouchsafed to us through Mohammed (SAAS), proves a blessing for the inhabitants of Pakistan and to what extent for the whole world.[8]

Pakistan become a reality on the 14 August 1947 and Mawlana Mawdudi migrated to Lahore along with his staff on 29 August 1947. The Jamaat headquarters had to be shifted from Paṭhānkoṭ to Lahore. The Jamaat-i-Islami was divided into two independent Jamaats, one for Pakistan and the another working in India. On reaching Pakistan, the Jamaat's workers started their activities which were at first confined to religious preachings and to undertaking relief work among the refugees, who were migrating from India. The Jamaat established mobile and stationery dispensaries to render medical aid to the poor and needy through 42 centres throughout Pakistan. More than a million persons benefited from such medical centre up to 1954 and the Jamaat had spent more than a quarter of million rupees on such centres. In the refugee camps of Lahore and other places the Jamaat workers cleared refuse, buried the unclaimed dead, distributed clothes, and medicines, etc.[9]

After a brief period of political dormancy the Jamaat-i-Islami plunged into active politics of the country from January 1948 by launching a campaign for the creation of an Islamic state. As a first step towards the realization of this ideal, Mawlana delivered a series of lectures at the Law College, Lahore. In his first lecture entitled "the Islamic law," Mawlana Mawdudi observed that the case of Pakistan, despite some

8. S.A.A. Mawdudi, *Our Message*, Delhi, 1989, pp. 44-45.
9. Ali Ahmad Khan, *Jamaat-i-Islami*, Pakistan Decca, p. 5.

similarities, is not the same as that of other Muslim countries, as the former has been achieved exclusively with the object of becoming the homeland of Islam.[10] And he also reiterated that the people of Pakistan were already committed before God, man and history for the promulgation of Islamic constitution and introduction of Islamic way of life in the country and no going back on it was possible.[11] The Mawlana also observed that if instead of the Islamic *Shari'ah*, the Western civil and criminal codes were to be the basis of the law, and a secular and Godless constitution was to be introduced in the country, there was no sense in the struggle for a separate homeland for the Muslims.[12]

In this lecture Mawlana Mawdudi tried to prove that Islamic laws could be enforced in any age. By saying so, he countered the misgivings that Islamic laws promulgated some 1300 years ago could no longer suit the requirements of the modern age. Elaborating his point, Mawlana Mawdudi said that those who raised these arguments assumed that Islamic laws had remained static and had failed to respond to the requirements of changing conditions of human life. However, Mawlana said, these critics have failed to realize that the laws propounded thirteen and a half centuries ago did not remain in vacuum, they formed a part and parcel of the life of Muslim society and brought into being a state which was run in the light of these laws. This naturally provided an opportunity of evolution to Islamic laws from the earliest days as it had to be applied to day-to-day matters through the process of *tawil, qiyas, ijtihad* and *istihasan.*

---

10. Mawdudi, *Islamic Law and Constitution,* Khurshid Ahmad, tr. and ed., Lahore 1960, p. 44.
11. Ibid., p. 45.
12. Idem.

Mawlana held that Islamic laws are of two types: the laws which are fundamental and unalterable and the second type of laws are alterable, which form a great part of the Islamic laws. It is these alterable laws, which could be modified as per the need and requirements of the time but of course taking into consideration the fundamental laws of Islam. And these same laws are evidence of the dynamism, adaptability and evolutionary character of the Islamic order.

As regards the objection that there were many schools of jurisprudence, which may not render it possible to evolve an agreed code law which might be acceptable to all the schools of thought, Mawlana pointed out that there were no differences with regard to the fundamentals of Islam. The differences were with regard to matters of detail, and that these could be accommodated within the framework of the Islamic law. Mawlana Mawdudi asked the votaries of modernity among the Muslims, if they believe in the values of Islam or in the values of the modern civilization. He made clear to them that if they believe in the values of Islam, they must have the Islamic law, whatever be the consequence, for if God is the sovereign, the Divine law must necessarily be enforced. On the other hand, if they have made their choice to accept the Western values, they disbelieve in Islamic ideology and as such have forfeited the right to be Muslims.

Mawlana Mawdudi delivered his second lecture at the Law College, Lahore on 19 February 1948. This lecture dealt with the introduction of Islamic law in Pakistan. In this lecture Mawlana Mawdudi observed that Pakistan could not become an Islamic state merely by declaring that it was so. He felt the task for the changeover to the Islamic law very difficult. He therefore called upon the scholars and administrators to give their best thought to the problem and to suggest practical measures to introduce the Islamic law in Pakistan in a systematic and scientific way.

Mawlana Mawdudi suggested that as the first step towards the introduction of the Islamic law in Pakistan, the Constituent Assembly should unequivocally declare:

(1) That the sovereignty in Pakistan belongs to God almighty and that the Government of Pakistan shall administer the country as His agent;

(2) that the basic law of the land is the Islamic Shari'ah which has come to us through our Prophet Mohammed;

(3) that all those existing laws, which may be in conflict with *Shari'at* shall in due course be repealed or brought into conformity with the basic law and nc law, which may be in any way repugnant to the *Shari'at,* shall be enacted in future;

(4) that the state, in exercising its powers, shall not be competent to transgress the limits laid down by Islam.[13]

The second step for the introduction of the Islamic law should be to transfer the power to such persons, who are capable for the task and this could be achieved through the democratic process of elections.[14]

The third step as suggested by Mawlana for the introduction of Islamic law should be to adopt and implement a comprehensive plan for thorough reform in all the departments of national life. The educational system should be re-oriented; all media of publicity should be used for

13. Ibid., p. 107.

14. Ibid, p. 108.

creating a new Islamic consciousness; and an incessant and systematic efforts should be made to mould the society and its culture into an Islamic pattern. The economic system is to be basically altered.[15]

In order to popularize and give practical shape to his four-point declaration, Mawlana Mawdudi appealed the to Muslim League, to the *Ulama*, the Muslim public and to the government of Pakistan.

Mawlana appealed to the Muslim League that as they had waged the struggle for Pakistan in the name of Islam, they should accept the four points demand and prevail upon the Constituent Assembly to pass a declaration accepting Islam as the objective of the new state . . ..

The Mawlana appealed to the *Ulama* to close their ranks and make a unanimous demand. He advised them not to fritter away their efforts in seeking petty concession such as a few seats for the *Ulama* in the assemblies or the creation of some offices to be held by the *Ulama*. They should concentrate on one basic demand only, namely an Islamic constitution, and all minor demands would be fully covered by that basic demand.

Mawlana Mawdudi observed that a constitution however Islamic would fail to work, if the people were not Islamic-minded. On the other hand, if the people were true Muslims, no un-Islamic constitution could be imposed on them. The Mawlana appealed to the Muslims to be true to Islam. . . .

The Mawlana appealed to the government that they should fulfil the promise that they had made before man and God. In some quarters it was held that in view of unstable conditions,

15. Ibid, p. 109.

it was too early to talk of an Islamic constitution. The Mawlana said that Islam was the only common factor between the various parts of the country, and Islam alone could vouchsafe stability for the nation. In some quarters it was objected that an Islamic constitution would alienate the minorities. The Mawlana said that there was no force in this objection as Islam fully protected the rights of the minorities. In some quarters it was objected that an Islamic government would be a government of the mullahs. There was no church in Islam, and as such the government would vest in the people and not in a particular class.[16]

Thereafter, for a few months, Mawdudi toured the west Pakistan, held public meetings propagating the need for an Islamic constitution; and by the middle of 1948 he had succeeded in popularizing his four-point demand and securing a general consensus in favour of an Islamic constitution for Pakistan.[17]

Mawlana on the Kashmir War

The Hindu dynastic ruler of Kashmir — Harisingh made Kashmir's accession to India in utter violation of the principles, on which the subcontinent was divided. The Pakistan government claimed it as rightfully part of Pakistan. There was a lot of excitement and a large number of tribesmen marched into Kashmir. Though Pakistan government encouraged local Muslims to resist Indian rule, referring to their struggle as *jihād*, yet it denied any direct involvement in the fighting.

---

16. Masudul Hasan, *Sayyid Abul A la Mawdudi and His Thought*, pp. 352-353.

17. Ibid., p. 353.

Mawlana maintained that there should be no ambiguity on the part of the government and every policy must be pursued with fairness and honesty. On being asked why he didn't participate in the jihād in Kashmir, Mawlana replied "If the government openly declares *jihād*, I would go in the front ranks. I do not consider it in accord with Islamic morality that while fighting secretly, we declare to the world that we are not fighting."[18] This view of Mawlana Mawdudi was published in a daily, wherein it was construed that the Mawlana had declared the *jihād* in Kashmir as unlawful. The government-controlled papers launched a campaign against Mawdudi wherein his patriotism was questioned. The mass media of India took advantage of the situation and campaigned against Pakistan in the international forums.

Mawlana Mawdudi, however, makes his position clear in June and August 1948 issues of the *Tarjuman ul-Qur'an*. In the former issue he strongly denounced the allegation levelled against him by the Pakistan press and maintained that all he had said was that as long as there was an agreement between the two governments, i.e. India and Pakistan, the *Shari'ah* didn't allow the Pakistanis to fight the Indians. By saying so, Mawlana held that it should not be construed to mean that he had in anyway condemned the *jihād* in Kashmir. While as in the latter issue of the *Tarjuman*, Mawlana Mawdudi pooh-poohed the Indian media. Mawlana declared in clear terms that from the geographical, historical, racial, economic, social and cultural points of view he regarded Kashmir a part of Pakistan. He declared that in his considered opinion by accepting the accession of the state at the instance of the Hindu ruler, India has violated the principle, whereunder it has justified the

---

18. Abul Afaq, *Sayyid Abul A la Mawdudi, Sawainh Afkar, Tehrik* Lahore, 1971, vol. 1, p. 372.

occupation of Jūnāgaṛh and Manavader. The Mawlana pointed out that after the evacuation of the Muslims from East Punjab, the accession of Kashmir to India would be a source of great danger to the Muslims of Kashmir. The Mawlana observed that he supported the Muslims of the state in the struggle that they were waging against the oppression and tyrannies of the Ḍogrās and the Indian forces. He regarded struggle as *jihād* from the Islamic point of view. He held that the people of Pakistan could help their brethren in Kashmir, but the armed forces of Pakistan could not fight in Kashmir as long as there was an agreement between the two governments.[19]

However, after the Government of Pakistan admitted the involvement of its armed forces in the Kashmir war, in a correspondence between the foreign minister of Pakistan and the Kashmir Commission in the United Nations, Mawlana declared that since the circumstances have changed, the war in Kashmir was a *jihād* for the people of Pakistan.

The Kashmir issue was followed by two other issues on which Mawlana Mawdudi and his party came into conflict with the Pakistan government. The first was regarding the oath of allegiances to the government, and the second pertaining to the recruitment to the army. Mawlana had been asked by a person to give his opinion about government employees taking an oath of allegiance to the government, to which he replied that a Muslim could not take an oath of allegiance to any one unconditionally except God.[20] This was interpreted by the government agencies to mean that Mawdudi was inciting the people not to take oath of allegiance to the state.

---

19. Quoted in *Mawlana Mawdudi and His Thought*, pp. 256-357.

20. Abul Afaq, *Sayyied Abul A'Lā Mawdudi Savanih, Afkar, Tehrik*, vol. 1, p. 369.

Before Independence the Jamaat-i-Islami had held that it was unlawful for Muslims to serve in the army under an alien government. The Jamaat's stand was brought in the new circumstances, when the country had attained Independence and it maintained that its previous view would remain unchanged till the government announced its decision to become Islamic. As a result, Mawlana Mawdudi was arrested along with some of his close associates on 4 October 1948.

The Objectives Resolution

Before his incarceration, Mawlana Mawdudi had led a delegation from his party to meet Mawlana Shabir Ahmad Usmani to explain Mawdudi's four-point declaration, which he had advocated should be adopted by the Constituent Assembly.[21] Mawlana Usmani is reported to have proposed appointment by the Constituent Assembly of a committee consisting of eminent *Ulama* and thinkers to prepare a draft constitution to be presented to the Assembly.[22] In this demand, it was felt that Mawlana Usmani was reiterating the opinions of Mawlana Mawdudi that only *Ulama* and those well-versed in Islamic law were competent to frame an Islamic constitution. The objectives resolution was moved in the Constituent Assembly on 7 March 1949 by the then prime minister of Pakistan, Liaqat Ali Khan. The objectives resolution was a statement of intentions of the principles on which the constitution was to be based; and the resolution was adopted on 9 March 1949.

The resolution provided that the sovereignty of the whole universe belongs to Allah, and the authority which He has

---

21. Leonard Binder, *Religion and Politics in Pakistan,* Berkeley and Las Angeles, University of California Press, 1961, p. 138.

22. Ibid., p, 141.

delegated to the state of Pakistan through its people for being exercised within the limits prescribed by Him is a sacred trust.

Among other things the resolution held that the principles of democracy, freedom, equality, tolerance and social justice as enunciated by Islam shall be fully observed; and that the Muslims shall be enabled to order their lives in the individual and collective spheres in accord with the teachings and requirements of Islam as set out in the *Holy Qur'an* and the *Sunnah.*[23] The religious parties including the Jamaat-i-Islami were delighted at the passing of the objectives resolution. The Jamaat members found in the resolution all the four points, which Mawlana had earlier demanded as a first step towards the framing of the Islamic constitution. Expressing his views regarding the objectives resolution, Mawlana Mawdudi said,

> In view of this resolution, the nature of the state has been completely transformed. The ideal of the Muslim nation and the state of Pakistan has now been defined in specific terms. As a matter of principle the state of Pakistan has now been transformed into an Islamic state. Now the service under the state is lawful and its laws are valid. It is now lawful to resort to the courts set-up by the state. It is now permissible to participate in the elections to the legislatures and other state institutions. With this constitutional change, the Jamaat-i-Islami has also changed its policy, and it would take part in the elections in the constitutional way, and try to make Pakistan Dar-ul-Islam in the true sense.[24]

The Basic Principles Committee of the Pakistan Constituent Assembly had constituted a board of Ta'limat-i-Islami to

---

23. *Constituent Assembly of Pakistan Debates*, vol. 1, 7 March 1949, pp. 1-2.

24. Mawlana Mawdudi, *Jamaat-i-Islami Its Objectives, History and Programme of Action* in Urdu, Islamic Publicities, vol. 1, also quoted by Masudul Hasan, op. cit., p. 368.

advise the committee on matters arising out of the objectives resolution. The board submitted its views to the parent sub-committee, which, however, rejected these recommendations.[25] Later in September 1950, the basic principles committee submitted an interim report, which contained nothing more than the Government of India Act of 1935, with the objectives resolution as a preamble, and a clause requiring that all Muslims must study the *Qur'an*.

The interim report aroused the opposition of the *Ulama*. Mawlana Mawdudi criticized the report vehemently and said that the recommendations were in violation of the objectives resolution. He held that the proposals were un-Islamic and un-democratic. In view of the strong opposition that the interim report met in the country, the prime minister of Pakistan announced on 21 November 1950, the postponement of the consideration of the report by the Constituent Assembly. The Prime Minister also appealed to the people and to the *Ulama* to send their agreed proposals about the constitution.[26] It is opined that in this there was a Conspiracy to divide the *Ulama*.

A meeting of the *Ulama* of all school of thought was convened at Karachi in 1951, through the efforts of Mawlana Ihtisham-ul Haq Thanvi. The meeting was presided over by Sayyid Sulaiman Nadwi. There was no fixed agenda, and all the participants except Mawlana Mawdudi had no concrete proposals for an Islamic constitution. Mawlana Mawdudi played the key role at the convention and his proposals were put up before the convention and later on unanimously adopted as the twenty-two points of an Islamic state with minor amendments. These points were:

---

25. Leonard Binder, *Religion and Politics in Pakistan*, p. 159.
26. Ibid., p. 202.

1. Sovereignty of the state vests in God.
2. The law of the land shall be based on the *Holy Qur'an* and the *Sunnah*.
3. The state shall be based on the principles and ideals of Islamic ideology.
4. The state shall promote virtue and suppress vice.
5. The state shall strengthen the bonds of unity and brotherhood among the Muslims of the world.
6. It shall be the responsibility of the state to guarantee the basic necessities of life for all people.
7. The citizens shall be guaranteed all rights conferred by the *Shari'ah*.
8. No one shall be punished without being given full opportunities of defence.
9. The recognized Muslim schools of thought shall have, within the Law, complete religious freedom.
10. The non-Muslim shall have, within the limits of law, complete freedom of religious and personal law.
11. All obligations of the state, with regard to non-Muslim by the *Shari'ah* shall be fully honoured.
12. The head of the state shall always be a male Muslim.
13. The responsibility of the administration of the state shall vest in the head of the state.
14. The head of the state shall be advised by a Majlis-i-Shura.
15. The head of the state shall have no right to suspend the constitution.
16. The head of the state shall be removable by simple majority vote.

17. The head of the state shall be responsible for his acts and shall not be above law.
18. The judiciary should be independent of the executive.
19. All citizens (officials or private) shall be subjected to the same law.
20. The propagation and publicity of such views and ideologies as are against the ideals of Islam shall be prohibited.
21. The various regions of the country shall be considered administrative units of a single state.
22. No interpretation of the constitution, which is in conflict with the provisions of the *Qur'an* and the *Sunnah* shall be valid.[27]

These recommendations of the *Ulama* convention dispelled the false notion that the difference among the various sects in Islam were too acute to make them agree on the fundamentals of the constitution. It was rather a big success in that the *Ulama* of various schools of thought had assembled at one place to spell out the basic principles of the Islamic constitution. Mawlana Mawdudi again launched a campaign for an Islamic constitution with his speech at Arambagh Park in Karachi on 8 May 1952. He alleged that the Constituent Assembly was not sincere in its duty and was making inordinate delay in the framing of the new constitution. He charged it for being more interested in functioning as a Legislature than as a Constituent Assembly, and that it had lost the confidence of the people. Mawlana held that the Constituent Assembly should seriously take the task of the constitution making and complete the exercise as early as possible. Mawlana made it clear that the task before the Constituent Assembly was not only to make a

27. Masudul Husan, op. cit., p. 425.

constitution ; rather it was to frame an Islamic constitution. Soon after it, Mawlana put forward an eight-point programme for a new constitution.[28] Jamaat-i-Islami launched a country-wide campaign with dissemination of posters and pamphlets and holding of meetings and demonstrations in favour of an Islamic constitution. The Jamaat also started signature campaign to the demand for an Islamic constitution. These signatures collected into a scroll were submitted to the Constituent Assembly in August 1952.

On 21 November 1952, one day before second report about basic principles was to be presented to the Constituent Assembly, the Jamaat-i-Islami organized a procession at Karachi. More than one lakh persons participated in the procession, carrying placards and banners demanding an Islamic constitution. This demonstration of a large number of people made the authorities to defer the presentation of the report to the Constituent Assembly for further considerations.[29]

Jamaat-i-Islami and the Elections

After the passing of the objectives resolution, the Jamaat-i-Islami had declared that since the country had become an Islamic state, all associations, including taking part in election, with the state were permissible. Accordingly, Jamaat-i-Islami decided to participate in the Punjab provincial election.

In a press statement issued on 17 August 1950, Mawlana made it clear that his party wouldn't put up its candidates on its own ticket; its object would be to educate the electorate and to purify the process of election so that the righteous

---

28. Mawlana Mawdudi, *Islami Riyasat*, ed. Khurshid Ahmad Lahore 1962, p. 458.
29. Abdur Rehman Abd, *Sayyid Abul A'Lā Mawdudi;* also quoted by Masudual Hassan, op. cit., p. 435.

candidates could be elected. He also said that Jamaat was against any person offering himself as a candidate.

The election board of the Jamaat-i-Islami met at Okara on 18 and 19 September 1950 to formulate the election policy of the Jamaat. The board decided to form panchayats in different localities, which would nominate righteous candidates. The candidates were not required to spend money for it. The job of campaigning and financing the election process was to be taken up by the panchayats.[30]

The Jamaat also issued its election manifesto, it explained the ideals of the Jamaat, of universal good and reconstruction of life on the basis of obedience to God in accordance with the guidance of the Holy Prophet (SAAS). The Jamaat aimed at running an ethical election campaign free from lies, manipulations and other corrupt practices. All the candidates elected through the panchayat system would form the Islamic parliamentary party and would strive to implement the manifesto. The laws like Safety Acts, Frontier Crimes Regulations, and Criminal Tribes Act were to be repealed. With regard to agricultural reforms the manifesto provided that all estates acquired in any way repugnant to the *Shari'ah* were to be taken free but all other estates were to be taken over in public interest on the payment of due compensation. The manifesto sought to ensure security for the tenants, and to fix their share in the agricultural produce. The manifesto also provided for the promotion of local industries and the prevention of monopolies. In the field of industrial relations, the manifesto laid stress on justice between the capital and labour.[31]

---

30. *Rudad-i-*Jamaat-i-Islami, Part V, Lahore 1956, p. 95.

31. Election Manifesto, Jamaat-i-Islamic, 1950 quoted in Masudul Hassan, p. 409.

Only one candidate out of 53 candidates nominated by the Jamaat was elected. The Jamaat accused the government of using unfair means to win the election. Addressing a meeting of the Jamaat-i-Islami in 1951 Mawlana hailed his party's participation in the election and said,

> If a proper assessment was made it would be seen that they gained in several respects. In the 37 constituencies the Jamaat received over 2 lakh votes, and that showed that although the strength of the Jamaat including sympathizers was barely 2000, its influence extended to 2 lakh persons. During the elections the voters were intimidated, coerced and subjected to other influences. If the elections had been held in a fair atmosphere the number of persons voting for the candidates of the Jamaat-i-Islami would have been much larger. We were also particular that the election expenditure should remain at the lowest.[32]

Soon after Mawlana Mawdudi put forward his eight-points programme, the whole of Pakistan got involved in the agitation against the followers of Mirza Ghulam Ahmad of Qadian,[33] known as the Qadianis or Mirzais. The demand for declaring the Qadianis as non-Muslims was first of all raised by the Ahrar[34] in May 1949; and by May 1952 it had become a public demand with *Ulama* joining the movement. A board of *Ulama* was set-up to chalk out the course of action; the board decided to call an All Pakistan Muslim Parties Convention.

---

32. Masludud hassan, op. cit., p. 419.

33. The Qadianis claim Mirza Ghulam Ahmad (d. 1906) of Qadian (Punjab) as a Prophet and the promised Messiah which goes contrary to the orthodox Muslim doctrine of the finality of Prophethood.

34. The Ahrar was the religio-political organization, which had opposed Pakistan movement before Independence. They were vituperative and abusive in denouncing the Qadianis.

An *Ulama* conference was held at Karachi in January 1953. Mawlana Mawdudi proposed that among other constitutional proposals, a proposal should be included requiring the declaration of the Qadianis as a minority. Simultaneously the All Pakistan Muslim Parties Convention was held at Karachi, which appointed an Action Committee to plan a course of action. The latter favoured a direct action whereas Mawlana Mawdudi was not in its favour. He said that any direct action against the Qadiani issue would hamper the demand for an Islamic constitution, which topped Mawdudi's priorities. He made it clear that if the demand for an Islamic constitution was conceded, all other issues including that of Qadiani issue would be automatically solved. However, an ultimatum was presented to the Prime Minister Khawaja Nazimuddin that unless their demands with regard to the declaration of the Qadianis as a separate community and the removal of Zafrullah Khan from the office of foreign ministry were accepted within one month they would resort to direct action.[35] The prime minister refused these demands and the Central Council of Action met at Karachi on 26 February 1953 to launch direct action, though Jamaat-i-Islami dissociated itself from direction action.

The government moved against the *Ulama* on 27 February 1953 and arrested many among them. Mawlana Mawdudi condemned this action of the government and declared that such movements could not be suppressed through force. The Majlis-i-Shura of the Jamaat-i-Islami met on 4-5 March 1953 and reiterated the demand for declaring Qadianis a Minority.

After Karachi, it was Lahore which witnessed the riots, and by 4 March 1953, the city was completely in the hands of

35. Masudul Hassan, op. cit., p. 441.

the rioters. The Provincial Government issued a statement that it agreed with the demands, and would soon forward them to the Central government with their strong recommendation for the approval.

On 5 March 1953, Mawlana Mawdudi's *Qadiani Mas'ala* was published, in which he justified the public demand regarding Ahmadiyyas. The next day, i.e. on 6 March 1953, Martial Law was declared in Lahore, and soon the situation was brought under control. Some of the prominent members of the Ahrar and some *Ulama* including Mawlana Mawdudi were arrested. A Martial Law Court was established which sentenced Mawlana Mawdudi to death, for writing the *Qadiani Mas'ala*. This created massive public outcry especially among the religious circles, and the sentence was later on commuted first to fourteen years rigorous imprisonment and then to two years imprisonment.

A meeting of the members of the Jamaat-i-Islami Majlis-i-Shura was convened at Karachi in April 1953, and later issued a press statement accusing the government of attempts to discredit the Jamaat because they didn't want an Islamic system, and that being the reason for arresting the Jamaat leaders.[36] According to the Jamaat-i-Islami, the reason why Mawlana Mawdudi was arrested was that he had mobilized the people in favour of the Islamic constitution and because he had put forward the nine-point programme of the Islamic government before the Constituent Assembly.[37]

The anti-Ahmadiyya movement in Pakistan, during this period, is thought to have created a void in the efforts of the

---

36. Kalim Bahadur, *Jamaat-i-Islami of Pakistan*, New Delhi, p. 72.
37. Ibid., p. 73.

Ulama to work jointly and make the Islamic constitution formulated for the country.[38]

Meanwhile, the Prime Minister of Pakistan began to be criticized for his failure to take immediate action in regard to the anti-Ahmadiayya agitation and for many other political issues. He was also held responsible for not being able to have the constitution framed. As a result, the Governor-General dismissed him on 17 April 1953. And by October 1954, a new constitution was prepared on the basis of the amended Basic Principles Committee Report, which bore the influence of the Jamaat-i-Islami and other *Ulama*.[39] The Jamaat declared the new proposed constitution to be Islamic in character to a great extent, and demanded its adoption without further delay. But soon the Governor-General declared a state of emergency in the country and the Constituent Assembly was dissolved on 24 October 1954.

After the dissolution of the first Constituent Assembly another was created, which held its first session in July 1955 and by 29 February 1956 a new constitution was adopted and enforced on 23 March 1956.

The Objectives Resolution of 1949 was incorporated in the constitution as the Preamble. The country would be a Federal Republic to be known as the Islamic Republic of Pakistan. Mawlana Mawdudi felt satisfied with the Preamble, Directive Principles of States Policy, and some other provisions in the constitution. According to him, this constitution had finally and unequivocally settled the eight years old struggle between

---

38. Sayed Riaz Ahmad, *Mawlana Mawdudi and the Islamic State*, Lahore, p. 70.
39. Leonard Binder, *Religion and Politics in Pakistan*, p. 345.

the Islamic and anti-Islamic-trends in favour of Islam.[40] Jamaat launched a countrywide campaign to welcome the 1956 constitution as an Islamic constitution. Jamaat leaders including Mawlana Mawdudi himself spoke to large public gatherings at Peshawar, Rawalpindi and Daska.

But it was not too long when in early 1958, the country under military rule, and with the exception of some brief periods, has remained under the control of the military. But Jamaat-i-Islami under Mawlana Mawdudi and after his death also continues to work for the strengthening of Islamic order in the country.

---

40. Sarwat Saulat, *Speeches of Mawlana Mawdudi*, Eng. tr. quoted in Masudul Hassan, p. 508.

5

Sayyid Abul Hasan Ali Nadwi's Educational Thought and Re-Orientation of History

Birth, Upbringing and the Making of Mawlana Nadwi

FAMILY BACKGROUND

MAWLANA Nadwi comes from a family, which has produced great scholars, thinkers and revolutionaries at regular intervals. Though his forefathers were not very rich in material terms; their scholarship is well-chronicled. Mawlana Nadwi is the proud descendent of luminaries like Mawlana Syed Numan, Mawlana Syed Fakhruddin and Syed Ahmed Shaheed.

Parents of Mawlana Nadwi belonged to the same clan. His paternal grandfather, Maulvi Hakim Syed Fakhruddin was not very well off. In contrast, his maternal grandfather Syed Shah Zia-ul-Haq Nabi was an effluent person. Syed Shah Zia-ul-Nabi was getting offers for his daughter from other influential persons but he preferred to marry his daughter into Fakhruddin's family. The family that did not have any large land holdings or other assets was known as an educated family, which could boast of producing many Islamic scholars. Maulvi Hakim Syed Fakhruddin's house was known as, or called Maulvi family — a mark of respect in Muslim society. By marrying his daughter, Syed Khair-ul-Nisa to Mawlana Syed Abdul Hai, Syed Shah Zia-ul-Nabi clearly gave preference to religious character and faith over material well-being. This decision was taken by Zia-ul-Nabi in spite of stiff opposition from his wife to the proposal. As the two families lived close-by and by virtue of being distant relatives, both families were well aware of financial situation and living standards of each other. Dismissing his wife's protestations and opposition, Zia-ul-Nabi said to her,

> Syed (common name by which Mawlana Nadwi's father was called) is youthful, pious, knowledgeable and able. I will not prefer anyone over him (to marry my daughter). To me, poverty and richness don't mean anything. The real thing to look out for is ability and knowledge.[1]

Knowledge, ability, piousness and devotion towards God were the yardsticks for the alliance, and not the more material things like wealth, position or large estates. Mawlana Nadwi was born to the couple who valued ethics, piousness and knowledge more than anything else and this was to dictate the way Mawlana Nadwi was brought up. The idealism of Mawlana Nadwi's parents was necessarily, to find a way in shaping up his life and this did happen, as we will see in coming chapters.

The marriage was consummated in CE 1904. Syed Abdul Hai started practising medicine, which was their family profession, after the marriage the fortunes of the family turned around. The mud house gave way to a big mansion and in that very house Khair-ul-Nisa gave birth to two daughters in June 1906 and 1907, and Mawlana Nadwi in 1914 (6 Muharram, AH 1333).

---

1. Sayyid Abul Hasan Nadwi Ali, *Karvaan-i-Zindagi* (Urdu), vol. I., Makataba Islami, Lucknow, 1984, p. 31.

Mawlana Nadwi's brother, Dr Syed Abdul Ali, who took up the responsibility of Mawlana Nadwi's education on the death of their fathers, was actually his half-brother, whose mother had died in CE 1901.

The family, Mawlana Nadwi was born in, was full of Islamic scholars and *hufaz* (those who can recite *Holy Qur'an* without any reference to the text). As there was no tradition of formal education for girls, the women in the family would learn the *Holy Qur'an* and study Islamics from their parents and brothers. At least five women — Mawlana Nadwi's elder maternal aunt, his mother, a paternal aunt, a cousin and another aunt (wife of his maternal uncle) were *hafiz*. The womenfolk in the family were inclined to learn the *Holy Qur'an* and *Hadith*, and they would compete amongst themselves to excel in Islamic studies. All the women had learned *Qur'an* from some *moharram*[2] (under Islamic tradition, a male, in whose presence a Muslim woman does not have necessarily to observe *purdah*/veil).

The family did not observe festivals other than the Islamic like two *Eids* and *Eid-i-Milad* (the birthday of Prophet Muhammad SAAS) and desisted from constructing concrete mausoleums or iron railings around graves of their dead.[3] By all standards, the family observed a very puritanical form of Islam in which anything or any practice contrary to the teachings of the *Qur'an* and the *Hadith* was strictly avoided. Keeping in mind that Mawlana Nadwi's father was also a scholar and a teacher, who had written many books on Islam, it was natural that he would be initiated into Islamic studies at a very tender age. The first book Mawlana Nadwi was taught had to be the *Holy Qur'an*. After completing the study

2. Ibid., p. 46.
3. Ibid., p. 38.

of *Qur'an*, Mawlana Nadwi was introduced to Urdu, Persian and modern Arabic.

In addition to these he started studying English language and arithmetic. At the age of 15, Mawlana Nadwi was swayed towards English and modern education as excelling in these brought along highest respect and position in the society. The desire to move towards modern education was accentuated by an event, which took place in 1929 when one of his relatives Hafiz Syed Hassani returned from London after qualifying Indian Civil Services (ICS) and the most of boys (men) in the family were studying modern English education. Again the family background played its part. Mawlana Nadwi's mother did not approve of his leanings towards English education and through many letters advised, suggested, pleaded, cajoled and coaxed him not to move away from Islamic studies. An excerpts from a letter written by his mother quoted in *Zikr-i-Khair* and *Karavaan-i-Zindagi*, vol. I, goes as follows:

> Ali, don't get swayed by what people are telling you. If you wish to receive the blessings of God and fulfil your duties towards me, then look at the people who spent their lives acquiring knowledge of Islam. What was their status? Shah Waliullah, Shah Abdul Aziz, Shah Abdul Qadir, Moulvi Muhammad Ibrahim, and among your ancestors Khawaja Ahmad and Moulvi Muhammad Amin, who were envied in life and revered after their death. Their life was enviable and when they departed, everyone remembered their qualities. How did they acquire such status and esteem? There are many people in the family, who have acquired respect and status by excelling in English education but they are no match to any of these Islamic scholars. . . . Ali, if I had a hundred children I would have liked all of them to go for Islamic studies only. Now there are only you, I pray to God that, may my sincere wishes come true and you may

> prove to be equal to a hundred. And by virtue of it I may also succeed and may be called (*Sahib-i-aulad*) Amen.[4]

These letters, particularly these words changed the course of Mawlana Nadwi's pursuit and life, as he dropped the idea to pursue English education. There are two more incidents, which to a large extend threw light on the environment in which Mawlana Nadwi was brought up and the kind of morals imparted to him. Mawlana Nadwi describes an incident as "A Joke and Test" in the biography, *Karavaan-i-Zindagi*. He along with another taught, was taking tutions from Sheikh Khalil Arab. One day as the teacher Arab had come straightaway from the university, he asked for a cup of tea. He was told that there is no sugar in the house. He gave a rupee to the other student and asked him to fetch a kilogram of sugar. The student, Hussain Ibn Muhammad Arab brought sugar and returned the change — around 14 *ānnās* (in todays' money around 80 *paisa*). The lessons/class continued and after a while the teacher enquired of Hussain, what happened to the change. The student insisted that he had returned it. But the money could not be found anywhere. The teacher said, "Only three of us; you, Ali and I are here, then where did the money go, It appears that you have fallen into some bad habits." The student kept saying that he had returned it. The lessons continued and afterwards the student went home. After a few days, Mawlana Nadwi found the money in one of his books, which was a big one with loose binding. This put Mawlana Nadwi, in his own words, in a fix. He was not sure what to do with the money. Later, he decided to tell the truth and return the money. Commenting on the incident, Mawlana Nadwi writes,

---

4. Ibid., p. 122.

> I don't know whether Arab (the teacher) believed me or not. He took the money without saying a single word. I always thank Allah for giving me the courage to act as I did. Moreover, whenever I remember that incident it makes me laugh.[5]

Another incident that needs a special mention is when in 1946, Mawlana Nadwi shifted to another house in Lucknow and started living separately along with his mother and family. That year he experienced significant financial problems.

> The year was full of constrains and problem. I was unable to understand the reason behind these hard times till the day I came to know that my brother is unhappy with my decision to live separately. He did not like that in spite of living in the same city, we should be housed in different houses. Though I had sought permission prior to shifting to another house. I apologized with tearful eyes and returned to our old house. Thereafter, I can't recall another time, when the times were so trying.[6]

EDUCATION

Having the advantages of being born into a family of scholars and intellectuals, the easiest thing that could come to Mawlana Nadwi was education. The family that virtually lived hand-to-mouth provided ample scope, and space for literary pursuits. Remembering that in early twentieth-century education was not common or as affordable as it might be nowadays, almost a hundred years later. All the male children in their family went to school (in those days formal education of girls was not socially acceptable). Mawlana Nadwi's education started at home with *Holy Qur'an*, Urdu, Persian, Arabic and English

5. Ibid., p. 324.
6. Idem.

followed at various stages of his life. The thrust area of his education chosen for him by his mother and to some extent by his brother was Islamic studies. He himself was interested in formal education that is science and other subjects such as social sciences and humanities, etc. By the glitter of the status and respect, the people mastering these commanded in the society. That was Mawlana Nadwi at the age of fifteen. An average teenager who was destined to face failure once in his life. And the time was approaching fast. As a young boy Mawlana Nadwi struggled to learn. His intelligence, pick-up and retention did not match other boys of his age. Mawlana Nadwi calls the early years of his life as "disappointing childhood.[7]

In August 1927, Mawlana Nadwi got admission into Fazil-e-Adab course in Lucknow University. The said course, in those days was seen to work as a sort of bridge or ladder for *madrassah* (seminary) students in acquiring or obtaining government jobs. Mawlana Nadwi at the time was barely fourteen years old, so he had very little role to play in the decision to sit in the exams. Mawlana Nadwi got admission in the course and appeared in the final examinations of April CE 1928. During the year at the University, Mawlana Nadwi did not discontinue the tutions of Sheikh Khalil Arab.[8]

Mawlana Nadwi's elder medico brother, Syed Abdul Ali, it must be said, did not subscribe to the idea of getting a university degree by sitting in formal university examinations. With a cursory glance at the situations and events leading to Mawlana Nadwi's admission to Fazil-iAdab course at Lucknow University, it is made clear that the driving force behind the decision was Sheikh Khalil Arab, the teacher who

7. Ibid., p. 38.

8. Ibid., p. 103.

gave Mawlana Nadwi tutions at home. Anyway, Mawlana Nadwi was too young, just 14 years of age, to take such a decision having far-reaching consequences. The event is very important in Mawlana Nadwi's life for two reasons. One, he tasted failure in his life and secondly, a smooth sail in examination may have changed the course of Mawlana Nadwi's life. The exams in the April of 1928 gave Mawlana Nadwi a lesson of his life — he failed. The news of his failure gave his mother and his elder brother, who was acting as his guardian, shock. Actually, Mawlana Nadwi's failure disappointed them to the point of dejection. Next year, Mawlana Nadwi passed the examination with flying colours as he topped the class by scoring the highest number of marks.

By virtue of securing first position in the examination, Mawlana Nadwi was entitled to "meritorious scholarship." To avail the scholarship, it was mandatory for the candidate to take admission in another class. As destiny had provided, for Mawlana Nadwi, he got admitted to *Fazil-i-Hadith* course whether it was resigning to fate or the pull of eight rupees a month scholarship; nothing can be said with absolute certainty. Though, Mawlana Nadwi received the *Fazil-i-Adab* certificate in the University Convocation in December 1929. He never bothered to collect the *Fazil-i-Hadith* certificate.[9]

It is more than surmiseable that the failure in *Fazil-i-Adab* examination played a very vital role in the life of Mawlana Nadwi. At least it nullified any changes of Mawlana Nadwi taking up a government job, which was the main objective of these university examinations and people went for these course mostly to pave way for securing a government recognized degree and subsequently a job.

9. Ibid., p. 104.

Besides Islamic studies, the thrust area in Mawlana Nadwi's education was Arabic. Both the modern and archaic nuances of language. To master the language, quite literally, Mawlana Nadwi started taking tutions from Sheikh Khalil Bin Muhammad Arab. Both the parents of this Bhopal-born Arabic teacher were of Yemeni descent. Sheikh Khalil was working as an Arabic Lecturer in Lucknow University.

The mode of teaching was very simple and to some extent archaic. There were only two students in the class, the other one besides Mawlana Nadwi, being the younger brother of the teacher. "For next few years only Arabic, language and literature, was taught to the students."[10]

While at the house of their teacher, the student would talk in Arabic only. Sheikh Khalil was an enthusiastic teacher who took pains to give his student the best. He will subscribe and teach only the latest books of elementary Arabic language, which was taught to children in Arabic-speaking countries like Egypt and Jordan. It would by no means be an exaggeration to say that the language over which Mawlana Nadwi acquired mastery was Arabic. This may be pointed out though again, that Mawlana Nadwi's tremendous command over Arabic and his lack of deep knowledge of sciences should differentiate him from his contemporary Islamic scholars, who invested a very large chunk of their energies in studying modern sciences, European languages and other social sciences. According to Syed Shahabuddin (former Member of Parliament of India):

> During the twentieth century, Muslim India has produced great Islamic theologians, interpreters of the *Qur'an*, scholars

---

10. Mawlana Sayyid Abul Hassan Ali Nadwi, *Puraane Chirag* (Vintage Lamps), vol. I, Maktaba Firdous, Lucknow, 1994, p. 216.

> of *Hadith*, Islamic jurists, historians, propagators of the faith, social reformers and educationists, but one cannot name another Islamic scholar, whose concerns covered the entire spectrum of the collective existence of the Muslim Indians as a living community universal respect, and who was accepted by the non-Muslims, at the highest level, as the legitimate spokesman for the concern and aspirants of the entire community.[11]

Notwithstanding the grumbles/complaints of a "disappointing childhood" (Mawlana Nadwi's words, referred to earlier) he was the scion of an illustrious family which had produced scholars and spiritual preceptors like Shah Almullah Naqshbandi and Syed Ahmad Shaheed. Mawlana Nadwi's father, Hakim Syed Abdul Hai, was an eminent scholar of his time, immortalized by his encyclopaedic work *Nuzhat-ul Khawatir* (in eight volumes) containing about 5000 biographical notes on Muslim scholars, theologians, jurists, etc. men of eminence of India. It is in Arabic, it is considered even in Europe, to be the most precious source book of its kind. His another book *As-Saqafat-ul Islamia Fil Hind* contains a complete history of the Arabic sciences and syllabi in India and detailed description of books and manuscripts left behind by the Indian scholars. It was published in 1957 by Royal Academy of Arts and Letters of Damascus. Born in AH 1333 (1914 CE) Mawlana Nadwi lost his father at the age of nine. His elder brother, Dr. Syed Abdul Ali Hasani who practised medicine at Lucknow, then brought him up. Mawlana Nadwi specialized in Arabic literature at Nadwatul Ulama, Lucknow, studied *Hadith* under Sheikh Husain Ahmad Madni at Darul Ulum, Deoband and *tafsir* (exegesis) under Mawlana Ahmad Ali of Lahore. At Lahore, he came in touch with Sir Muhammad Iqbal, whose

11. *Fragrance of East*, vol. II, no. 1 and 2, January-June, 2000, p. 85.

poetry left an abiding impression on him. Besides literary and theological studies, Mawlana developed keen interest in Islamic history and also learnt English.

He taught Arabic literature and *tafsir* at the Nadwatul Ulama for ten years. After the demise of his elder brother, he became the Secretary of Nadwatul Ullma and subsequently the Rector of the institute. In 1947, he decided against migration when many of his relatives and friends including his mentor, Syed Sulaiman Nadwi chose to migrate to Pakistan.

In his formative years, Mawlana Nadwi was associated with the Jamaat-i-Islami for a few years after its establishment by Mawlana Abul A'Lā Mawdudi. Then he turned to the Tabligi Jamaat founded by Mawlana Ilyas, whose approach and method of working appealed to Nadwi more than any other. Therefore, continued to remain with the programme of Tabligi movement till last.

Spiritually, Mawlana Nadwi was the disciple of Mawlana Abdul Qadir Raipuri[12] and Mawlana belonged to the *Sūfi sisila* Qadiriyya Naqshbandi. Apart from his long association with Nadwatul Ulama, he served on the *shura* (grand council) of the Darul Ulum Deoband, chaired the Managing Committee of Darul Musannifin and established the Academy of Islamic Research and Publications at Lucknow. (See Appendix II.)

A prolific writer preferred to write mostly in Arabic language and Urdu, has written about fifty books on the subject related to Islamic faith, literature, history, and on problems confronting the Muslim in the present time. His works have been prescribed in the courses of study in a number of Arab universities. His notable Arabic work *Maza Khasera al-Alam*

---

12. *Purane Chiraga* (Vintage Lamps), op. cit., vol. 3, p. 132.

b'inhitatil-Muslimeen (what has the world lost by the decline of the Muslims?) was widely acclaimed in the Arab world. This book immediately became a best seller and was warmly received by a great number of Muslim men of letters, particularly in Egypt, where it was first printed, before its translation into Urdu in 1954. Later translated into English under the name of *Islam and the World*. In 1951 Sayyid Qutb (1906-66) wrote an introduction of this book in which the term *jahilliyya* (religious ignorance) as a description of contemporary European civilization is singled out. This book, like many others served to heighten Qutb's idea of the exclusive nature of Islam. As its title indicates, the book primarily seeks to explain the decline of Islam by offering a historical account of its rise, expansion and gradual regression. Nadwi's depiction of "Muslim decadence" which is seen to have taken place under the Ottomans, is followed by a grim description of the genealogy of Western civilization, embracing the Greeks, the Romans, Christianity, materialism, the theory of evolution, nationalism and scientific progress. His verdict is unambiguous: "Christian Europe" has become in its entire civilization "Pagan and Materialistic" (*jahilliya-madiyya*). Nadwi in this book points out that the Muslims have been forced to join in this mad pursuit of materialism, turning into "mere passengers" in a train driven by west. Nevertheless, he asserts, the Muslims are essentially immune to outright "Pagan Materialism" since their spiritual heritage is still "Preserved in its pristine purity."[13] The book aims at to stir the Muslims into an appreciation of Islam's glorious role in the story of human progress, and to instill in them, thereby, a desire to look into

13. Abul Hasan Ali Nadwi, *Mazaha Kasir-al-'Alam bi Inshitat al-Muslimin*, 10th edn., Dar al-Ansar, Cairo, 1977, pp. 279, 85 or see English translation *Islam and the World*, tr. by M. Asif Qidwai, The Academy of Islamic Research Publication, Lahore, 1961, p. 181.

themselves, with a view to finding out how far they have been true to their duty and mission to the world. It presents Islam as an eternal reality and a programme of life which can never grew obsolete.

A number of his Arabic and Urdu works have since been translated in English, Turkish, Bhasha Indonesia, Persian, Tamil, etc. He was awarded Shah Faisal International Award for his service to the cause of Islam in 1980. Some of Mawlana Nadwi's works in Urdu are *Karavaan-i-Zindagi,* his autobiography in eight volumes, and *Purane Chiragh* (Vintage Lamps), his biography of Syed Ahmad Shaheed, his biography of Hazrat Ali, (RA) and *Tarikh-e-Dawat-o-Azimat* (Saviours of Islamic Spirit), are worth mentioning. Mawlana Nadwi has been a honorary member of the Academy of Art and Letters, Damascus and Academy of Arabic language, Amman and served as a Visiting Professor in various Arab universities (see Appendix II). He carries the distinction of being one of the Founder Members of the Rabita-Alam-il-Islami, Mecca besides serving on the Higher Council of the Islamic University, Rabat and as the Chairman of the Board for the Centre of Islamic Studies of the Oxford University. Mawlana Nadwi was never involved in active politics nor did he participate in electoral politics. He did not even join the All India Muslim Majlis, established by his protégé Dr. A.J. Farid in 1967, as it took to electoral politics. Mawlana Nadwi was one of the founders of the All India Muslim Majlis-i-Mushawrat (1964), the All India Muslim Personal Law Board (1972) and the All India Dini Talimi Council. He presided over the Milli Convention in 1979.

To promote communal harmony, Mawlana Nadwi became one of the founders of the FOCUS, which was later transformed into Society for Communal Harmony. He also established a

Movement called "Payam-i-Insaniyat" (The Message of Humanity) to preach universal love and brotherhood.

Educational Thought

Mawlana Abul Hasan Ali Nadwi was destined to become a religious scholar, circumstances as well as he himself consecrated his whole life to the learning and teaching of religious education. Mawlana Nadwi belonged to the family of Syed Ahmad Shaheed (1786-1831) which produced a number or renowned scholars and Mujahidin in the subcontinent. His father Mawlana Hakim Syed Abdul Hai, was a reputed writer, physician, as well as an erudite Islamic scholar. His published works include an eight-volume literacy encyclopaedia in Arabic, *Nuzhatul Khawatir*, and two historical works in the both Arabic and Urdu, on the History of Islamic Culture in India and India during the Islamic period. His mother, Khayr un-Nisa Begum, who had memorized the *Holy Qur'an* by heart (a *hafizah*). As his father died in early age, it was the desire of his mother as well as his elder brother Hakim Hafiz Dr Abdul Ali (1901-61) who directed and guided him single-mindedly in pursuing religious education.

Mawlana Nadwi was educated in Darul Ulum Nadwatul Ulama, Lucknow, Qasimul Ulum, Lahore and Darul Ulum, Deoband. These three were amongst the most eminent colleges of Islamic education in the northern India. He specialized in Arabic literature at Nadwatul Ulama Lucknow, studied *Hadith* under Sheikh Husain Ahmad Madni at Darul Ulum, Deoband and *tafsir* under Mawlana Ahmad Ali of Lahore. Apart from other institutions of learning Nadwatul Ulama, Lucknow was his main centre of learning, He entered Nadwa in 1929 where he had opportunity to study under some illustrious teachers such as Sheikh Khalil Bin Muhammad Ansari (d. 1966) Professor Taqvi al-din Hilaly (d. 1987) and visiting professors like Sayyid Sulaiman Nadwi (d. 1373/1953) later in August 1934. Mawlana Nadwi joined the Nadwa as a teacher of *adab* and *tafsir* (literature and *Qur'anic* studies) though he bloomed as polymath— scholar, writer author, historian, leading spokesman on India and International scene as well as his sense of duty and consciousness towards Islam and Muslims. He was by inclination, a teacher in the tradition of classical Islamic tradition of history. Despite his all other activities and engagement at national and international level Nadwa remained his main concern throughout his longevity.

Nadwa was his *alma mater* and had some sort of family connection with it. His father Sayyid Abul Hai, had helped, together with Mawlana Sayyid Muhammad Ali Monghyri and Allama Shibli Numni (d. 1914) to found in 1311/1893 Nadwatul Ulama (scholars society) prescursor of Darul Ulum, Nadwatul Ulama, Lucknow. He had also served as Secretary General of the Islamic school Dar ul-Ulum Nadwatul Ulama which was founded by Nadwatul Ulama in 1316/1898. Mawlana Nadwi's elder brother and guardian Dr. Abdul Ali served as rector of Nadwatul Ulama, Darul Ulum for thirty years from 9 June 1931 uptill his death 7 May 1961.[14] After his death Mawlana Nadwi assumed the rectorship of Nadwa till death.

Therefore, the educational thought of Mawlana Nadwi reflects thought in essence assumed by the *nadawah* itself. Nadwatul Ulama was conceived as a middle of the road institution between the extremes of Aligarh's "secularism" and Deoband's rigid conservatism.[15] If Deoband symbolizes Muslim conservatism, Aligarh represents Muslim modernism

14. Mawlana Nadwi's Address to Executive Congress (Report) of Nadwatul Ulama held on 18 June 1961, p. 5.

15. Aziz Ahmad, *Islamic Modernism in India and Pakistan* 1857-1964, Oxford University Press, London, 1967, p. 109.

in the nineteenth century. Deoband from its inception was oriental and Islamic in character, and has given Persian and Arabic the same privileged position that medieval institutions of higher learning had given them. This institution was established after the failure of the uprising of 1857 with the purpose of establishing a centre, not only a response to the challenge of Western knowledge alone, but the response to a whole gamut of challenges that were posed before the Muslims in the nineteenth century as a result of their exposure to Western culture.[16] Therefore, anti-British from its inception as is evident from the life and work of its veterans like Mawlana Qasim Nanwati (d. 1880), Mawlana Rashid Ahmad Gangohi (d. 1905), Mawlana Mahmud Hasan (1851-1921), Mawlana Obaidullah Sindhi (1872-1944) and Mawlana Husain Ahmad Madani (1879-1957), Aligarh, on the other hand, professed itself to be modern and secular institution, where English held the position of privilege. It was pro-British from the outset as a matter of policy, and remained so all long despite many efforts to change its stand, especially during the period of Balkan war and *khilāfat* movement.[17] In spite of being diametrically opposite in almost all major areas related to education and political life of the country Deoband and Aligarh had some common basic points. Both of them were responses, though vastly different from one another, to the same challenge that was posed by the Western knowledge and culture during nineteenth century. Therefore, both were part of the same educational movement, which started in response to the challenge of Western education. The second common point

16. Sayed Masroor Ali Akhter Hashmi, *Muslim Response to Western Education*: A Study of Four Pioneer Institutions, Commonwealth, Pub., New Delhi, 1989, p. 38.

17. Ibid., p. 73.

between the two was their profession of being institutions established for the cultural and educational upbringing of Muslim youth. Their difference lay in their interpretation of the terms "culture" and "education."[18]

Establishment of Darul Ulum Deoband in 1867 and M.A.O. College in 1875 were Muslim response to the challenge of Western education and culture. However, in education and politics they had taken different stands. Deoband was too conservative to give any allowance to liberal arts, modern sciences and English language. Aligarh was progressive enough to give position of privilege to these secular studies. These institutions provided reference models for the future Muslim educational institutions, which tried to strike some sort of balance between the two institutions, so was Darul Ulum Nadwatul Ulama.

Mawalana Muhammad Ali Monghyri (1846-1927), Mawlana Shibli (1857-1914) and a group of other *'Ulama* founded Nadwatu al-'Ulamā', congregation of *'Ulamā*, on the occasion of annual convocation (*dastarbnadhi*) of Madrasah Faid-i-Am Kanpur in 1892, with a purpose of reforming the old educational system and bringing about unity among *'Ulamā* holding different views on religious matters, with Mawlana Muhammad Ali Monghyri its first organizer. In his first congress address Mawlana Shibhli stressed *Ulama* to play a viable role in the society, keeping in view the practicalities of space and time and to equip themselves with necessary requirements to face the challenges of modern times.

> Unprepared to re-adjust their role and their learning to this challenging state of affairs, the *'Ulama* of Muslim India had sunk into apathy and fossilized dogma, concerning

18. Ibid., p. 74.

> themselves exclusively with insignificant minutiae of ritual and in fruitless disputations. Instead they might have given the Muslim community in India a moral lead. They might have continued the reformist mission of *Wali-Allah*, preaching against superstition and extravagance. They might have tried to propagate a broad-minded view of Islam among the masses.
>
> It was clearly the responsibility of religious leaders to counterbalance the scientific trends of agnosticism, scepticism, and atheism and they should strive to offer an enlightened interpretation of religion. . . . Their principal intellectual responsibility was, however, to develop a new *ilm al-kalām*, a modern system of theological dialectics to meet the challenges of atheism, just as the medieval scholars al-Razi, al-Ghazzali and Averroes integrated Greek thought into a framework which was as rationalistic as it was basically Islamic.[19]

The essence of the letters of Mawlana Monghyri reflected the same idea, which he despatched to *'Ulamā* for acquittance with the aims and objectives of the Nadwatul 'Ulama and an invitation to join hands with. The gist of those letters were:

> Those students who complete their education in Arabic *madrasahs* are only ignorant of the ways of the world, and so dependent of others, but are also ignorant of the religious knowledge essential for modern times. This organization, therefore, wants to recognize the system of education in a manner so that the students may be educated on proper lines.

---

19. Mawlana Shibli Numani, Address to First Congress of Nadwatul Ulama held on 12 April, 1895, reprinted in Rasail (Amritsar, 1911), pp. 1-16. quoted from Aziz Ahmad, *Islamic Modernism*, pp. 109-10.

> Further, the organization will try to bring the *'Ulama* closer to each other, as the difference between them serve no useful purpose and humiliate Islam in the eyes of its foes.[20]

The whole of the idea was later promulgated into six specific objectives such as: progress of education; reform in the system of education; moral regeneration; propagation of Islam, removal of mutual differences; and knowledge of welfare of the followers of Islam.[21]

Finally, Darul Ulum Nadwatul 'Ulama was established in 1898 in Lucknow. It is curriculum was framed to meet the challenges of modern times. Till then the Arabic *madrasah*s used to impart religious education of a general nature. It was thought that the courses of studies framed some two hundred years ago by Mulla Nizamuddin, known as Dars-i-Nizami, had lost much of their usefulness with respect to modern challenges facing Muslims. Therefore, a sustained effort was made by the founders of Nadwatul Ulama to reframe the courses of studies prevalent in Arabic *madrasah*s. The curriculum engaged the attention of the Ulama of Nadwa so much that many times syllabus were reframed and revised. The course of studies of the Darul Ulum was revised several times during the Nizamat of Mawlvi Syed Ali Hasan Khan and that of Syed Abdul Ali.[22] In spite of numerous efforts, the course of studies in the Nadwatul Ulama could not go far from Dars-i-Nizami, especially in the area of theology. There are many reasons for

---

20. Re*port of the Nadwatul Ulamā'*, part I, 1894, Intizar Press, Kanpur, pp. 23-24. quoted from Sayyid Mansoor, *Muslim Response*, pp. 120-21.

21. Dasturul Amal Nadwatul Ulama, Article, 4, p. 2, included in the report of the Nadwatul Ulama, 1915, Shahi Press, Lucknow, n.d.

22. Mawlana Abdus Salam Qidwari, *Nadwatul Ulama ke Pachasi Sal*, Daftar-i-Ijlas Nadwatul Ulama, Lucknow, 1975, pp. 17, 19.

it, one may be reluctance on the part of many conservative *'Ulama* to switch over to new courses. Whatever may be the reason but the absence of worthwhile books on modern subjects would also have contributed to delay in inclusion of new subjects in the course of studies.[23] Notwithstanding, its commitment to response modern challenges. In the eyes of some scholars it drfited towards conservative orthodoxy, in time its scholars and their work became indistinguisable from those of Deoband.[24] Finally in Nadwah the course in rational sciences was considerably reduced and more emphasis was laid on Arabic literature and Islamic history. English language paper and sometimes Sanskrit were also included in the syllabus to equip students to meet the challenges and defend Islam against the critics. Emphasis on Arabic literature and language in Nadwah, has therefore, augmented the competence of the students in writtings and spoken Arabic. It served the purpose of helping the students to study the religious texts in more meaningful manner, and to interact with Arabic world.

It should, however, be acknowledged that the Darul Ulum Nadwatul Ulamā', endeavoured to frame a course of studies, which might represent sufficient elements of the new education in it. It made some experiences in the field of the education and remained less rigid in accepting reasonable changes in the courses and methods though with some very specific and limited purposes. In contrast to Deoband and other *madrasahs*, Nadwah meant a rapprochement between the old and the new.

Dr. Hakim. Mawlana Sayyid Abdul Ali who served as the rector (*nazim*) of Nadwah for 30 years was a Doctor (M.B.B.S), Hakim (Unani medicine expert) also on *hafiz* (memorized

23. Sayed Masroor, *Muslim Response*, pp. 130, 133.

24. Aziz Ahmad, *Islamic Modernism*, p. 112.

Qur'an) *qari* of the holy *Qur'an* and had acquired a comprehensive knowledge of religious and traditional sciences at Deoband as well as an excellent student of Sheikh ul Hind Mawlana Mahmud Hasan. A multi-faceted personality, whom Mawlana Abdul Hassan Ali Nadwi cherished as living role model of Nadwa, in him the traditional and modern were combined. He was a practical example what the founders of Nadwa had thought 60 or 70 years before. He was an authority on religious sciences as well as modern sciences, a practising physician. He was a culmination of endeavours to bridge the gap between religious and modern education as well as paragon of piety and conscientiousness.[25]

These are the role models, which formed the educational thought of Nadwah as well as Mawlana Nadwi. Two other personalities who influenced Mawlana Nadwi were Allama Iqbal (1875-1938) and Mawlana Muhammad Ali Jawhar (1878-1931), both were educated in West but returned without losing to Western culture. They were not like those who lost everything to West, who became westoxicated and renegaded against their own culture and community. Iqbal and Muhammad Ali Jawher instead returned triumphat and served their own culture and community. Mawlana Nadwi took pride in the fact that of those from Muslim world who had gone to British universities particularly to Oxford and Cambridge and these both personalities of East had returned as rebels, untainted and uncorrupted by any un-Islamic influence or affection. He did not know of any such "rebels" in other countries.[26]

Mawlana Nadwi was not against the modern education rather the education, which turns a person against his own

25. Mawlana Nadwi, Address to Executive Congress (Report) of Nadwatul Ulama, held on 18 June 1961, pp. 1, 3.

26. Mawlana Nadwi, *Dawati Fikr wa Amal* (Urdu), Majlis Tahkikat wa Nashriyati Islami, Lucknow, 1999, pp. 126, 29.

culture and thought. He contends the education and university both serve the purpose of particular culture and culture represents the world-view. Therefore, the philosophy of education of a given society should be in the context of its own culture. It should not create tension and confusion in a society.[27] He stresses that university should also work for personality and character building instead of producing only experts of particular subject.[28] According to him, the aim of education is to provide self-sacrificing Islamic intellectual leadership that can take efficiently and skilfully the complex problems of modern Muslim society from an Islamic perspective and can provide workable and viable Islamic structures and institutions for the establishment of justice in the society.

As Mawlana Nadwi asserts "the foremost task of the university in character building. Their endeavour should be to produce men who, in the words of Allama Iqbal, may not be willing to sell their conscience for 'a handful of barely' . . . the real success of university lies in moulding the personality of its scholars in a way and giving such citizens to the society who do not put themselves up to auction nor can be lured away by a destructive ideologies or misguided movement — secondly, our universities ought to send forth men who may be ready to sacrifice their lives for the sake of truth, knowledge, reform and uplift, and derive the same satisfaction from going without food as people, generally, do from eating and drinking to their hearts content, and to whom loss appears to be more worth while than again."[29]

27. Ibid., pp. 112-13.

28. Ibid., pp. 120-21.

29. Ibid., pp. 121-22, also seel Mawlana Nadwi — The Place of Knowledge and Responsibility of those who acquire it. (Speech delivered by him at the seventh convocation of the Univesity of Kashmir, held on 29 October 1981, pp. 12-13.

In its totality, the concept of *'ilm* in Islam is very vast. It ranges in meaning from a *sūfī*'s deep understanding of truth (*marifat*) to the scholar's interpretation of knowledge as it concerns the everyday activities of the individual. *Ilm,* in general, is divided into two categories; revealed knowledge, which basically includes the *Qur'an* and the *Sunnah,* and the knowledge that is acquired through experience, observation and systematic research. *Ilm* is mentioned in the *Qur'an* with unusual frequency and has been paired, in verse 30: 56 with *iman* (faith), which accordingly in the verse 3: 71 follows knowledge. The pursuit of *ilm,* according to a *Hadith,* is incumbent upon every Muslim.[30] However, *ilm* becomes a value only if it is pursued within the value-framework of Islam. Unlike the hackneyed Western phrase of "knowledge for knowledge's sack" or the convoluted assertion that "all knowledge is good." Islam considers *ilm* as a value and an act of *ibadah* only when it is pursued for the benefit of the individual or the community and ultimely, to seek the pleasure of Allah. *Ilm* has to be value-based and must have function and a purpose. In other worlds, knowledge is not for its own sake but serves as a way to success in this life and in the next, and not all kinds of knowledge would serve that purpose. Therefore, according to Nadwi, "the universities should see to what extent they are being successful in producing men of real worth and merit. The greatness of a country does not depend on the number of the universities it has. This criterion has, now become outdated. The real thing is how many of its citizens are endowed with an awareness of their duties and obligations and come forward to dedicate themselves to the attainment and promotion of knowledge, growth and development of moral virtues, and suppression of evils like

30. Al-Tabarani, al Mujam al-Awsat, 4: 245.

corruption, greed, cruelty and injustice. How many of them are able to rise above personal considerations and lift the country to a higher cultural and spiritual level."[31] This is only possible, when education is value based . . . therefore, purposeful knowledge.

In contrast to some conservative *Ulama* Mawlana Nadwi regards no division or compartmentalization of education into religious and mundane (secular) rather held the view that the knowledge is reality or human experience. In Mawlana Nadwi's words:

> Knowledge, I believe is one and indivisible, and to separate it into parts, into ancient and modern, religious and secular Eastern and Western, and ideological and practical is incorrect. As Iqbal has said 'talk of modern and ancient is the sigh of narrowness of vision' I regard knowledge a truth, which is gift of God and does not and should not belong to a particular race or community. I see unity even in its diversity. That unity is truth, the search for the truth, the aptitude for it, and the joy of its realization. [32]

Therefore, according to Mawlana Nadwi, it can be implied that all sciences should be taught from a holistic perspective. Islam provides guidance for human life in such a way as to achieve peace, honour and dignity in the present life and success in the next. Thus the whole system of education needs to be infused with the spirit of Islam.[33] Then only there will be peace of mind and soul. It Seems That Mawlana Nadwies Views regarding education Concurs whith the scholars who believe that there is misunderstanding in certain section of Muslims

31. Nadwi, *The Place of Knowledge*, pp. 13-14 and also see his *Dawat Fikr wa Amal*, p. 122.
32. Nadwi, *Dawat Fikr wa Amal*, p. 107, and also Nadwi, *The Place of Knowledge*, op. cit., pp. 7-8.
33. Ibid., pp. 110-11.

about the character of proper Islamic education. Most Muslims nowadays speak of religious education as something quite apart from education as a whole, as if it meant the teaching of *fiqh* only. From the proper Muslim standpoint, all education is alike religious. In a real Muslim school there would be no separate religious instructions, just as in a real Muslim state there would be no separate religious institutions. The state itself would be religious institutions. In the same way the school itself would be religious institution. All the point of *fiqh* would be brought out in the course of teaching other subjects.

Islam is the religion of daily life. It includes a man's whole life and it includes a man's whole education. At present it is made to seem something apart from the mainstream of life, requiring separate instructions and a different attitude of mind. That is altogether un-Islamic. No such terms as "secular" and "religious" exist in proper Muslim phraseology. The terms in which we have to think are "good" and "evil." We have to bring religion back to daily life and that can be done only by claiming modern education as our own and making it — the whole of it — Islamic.[34] This has been the endeavours and philosophy of education of Mawlana Nadwi as well as the many Islamic thinkers.

Mawlana Nadwi asserts that this religion of Islam could never be separate from knowledge, because the first message Muslim received is *iqra* read.

Read (O Muhammad SAAS): In the name of thy Lord.

Who created

Created man out of a (mere) clot of congealed blood,

---

34. Marmoduke Pickthal, "Education — A Comprehensive View" *Harmony*, April–June, 2000, p. 40.

Read: And thy Lord is Most Bountiful

He who taught (the use of the) pen,

Taught man that which he knew not.[35]

Even in this first Qur'anic verse Muslims are instructed to read, acquire knowledge. Therefore, a real Muslim cannot remain without knowledge, which is indispensable.[36] Furthermore human intelligences was hallowed and exalted in Islam. Again and again, in the *Holy Qur'an*, Muslims are adjured to use the mind, which Allah has given mankind in order to discriminate in matters of religion and belief. Mawlana Nadwi says,

> Even in this initial instalment of the Revelation, this first shower of the Rain of Mercy, the lord and cherishes of the worlds did not put off the proclamation that the destiny of learning was bound up with pen. The Revelation is sent down, for the first time, to the unlettered Prophet in an illiterate country, where what to speak of educational institution, even bare literacy was rare, and contacts is established, after hundreds of years, between sky and earth, and it begins with Read. He who did not know how to read or write is being commanded to Read. It signified that the community that was given to him would not be a mere student, but teacher of the world and bearer of knowledge. It would promote learning among the mankind. The era that had been granted to him would not be an era of darkness and ignorance, but of progress and enlightenment.[37]

According to him,

> It, further, unfolded the great reality that knowledge was

35. *Al-Qur'an*, XCVI: 1-5.

36. Nadwi, *Dawat Fikr wa Amal*, pp. 116, 118.

37. Idem and also Nadwi, *The Place of Knowledge*, pp. 9-10.

> infinite. It was without end. He taught man that which he knows not. What is science? What is technology? Man is going to the moon. We have conquered space, and pulled the rope of the earth. It is not a miracle.[38]

Therefore he asserts when the foundation of the message of religion is laid with this concept, how it can be indifferent to knowledge and science.[39] Furthermore, whatever is needed, is that the knowledge and science should not go astray from the fundamental concepts and belief rather should develop from it and there should not be any doubt or confusion between heart and mind. Thus, the whole system of education needs to be infused with the spirit of Islam.

In the worlds of Mawlana Nadwi, the urge of knowledge is natural in man. It is in his instinct to have knowledge. It is God's gift. It is the need of the world. God created it to develop and flourish.[40] In contrast to other religions, Islam always encouraged its followers to acquire knowledge. Human intelligence was hallowed and exalted in Islam. While as in Christendom it was regarded as an enemy to religion for the simple reason that it questioned, seeking truth, as against dogma; so the priests condemned it. Church tried to suppress knowledge and lost the battle. The conflict between religion and science was in west. In Europe and America science was in conflict with religion and they gave rise to the thought that religion and knowledge cannot progress together. Islam had nothing to do with it.[41] There is no reason for such conflict in Islamic countries. There was no such conflict in the hey-day

---

38. Ibid., pp. 119, and ibid., p. 12.
39. Ibid., p. 119.
40. Ibid., p. 114.
41. Ibid., pp. 113, 115, also see Mawlana Nadwi, *Ek Aham Takreer* (Urdu), Deeni-Talimi Council, Lucknow, 1972, pp. 7, 9.

of Islam, when science was pursued as religious duty. Islam has always emphasized the acquisition of knowledge as obligation and that it has to be acquired in the name of and for the sake of Allah. Therefore, it is understandable why the mosques emerged, *inter alia*, as active centres of learning, and have remained so throughout the last fourteen centuries. The mosque-related educational institutions such as those centred in the mosques of Medinah and Mecca, al Fustat Mosuq (in old Cairo), al-Zaytunah in Tunis, al-Qarawiyyin in Fez, Morocco, (in Qurtubah (Cordova) Mosque in Spain and al-Azhar in Cairo preceded the known formal universities outside the Islamic world by centuries. Quite a few of these institutions are still intact and functioning.

During the first five centuries of Hijri era (from the seventh to tweleth century CE), Muslims exhibited an insatiable desire as well as immense capacity to learn, which led to a phenomenal efflorescence of Islamic thought. In the early period of Islam, while the learning of Arabic language and Islamic studies was considered of vital importance, Muslims also assimilated the entirety of knowledge available at that time. Thus the Muslims acquired in a short period of time the contributions of a number of civilizations — Indian, Persian, Iranian, Egyptian, Greek and Roman. This open-minded attitude stemmed from the realization that knowledge is the legacy of all humanity, and it is the duty of every intelligent human being to critically review, appropriate and preserve it. Hence Muslims tried hard to have access to all available knowledge which seemed to be of any use, and once they had done so they further enriched it by their numerous contributions. In the course of time Islamic civilization reached it zenith and made most significant advancement in almost all fields of knowledge, including the natural science. It is pertinent to recall that in their scholastic pursuit Muslims had recourse to the empirical method, which they developed and refined.

If there is something wrong with science as applied today, that is not due to science itself but to the divorce of science from religion. The use of scientific discoveries which ought to be of benefit to all mankind, for selfish individual or national gain, for the advantage of one individual or group at the expense of others, or the enslavement or destruction of one national by another, happens because the people using such inventions have not the Islamic ideal of progress of mankind as a whole. They have no supreme, religious, thinking head, no sacred law of undenied authority. In short in Qur'anic phrase, "without guidance" in such matters; which are regarded by them as outside the provision of religion.[42]

As a matter of fact, in Islam there is no concept of science for its own sake nor of knowledge for its own sake. Everything is for an end, which is to use knowledge for the good of humanity and to earn the pleasure of Allah. The Islamic approach to the cultivation of knowledge has always been holistic, an approach that seeks to integrate the sacred and the temporal. Muslim philosophical thought and scientific knowledge have essentially had a moral and religious base. Therefore, Muslim scientists in their golden era were always guided by moral purposiveness and, consequently, were not disposed to the deployment of scientific knowledge for exploitive and destructive ends.

According to Mawlana Nadwi,

> Being a "natural" religion, Islam lays a great stress on the pursuit of knowledge and urges mankind to take the fullest advantage of all the useful branches of learning. It calls

42. Marmaduke Pickthall, op. cit., p. 41.

> upon its followers to be ready to defend the faith and to build-up their strength so much as to act as a deterrent to the wicked ambitions of the enemies of truth and other self-seeking adventurers.[43]

Substantiating his statement with the Qur'anic verses (Aal-i-Imran 90-91 and Al-Anfal: 60) and similar tradition of Prophet (SAAS) which reads as "knowledge is the last property of the Muslim. Wherever it may be found, it is his (*Tirmizi*). Mawlana Nadwi insisted upon the Muslims to take lead in acquiring modern scientific knowledge, which is in accordance with the Islam. Therefore, according to him:

> A country which seeks to ignore the challenges of modern civilization by withdrawing into its shell and shutting its mind to the mighty changes that are taking place around it has no future in the present context of things. . . . Human nature never looks back, nor does it tolerate a vacuum. It is always looking ahead, moving forward. It neither tires nor halts nor gives way to despair. It always on the lookout for the fresh and the new. Adventure is into its blood. It believes in constant struggle and relentless endeavour. All the time it is in quest of advancement and supremacy, of new and newer glory.

The attitude of rejection and withdrawal is emphatically futile. It is bound, ultimately, to fail. It cannot confer immunity against the mounting pressure of modern civilization to the country, which adopts it. It cannot hold back from it the tide of Western civilization, which will at first seep into it through the crevices and then sweep over it once the breach has been made.[44]

---

43. Nadwi, *Western Civilization — Islam and Muslims*, Academy of Islamic Research and Publication, Lucknow 1969, pp. 7, 8.

44. Ibid., pp. 8-9.

Therefore, the attitude of negation and rejection and strict refrain from making use of the fruits of culture and civilization offered by the West including even such branches of knowledge in which the Western people enjoy a monopoly, as for instance, the martial sciences and technology, will be potently foolish and short-sighted. Consequently, such attitude results in further backwardness and total isolation from the main current of time.[45]

However, there is misunderstanding concerning the nature of modern scientific education. Marmaduke Pickthall (an early convert to Islam from Europe who lived in pre-Independence India, he is the author of many valuable books on Islam, including a comprehensive translation of the *Holy Qur'an*) puts this misunderstanding into these words:

> Those Muslims who regard modern scientific education as something altogether foreign to Islam are hardly less absurd than such a man, who refuses to acknowledge his own son merely because that son had grown to manhood since he last beheld him; who used such arguments as these. My son was small and weak, he had a little voice, and no hair on his face. This creature, on the other hand, is big and strong, he has a deep loud voice and wears beard. Therefore, he is quite a stranger to me.

For this great forward movement is not child of Christendom. Medieval Christendom contained no germ of such a thing. It is the offspring of the old enlightened days of Islam. It was the Muslim scientists, who first hit on the inductive method of reasoning, to which this great material advancement is mainly due. That method can indeed, be traced to the *Qur'an* itself. It was the contact and example of Islam. It was the

45. Ibid., pp. 6-7.

teaching of the Muslim universities, which gave that shock and impulse to Christendom, which resulted in the renaissance and the reformation; liberating Europe from the bondage of ecclesiastics and leading to the era of free thought and free enquiry.[46]

Furthermore, Islam has never proved to be barrier to progress and science. History cannot cite the instance of any other religion, that has given such encouragement to scientific progress as Islam did. Who, indeed, can know this better than the Europeans themselves, for, is it not to Islam and to the Muslims that Europe owes its intellectual and cultural rebirth after it had been sinking deeper and deeper in barbarism from the fifth to the tenth centuries? In the words of Robert Briffault,

> It is highly probable that but for the Arabs modern European civilization would not have arisen at all, it is absolutely certain that but for them, it would not have assumed the character, that has enabled it to transcend all previous phases of evolution.[47]

Keeping in view the whole contemporary scenario, advancement of West and decline of Muslims, Mawlana Nadwi suggests,

> The educational system ought to be reorganized soon in the light of a harmonious blending between contemporary knowledge and needs and aspirations and the basic ideals of Islam. It should be made true representative of the spirit of the faith as well as of the times so that the rising generations of Muslim may be equipped properly to meet the demands of both, and can be firm like a rock where spiritual belief, morality, constancy, honour and self-

46. Marmaduke Pichthall, op. cit., p. 40.
47. Quoted from Nadwi, *Islam and the World*, p. 9.

> reliance are concerned and, at the same time, be lagging behind no one in matters of knowledge, creativeness and intellectual maturity, and, able to respond to the challenges of the West with courage, faith and vision.[48]

As conceived by Mawlana Nadwi, there can be no other way to the resolution of contemporary crises in the Muslim mind to the peace, progress and self-reliance than the appreciation of the hard relatives of the situations and in meeting them with courage, foresight and genuine Islamic understanding. Its aim is to provide to the Muslim *ummah* a vision, and a sound and ideologically-oriented methodology to confront the contemporary challenges. Islamic re-awakening and moral and spiritual re-orientation according to the Islamic world-view and the absolute values of Islam needs to be implemented.[49] With regard to the Western civilization he advocates its critical appraisal rather than severing all the links with it, or spurning all its achievements. As he writes,

> The components that had gone into the making of Western civilization were good as well as bad, true as well as false and beneficial as well as harmful. There were found among them intellectual conclusions, that were the fruits of profound study and observation and also those which could only be described as immature, slipshod and puerile. Some of their ingredients like the experimental science transcended the barriers of race, geography and politics and were universal in their scope while others were typically Western, both in the form and character and bore exclusively the stamp of Western social and historical experience.[50]

---

48. Nadwi, *Western Civilization*, p. 29.
49. Ibid., pp. 28-29.
50. Ibid., p. 6.

Therefore, Mawlana Nadwi suggests to be selective in adopting from West, only good, useful and compatible with moral and spiritual heritage are to be taken. Anything which can contribute to the strength and stability or prove helpful in the preaching and propagation of the word of God must not be rejected simply because it is foreign or Western.[51] As far as cultural and civilization interaction between different nations is concerned, Islam not only considers it to be legitimate but even encourages it. Islam does not erect barriers of prejudice between nations that would preclude "cultural exchange" between them.

However, Mawlana Nadwi vehemently criticized the blind imitation and servility to Western civilization and its social cultural ideals and materialistic form of life. He opposed the wholesale Westernization but not to acquiring Western knowledge as such. In one of his famous booklet entitled *An Apostasy that has no Abu Bakr for it.*[52] He pointed out the dangers of a new kind of apostasy that had appeared in the wake of Western cultural onslaught on the world of Islam. It was coming along with the modern education. It was the most massive ever apostasy movement since the time of the Prophet (SAAS). As against previous waves of apostasy. This one had a different character. Those who had become apostates under its influence did not deny God, and did not go to a church, temple or elsewhere to announce of their change of religion. Nor does the Islamic society take any notice of someone, who betrayed the signs of this new kind of apostasy. No Muslim

51. Ibid., pp. 29-30.

52. Originally two editorials that Mawlana Nadwi wrote during 1958, for the magazine Al-Muslimun brought out from Damascus, later were combined into one entitled "An Apostasy that has no Abu Bakr for it."

ever boycotts them and no one ever sees any difference between this apostate and the true Muslims. A large number of the educated class had already caught the disease, and seemed to be beyond cure. But the new generation had to be saved. He pointed out the dangers of neglecting the new, stealthily but fast-advancing melody which would eat away at Muslim *ummah*'s root and branch from within like termites eat away at wood. What was required was a firm resolve to fight it out, with new educational institution, new literature and most of all, new resolve.[53] This shows his concern about the Western educated (westoxicated) and Western education, which not only is against Islamic ideals but also adamant to destroy it therefore, need to be contained.[54]

The West has developed a particular system of life with its starting points and hypotheses, which it naturally regards as valid. Islam is at odds with it since it has its own philosophy and concepts, its own vision and world-view. The Islamic theory of knowledge is based upon a spiritual conception of man and the universe which is his habitat, while as Western theory of knowledge is secular, whose metaphysical basis lies in the ontological barrier separating man and God. It affirms the applicability and empirical and scientific methods to every field of inquiry. It also rejects every form of knowledge that has its basis in the assumption that there is any reality beyond our worldly existence. It basis its instrument of knowledge exclusively upon the senses and human reason, which enable man to discover laws of development inherent in a rationally ordered world. It not merely separates reason from revelation but also tends to down play the latter as a means of knowledge.

---

53. Mawlana Nadwi, An Apostasy that has no Abu Bakr for it.
54. Mawlana Nadwi, *Dawat Fikr wa Amal*, p. 130, 136.

Furthermore, it has eschewed moral and ethical question and has aspired to make science objective and value-neutral. It tends to describe all phenomena in terms of the observed and the observable. Consequently, first of all philosophy came to be regarded as the product of reason alone. This led to a world-view in which no place could be assigned either to the spirit or to spiritual values. Therefore, the subjects such as history, political science, economics and law, which are immersed in an attitude antithetical to the spirit of Islam.

Marmaduke Pickthall has aptly put this whole phenomenon into these words:

> You need the learning and the practical example of the West, but you do not need the ethical, political and social system and ideals of the West, for the West is thirteen hundred years behind Islam in all such matters. The systems and ideals of the West are always changing, still seeking for the synthesis which was revealed thirteen hundred years ago in Arabia. You have your own unchanging social and political ideals, which have stood the test of centuries, and you should return to them, making that return to true Islam a great part of your modern education; purging your community of all those superstitions, vices and abuses which have overgrown the real Islamic structure, and above all purging it of ignorance. Muslims must go to school to the West for the scientific and material progress necessary to their healthy growth. But for social peace and for political security the West must come to school to Islam. The East gave the West the awakening shock, the knowledge and the practical example which started modern Western civilization; the West is paying back that debt today by rousing up the details of observances.[55]

---

55. Marmacluke Pickthall, op. cit., p. 48.

In so many words Mawlana Nadwi suggests that, for the Muslim east, there can be no other way to peace, progress and self-realization. Nothing apart from it can hold out to them the assurance of continued adherence and loyalty to the Islamic ideals and programme of life.[56]

Mawlana Nadwi vehemetanly endeavour to maintain and further Islamic religious educational institutions of Indian Muslims, which he feared of being swayed over by the Western education and disparaging government policies. Under the banner of "Deeni Talimi Council" (Religious Educational Council) of which he was member as well as president for some time, Mawlana Nadwi made several addresses, which shows his concern for religious education especially in India. He stressed the importance of religious education for the survival of Muslims in India and the survival of future generation of Muslims. As Muslim he points out that:

> Neither Islam nor the Muslim could possibly exist without the fundamental knowledge of the faith. If one wanted to remain a Muslims it was essential to obtain the requisite knowledge of basic Islamic truths, and, thereby to develop in himself the ability to carry out the obligations and duties that flowed from the acceptance of the faith.

and furthermore:

> In whatever country the Muslims may be placed, no matter whether they are in a majority there, or in a minority the first and foremost question before them always is what arrangement obtains there for the religious instructions and training both for the children and adults.[57]

---

56. Mawlana Nadwi, *Western Civilization*, p. 30.

57. Mawlana Nadwi, Presidental address State *Dini Talim* Conference, Lucknow, 4-5 June 1961, published by Reception Committee State Dini Talimi Conference Lucknow, 1961, p. 9.

Because according to him,

> Islam is not the name of natural association springing from factors like caste, nationality or statehood, in which the choice or violation of the individual does not have a hand. It is a well-considered decision, a chosen way of life and a voluntary creed, which calls for proper awareness, enlightened will and correct knowledge and endeavour, an amalgamation of men whose origin and existence is dependent wholly on a distinctive plan of faith and programme of life. The existence of such a community can scarcely be visualized without a knowledge that can invest it with an awareness of the foundational principles of its creed and the ability to fulfil the obligations, which accrue from the acceptance thereof . . . It is because of these reasons alone that Islam has attached so much importance, sacrosance and dignity to knowledge as to proclaim, it is not possible to realize God without knowledge.[58]

Therefore, according to him; religious education of Muslims is indispensable for Muslims as a nation as well as Islam itself. He called it matter of life and death for Muslims of India and asked for struggle and sacrifice for maintaining religious education.[59]

Mawlana Nadwi laid special importance to the study of Arabic language "the language of Muslim culture" without, Muslims will not be able to have direct access to the *Qur'an* and the *Sunnah*. Therefore, prone to committing shocking errors.[60] In order to make Arabic language popular and easy

58. Ibid., p. 7.
59. Mawlana Nadwi, *Ek Aham Takreer* (Urdu), Deeni Talimi Council, Lucknow, 99, May 1972.
60. Mawlana Nadwi, *Islam in a Changing World*, Academy of Islamic Research and Publication, Lucknow, n.d. p. 19.

for learning, he contributed several books while teaching Arabic language at Nadwa. He produced *Al-Qiraat al Rashidah* in three volumes in about two years of time. It won appreciation by way of inclusion in the Arabic courses. By 1944 he also brought out another set of children's book for the religious courses titled *Stories of the Prophets* (*Qusasul Nabieen*) for children in Arabic. This one won the appreciation of even Sayyid Qutb, who wrote a Foreword for its second publication. The book was soon included in the syllabi of various countries including Saudi Arab. A forth in 1975 and fifth in 1977 followed the first three volumes of this work. The five (vols.) together cover all the major Prophets mentioned in the *Qur'an*. A little later he followed up the children's series with the life of the Prophet, also in Arabic, for people of all ages. It was also well-received and was included as a course material by various universities of Arab world.

Mawlana Nadwi's Re-orientation of Islamic History

History has always been a tricky subject, as all historians have been alleged of some sort of bias and prejudice towards their subject. Even those historians who seem to be wholly objective, devoid of vested interest and as well had not any direct personal connection — physiological, physical or material — with the subject, have been unable to escape the tag or prejudice. These allegations are not always unfounded as historians, even if they themselves may take detached and non-partisan posture, have to rely on others (source) for information and nobody can guarantee/assure that the person, who is one's source of information is free of any kind of prejudice. According to E.H. Carr:

> In the first place, the facts of history never come to us 'pure' since they do not and cannot exist in a pure form: they are always refracted through the mind of the recorder. It follows

> that when we take up a work of history, our first concern should be not with the facts which it contains but with the historians who wrote it.[61]

Mawlana Abul Hasan Nadwi had particular style of writing history. Essentially a religious scholar he used writing history as a tool to bring home the achievements of Islam throughout its history, highlight the role of eminent personalities and describe their accomplishment in the field of Islamic revival and renovation. In his book, on The Sociology of Islam, 'Ali Shariati writes that:

> According to the Islamic school of thought, the philosophy of history is based on a certain kind of historical determinism. History represents an unbroken flow of events that, like man himself, is dominated by a dialectical contradiction, a constant warfare between the two hostile and contradictory elements that began with the creation of humanity and has been waged at all places and at all times, and the sum total of which constitutes history.[62]

Based upon the *Qur'an*, it sees the entire of history as a conflict of forces; in the same way that man himself is the battleground for the competing forces of his lowly origin, his lowly bodily nature, and the element of divine spirit contained within him, history is also battleground where *tawhid* and *shirk*, justice and injustice, have continually opposed each other. Therefore, there is continuous struggle throughout history between two different types of man, two different types of society, two different types of world-view. The struggle has always been between belief and unbelief, paganism and godliness, or Islam, as last and only religion, and all other varieties of erroneous

61. E.H. Car, *What is History*, Penguin Books, 1964, p. 22.
62. Ali Shariati, *On the Sociology of Islam*, Cresent Publishing Company, 1919, p. 97.

and false doctrines. To Sayyid Qutb, the confrontation against Islam has always been motivated by one overriding objective — the destruction of Islam and its doctrines.[63] Moreover, this hydra-type conspiracy is considered by him to have come into being with the foundation of Islam itself. The methods used and the individuals involved may vary from age to age, but the objective has always been the annihilating of the only authentic religion ever preached to mankind. The same enemy masquerading under various disquisies. Polytheists, hypocrites, the Jews, Christians, secular rules, communist states, and capitalistic system, have all conspired one after another to undermine the foundation of Islam.[64]

According to Nadwi,

> Who also reinterpreted Islamic history and tradition to respond to the Sociol historical conditions of the twentieth century, comments that,
>
> From the very inception of its career on this planet, Islam has been singlled out for such fatal attacks as no other religion would have been able to withstand. There have been religions, which had once conquered the then known world but they could not survive under an offensive much less serious than that Islam had to face. Unlike, others, Islam not only overcame all its adversaries but was also successful in maintaining its original form and purity.[65]

He cherishes inherent qualities of Islam preserved in its pristine purity and role of reforms, who endeavoured to

63. Sayyid Qutb, *Ma'alim fi al-Tari*, Dar al-Shurq, Beirut and Cairo, 1981/1401, p. 202.
64. Sayyid Qutb, *Fi Zilal al Qur'an*, rev. edn., vol. 2, Dar al Shurq, Beirut and Cairo, 1981, pp. 924-25.
65. Sayyid Abul Hasan Ali Nadwi, *Saviours of Islamic Spirit*, vol. I, Islamic Research and Publication, Lucknow, 1986, p. 3.

uphold that against all odds. He further explains that Islam, not only survived in the face of all these internal and external threats to its very existence, but was also able to gain victories in entirely new fiels.[66] The conscience of its followers always refused to strike a compromise with the evil,

> In every age, its produced a man of God, who attacked the innovations and deviationist tendencies with the full weight of unshakable conviction and restored the true spirit of the faith; reaffirmed the *Sunnah* of the *Holy* Prophet against the heretical rites, customs and foreign influences; propound the teachings of Islam to contradict speculative thoughts and materialistic precepts; raised the banner of revolt in the face of despots and emperors; condemned opulence, luxury and indolence of the rich and enunciated the teachings of Islam as the sole valid source or religious, moral and political advancement, they provided a new driving force, a new life to the Muslims of their time. These scholars of impeccable worth and ability possessed the priceless gift of intellectual, moral and religious capabilities and were beacons of light for their contemporaries. Each one of these was capable enough to expose the manifestations of the ignorance of his age and to bring into light the correct and unalloyed teachings of Islam before the people.[67]

Mawlana Nadwi asserts that, this tradition of struggle against un-Islam, the spirit to preserve and renovate the pristine teachings of the faith and the effort to infuse people with revolutionary spirit to re-assert the divine message are as old as Islam itself. He writes

> History bears a testimony to the fact that there has never been a spell, however brief, during the past one and a half

66. Ibid., p. 3.

67. Ibid., pp. 3-4.

> thousand years, when the message of Islam was eclipsed or its teaching were engulfed by heresy and the Islamic conscience became dormant enough to accept a contaminated faith. Whenever an effort was made from any quarter whatsoever to distort the tenets of Islam, pervert or falsify its teachings or it was attacked by Sensuatist materialism, someone invariably came forward to accept the challenge and fight it out to the grief of Islam's adversary . . . finally, however, it was Islam which gained ascendancy over these contending forces."[68]

To understand fully the process of *tajdid* and *islah,* and looking back upon our history determine to what extent and in what ways have the different leaders accomplished this work, there has always been demand to compile a comprehensive history of religious preaching and the revivalist movement. The absence of any work on this subject had provided chance of misconceived notion among many people that there was no continuous attempt at rejuvenating Muslim society. It was commonly held that Islam did not produced towering personalities, barring a few luminaries who were born after centuries. There was also a deliberate attempt to slur or misrepresent the continuous effort made during the past 1300 years for stimulating a spirit of reawakening among the Muslims. Therefore, to bring into light those eminent savants who rose to the defence of Islam in order to arrest the onslaught of evil forces, and gave birth to various movements for upholding the Islamic morals and values and, finally, whose efforts made it possible for Islam to survive to this day. Mawlana Nadwi used his pen and energy to accentuate the positive contributions of these remarkable men of Muslim history. He writes:

---

68. Ibid., p. 11.

> Unfortunately we find either a glossary of events with kings and emperors as the central figures or biographical accounts of certain eminent luminaries in the vast treasure of Islamic literature but no account of the revivalist movement or intellectual history of the Muslim people encompassing the academic and speculative achievements of all those savants who have left an indelible mark on the world of Islam. These scholars have relentlessly fought against the forces of corruption, defended the Islamic precepts and teachings and rejuvenated the spirit of Islamic revival besides making valuable contributions to the intellectual and academic treasure of their people.[69]

However, he further asserts that,

> In fact there is no gap at all in the intellectual history of Islam; it is only in the presentation of the history of its people, which needs urgently to be filled in. A history of religious revival and preaching in Islam would also be an account of the intellectual and academic movements, which have seen successive ebbs and flows of Islamic re-awakening in the past.[70]

Under this compelling context Mawlana Nadwi adopted a unique style of writing history, which bear distinct historical roots and reflect an in-depth study of the subject, Islamic history in particular. May it be the penning of a biography or a thesis recounting the rise and expansion of Muslim power; or lamentations on civilizational maladjustment following the waning fortunes of Muslim; or the multi-splendoured achievements of the Muslim in India; or the obligations to pay literary tribute to the spiritual orders, Mawlana Nadwi derives an inherent satisfaction in heaping himself with the debris of

69. Ibid., Preface, p. X.
70. Idem.

history to sift the chaff from core. He took the responsibility of bringing to light the memorable chapters of Islamic history, to clear the haze on "views" taken for granted and to report on "events" of history hitherto ignored by the historians at large. As he writes:

> A vast treasure of information on the social, political and historical events of the bygone days is in fact to be found in the religious works, which can serve as a valuable source of history. These are the writings of the religious savants and scholars wherein they have laid bare their innermost feelings, given numerous accounts of the incidents they or their contemporaries had come across, quoted their teachers and mentors and recorded proceedings of the profounded and heartful reunions of their masters and fellows. There are compilations of letters and discourses from which we can gain access to the thoughts and ideas, feelings and emotions of their writes. There are also monographs written for the refutation of innovations and deviations or to censure the wayward sections of society. If one could extend his vision to all these writings and had time to cut out relevant data from these works, a complete and detailed history of Islamic missionary effort could be written to show that the effort to re-kindle the fire of religious ardour and dynamic energy into the followers of Islam has never ceased for a movement and the Muslims too have never remained cold or indifferent to the call.[71]

Mawlana Nadwi's first literary endeavour and debut as a historian was his historical biography a Sayyid Ahmad Shaheed written in 1938-39. Earlier he had also published an article on "Sayyid" in reputed Arabic journal *Almanar* of Syed Rashid Raza during AH 1349-50 (CE 1931). The book *Sirat Saiyid Ahmad Shaheed* is a memoir of the life, work and achievements of the

71. Ibid., p. 12.

founder of the greatest revivalist movement known to Indian history. It is the comprehensive, well-researched and painstakingly portrayed, documenting the vast material existing on the subject. The author claims,

> Fortunately, I have also had the advantages of having access to certain original sources, not available to others, and also the opportunity to study the Saiyid's life and mission from close quarters. I had, therefore, been giving thought to the matter from comparatively early age and also written a monograph on the subject.[72]

Therefore, utilized all existing sources on the subject to produce a worthy work to understand the real worth and value of the Sayyid's movement and the place he occupied among the lumanaries of Islam. The book made an instant success and received wide acclaim, both within and abroad. Written originally in Arabic, then Urdu. The way this work was received was a indication of the popularity of Sayyid Ahmad Shaheed and the urge of the people to know more abut him. Political situation then prevailing in India had created an upsurge in the Muslims, who were eager to re-assert their identity and to see Islam strong and powerful in the world. Naturally, the Saiyid's message of hope and faith, of self-confidence and self-realization, contained in the book, was enthusiastically welcomed by them.[73]

Mawlana Nadwi's book and other related writing on Sayyid Ahmad Shaheed, in addition, proved to be a rebuttal and cleared the many misconceptions about the Sayyid Ahmad and his movement disseminated by some Western writers, such as P. Hardy, *The Muslims of British India*. W.W. Hunter,

72. Nadwi, *A Misunderstood Reformer*, Academy of Islamic Research and Publication, Lucknow, 1978-79, p. 6.

73. Ibid., p. 40.

Indian Musalmans and some apologetic writers. As Nadwi claims,

> I drew attention to and protested against the biased and extremely intolerant attitude of the Western writers, in regard to the Sayyid and his mission. I tried to show that dearth of material was not the cause of their partisan and unwarranted observation, as it so often happens in depicting the true character and achievements of the reformers of old. For, in such cases, the writers usually exercise their whimsical speculations to present a character sketch.[74]

But according to Mawlana Nadwi, it seems that the chroniclers never wanted to ascertain true facts; they gave credence to every groundless rumour without evaluating the relative evidential value of the report reaching them. Therefore, on their part it was sheer shadow of narrow-spiritual uncharitableness bequeathed by the crusades, which was not expected of the present age persons professing to be rationalists.[75]

Mawlana Nadwi wrote several historical biographies of some outstanding personalities, who played important role in the society. As a historian, he understood the importance of extensive research to produce any meaningful work having far-reaching benefits for future generations. The biographies of two saints Mawlana Fazlur Rehman, *Tazkirah,* and that of Mawlana Mohammad Zakariya *Biography of Zakariya* fall in the same category of writing Islamic history through the media of biography, each book provided a valuable source of information for the reader and research scholar alike. Mawlana Nadwi wrote biographies of his two spiritual mentors, who

---

74. Ibid., p. 7.
75. Ibid., p. 35.

had influenced his life, more than anybody else. The biography of Shah Abdul Qadir Raipuri and that of Mawlana Ilyas (founder of Tabligi movement) is his spiritual and literary tribute to the great divines of the era, whom he held with high reverence. Writing biographies of these spiritual personalities, he felt it an obligation to present these personalities to future generations, to make a close study of their accomplishment impartially and justly, so as to allocate them the place they deserve in the history of Islam. In the biography of Hazrat Mawlana Abul Qadir Raipuri, Mawlana Nadwi in addition to many other things related to biography, throws light on the most important political issue of the time, the Partition of India and aftermath. Mawlana Abdul Qadir never supported the Partition and concurred with Mawlana Hussain Ahmad Madni, Mawlana Muhammad Zakariya and many other Deobandi *'Ulama* on this particular issue. Mawlana Nadwi cherishes the role of these three personalities during the trying situations of Partition for counselling Muslim especially that of UP and adjacent areas to remain in India. As a result of their steadfastness in staying in India, Mawlana Nadwi believes Muslims in India are once again a reality.[76] With regard to there writings, which otherwise would have been lost, Mawlana Nadwi's writing have become indispensable.

Mawlana Nadwi's another important book on history, which deserves special mention is *Hindustani Musalman* originally lectures in Arabic and afterwards translated into Urdu and later into English as *Muslims in India*. The role of Islam and Muslims in the history of India has been deliberately distorted, first by the Western writers, to serve their vested

76. Mawlana Nadwi, *Sawaniah Hazrat Mawlana Abdul Qadir Raipur* (Urdu), Maktaba Islami, Lucknow, 1994, pp. 144 ff.

interests in India; by the socialist and secular historians blinded by ideological baggage, Hindu extremist writers because of their jaundiced views about it and as well as by the Muslim apologetic writers. As Mawlana Nadwi himself writes:

> The tragedy, however, is not confined only to ignorance what is worse and more disconcerting is that there has got created in our country a powerful tendency to blackout and reject the history and the cultural stock of a whole community, its past achievements and the glorious contribution it has made to the national fight for Independence. There is afoot a campaign to present the history of our land in a manner as if the Muslim era in India was an era of foreign, imperialistic domination; it was devoid of all virtue and greatness and failed miserably to produce a single noteworthy personality, a single remarkable achievement in the domains of thought and culture, a single act of unpolluted, selfless service to the country's welfare and development of which the nation could be proud, and that in the long-drawn battle for freedom against the British, the Muslims were nothing more than disinterested spectators, and if they did, accidentally, take part, it was not worthy of attention. . . . Though it is entirely in opposition to what history tells.[77]

To dispel misconception created by misinformation about the role of Muslims in India, Mawlana Nadwi's book may be said to be most useful publication on the subject, which has given a befitting reply to those historians, who consider the period of Islamic dominations as a dark age in the history of this subcontinent. Published in precise time, in 1953, when Muslims in India were in desperate search for such objective writing,

---

77. Nadwi, *Muslim in India*, Islamic Research and Publication, Lucknow, 1980, pp. 2-4.

which would project the real image with accuracy to help ward off senseless onslaughts on their identity and existence in their very homeland. As well as because it is not possible for all to read voluminous work in Persian and even in Urdu of the old style to enquire into the manifold cultural, literacy, material, and political achievements of Muslim period in Indian history. This brief, perspicuous, easy to read, book of Mawlana Nadwi gives detailed exposition of Muslim genuineness that has gone into the making of Indian history and culture. Their presence at every form of life throughout the most important period of Indian history drew out the best in them, laying the foundation of a broad-based and composite culture. The contribution of Muslims at all levels of life and society left its multi-dimensional impress on almost all human activity, including statecraft and land management. He demonstrates the part played by Muslims in the progress and development of the motherland, the achievements of Muslim scholars and their contribution and role of Muslims in the freedom struggle of India. In the words of Mawlana Nadwi,

> They gave India and Indian civilization a new lease of life and a new dimension and awakened its people to a new set of moral and spiritual values. Every path of its land and every particle of its soil bears the imprint of their greatness and is a monument of their industry, earnestness and creative genius. In every aspect of Indian life and civilization can be seen evidences of their noble aestheticism and cultural richness.[78]

Mawlana Nadwi's two voluminous books *Purane Chiragh* (Old Lamps) and *Karavaan-i-Zindagi* (March of Life) are profound contribution to the history as well as Urdu literature. *Purane*

---

78. Ibid., p. 5.

Chiragh is a life-sketche of contemporary personalities personally known to Mawlana Nadwi, therefore, recorded facts and information. He has preserved precisely his reflections, impressions of some important personalities who had passed away and were personally known to him. He assesses at length their respective talents and specific achievements, dedication and excellence in their respective fields. While reading three volumes of *Purnane Chiragh* one comes in direct contact with the saints the philosophers, the poet, the writer, the editor, the pacifist, the revolutionary, the teacher, the social worker, the statesman and the administrator, keeping the reader at pace with the unbroken chain of history. Likewise *Karavaan-i-Zindagi* is his autobiography in eight volumes but as a matter of fact is more than that, a glance at the history through his eyes. These writings will not only serve as record on lives surveyed but also act as good source material for the student of the future years.

Mawlana Nadwi's personality and vision seemed largely defined by his six-volume *magnum opus, Tarikh-i-Dawat wa Azimat*, translated into English as *Saviours of Islamic Spirit* (4 vols.). In these volumes, he has extensively potrayed the intellectual and religious efforts of Islam, its social history and revivalist and reformative endeavours and has introduced in a copious way the leaders of such movements and has categorically stated in the introduction to the book that in Islam there has been a continuity of reformative movements and there were no long interregnums of suspense or in action. The *Tarikh-i-Dawat wa Azimat* answers the key questions in Islamic history. viz, what's there in Islamic society which, despite all the vicissitudes and debacles, explains its undiminished resilience? The Islamic history is a history of *dawah* and fortitude and which keeps on refreshing and reviving itself through *tajdid, islah* and *jihād.*

Tarikh-i-Dawat wa Azimat provides an alternative view of looking at Islamic history as a history of *'Ulama* and intellectuals instead of as a chronicle of sultāns and regimes some noble and horrible. Depending upon their respective circumstances some of the *'Ullemas* took part in or even led *jihād*, others concentrated on winning the hearts and soul of the people. Not surprisingly Islamic society has suffered more by the decline of the *'Ulama* than the disloyalty of its *umara*.[79]

Much acclaimed book of Mawlana Nadwi *Mazaha Kasir-al-alamo bin-hitaal al-Muslimin* for which he received accolades throughout, especially Arab world where it was first published in 1951, with a Foreword by the leading modernist writer Ahmad Amin (d. 1954). However, many who read the book, including king Abdullah I of Jordan (d. 1951), felt that Ahmad Amin's Foreword lacked a fuller understanding of the book's driving theme.[80] The second and subsequent editions of the book carried a new Foreword, this one by Sayyid Qutb (d. 1966). The book was later translated into English under the title of *Islam and the World* and into Urdu, Persian and Turkish.

What mankind has lost because of Muslim decline was the subject matter of this book. The book traces the history from antiquity especially before the advent of Islam. Describing the conditions, the state of affairs, and intellectual temper of man from the east to west and from north to south. The picture that the book presents of that age is clear-cut and delineates

79. M.H. Faruqi, "Abul Hasan Ali Nadwi," in Impact International, reproduced by *The Fragrance of East*, January-June 2000, p. 130.

80. Ibid., p. 136.

its features with accuracy and insight. The author has supported his statements by references to admittedly reliable authorities to provide an elaborate account of religious, social, moral and political state of that moribund period of human history, particularly on the eve of the prophethood of Muhammad (SAW). According to Sayyid Qutb,

> The book in its style and treatment does not however, ponder to mere sentiments or excite passions of dogmation. The claims that it makes are sustained by solid scholarship and objective research in a manner that appeals both to the mind and the heart. The enlightened and unprejudiced mind of the author is clearly revealed by the scrupulous care and deep concern from truth with which historical events and their sequences are recorded and environmental effects and ramifications analysed. Decisions are left to the discernment of enlightened minds and a conscience that is sensitive to truth. Topics have been discussed, arranged and interfered in such a manner that no conclusion is ever forced on the reader.[81]

After describing the age as the age of ignorance (*jahilliyyah*), in its salient feature, the author has outlined the part played by Islam in the reconstruction of humanity. Delineates upon the role of Islam in saving the human society from decadence and degeneration, in liberating the soul of man from superstitions and banalities, emancipated him from the evils of slavery and degradation, and liberated man from the tyranny of kings and the dominance of priests. It striked a harmonious balance between the world of faith and the world of action, therefore Islam never proved to be barrier to progress and science. It was Islam that made earlier Muslims great but later generations deviated from the teaching ɔf Islam

81. Sayyid Qutb, in Foreword to Nadwi's *Islam and World*, p. 2.

resulting in the decline of Muslims fortunes. The author describes succinctly the reason for the material and spiritual decay in the Muslims and points out that the harm the Muslims sustained was by deviation from the principles of their faith and turning away from the responsibilities it entailed.

Thus according to Mawlana Nadwi, with the failure of the Muslims to sustain and discharge efficiently the great responsibility of the trusteeship of mankind which Islam enjoined upon them, Islam lost its world leadership. Paving the way for West to take the leadership of world, which is sheer materialism. Therefore, ignorance, which prevailed before Islam reigned again in garb of Western civilization. Then he, explains the cruel and catastrophic consequences of the transfer of world-leadership from the Muslims to the Western people, whose appetites are purely material and who have, thereof, built-up a structure of which is utterly inimical to the needs of human mind and spirit. Mawlana Nadwi has objectively delineated on the subject of Western civilization and its impact also in his another book translated into English under the title of *Western Civilization Islam and Muslims*.

Mawlana Nadwi through this book *Mazaha Kasir-al-alamo bin-hitaal al Muslimin* re-instills hope of revival of Islam on the seat of world leadership. In the words of Sayyid Qutb:

> The historical analysis the author (Mawlana Nadwi) gives, compels one to believe strongly that a time has come when the present leadership should be changed and humanity brought back to the real fountains head of guidance, which aims at leading man from darkness to light and from ignorance to knowledge and wisdom. The reader of the book soon realizes how much important such a guidance is to the world today and what a terrible loss humanity has suffered in losing it. This loss is sustained not by the

> Muslims only but is shared by the whole world . . . if by reading this book, the Muslim is filled with the shame and contrition for his criminal neglect and carelessness, he also becomes acutely aware of the tremendous potentialities, that have been given to him and begins to feel an overpowering desire to regain the world leadership he lost through his own neglect and lack of appreciation of its quality.[82]

Also from the methodological point of view Sayyid Qutb cherishes the Mawlana Nadwi's approach to history he writes,

> The books are not only a refreshing example of religious and social research but of how history can be recorded and interpreted from the wider Islamic point of view. The scholars of the West have written the history of the world from their own Western point of view. They could not, naturally escape from being conditioned by their upbringing, their philosophies and their national and religious prejudices. Because they forget or underrated, consciously or unconsciously, certain important values of life, the history writings by them contains many observations and travesties. Unless these values are understood and appreciated properly, no history of man can be recorded in its completeness nor can facts be interpreted and conclusions deduced from them, correctly. . . . The book has kept all these considerations steadily in view and given special attention to movements and values that have conditioned and influenced man and his life. Nothing has been left out which had any effect on life.[83]

Furthermore, Mawlana Nadwi has discussed some methodological issues while writing historical biographies. In his Preface to *Saviours of Islamic Spirit*, he has explained few

---

82. Ibid., p. 4.
83. Ibid., pp. 5-6.

points, which he personally adopted in writing these volumes. He writes,

> For presenting the viewpoint of any particular person or a movement started by him, his own writings, or sayings have been relied upon. If these have been found inadequate, only then help has been taken from the writings or descriptions left by his friends, contemporaries and pupils. In the latter case more reliable and authentic sources have been given preference without placing undue reliance on those writers who were nearer to him in time; trustworthy material has been used whenever it could be found, after careful verification of the facts.[84]

He emphasized before analysing and discussing a personality and in order to make correct assessment of the achievement of the subject concerned in its true perspective. It is necessary to cast light on the intellectual, cultural and academic temperament of the time. The scholar should be able to understand the particular contemporary situation and circumstances in which the personality under discussion has endeavoured. Assessment of any character, out of its own context of time and place, according to modern concepts and values might appear to be a work of critical study but it will be injustice to the personality so evaluated.[85] Therefore, Mawlana Nadwi claims of having adopted realistic approach and of having elucidated the real picture of the personality and the situations under which they struggled rather than relying on same critical approach or dryly objective method to appease others.

---

84. Nadwi, *Saviours of Islamic Spirit*, p. XI.
85. Idem.

In the words of Sayyid Qutb,

> It is a remarkable example of how history should be recorded. It shows how a Muslim can take up his pen to record historical events and discuss their sequences without borrowing from the European historians and copying their style which often lacks balance, historical veracity and adequate scholarship and research.[86]

---

86. Sayyid Qutb, op. cit., pp. 6-7.

6

Sayyid Abul Hasan Ali Nadwi's Response to the Issue of Muslim Community in Independent India

1857 marked the end of the Muslim rule in Indian subcontinent and beginning of their suffering and agony. After the collapse of the movement, they had to pay a heavy price. The post-1857 policy of the British government in India was decidedly anti-Muslim. Many of their leaders had been killed in the first war of Independence (1857-59) of those, who had survived the struggle and quite a few had gone into voluntary exile to escape the tyrannous hand of British retaliation. The failure of the uprising of 1857 had inflicted a blatant blow to their morale and prestige, as a result of which a host of new and terrifying problems had cropped-up for them. Multitudinous charges were being levelled against them. They were being treated with suspicion and mistrust on all sides.[1] British government looked upon Muslims as the perpetrators of rebellion (mutiny) therefore unleashed reign of terror and persecution against them. With the end of Brutish rule in subcontinent and the Partition of the country. Muslims who decided to remain in India, instead of enjoying and rejoicing freedom, were disenchanted. They were subjected to more

---

1. Sayyid Abul Hasan Ali Nadwi, *Western Civilization Islam and Muslims,* Academy of Islamic Research and Pub., Lucknow, 1969, p. 56.

tribulations and agony than ever. They found themselves in critical situation in the wake of poignant Partition, and in the Independent India, Muslims had to endure more than they had in the British India.[2]

Educational Concerns

Mawlana Nadwi chose to remain in India, his own country of birth; therefore, witnessed the poignant aftermath of the Partition and incessant impediments and tribulations, which Muslims had to face in Independent India. Despite apolitical and non-partisan approach, he could not shut his eyes to the desperate problems of Indian Muslims. Like many other leaders of Muslim community, he remained at forefront to address the issues, which Muslim community faced time and again. In addition to religious and academic pursuits, he remained alert and in vanguard to safeguard the religious and cultural identity of Muslims in India. For Mawlana Nadwi, the foremost and necessary thing to pursue in order to preserve identity of Muslims in secular India, is Islamic religious education. Therefore, for the survival of Muslims as Muslims in India in the eyes of Mawlana Nadwi; the educational system is very important, else they will go astray, will loose their identity — cultural as well as religious.[3] From the platform of Dini Talim (Muslim Religious Education) Conference of whom Mawlana Nadwi remained president for most of the time, he asserted for Muslim religious education and opposed the nationalization of educational system in multi-religious and multi-cultural state like India.

In his presidential address of "State Dini Talim Conference" at Lucknow, he asserts:

2. Nadwi, *Khutba Sadarat 'Riyasati Dini Conference'* 14-15, June 1969, pp. 14-15.

3. Nadwi, *Karavaan-i-Zindagi,* vol. 1, pp. 459, 462.

> Why should it be necessary for Muslims to provide for their Children a system of education, that may be calculated to inculcate in them Islamic consciousness and faith in the fundamental truths of their Islamic virtues and the basic attributes of Islamic character. And, conversely, why should a system of education, which clashes with the fundamental articles of their religion, propagates the teachings of parallel structure of spiritual belief, and aims at tearing them apart from the universal Islamic culture and the international brotherhood of the clan of Ibrahim (Abraham) be an absolute lethal in its effects for them. Furthermore, should such an educational system get established — as part of a pre-conceived plan or through ignorance or thoughtlessness in a country which Muslim have decided to make their homeland — why must it become for them a question of extreme concern and a matter of life and death?[4]

While explaining these concerns, he accentuates that the Islamic *millet* owes its entire existence to a certain creed and system of spiritual truths, which according to its belief were brought into the world, from time to time by the Prophets, attaining their perfection, their final, complete shape, their full elaboration with the raising up of the last of the divine apostles, Prophet Mohammad (SAAS). The identification of Muslim *millet* with this creed is so obvious and complete and its existence is so thoroughly and permanently linked up with it that God and the Prophet have declared. The fact of the affirmation of and obedience to it to be its collective denomination and title.[5] Furthermore, according to him:

---

4. Nadwi, Presidential Address State Dini Talim (Muslim Religious Education) Conference. Lucknow, 4-5 June 1961, published by Reception Committee State Dini Talim Conference, Lucknow, 1961, p. 1.
5. Ibid., p. 2-3.

> Islam is not the name of a natural association springing from factors like caste, nationality or statehood in which the choice or volition of the individual does not have a hand. It is a well-considered decision; a chosen way of life and a voluntary creed, which calls for proper awareness, enlightened will and correct knowledge and endeavour, an amalgamation of men whose origin and existence is dependent wholly on a distinctive plan of faith and progamme of life. The existence of such a community can scarcely be visualized without a knowledge that can invest it with an awareness of the foundational principles of its creed and the ability to fulfil the obligations, which accrue from the acceptance there of.[6]

And also he proclaims that:

> Just as Islam is most generous and large-hearted in the universality of its massage and management of its international relations, it's extremely jealous and sensitive where its fundamental articles and basic laws are concerned. In the matter of fundamental doctrines, it is not prepared to make the slightest concession or indulge in the least self-deception for the sake of anyone what ever high and mighty he may be or in any circumstance of emotional tussle.[7]

According to Mawlana Nadwi, it is because of these reasons alone that Islam has attached so much importance, sacrosanctity and dignity to knowledge as to proclaim "it is not possible to realize God without knowledge" and term used in *Qur'an* and in Islamic chronicles in opposition to Islam in ignorance. That is why, it was not permitted to Muslims to live in an environment in which the means to acquire requisite

6. Ibid., p. 7.
7. Ibid., p. 4.

religious knowledge and understanding and the freedom to fashion their lives accordingly were not forthcoming. The spirit underlying the permission and institution of *hijrat* (migration) denotes nothing else.[8] He asserts after explaining certain historical evidences, that neither Islam nor the Muslims could possibly exist without the fundamental knowledge of the faith. If one wanted to remain a Muslim, it was essential to obtain the requisite knowledge of basic Islamic truths, and, thereby to develop in himself the ability to carry out the obligations and duties that flowed from the acceptances of the faith. In whatever country, the Muslim may be placed, no matter whether they are in a majority there or in a minority, the first and foremost question before them always is what arrangement obtains therefore the religious institution and training, both for children and adults.[9]

He reiterated the importance and indispensability of religious education among Indian Muslims, throughout all his addresses organized by *Dīn-i Talim* Conference and like a crusader endevoured along with other leaders and *'Ulama* to protect it and disseminate it among the Muslim masses. More importantly, he perceived that the responsibility becomes all the more grave and urgent in situations like India. Where the position is loaded with the ideas adverse for Muslims and the system of education in force, which uphold and propagate a religious creed that is at variance with the basic principle of Islam and cuts across the fundamental concepts of divine unity and Apostleship, and which compel the Muslim children to study the mythological lore of another religious community after being influenced by which no Muslim can remain a

8. Ibid., pp. 6, 9.

9. Ibid., pp . 8-9.

Muslim by any stretch of imagination.[10] According to him, a system of education and a syllabus of study, which presents the personality of the Prophet in such an incorrect and unbecoming manner that to read it is a source of the greatest spiritual agony and religious peril to them; and makes a caricature of the heroes of Islamic history and show them in such false and disgraceful colours that it is sure to make Muslim children ashamed of their past; and which permit the use of terms in respect of Muslims, who are an important part of the country's population and citizens of a full stature, that are generally applied to aliens or depressed classes and untouchable.[11]

Keeping in view such a terrible state of affairs, he appealed to the Muslims of India to make a permanent arrangement for the religious instituition for their children's irrespective of the fact that such a situation continues to prevail or not and to adopt democratic means to protect their rights, which Constitution of India has provided. He asserts that for Muslims to live in circumstances in which their future generation are caught in the grip of religious and cultural apostasy, with the foundations of their faith shaken and polytheistic beliefs holding sway over their minds and hearts. And even for a defaulting Muslim the prospect of leading a religiously paralysed and mutilated life and his children being deprived of the heritage of Islam is more terrible then the keeping a community permanently under the pangs of hunger and thirst, which constitution of any country could not permit.[12] He

10. See also Nadwi, *Kutba Sadarat Riyasati Din i Talim* Convention Aligrah, 27 April 1998 (All India Talim Counsil, Aligrah, 1998), p. 9.

11. Nadwi, Presidential Address, 4-5 June 1961, p. 10.

12. Ibid., p. 12.

emphasizes that we have resolved to live in this country without giving up our individual characteristics, our religious creed and our Islamic civilization. These characteristics, this creed and this civilization are more precious to us than ties of blood. This is a natural corollary of faith without which we cannot consider ourselves to be men of faith and deserving of divine assistance.[13] And after all in the words of Mawlana Nadwi,

> We are not only permitted by the law of the land to take recourse to all peaceful constitutional steps in this regard but the secular spirit of our constitution and our bond of loyalty to it demand us that we must do so[14]

Mawlana Nadwi insists that

> It is also for the well-being of this country as, when we have decided to make India our home along with our religious beliefs and other cultural and Islamic characteristics we also, naturally, took upon ourselves the responsibility that go with it. Therefore, according to him, that we (Muslims of India) have not only to safeguard our own religious future and the religious survival of our coming generations but also to leave a permanent mark of our genius — our correct and unserving patriotism. . . . We have to participate whole-heartedly in the making of the new India with all propensities granted to us by God and nurtured by Islam and to carry it to great heights of progress and prosperity. We have to raise India high in the esteem of the world and furnish an irrefutable proof of its secular and democratic character by proving to everyone that we can live and prosper here with our faith and other social and cultural characteristics intact.[15]

13. Ibid.
14. Ibid., p. 11.
15. Ibid., p. 14.

At the same time he voiced the apprehension, that

> When this most important article of our faith falls in jeopardy, it will be hard for them [to our fellow countrymen and educational authorities] to understand how painful and purposeless will our life in any country become conversely. Instead of participating in the development of the country. We will get caught in such mental unease that, we will no longer remain in a fit state to take part in the task of the country's development. We will never be able to reconcile overselves to this injustices or regard with satisfaction our citizenship of the land.[16]

These disparaging state policies, fears Mawlana Nadwi will harm not only the Muslim community in India but when one major section of the country is inhabited to take active part in its development will consequently have damaging effect on the development and prosperity of the country on the whole. He vehemently opposed the national Educational policies dominated by particular thought.

He apprised the Muslim community about the defects and deficiencies of the officially prescribed textbooks and Their damaging consequences upon the community. He impelled the Muslim community of India to give greater importance to the religious education of their children than to food and drink and established *maktab*s (schools of imparting religious education) with greater sincerity and fervor than they do the Masjids for in the final analysis the attendance in the Masjids, will depend on these *makatab*s.[17]

Muslim Community in India

Hindus and Muslims have been living in India side-by-side,

16. Ibid., p. 11.
17. Ibid., p. 15.

as neighbours, for more than a thousand years but how much the people know about each other? Many researchers have been disappointed to see that the people in India lack elementary knowledge about other religions. In the absence of knowledge, myths and suspicion occupy the place in the back of mind. These myths about other people's religions, which Hindus have of Muslims and Muslims about Hindus, creates walls of hostilities among these communities. In a communally charged atmosphere in India it is a common phenomenon when on very trivial matters, riots have broken out causing wide scale loss of life and property. These walls of hostilities are ready ammunition to indulge in hate campaign against the other communities. How do you tackle it? This puzzled Mawlana Nadwi.

Mawlana Nadwi was perturbed by the fact that there was a complete absence of knowledge about each others religion among the two communities. As the best, and only, way of tackling ignorance is knowledge, he wrote a book *Indian Muslims at a Glance* (*Hindustani Muslaman*: *Ek Nazar Mein*), to acquaint Hindus about the way of life of their Muslim countrymen — their neighbours. Explaining the reason and goal of writing such a book Mawlana Nadwi writes in the Preface of the book:

> As far as history of Muslims is concerned or their role in the making of this country (India) and their contribution towards culture, tradition, poetry, literature and other fine arts many good books have been written by both Hindu and Muslim writers. . . . But such works are of the interest of students and researchers only. The need, on the contrary, is more common and more widespread. The times demand a book which presents the present picture of Muslims, as and how they are, without prejudice of as how they should be. The account should be detached and true irrespective of

> whether anybody likes it or not. . . . It should be factual and not argumentative.[18]

By giving an introduction of the religious, cultural and social life of Muslims including their beliefs, prayers, festivals, the tradition and their distinct features, acquired by virtue of being Muslims, Mawlana Nadwi tried to start a dialogue between these two communities in particular and other religious groups in general.

In starting a dialogue, Mawlana Nadwi had to represent the side of the Indian Muslims. He continuously fought for a proper place for Muslims in the Indian society. This earned him many adversaries and enemies among both Muslims and Hindus. At times even the media was very unfair to him and painted him as a "fire-breathing communal Muslim." Syed Shahabuddin, a prominent politician and Member of Parliament, castigating such allegations writes:

> The Mawlana was the very antithesis of the media image of the fire-eating (fire-breathing), narrow-minded *mullah*. Orthodox as he was, he was far from being conservative in his approach. *Ummah*-conscious as he was, his love of the motherland knew no bounds. He preached *Jihad* to restore Muslim dominance; He stood for mutual respect, for peaceful co-existence, for human values, for establishing a social ambience based on tolerance and harmony in India and in the world at large.[19]

All his life, with Lucknow as his base, he wandered ceaselessly, not only within the country but in the Arab-Islamic world

---

18. Mawlana Sayyid Abul Hasan Ali Nadwi, *Hindustani Musalmaan: Ek Nazar Mein* (Urdu), Majalis Tahkikat wa Nashriyati Islimi, Lucknow 1985, p. 15.

19. Sayed Shabuddin, "Defender of Islamic Identity" in *The Fragrance of East*, vol. 11, no. 1-2, January-June 2000, p. 86.

and the West, in a constant search, apparently, for reconciliation between Islam, and the West, between rival ideologies in the Arab-Islamic world, between India and Pakistan and between the Hindu and Muslim Indians.

His constant endeavour for interreligious dialogue and for reconciliation and harmony, he commanded universal respect for his moderation, learning and integrity, for his influences in the Muslim community and for his outreach in the Islamic world. Mawlana Nadwi acted as the bridge between the government and the national parties, on the one hand, and Muslim community, on the other. Shabuddin writes: "The Mawlana, it has been correctly observed, stood for social reform, religious revival and political awakening but not for Islamic revolution. He was realistic enough not to chase mirage or instant solution. He saw clearly that the destiny of Muslim Indians was intertwined with that of the Indian people as a whole and that, in the age of democratic pluralism, an Islamic revolution or the revolution of Islamic power was out of the realm of possibility but it was possible for the Muslim Indians to lead an Islamic life and at the same time participate in managing the affairs of the country and contribute to its progress and development. This was the basis of his efforts to minimize the distance between the Muslims and Hindus, to demolish the wall of distrust between them and to create bonds of understanding and co-operation in rebuilding relations on the terms of common values of the society, which he saw as being engulfed by dark forces of hatred and violence."[20]

Muslim Personal Law Board

The two most painful events in the religious life of Muslims of

20. Ibid., pp. 89-90.

India are undisputedly the Babri Masjid–Ram Janma Bhumi dispute and the call for a Uniform Civil Code from a section of Hindu population. *Shari'ah* or the Islamic code of jurisprudence, for Muslims, is an inalienable integral part of Islam. Its followers must follow all commandments as detailed in *Holy Qur'an* and *Hadith.* Islam is not confined to acts of worship alone. It is much more. Islam encompasses the whole life of a follower.

The whole process started with the famous court case called *Ajmal Khan* vs *Shah Bano* more commonly known as Shah Banu case. Shah Banu, a divorcee demanded maintenance for life from her former husband in contravention of Muslim Personal Law. The *Shari'ah* laws, Muslims in India are allowed to follow. The litigant, Shah Banu was supported by many Hindus and a section of "liberal" Muslims like Danial Latif and Dilwai. The case turned into a full-fledged political controversy as its supporters hailed it as justice to women and eradication of bias towards females. The Supreme Court, the highest court of law in the country, decided the case in favour of Shah Banu, which most Muslims believe, is against Islamic tenants. Muslim scholarship was unanimous in opposition as can be gauged from the fact that almost all sects and sub-sects of Muslims Sunnis, Shias, Bohras, Bareilvis . . . came together to fight against the Supreme Court order.

Muslim Personal Law Board came into being in reaction to the demands of Uniform Civil Code from various segments of population in India. Muslim theologians and majority Muslim population opposed the move as they felt that it would erode Islamic values from their community. In Mawlana Nadwi's words,

> This (Uniform Civil Code) will be a rebellion (of Muslims) against (Islamic) culture and *Shar'ih* besides being harbinger

> of end of blessings of the religion Islam. So far the Muslims are concerned, it is part of their faith and belief that their personal law is Divine and ordained by the same God who revealed the glorious *Qur'an* and fundamental beliefs and the system of worship and without which one cannot remain a Muslim. It means law has been decreed by all-knowing God, who has created man and who knows his natural wants and weaknesses.[21]

Preservation of Muslim Personal Law in India was very close to Mawlana Nadwi's heart. Mawlana Syed Mananat-ul-llah Rehmani, Amir Sharia Bihar and Orrisa, played the leading role in the movement for preservation of Muslim Personal Law in India. His initiative was backed by Muslim Majlis Mashawarat, Jamaat-i-Islami, Darul-Ulum Deoband, Mazahar-ul-Ulum Nadwat-ul-Ulama' besides many other organizations. It was decided that a convention (Muslim Personal Law Convention) would be held at Mumbai (then Bombay) on 27, 28 December 1972.

Mawlana Nadwi along with Mawlana Mohammed Manzoor were at Hejaz to attend themeeting of Rabita Conference. As Rabita Conference is held in the month of Zi-Qadah, Mawlana Nadwi intended to return after performing *haj*.[22]

But on the insistence and repeated messages of Mawlana Muhammad Yousuf of Jamaat-i-Islami, and other friends Mawlana Nadwi, who had performed *haj* many times earlier decided to attend the Muslim Personal Law Convention at Mumbai on 27, 29 December 1972.[23]

---

21. Mawlana Nadwi, Islamic Code of life and Uniform Civil Code, All India Personal Law Board, Nadwatul Ulama, Lucknow, 1992, p. 6, and also see *Karavaan-i-Zindagi,* vol. 3, pp. 111, 186.
22. *Karavaan-i-Zindagi,* vol. 2, p. 137.
23. Ibid., pp. 137-38.

Mawlana Nadwi's decision to return from Hejaz without performing *haj*, which was just two to three weeks ahead to attend the Muslim Personal Law Convention shows how much of importance he gave to this issue. The core of Mawlana Nadwi's pursuit was that the climate of fear, distrust and confusion should be brought to an end as, he felt, it was imperative for the progress and development of the country.[24]

Mawlana Nadwi vociferously advocated utmost religious freedom where no section of the society "may harbour doubts about their religious tenants, laws, rites and rituals without which it would be difficult for them to live as true followers of their religion."

Mawlana Nadwi considered Muslim Personal Law Board as a Jugular vein for Muslim society. Mawlana Nadwi's name was proposed at the Ranchi convention in 1977 for the presidentship of the Muslim Personal Law Board, but he declined it, saying, "When the ship is sinking you don't change the captain."[25]

Mawlana Qari Mohammad Tayyab continued to head the Muslim Personal Law Board till he passed away on 17 July 1983, Mawlana Nadwi did not participate in the Madras convention of All India Muslim Personal Law Board, due to ill-health. Though Mawlana had made all preparations to participate, a serious attack of gout barred him from joining the convention. In his absence, Mawlana Nadwi's name was proposed for president and accepted unanimously.[26] To which Mawlana Nadwi reacts as :

---

24. Mawlana Nadwi's address to 10th Annual session of All India Muslim Personal Board, New Delhi, 23-24 November 1991.

25. *Karavaan-i-Zindagi*, vol. 3, p. 111.

26. Ibid., p. 112.

> If it had been (the presidentship) the case of a high office bestowed by a political organization or social or religious organization, I would have declined without any second thoughts but the importance and complexity of the issue, which I consider an integral part of my faith and a jugular vein of Muslim life, besides out of respect for Mawlana Syed Manatullah I could not say no.[27]

The first presidential address of Mawlana Nadwi at Calcutta (now Kolkata) convention on 6 April 1985, was not in a written form. Mawlana opened the address by apologizing for not being able to prepare a written speech citing his hectic travel schedule within and outside the country as a reason.

Mawlana Nadwi outlined some reason for opposition to a particular issue as opposition for opposition, enmity, political expediency or personal interest besides misunderstanding, lack of knowledge or ill-information. "I believe that" says Mawalna Nadwi, "those people or a school of thought, who oppose Muslim Personal Law or are in favour of a Uniform Civil Code, do not simply do so for opposition or with a spirit of enmity but, I think, misunderstanding and ill-information play a vital role in it."[28]

Mawlana Nadwi highlights the need to educate people about Islam and *Shar'ih*. Dismissing the argument that a Uniform Civil Code will bring amity between various sects of people and help in national integration, Mawlana Nadwi posed a question, "If Uniform Civil Code is such a panacea, why did Germany and Britain went to war with each other, when both nations were Christian, actually both of them Protestant Christian nations?"[29]

---

27. Ibid., p. 113.
28. Mawlana Nadwi's address at Calcutta Convention, 6 April 1985.
29. Ibid.

Mawlana Nadwi, who all along has been a vociferous supporter of Muslim Personal Law said in the concluding part of his presentation address at Calcutta Convention, "We (Muslims) consider imposition of any other Civil Code an invitation to apostasy, as the economic, cultural, social setup in Islam is an integral and necessary part of the religion, as is the case with any other religion."

In his book *Karavaan-i-Zindagi* Mawlana Nadwi writes:

> I purely addressed the Muslim audience with unbiased introspection. I told them how many un-Islamic rituals they have ingrained into their lives, how little do they follow *Sharia* and the Muslim Personal Law in their daily life. . . . As the basic and fundamental objective of the creation of All India Muslim Personal Law Board was reformation in Muslim society and inviting/making Muslims to adhere to the orders of God in their social, cultural and civil life.[30]

Mawlana Nadwi explained the need of preservation of Muslim Personal Law and the objectives of Muslim Personal Law Board again at Delhi Conference, the 10th Annual Session of All India Muslim Personal Law Board held at New Delhi on 23 and 24 November 1991. Mawlana Nadwi always held democracy and freedom in high esteem and close to his heart. The Delhi convention was held at a time, when political developments had subverted the atmosphere in the country. The country was experiencing unprecedented divisions among its society. Mawlana Nadwi opened his address with a fervent appeal:

> I wish that all the truth-loving and conscientious persons and all those, who have the good of the country at heart should take notice of this Convention, as without such

30. *Karavaan-i-Zindagi,* vol. 3, pp. 114-15.

> analysis and deliberations democratic values cannot continue for long.[31]

He emphatically reiterates in this lecture that:

> It is necessary for the progress and development of the country that the climate of fear, distrust and confusion should be brought to an end as no country can move forward when the different sections of its population may harbour doubts about their religious tenets, laws, rites and rituals without which it would be difficult for them to live as true followers of their religion. There can be nothing worse than that the energies, which ought to be utilized in strengthening and advancement of the country should be spent in dispelling doubts and suspicions. I will go further and say that we have an apprehension that if our future generations do not hold the beliefs which are dearer to us than our lives, then there will be uncertainty and confusion among the Muslims, which will not only be harmful to them but to the country aswell.

Further more he emphasizes that:

> Secondly the wide scope of Islam should also be kept in mind. The difference in religions is not confined to minor rites and rituals but in the fundamental principles of religions themselves. There are religions, which were founded on revelations and Prophethood, but their followers confined them to acts of worship alone. There is no such thing in Islam. It encompasses the whole of a life of Muslim. It is a basic reality which cannot be appreciated without realizing the relations between the Creator and the created.

31. Mawlana Nadwi. Islamic Code of Life and Uniform Civil Code or 10th Annual Session of Indian Muslim Personal Law Board held at Delhi on 23 and 24 November 1991, All India Muslim Personal Law Board, Lucknow 1992, p. 1.

> Every Muslim is an obedient servant of God and his relationship with him is eternal and all-embracing:
>
> O Ye who believe ! come, all of you, into submission (unto Him); and follow not the footsteps of the devil. Lo ! he is an open enemy for you. — *Surah Baqarah*: 208

It should be clearly understood that the religion of Islam owes its origin to revelation and the last Prophet Muhammad (SAAS) himself has been directed to follow it. The glorious *Qur'an* lays down:

> And now have we set thee (O Muhammad) on a clear road of (Our) commandment; so follow it, and follow not the whims of those who know not. — *Surah Jathiya*: 18

When the innocent and beloved Prophet (peace be on him) is being directed to follow it, how then can it be demanded from his followers to change or accept any change in it?

These are the two basic realities, which when understood in their correct prespective, there would be no such demands from the Muslims. They would be saved of an avoidable embarrassment and their faculties and energies would not be spent in refuting such unnecessary demands and the government would save time to spend on useful pursuits."[32] After explaining it, he explodes the myth that the Uniform Civil Code will bring unity and goes on to say:

> We are told that for the sake of unity and integrity of the country we may accept Uniform Civil Code. I ask a question which a school-going child can answer. The First World War was fought, at the beginning, between Britain and Germany. The Britons and Germans are not only Christians but Protestants and their Personal Law is also the same.

32. Ibid., pp. 1, 3.

> Why then they fought? If Uniform Civil Code could stop fighting, it should have stopped them. The Second World War is another example. They were both Christian and Protestants and their Personal Law is the same. But they fought as blood-thirsty enemies bent on annihilating each other. If we go to law courts we find there are law suits between Muslims and Muslims, Hindus and Hindus. The complainant wants to seal the doom of the respondent and vice versa. Their personal law is the same and at times, they belong to the same caste and family, in some cases they are blood-relations. In fact, the cause of enmity is selfishness, greed and materialism. It is on account of the wrong system and curriculum, which has neglected moral teachings. I can say, indeed challenge, that there would be no change in morality even after introduction of a Uniform Civil Code. Why then Uniform Civil Code is mentioned time and again that there be unity by it.[33]

Mawlana Nadwi was a vehement supporter of religious freedom, which in his views was necessary for peace of mind and to avoid confusion in the society, therefore he proclaims that:

> We should also keep in mind that if any law clashes with the fundamental beliefs of any section of population, sect or religion then it would not create unity, co-operation, sincerity and peace of mind but create confusion, lack of interest and a sense of compulsion and serfdom, which is detrimental for the unity of the nation and the country.[34]

Babri Masjid Demolition

If any person in India is asked to identify one most important factor responsible for continuous tension between Hindu and

33. Ibid., pp. 3-4.
34. Ibid., p. 5.

Muslims, it is most likely that he or she may point out the Babri Masjid dispute. The reason is simple; the other reasons that might have been cited by people say thirty years back are too old for common memory not to speak of collective memory. What happened before, during and after Partition may have been very close to the generations that experienced it. But that era has passed that happened almost three generations back, the Babri Masjid-Ram Janambhoomi dispute comes from the same era. It may have started before but the movement for Ram Janambhoomi got some mom in 1940s itself.

A section of Hindus claim that Lord Rāma, a mythical figure of Hindu religion, was born at Ayodhyā, a town in the largest state of India, Uttar Pradesh, where a seventeenth-century Zahir-ud-Din Babur era Masjid stood. The Masjid was razed to ground by a frenzied mob, who had congregated at the place coming from various parts of India. The rally/public meeting was organized by the Bhartiya Janata Party and other Sangh Parivar outfits like Rashtriya Svayamsevak Sangh, Vishva Hindu Parishad, etc.

Babri Masjid was brought down on 6 December 1992. There was rioting and communal clashes took place almost all over the country. The demolition of Masjid came as a double shock as Muslims were fighting a long tiring battle towards safeguarding the administration of Muslim Personal Law in the country.

Mawlana Nadwi was actively involved in the various efforts made to settle the dispute, though, everybody knows, without success. He was even accused by some persons of striking a deal with the central government over the Babri Masjid issue. However, these allegations were strongly refuted by Mawlana Nadwi.[35] Describing the demolition of the Masjid at Ayodhya.

35. For the response to these a allegations, see *The Fragrance of East*, pp. 219-20.

Mawlana Nadwi writes in his biography:

> With the passage of time the BJP government in the State (U.P.) headed by Chief Minister Kalyan Singh and, other leaders of the party Mr. L. K. Advani, Mr. M. M. Joshi, Mr. Vajpayee and their associates launched a countrywide movement for demolition of Babri Masjid and construction of Ram temple at the site. It (building of the temple) had been made into a point of prestige of free India not to mention of Hindu community. The propaganda of the campaign was so vicious that the whole country seemed to be on fire. An army of *Karsevaks* (volunteers) was ready to perform the act (of demolishing of the Masjid). They felt it was their religious duty. . . . As a result the Masjid was brought down in a cruel way with religious fervour accompanied by deep-rooted hatred.[36]

With the same feeling of resentment and desperation he later on in the same book alleges,

> (Later) it was proved that rehearsal of the demolition of the Masjid was going on from a week. P.A.C (Armed Police) and *Karsevaks* were as friendly as BJP & RSS.[37]

The most of the political battles of Indian Muslim community during the last decades of the century were fought under the guidance of Mawlana Nadwi. The All India Muslim Personal Law Board launched in 1985 the movement for legislative nullification of the Supreme Court judgement in the Shah Banu case, which most of the Muslims in India saw as the thin end of the wedge for interference with the *Shari'at* and for distorting the Islamic identity of the community. The Muslim Women (Protection of Rights on Divorcees) Act, 1986 was its

---

36. *Karvan-i-Zandagi*, vol. 5, p. 109.
37. Ibid., p. 109.

fruit, though it had several in-built flaws, which landed the community subsequently in endless litigation. With the Mawlana's consent in 1986, the AIMMM and the AIMPLB took up the question of restoration of the Babri Masjid when the unlocking of its doors in January 1986 for regular *darśana* and *pūjā* converted it into a *de-facto* temple. Though he did not directly involve himself in the Babri Masjid Movement (whose co-ordination Committee was later split to form the All India Babri Masjid Action Committee), he guided it at all critical points and participated in negotiations with the government as well as Hindu representatives. Subsequently to the demolition, the AIMPLB, under his presidentship took the question in its own hands including the direction of the proceedings in the title suit, the criminal case and the inquiry.

The Muslims of Indian subcontinent right from the inception of British rule could not keep themselves aloof from the issue of international concern particularly the problems and issues faced by *ummah* across the Muslims world. After India became independent in 1947 the Indian Muslims, who were subjected to many forms of brutality back home could certainly feel the tears of agonies of suppressed Muslim communities world over. This becomes clear from the fact that Indian Muslims always reacted strongly and publicly against Israeli brutalities inflicting upon Palestinians.

Therefore, in its response, Mawlana Nadwi not only expressed his views *vis-à-vis* such issues of international concern but also made the general masses to comprehend the real nature and the vitality of those issues.

Mawlana's Response to the Palestine Issue

Though as theologian, Mawlana Nadwi was more concerned with the societal or collective apostasy of Arab people, he could not betray his feelings regarding occupation of Palestine. Describing the occupation of Al-Aqsa Masjid, *qibla* Awwal (first *qibla*) of Muslims and Palestinian land and people as the darkest day in the history of Muslims in his book *Latest Catastrophe of Arab World*, Mawlana Nadwi writes, "June 9, 1967 (Safar 29,1387 H) came as such an ominous day for Muslims, which hanged their heads in shame and they couldn't look into the eyes of anyone even their own countrymen."[38] The pain in Mawlana Nadwi's words could not have been more palpable.

Islam calls Jews and Christians as *Ahli-Kitab* (people whose prophets were given/bestowed a book of revelations) This kind of kinship resulted into some bloody wars and oppression.

More than 800 years ago, during crusade, Muslims lost the control of Al-Aqsa Mosque. But Salah-ud-din Ayubi (R.A.) won it back from crusaders. Mawlana Nadwi about the first occupation of Al-Aqsa Mosque by crusaders says:

> When Al-Aqsa Masjid fell into the hands of crusaders, Muslims were restless till they won it back. The miseries of Palestinians give pain to every Muslim in the world. As Islam is a faith which envisages brotherhood (amongst its followers) and the concepts of *Millat* (*Milah*). It is natural that Muslims even living far away from the scene of conflict are aggrieved by the happenings in Palestine. The 1967 defeat of Muslims at the hands of Jewish Israel left deep scars in the hearts and psyche of the Muslims all over the world.[39]

Mawlana Wahidudin Khan, the renowned Islamic scholar of India in an article, in the *Milli Gazzette*, titled "The Importance

38. Mawlana Nadwi, *Aalam-i-Arabi ka Almiya*, Majlis-Tahkeekat-Wa Nashriyati Islami, Lucknow, 1980, p. 26.

39. Ibid., pp. 26-27.

of Unity" writes, "to fight one's friends is to become one's own worst enemy. It is to destroy oneself as one's enemies are always seeking to do."[40] In the article Mawlana Wahiduddin Khan cites Moshe Dayan, the former Israeli defence minister, from his autobiography, *The Story of Life*', "The Arabs, disunited and at odds with one another over every issue, big and small, pose no threat." Mawlana Wahiddudin Khan in his Islamic scholarship of highest order was the contemporary of Mawlana Nadwi. While Mawlana Wahiddudin Khan laid stress on unity among Arabs to put an end to miseries of Palestinians, Mawlana Nadwi saw other things such as irreligious behaviour of Muslims, rise of nationalism, etc. as the bigger evils, which needed to be dealt with to free Palestinians from the cruel hands of tyrannical Israel.

Mawlana Nadwi opines that the three basic factors in the defeat of Arabs at the hands of Israel were:

1. The influence of Western culture and materialism on Arabs,
2. Rise of Arab nationalism, and
3. Military governments/rule in almost all Arab countries which gave rise to revolutions and rebellions and conspiracies.

If these factors are studied with some degree of detachment it can be easily concluded that Mawlana Nadwi was distressed and disgusted with the irreligious way of life of the Arabs.[41]

Western civilization had an impact on the Muslims throughout Islamic world therefore, Mawlana Nadwi like

---

40. *Mili Gazette* (journal), 16-30 September 2000.
41. Mawlana Nadwi, *Alame-i-Arabi ka Almiya,* pp. 32, 56.

Mawlana Maududi could not escape to respond this growing threat. He explored its positive as well as negative effects.

Islam and the West

The many factors that prevent, desist, dissuade the Easterners from any proper appreciation of the West, in Mawlana Nadwi's views were due to the fact that during nineteenth century the West, driven by political and economic considerations invaded the East with all it had — its civilization, its sciences, its culture and its scheme of state organization. The East was dumbfounded by this onslaught and even now could not get into right frame of mind to attempt an effective understanding of the West. Another factor for this aloofness of Easterners towards the West could be traced to the nature of Western civilization; which on a whole is a materialistic view of the world and contained more or less all that is characteristics of a civilization, whose religious impulse has suffered atrophy. Also the feeling of racial superiority in individual behaviour and general policies of Westerners, which are incompatible with human dignity created hurdles in proper understanding and appreciation of the West.[42]

The above-chronicled factors or reasons were described as impediments in proper appreciation of the West by Mawlana Nadwi in his opening remarks in the speech delivered by Mawlana Nadwi at seventh convocation of the University of Kashmir on 29 October 1981, he said, "knowledge, I believe is one and indivisible, and to separate it into parts, into ancient and modern; Eastern and Western; and ideological and practical is incorrect." Further down in the address he went on to say, "I regard knowledge a truth which is a gift of God

42. Mawlana Nadwi, *Speaking Plainly to the West*, Academy Islamic Research and Pub., Lucknow, 1973, pp. 7, 9.

and does not and should not belong to a particular race or community. I see unity in diversity. The unity is truth, the search for truth the aptitude for it, and the joy of its realization."[43]

These words should allay the fears, if any, of Mawlana Nadwi being a critic of West. Obviously, he stood for and propagated a proper understanding and appreciation of the West. The biggest reason Mawlana Nadwi feels was responsible for the humiliating walk over of the East by the West in the nineteenth century with ease was that the West had outpaced East in knowledge and education.[44]

In short, Mawlana Nadwi was not averse to the West, rather he did not look down upon the West as something from which one should distance himself or herself. This in no way is meant to suggest that Mawlana Nadwi was for blind imitation of the West. Actually, Mawlana Nadwi strongly advocated against such human tendencies. As he writes:

> There arose a trend of blind imitation of the West (among Easterners), which robbed the peoples of East of their distinctive personality as well as of their self-respect. The aping of the West in all walks of life pushed the Easterners into the background, reducing them to the position of mere camp-followers.[45]

Mawlana Nadwi spoke these words on 11 October 1963, at the University of London. "Blinding imitation" did some serious damage to the self-respect, esteem and psyche of the peoples of the East. The wedge between the East and the

---

43. Mawlana Nadwi, *The Place of Knowledge and Responsibilities of Those who Acquire It*, pp. 1, 7.
44. Idem.
45. Mawlana Nadwi, *Speaking Plainly to the West*, p. 9.

West was growing, as was the difference between other things or assets like wealth and knowledge. This necessarily meant that people would get swayed to the powerful, wealthy and the learned. The Easterners who were, in Mawlana Nadwi's words, robbed of their self-respect and personality did not care to retain whatever they had inherited in the form of culture, knowledge, or other assets. The Easterners, speaking plainly to Muslims, lost their sense of history and succumbed meekly, painfully, idiotically, reprehensibly to the West — including its (West's) culture, economics, lifestyles and everything else except religion. The meek surrender of the Easterners culminated in the West treating the East with disregard and outright contempt:

> This aping of the west in all walks of life pushed the easterners into the background, reducing them to the position of mere camp-followers. Consequently the West could not look upon the East with any sense of equality and respect much less of admiration and esteem; nor could it look to the East for inspiration or guidance or anything original or creative. Eventually matters came to a pass where complete dissolution threatened the fading away of the East into the West.[46]

These remarks were made in October 1963, when the humiliating six-day war, which was the final nail in the coffin of esteem, self-respect and, perhaps, myths, of the Muslim East, was yet to come. Even at that time Western lifestyle had overwhelmed the East. In the aftermath of the war, Muslim world was in chaos — psychologically, politically as well as intellectually. Though the sense of defeatism and servility had made inroads much earlier into the hearts and minds of Muslims all over the world especially in the Arab world.

---

46. Idem.

According to him:

> In the contrast to the attitude of exclusiveness and denial there is the philosophy of defeatism, capitulation and servility. Its advocates are among the most enthusiastic and ardent, though immature, disciples of the West. They are of the view that a section of the public opinion in the some part of the Muslim world should adopt whole-heartedly the materialistic and 'technological' civilization of the West, along with all its cultural, social and intellectual implications, and then strive to establish it in its country, at all costs and whatever the suffering.[47]

Mawlana Nadwi strongly advocated the safeguard of Islamic culture. He was of the view that totalitarian and dictatorial regimes, who currently govern most of the Muslim countries especially in the Arab world were not in the interests of Islam and could not help in safeguarding the Islamic culture. Mawlana Nadwi always criticized state-control over mass media. And at many places listed/rated it as an impediment in enhancement of Islamic culture and progress of these countries.

> Bayonets and machine guns, tanks and aeroplanes, totalitarianism and regimentation cannot save the Islamic countries from the destiny which is staring them in their face. The state-controlled radio and the newspapers, the buying of the hearts and souls of men, with money or political patronage, glittering banquets and other celebrations at their diplomatic offices in foreign land, half-hearted attempts to appease religious sentiments of the people through holding Muslim conferences or other similar demonstrations of Islamic feeling cannot remove inner discord and discontent from them nor pave the way for

47. Mawlana Nadwi, *Western Civilization — Islam and West*, Academy of Islamic Research and Pub., Lucknow, 1969, p. 31.

> peace, stability and progress.[48] The civilization, which originated in lands far away from the hot land of Islam. These engines of Westernization are driven by the people whom Mawlana Nadwi calls; the most enthusiastic and ardent, though immature disciples of the West.

Apart from material and technological progress of the West there are other factors within the Muslim society, which makes Western culture appealing and the Muslim culture unattractive. These factors include the rule of totalitarian, military and undemocratic regimes prevalent in most of the Muslim world. The huge difference between the rich and the poor in these countries. Absence of a free media and other such factors.

Mawlana Nadwi, it can be gauged from his various dilations on the West, was not against the West. He can not be accused of Westophobia. But he on numerous occasions, stressed the need for conservation of Islamic culture. The problem of Westernization in Mawlana Nadwi's view emanated from within, which had little to do with the outside. So Mawlana Nadwi professed corrective measures from within and was against the concept of hatred of the West.

Mawlana Nadwi also suggested some remedial measures, which out and out are a theologian's view, who has a reasonable understanding of ground realities as well, as proper approach to the problem. Therefore he writes:

> The road to their salvation lies only in the appreciation of the hard realities of their situation and in meeting them with courage, foresight and genuine Islamic understanding. The Muslim countries must honestly strive for a radical and all round reorientation of their socio-political structures as demanded by true dictates of Islam. All the things that

48. Ibid., p. 28.

> call for axe should be rooted out without mercy and the necessary changes should be introduced and wholesome reforms and other measures of advancement launched without delay. The principles of equity and justice must be established in Muslim society as taught by Islam and practised by *Holy* Prophet (SAAS). Steps must be taken immediately for the amelioration of the living conditions of the common man. The basic necessities of life must be assured to everyone. Extravagance and wastefulness, which have no place in Islamic way of life will have to be eschewed before a solid economic reconstruction of Muslim world can be taken in hand. The wealthier sections among Muslims should learn the Islamic lesson of self-denial and austerity and the poorer ones that of dignity, contentment and hard work. The educational system ought to be re-organized soon in the light of a harmonious blending between contemporary knowledge and needs and aspirations and the basic ideals of Islam. It should be made truly representative of the spirit of the faith as well as of the times so that the rising generations of Muslims may be equipped properly to meet the demands of both, and can be firm like a rock where spiritual belief, morality, consistency, honour and self-reliance are concerned and, at the same time, be lagging behind no one in matters of knowledge, creativity and intellectual maturity, and, should be able to respond to the challenge of the West with courage, faith and vision.[49]

Mawlana Nadwi did not ever in his life suggested that the Muslim world should take a path of confrontation with the West or isolate itself from the West. It can be safely deduced that Mawlana Nadwi did not foresee a clash of civilizations as envisaged by many intellectuals such as Samuel Huntington. He, gauging from his works and speeches, firmly believed

49. Ibid., pp. 28-29.

that various cultures could co-exist at the same time. What he was against was the destruction/fading of Islamic civilization by presently more dominant Western civilization. The preservation of Islamic culture or adherence to roots was what Mawlana Nadwi professed as the road to salvation. The wining back of glory needed to be preceded by sound progress in all spheres of life. Democratic, people-friendly governments must replace the existing totalitarian scumbag regimes, equity and justice must be restored in the society, adherence to the much professed path of austerity backed by sound education were described as some of the measures by Mawlana Nadwi, which may help the Muslim world get out of the mess they presently find themselves in.[50]

To sum it up in Mawlana Nadwi's words:

> Dr. Sulaiman Dunya, from whose writings I (Mawlana Nadwi) too, have profited has very aptly remarked that Islam is not exclusive to any country. I wholly agree that Islam is not a territorial faith, yet, it also needs a distinctive environment, a congenial climate and a predisposition that may transcend personal, cultural and intellectual standards and give forth, as one would say, the aroma of Islam. It requires an Islamic homeland for it is neither a mystical doctrine nor a philosophy nor a collection of soulless beliefs and rituals but a real, living and all-embracing faith.[51]

Though these words were said in a different context but by reading between the lines one can find Mawlana Nadwi elucidating the "why" of preserving the Islamic culture.

Mawlana Nadwi continuously, relentlessly criticized Arabs

50. Ibid., pp. 5, 30.

51. Mawlana Nadwi, *From the Depth of Heart in America,* Academy of Islamic Research and Pub., Lucknow, 1978, pp. 58-59.

when addressing them during the time he spent in Hejaz and other parts of the Arab world between 1947 to 1951.

He was disgusted with the Muslims over their outlook towards the challenges they were facing. In his views the following weaknesses were taking roots in the national character of Muslim societies:

(a) A tendency to give preference to personal interests over those of the nation at the cost of principles.

(b) Refusal to accept the challenge the West had thrown at them.

(c) Refusal to act and work hard.

(d) The demonstration of cowardice.

(e) Unconditional following of the secular and national leadership.

(f) Outpouring of emotions and sentiments in writings and speeches.[52]

He pointed out that the depth of intellectual and moral decline of the Muslims had reached such levels that seemed to gloat over the calamities of their enemies and almost waited for them to occur. Their moral bankruptcy had suffered such decline that they were not ready to concede that their adversaries had anything good in them. Because of their inaction, they seemed to be so dispirited that they over estimated the power and capabilities of their adversaries.

Mawlana Nadwi's Response to Muslim University (Amendment) Act of 1972

Mawlana Nadwi has always lived in the contemporary world. He has never been found wanting in his duties towards the

52. Mawlana Nadwi, *Alam-i-Arabi ka Almiya*, p. 33ff.

issues facing Muslim society. Mawlana Nadwi has always guided people showing them the right path, which at times was not the popular path.

Mawlana Nadwi's appeals for peace and restraint after communal flare up in Rourkela and other areas were not perceived to be the best option especially by the Muslim youth, but Mawlana Nadwi never wanted to be a populist figure. Though the main area of interest and works of Mawlana Nadwi were theology and explanation of various aspects of Islam through his books and speeches (*tablig*), he always responded to current issues facing the Muslim society in India in particular and the whole *ummah* in general.

In his inaugural address to Aligarh Muslim University Old Boys Convention of 10, 11 March 1973 at Delhi, Mawlana Abdul Hassan Ali Nadwi deliberated on the Muslim Universities (Amendment) Act of June 1972.

Deep understanding, wide vision and clarity of thought have, all along, been hallmarks of Mawlana. It was his interest, typical style, be it his writings or speeches — wherein he will explain the problem, the genesis of the problem, its repercussions and the way out or remedies, if any. Mawlana's always used to be lucid and forthright.

Mawlana opened his address by describing "How and Why" of the making of Aligarh Muslim University and went to discuss the gains, which were made because of the independent character of the University and goes on to say:

> What I aim to stress here is that its founder, Sir Syed Ahmed Khan wanted it, from the first day, to be an independent Muslim university. He firmly believed that unless the education of the Muslims was free from governmental control and its management and organization was directly in their own hands they could not derive much benefit from

> it. The Muslim educational scheme published by his illustrious son, Syed Mahmud, in 1873, was wholly representative of his views. It envisaged the establishment of a university on the pattern of the Oxford and Cambridge Universities and free from official interference. After the death of Sir Syed his colleagues adhered to the same ideal as was evident from the proceedings of the Mohammedan Educational Conference held at Lahore in 1898. Sir Syed wanted to popularize modern education among Muslims not only so that they could qualify for government jobs. He had a much higher objective before him, which was that through it he hoped to erase the moral and psychological effects of the disaster of 1857. He wanted to pull them out of the morass they had sunk into and to reawaken in them the qualities of leadership, re-soluteness and self-confidence that had enabled them to rule over the country for 800 years, to play a vital role in its advancement and progress and to leave such magnificent monuments — both of a literary and architectural character — that prompted Sir Syed to write Aasar-*Us-Sanadid* (Great and Lasting Monuments) in order to preserve their remembrance.[53]

Being a man of perfection and a scholarship *par excellence,* Mawlana Nadwi lamented about the non-availability of history of Aligarh Muslim University in written form. This was no bragging as it came from a man, who has devoted major part of his life to research and writing. In his indomitable style he went on to say:

> The story of the establishment of the Aligarh Muslim University is a long one, full of bitter and sweet memories . . . replete with legal and constitutional debates and

53. Mawlana Nadwi's Inaugural Address, Aligarah Muslim University Old Boys Convention, 10-11 March 1973 at Delhi, published by Majlis Istiqbaliah all India Aligarah Muslim University Convention, Delhi n.d., pp. 5, 7.

> controversies. It forms a vital part of the history of Indian Muslims. Unfortunately, the history of the Aligarh Muslim University has not yet been written but fragments of it can be seen in the files of Al-Hilal. It is not necessary to recapitulate it here. In brief, the efforts of those who were striving for it . . . among whom the Raja of Mahmudabad and the Agha Khan were in the forefront bore fruit and, in 1920, the Charter was granted to Muslim University by the British government. Though the Constitution of the University fell short of the expectations of Nawab Viqarul Mulk and Mawlana Abul Kalam Azad the Court was recognized as its supreme governing body and it was provided that its members will be elected by the different Muslim associations and schools of thought and donors and sympathizers and members of the staff of the University. There were to be the Academic Council and the Executive Council but the last word rested with the Court which alone could select the Vice-Chancellor.
>
> In its autonomous atmosphere their latent potentialities were developed and they grew up to be fearless and self-reliant. Every field of national endeavour was enriched by them. A direct relationship obtained between the University and Muslim intelligentsia and it sent forth new blossoms, which is the hallmark of a free and national seat of learning.[54]

Mawlana Nadwi fearlessly in a straightforward and uncompromising manner, spoke about aspirations and hopes of people in an independent and democratic country. Again, it was not politically correct statement to make but Mawlana Nadwi seldom cared about anything except truth and justice.

After India attained Independence in 1947 it was hoped that the democratic and autonomous character of the

54. Ibid., pp. 11, 13.

University will be maintained for the chief advantage of freedom lies in the fulfilment of the urges and aspirations of the people and in safeguarding not only the life, property and honour of all the classes and communities, irrespective of their numerical strength, but also of their creed, ideals and social and cultural characteristics.

The hope was not only realized but the rights that had been granted by the alien government began to be withdrawn one by one. By the amendment of 1965 the administration of the Muslim University was handed over to a new Executive Council which consisted of nine members, all nominated by the government. The old University Court, Academic Council and Executive Council were superseded and their powers were vested in the new Executive Council, which was to function under direct governmental control. Then in June, 1972, the Muslim University (Amendment) Act was rushed through the Parliament with unseemly haste.[55]

Explaining the cause and repercussions of the move, i.e. amendment of in the Muslim Act, Mawlana adds:

> It is a great tragedy of modern politics that the springhead of thought and morality, the laboratories of personality and character and the watch-towers of life are being exploited for ruthless political ends and electoral expediencies. Notwithstanding the fact that a national government is nearer and more sympathetic to popular needs and urges than an alien government and that the functions of the government are now not confined only to the maintenance of law and order, defence against foreign aggression and collection of taxes. I make bold to say that to infer about educational institutions on the basis of industrial mills and

55. Ibid., pp. 12-13.

> factories, to destroy their autonomy and to sever their bonds with the community or group that founded and maintained them is wrong, unjust and un-equitable. Any attempt at the regimentation of hearts and minds, any endeavour to produce the same type of men and any effort to cast all the classes and communities into the same political mould can be extremely harmful for the society.[56]

Mawlana Nadwi vehemently asserted for the independent character of Muslim University and educational system. He found it important for preservation of Muslim culture and society at large.

Message of Humanity (Payam-i-Insaniyat)

Mawlana Nadwi was associated with many parties and movements to ameliorate the problems faced by Muslims throughout the world in general and in India in particular. "Message of Humanity" is the only movement, which was conceived and run by Mawlana Nadwi. "Message of Humanity" was/is intended to bring together peoples of different faiths, colour and creed, on a common platform to address the common cause. Its aim were:

1. To promote an environment of love and brotherhood.
2. To weed out corruption, hoarding, sectarianism and communalism, economic exploitation and licentiousness from the society.
3. To try to remove wrong and tyrannical customs and traditions from the society.
4. To reach out to and help poor and downtrodden people of the country without the consideration of colour and creed.

56. Ibid., pp. 14-15.

5. To inculcate ideas of social service and seriousness in youth especially students so that the country can be saved from the problems which are/may be arising from waywardness/licentiousness of the younger generation.
6. To try to create an atmosphere of camaraderie/ brotherhood in one's area of influence, *mohallah,* area or city.[57]

Post-Partition India saw a lot of bloodletting as Hindus and Muslims clashed many a time. The vitiated atmosphere in the country and distrust between the communities in India was hampering the progress of the country and rendering a peaceful life virtually impossible. In an answer to the question, what is the driving force and motivating factor behind the "Message of Humanity" movement? Mawlana said:

> It is natural, and an instinct, that a person cannot see the destruction of his home, which has been built and decorated by the best of his efforts and energies and those of his forefathers. Nor can a sane person let anybody make a hole in the boat in which he is travelling.[58]

Commenting on the state of affairs at that time Mawlana Nadwi adds in his autobiography *Karavaan-i-Zindagi,* vol. 2:

> Observation of daily happenings suggest that this country is fast going into the lap of 'moral anarchy' rather collective national suicide. Meanness and selfishness can be found in extreme proportions (barring some on whom religion and morality enjoy a hold). Respect of other people's honour,

---

57. Mawlana Nadwi, *Tehreek Payam-i-Insaniyat ke Agraz wa Maqasid* (tr. from Urdu).

58. Mawlana Nadwi, *Tehreek Payam-i-Insansiyat* (Urdu) And interview by Mawlana Ishaq Jalees Nadwi [*Halka Payam-i-Insaniyat* Lucknow 1988, pp. 6-7.

> dignity life and property is vanishing fast. Collective and national interest is sacrificed over petty self-interest. Rife corruption, absence of work culture, lack of responsibility and accountability, hoarding and other ills are the fruits of this phenomenon. All this has made life a hell. Even in an independent and sovereign country, living freely has become a dream.
>
> These ills and shortcomings were present during English (foreign) rule. It wouldn't be wrong to say that rule and educational system played a vital role in creating on enhancing these ills. But the presence of a tyrant foreign rule, an alert administration and sheer powerlessness and haplessness had suppressed these. And like by removing the lid from boiling broth, these ills come out as vapours. The freedom struggle and throwing out of foreign rulers did not leave any time for national construction and character-building. Though the country became free, the consciousness continued to remain as a slave; A slave not of any foreign power but of money and power, narrow-mindedness. The governance of such a big country, bickering among political parties and to cling to the power did not allow any time for moral and character-building of the nation. Our political leadership (with a few exceptions) did not even feel it (moral and character-building) as having any importance.[59]

Under these compulsions and demand of time and personal conscientiousness, Mawlana Nadwi charted out programme of reforming humanity which he called *payam-i-insaniyat*. As he writes:

> After waiting for a long period, we decided to take the problem head on and approach all people without any

59. Mawlana Nadwi, *Karvan-i-Zandagi*, vol. 2, pp. 110-11.

> distinction of colour, creed or race. Though we were well aware of our limitations and lack of resources. When a neighbourhood or a village is on fire nobody looks for his or her handicaps or weakness, even dumb people shout and handicapped start to run.[60]

The excerpt from the interview, which has also been published in *Karavaan-i-Zindagi,* vol. 2, *in toto* outlines the need and urgency for a movement like "Message of Humanity." The basic objectives of "Message of Humanity" are not political in strict sense of the term but cover a wide array of issue, which is central to the progress, peace and prosperity of all sections of the society. The discipline and dedication demanded from the students, employees, and businessmen speaks volumes about what "Message of Humanity" tried to achieve. "Message of Humanity" movement tried to create an ideal atmosphere, where all sections of the society lived in amity and peace.

In a Lecture at Message of Humanity Conference held at Hyderabad, 29 December 1988 Mawlana Nadwi says:

> I would like to tell you without any preliminaries or philosophical and learned explanations that every man has two homes. One is his own house in which he lives with his family and children. It is essential that there should be peace and security and affection and atmosphere of harmony and fraternity in every house. There is another home a bigger one, and this is his country. But we all often forget that both these are our own homes — the similar one in which we live with our family and the bigger one composed of innumerable small houses in which reside our kins and countrymen. Just as we are a member of our small family, we also belong to the larger family — the society and the country. We also lose sight of the fact that both these homes are fated to go

60. Ibid.

> together. Or, the fact is that the future of the bigger home does not hinge on our smaller house to the same extent as its fate rests on the bigger one. If this bigger house has peace and harmony, if its members have love and regard for one another, everyone is aware of his duties and obligations to the other, has a respect for the life and property of the other and is willing to defend it, then that house or country is fortunate, it is then a home worth living and dying for, and safe for every danger. But if we do not recognize this bigger home — the country — as our own house, or remain indifferent to it, or make no effort to create an atmosphere of peace and harmony and mutual trust in it, or else we fail to adore it as our own house, then our own smaller house will neither be safe nor have any future.[61]

Lamenting upon the covetous and individualistic thinking of the people, he says:

> But this is an apparent and indisputable fact that this bigger home often slips from our memory. Our own personal house which is no more than a doll's cabin in comparison to the country, becomes the sole object of our care and attention. We begin to consider it as our world, confine our aims and attention and activities to its precincts and consider our destiny linked to those living in it. We close our eyes to the bigger home and forget that our house will not be safe if a tempest is raging outside or there is a devastating fire or flood engulfing the locality. In such conditions no house will be safe. The principles of engineering and architecture and the strongest iron gates will not be able to protect this house against such calamities.[62]

---

61. Mawlana Nadwi, *Tehreeke Payam-e-Insaniyat* [massage of Humanity] Confrence, Hyderabad, 29 December 1988, Message of Humanity Forum, Lucknow, n.d., pp. 1-2.

62. Ibid., p. 3.

Mawlana Nadwi points out that in the country like India, where life, property every thing is always in danger, one community suspicious of other communal riots and pogrom is constant affair. The programmes of development, progress, education prosperity and intellectual devlopments seems improbable.[63] Though the "message of humanity." Mawlana Nadwi in his typical and lucid style touched basic problems, like immorality, extravagance which were alien concepts in the country but had made deep inroads in the society. Being a scholar of theology and history Mawlana Nadwi extensively quoted *Qur'an* and history to co-relate immorality and corruption to downfall of empires. Mawlana Nadwi considered these evils — immorality, corruption, extravaganza, show of wealth — ingredients of a rat race among people, which harm society and the country. He addressed these issues in the presidential address of Message of Humanity held at Hyderabad on 29 December 1988. According to him:

> Immorality in any society, disregard for ethical norms and values, self-gratification, excessive greed, violence and operation do not have a corrupting influence only on those who commit these evil deeds but work upon the entire society and vitiate the whole atmosphere if no effort is made to check them. The society which closes its eyes to these inquities falls a prey to them.[64]

In the words of Mawlana Nadwi:

> History tells us that there had been many powerful empires and flourishing civilization, which were once at the

63. Mawlana Nadwi, *Karavaan-i-Zindagi*, vol., 2, pp. 112-13.

64. Mawlana Nadwi, *Dangerous Situation in over Country and Responsibility of Patriots*, Massage of Humanity Forum, Lucknow, 1988, p. 5.

> pinnacle of their glory but in due course of time they yielded to mental confusion, moral degradation, dissoluteness and self-indulgence. Cupidity become their ruling passion. Human dignity was rendered meaningless, personal aggrandizement became the chief object of human effort and intelligence and moral values and religious teachings became in opposite, ridiculous. The houses of rich turned into dens of dissoluteness, presenting the picture of the adage: "Rome burnt while Nero fiddled." Those nations and thinkers, philosophers, litterateurs and poets but they were all busy in their own persuits displaying their skill and proficiency, while the society, different class and families, in short, every facet of social life was showing signs of decay and was falling apart. When decay once cropped up into the Roman society, its vast possessions, firm administration and the exquisite Roman Law could not protect it against the eternal law governing the rise and fall of nations which has thus been enunciated by the *Qur'an*.
>
> And how many a city have we destroyed that exulted in their living, and yonder and their devilling which have not been inhabited after them save for a little while; and verily we have been the inheritors. Q. XVIII: 58.[65]

Mawlana Nadwi laments the general apathy of responsible and intellectual persons of society towards these exigent social issues which have resulted in the anomie. He perceives that this anomic condition if left unaddressed will ruin country therefore reminds that:

> The gradual degeneration and the final decay of Roman civilization can be seen in Gibbon's classical work *The Decline and Fall of the Roman Empire*. In India we are persistently ignoring the fact that today we are all concerned

65. Ibid., pp. 5-6.

> with our own hearths and homes. Everyone has become so ego-centric that all the ethical values, humanitarian considerations and interests of nation and country have been relegated to a secondary place. Everybody seems to be selfish and self-absorbed, after his own petty ends. Everybody is concerned only with what he earns in a day or a month and what more can he get through unfair means. Excuse me if I (Mawlana Nadwi) say that the income through unfair means has these days become a qualification, a criterion for determining the status of any man, specially on the occasion of settling marriages. people unashamedly ask how much the prospective bridegroom earns besides his salary. Those who depend merely on their lawfully earned income are exception these days.[66]

Even small things can be very important indicators of the health of society. Little things describe the psyche of society on the whole. "People unashamedly ask how much the prospective bridegroom earns besides his salary. Those who depend merely on their lawfully earned income are exceptions these days." What seemingly perturbed Mawlana Nadwi was the acceptance of evil or unlawful as a normal affair. How can a theologist whose actions were dictated by his religion, and who all through his life believed that he is accountable for all his deeds in this life and hereafter, not be pained with such state of affairs, where people don't consider themselves accountable to any. Or people feel that a thief is not the one who steals but the one, who is caught after stealing. One of the basic tenants (faiths) of Islam is that every deed of a person is watched and recorded and that a person will have to answer for his every misdeed and will be rewarded for every good work he or she does in this world, irrespective of the rewards and benefits he or she gets in this world for a particular deed.

66. Ibid., pp. 6-7.

Message of Humanity movement was by and large driven by the anxiety brought about by riots in independent India. The communal riots, which occurred in the country at periodic intervals, vitiated the atmosphere and made peace and tranquillity a rare commodity. Anxiety and suspicion of the other community overtook the place of peace. Even a simpleton can understand the need of peace in a society or country but only stalwarts and man of vision strive for it. Mawlana Nadwi by starting the Message of Humanity movement tried to bring back peace and trust in the society overridden by fear and suspicion by building bridges between communities. His conscience compelled him to start this movement. As he mentions:

> I had once asked in one of my press conferences what they would think about a country where people were not delighted to see their own children? Instead of finding any pleasure in them, anxiety overtook them about the future of those children, about the riots and disturbances, which might send them to sleep forever. Surely, this appears to be somewhat abnormal and aberrant situation. A man not belonging to this country is most likely to reject it as unbelievable. But it does happen here. Why? Because we have no sense of human dignity, no respect for life of a man and no conviction that entire humanity is like a family. We never realize that whatever exists in the country constitutes its wealth which, in one way or the other, can be beneficial to each one of us.[67]

Mawlana Nadwi through Message of Humanity movement wanted to inculcate the conviction that "entire humanity is a family," in the society. He explains in his words: "this country has the honour of giving birth to those great men who had

67. Ibid., pp. 8-9.

preached the message of love to the whole world. love is an essential ingredient in the texture of this country." Quoting Khwājah Nizam-ud-din Awliya [Delhi], once he said, "the custom generally followed is to be genial with the gentle and tough with the rough but our elders used to be genial with both the gentle and rough." Then be added, "if anyone sows one thorn in my way and I also put another thorn in retaliation, the entire path would soon be full of thorns therefore, put a flower in return for a thorn and you will find the path full of flowers."[68]

This was the message Mawlana Nadwi wanted to popularize through the programme of *payam-i-insaniyat* (message of humanity) and the only way in his mind to save this country from yawning gap. This message voiced though the platform of *payam-i-Insaniyat* was to all the citizens of India irrespective of cast, class and religion. He invited every section of the society to take their share in reforming the society by the circumstances.

For the Muslims of India who were dejected by the prevailing circumstance, he delineates the massage as, "the Muslims are not only citizen of an equal status with anybody in India; they are also among its chief builders and architects, and hold position second to none among the people of the world for selfless service to the motherland. They gave to India and the Indian civilization a new life and a new dimension and awakened its people to a new set of moral and spiritual values. Every patch of its land and every particle of its soil bears the imprint of their greatness and is a monument to their industry, earnestness and creative genius. In every aspect

68. Ibid., pp. 9-10.

of Indian life and civilization can be seen evidences of their noble aestheticism and cultural richness."[69]

Indian Muslims initiated the struggle for national freedom and took a leading part in it and their sacrifices on the whole, in the course of it, were greater than those of any other community if one judged them in proportion to their numerical positions.[70] In view of these self-evident truths, he propounds that the Muslims in India should have been enjoying in practice all the rights and opportunities, which are there in principal so far as the law and the constitution of the land are concerned, the notions of majority and minority would have disappeared from the Indian mind and everyone would have begun to be regarded as an Indian and nothing more and nothing less than this.[71] Believing the adverseness of situation, he brings succour to India dejected Muslim community and proclaims:

> We firmly and, clearly, declare that in many respected, the Muslims in India are discontented, they have many just and legitimate grievances and they are passing through a most critical period of their history. But we have lost faith neither in the mercy of God, nor in our strength and ability to live, nor in the destiny of India, nor in the future of democracy, nor in the spirit of our constitution. We have resolved to live here and nowhere else, and to tell you the honest truth . . . weren't we born here? Have we not been living here for a thousand years? Is not our existence a greater reality and far more enduring than the Himalayas or the ganges? We are older than the Qutb Minar and Taj Mahal

69. Mawlana Nadwi, *Muslims in India*, Islamic Research and Pub., Lucknow, 1980, p. 5.

70. Mawlana Nadwi, Welcome Address to All India Muslim Consultative Convention, Lucknow, 8-9 Agust 1964, p. 3.

71. Ibid., p. 4.

> and our claims on India is stronger than of these monuments, which we ourselves gave to the motherland. They owe their existence to us. We must and we shall solve all the problems and difficulties that are plaguing the country at present. We are an inseparable part of Indian nationality, Indian culture, and Indian civilization. We will complain and protest a thousand times; we get angry and we will forgive and forget and be friend again. In any case, we have got to live in this country and with all our distinctive attributes and characteristics. And we are confident that it will be possible for us to do so. The clouds that darken the horizon today will ultimately disappear. Communal peace and society are bound to return to the land.[72]

These words of Mawlana Nadwi were not only to restore courage and confidence among the Muslims but also to revive that spirit of peace, co-operation and humanitarianism, which Islam has blessed them. The message of love and faith and selfless service of mankind earlier preached and propagated by Khwaja Moinuddin Chisti and Khwaja Nizamuddin Aulia and hundreds of other Muslim saints and divines. Further more, believing that India as their home and the home of their ancestors and they have been chosen for India and India for them by God, he encourages Muslims to take active part in reforming, development, progress and prosperity of this country. Instead of drifting away from the currents on national life, they should join them and guide them towards the right direction.[73]

---

72. Ibid., pp. 10-11.
73. Ibid., pp. 11-12.

7

Comparison of the Two Paradigms of Islamic Thought

MAWLANA Sayyid Abul A'Lā Mawdudi (1903-79) and Mawlana Sayyid Abul Hasan Ali Nadwi (1914-99) are the luminaries and most influential figures of Islam in the recent past. They exercised a great influence on the Muslim revivalist thought in their own capacity throughout the Muslim world particularly Indo-Pak subcontinent. Both were prodigious writers, whose books have been translated and circulated widely throughout the Islamic world. Mawdudi's writings have been translated from Urdu into Arabic, Farsi and English, while as Nadwi preferred to write in Arabic as well as Urdu. Through their writings they provided an ideological foundation to the contemporary Islamic revivalism. They identified and responded to many of the concerns, which continue to trouble contemporary Muslim in executing Islam in day-to-day life. Their assiduous writings on incompatibility of Western culture, thought and ideologies *vis-à-vis* Muslim society and emphasis on Islam as a comprehensive and transcendental world-view, obviated to a large extent the overwhelming influence of West. Influence of their writing crossed the boaders of subcontinent, most importantly Egyptian Sayyid Qutb (1906-66) Ideologue of Islamic resurgence got benefited from them. While the Nadwi's writings constitute a primary source for Sayyid Qutb,

Mawdudi's writings served to heighten Qutb's idea of the exclusive nature of Islam and formulating the ideology of Islamic radicalism.[1]

Mawdudi as well as Nadwi consecrated their whole life for the cause of Islam. They were pious, committed Muslims whose upbringing and education exposed them to Islamic education, modernist thought and Western learning though in different styles and ways. Both were raised in the shadow of British colonialism in society where impact of Western civilization on the one hand and anti-colonial national independence movements on the other hand were active. They whole-heartedly endeavoured to revive and restore Islam and rekindle the fire of religious ardour and dynamic energy into the followers of Islam. Their effort was in fact continuation of mission of predecessors like Shah Waliullah, Shah Abdul Aziz, Sayyid Ahmad Shahid, Jamil-ul-Din al-Afghani and Allama Iqbal but in a different situation and given the fact that Islam has never ceased for a moment and that the Muslims too have never remained cold or indifferent to the call. The Western domination of much of the Muslim world stirred political as well as cultural chaos and confusion. Almost all the Islamic countries since its inception remained griped in acute intellectual crisis. With the result, an unrelenting battle of ideas and ideals started throughout the Muslim world. So to say a clash between the Islamic and the Western concepts of life, values and traditions became ubiquitous.[2] A variety of responses emerged from Muslim self-criticism and reflection

1. Youssef M. Choueiri, *Islamic Fundamentalism,* CBS Pub. & Distributors, New Delhi, 1991, pp. 95, 105.
2. Abul Hasan Ali Nadwi, *Speaking Plainly to the West,* Academy Islamic Research & Publications, Lucknow 1973, P-I & Abul Hasan Ali Nadwi, *Western Civilisation: Islam and Muslims,* Lucknow, 1969, pp. 1, 3.

on the cause of decline. Their actions spanned the spectrum, from adaptation and cultural synthesis to withdrawal and rejection. This question has exercised the minds of Muslims ever since the opening decades of the nineteenth century, when they found themselves enfeebled by decadence within and confronted by progressively expanding West.

The failure of early efforts to stunt the Western imperialistic designs further precipitated a religious as well as political crisis. With the result, Muslim community largely lost its self-confidence and its impact became obvious day by day. In fact, both the groups — those protesting against external encroachment and those condemning internal deterioration — failed to correctly estimate the real dimension of the problem. None of them could adequately assess the ambitions, roots and causes of exuberant Europe nor could anyone forge a comprehensive response to it.

Mawdudi as well as Nadwi, responding both to South Asian experience as well as the general conditions of Muslims throughout the world, called upon Muslims to restore Islam's primacy in private as well as public life. They were convinced that Islam is a comprehensive way of life, and wrote extensively on the holistic nature and character of Islam as guide and panacea to all human sufferings. They called for a social order based not on modernist acculturation but on a self-sufficient Islamic alternative. Both reviewed the situation in comprehensive terms in its true perspective and advocated that the vitality and skill of the West should be appropriated rather than accepted. They wanted East to be enlightened rather than intoxicated by the West. Through their writings, they urged Muslims to maintain its distinctive individuality — its faith, its moral integrity and fervidness of heart and spirit. Since, on its ability to do so depends its capacity to play a useful role for itself, as well as for the West and for the humanity at large. Their analysis of Western civilization, revealed that the modern West is moved by the philosophic vision of the ancient Greece, which demands a complete separation of all institutions, customs, ideas, arts and sciences from religion, rejects everything beyond the visible and tangible and makes man a measure of all things. They brought about how these bases of Western thought and culture are antagonistic and incompatible with the values and ideals cherished by Islam as well as destructive to the West itself.[3]

In the beginning, Mawlana Nadwi was influenced and attracted by the articles written by Mawlana Mawdudi in his journal *Tarjuman-ul-Qur'an* especially (Future Revolution) *Aana-wala inqlab* (Muslims and present political struggle). How Islamic government is established, *purdah, usury, sood,*[4] etc. Especially, the writings of Mawlana Mawdudi written in response to Western culture and civilization, which had challenged the Muslims, these writings of Mawdudi influenced

---

3. For detailed study of Mawdudi's and Nadwi's views on West see:

   Mawdudi, *West versus Islam* M. M. Islami Pub., 2000,

   Mawdudi, *Our message* M. M. Islami. Pub., Delhi, 1981,

   Mawdudi, *Let us Change Word,*

   Nadwi, *Islam and the World,* tr. M. Asaf Didawai, The Academy of Islamic Research Pub., Lahore 1961.

   Nadwi, *Western Civilization Islam and Muslims,* The Academy of Islamic Research and Publications, Lucknow, 1969.

   Nadwi, *Speaking Plainly to the West,* Academy Islamic Research and Publications, Lucknow, 1973.

4. Mawlana Abul Hasan Ali Nadwi, *Karavaan-i-Zindagi,* Urdu, vol. I, Maktaba Islami, Lucknow, 1995, pp. 231, 233 and also see, Nadwi, *Purane Chirag* (the Old Lamps), Urdu, vol. II, Maktaba Firdousi, Lucknow, 1995, p. 304.

and became reason for Nadwi's attachment to him and Jamaat-i-Islami literature.[5] He writes about Mawdudi:

> Resistance to Western thinking and values was growing in its own way when in the first half of this century the articles of Mawlana Sayyid Abdul A'Lā Mawdudi published in his esteemed journal *Tarjuman-ul-Qur'an* from Hyderabad, which were written not in any defensive but in an aggressive way against Western civilization and philosophy of life, attracted the attention of the educated Muslims. Those articles had confronted the movement of modernity bred by Western education and had opposed rank nationalism. He also wrote powerful and well-reasoned articles on Islamic *Shariat* and laws which had become the target of attack like *usury, purdah, jihād*, sacrifice, slavery, *Hadith* and *Sunnah*. Through those articles, which later on appeared in the shape of bound volumes, and his other books and treatise, he moulded the thinking of recipients of modern education and restored in them confidence in Islamic values and thinking and rescued them from any sense of inferiority or defeatism. That was sterling work indeed which must be acknowledged and because of it many men of letters gave him the little of "*Mutakalim* Islam [spokes man of Islam].[6]

The popularity and reputation of Mawdudi's writings influenced Nadwi so much so that he also wrote two articles in *Tarjuman-ul-Qur'an* on the exegesis of *Sura Al Kahf* and another *Dīn* and *Siyasat* [Religion and Politics], first article was published from Hyderabad and another from Lahore where Mawlana Mawdudi later shifted.[7] In these articles

5. Nadwi, *Purane Chirag*, vol. II, Urdu, Maktaba Firdoos Lucknow, 1995, p. 113.
6. Mawlana Nadwi, *Asr-i-Hazir ma Din ke Tehfeem wa Tashri* (Urdu), Darul Asfat, Lucknow, 1980, pp. 19-20.
7. *Purane Chirag*, p. 304.

written by Nadwi we find Mawdudian idiom and expression. Nadwi, continued to have correspondence with Mawlana Mawdudi and held several meetings with him on many occasions. Mawlana Mawdudi in a letter written in 1940, expressed his desire to Mawlana Nadwi to translate his book *Purdah* into Arabic. On the insistence of Mawlana Manzoor Nomoni in 1941, Mawlana Nadwi joined Jamaat-i-Islami of Mawlana Mawdudi and served as the (*amir*) President of Lucknow Unit for about three years. It was on his request, Mawlana Mawdudi during his visits to Lucknow delivered Lectures, one in Darul-Ulum Nadwat-ul-'Ulamā and another in Lucknow University on "New Educational System" (the article has been now published in book the Education, English rendering of Mawdudi's book *Talimat*) and *Economic Problems of Man and Its Solution*.[8] During those days, Mawlana Nadwi remained active in the programmes of Jamaat-i-Islami. He also participated in the executive meeting of Jamaat-i-Islami held at Lahore on 1942, in which some members of Jamaat were demanding resignation of Mawlana Mawdudi as Amir (President) of Jamaat-i-Islami and wanted to elect Amin Ahsan Islahi.[9] In his place, owing to some organizational dispute. In that meeting Mawlana Nadwi supported and voted for Mawdudi, to continue as Amir of Jamaat-i-Islami. Because according to him, "it was Mawlana Mawdudi's endeavour and writings that Jamaat was founded."[10] This turned to be the opinion of Majority and Mawdudi continued to be Amir of Jamaat-i-Islami. Mawlana Nadwi attended several executive meetings and accompanied Mawdudi on several occasions. As a matter of fact it seems during those days Mawlana Nadwi

8. *Karavaan-i-Zindagi*, pp. 241-42.
9. Ibid., p. 242 and also see *Purane Chirag*, p. 310.
10. Ibid., p. 243 and see *Purane Chirag*, op. cit., p. 310.

was in consonant with the programme of Jamaat-i-Islami and actively participated in it. Mawlana Mawdudi even ought to publish an Arabic journal under the responsibility of Mawlana Nadwi, but it was later decided only to translate Articles into Arabic. The name of Masood Alam Nadwi was suggested by Mawlana Nadwi for this job of translation into Arabic, which was excepted and proved fruitful.[11] Mawlana Nadwi's active participation with Mawlana Mawdudi and Jamaat-i-Islami would have been envisaged a great good fortune of Islam and the Muslims of the subcontinent but unfortunately it did not last long.

Moreover, despite all these affinities and amity Mawlana Nadwi left Jamaat-i-Islam just after three years. He pointed out certain apprehensions, which finally led him to relinquish Jamaat-i-Islami. During his days with Mawdudi and Jamaat he became conscious of the way people started treating Mawdudi. According to him, people, especially modern educated class, who were having very little knowledge of Islam and whatever awareness about Islam they had achieved was only through the writings of Mawlana Mawdudi. They had started revering Mawdudi to the extent, as if there was no other scholar and writer on Islam better than him. Their veneration to Mawdudi had reached to the extent of disparaging all other *'Ulama* and scholars of Islam. It was an evidence of the personality cult that was surrounding him[12] and was not in accordance with Islamic spirit. Second thing, which striked Nadwi was the rising criticism among them against the *'Ulama* and religious circles.[13] Thirdly, he felt that

11. *Purane Chirag,* pp. 310-11.

12. *Karavaan-i-Zindagi,* vol. I, p. 244.

13. Idem.

the spiritual dimension of Islam was becoming cinderella. Lack of insistence on the inner self-discipline of the individual and also Lacuna of training programme to inculcate scrupulous self-piety and quest for union with God among the Jamaat's cadre.[14] Furthermore Mawlana Nadwi mentioned that his personal estimation and impression he had conceived of Mawdudi after going through his writings only, did not remain same after having close acquaintance with him. His perception about Mawdudi changed. He thought it was because of his rich spiritual family background that disinclined him to get influenced or persuaded by less prominent spiritual and charismatic figures.[15] Instead, Mawlana Nadwi claims that he became more inclined towards Mawlana Mohammad Aliyas (1303–1363 AH/CE 1885–1944) founder of Tabligh movement. His influence appealed to Nadwi's heart rather than head. He found Mawdudi's writings beneficial only for the particular educated class and not for the Islamicists like him, who could have excess to original and primary sources.[16] Accordingly to Nadwi the nature and approach of Mawlana Aliyas was more inline with the spirit of Prophets and his mission more in accordance with the way of Prophets. This impression of Mawlana Aliyas' personality attracted Nadwi towards Tabligh Movement than the Mawdudi and his Jamaat-i-Islami.[17] To which (Jamaat) he now termed as only eruditionistic and a reaction against particular intellectual and philosophical system.[18] This depicts Mawlana Nadwi's traditional and Sufistic temperament and his inclination towards this particular

14. Idem.
15. Ibid., pp. 244-45.
16. Ibid., p. 246.
17. Ibid., p. 245.
18. Ibid., p. 247.

attitude owes much to his family background and his traditional educational background.

Mawlana Nadwi began his educational career at Nadwatul Ulama, Lucknow. It was conceived as a middle-of-the-road institution between the extremes of Aligarh's "Secular and Deobands" rigid conservatism. However, as envisaged, with rare exceptions, could not hold its own, in its drift away from Aligarh modernism towards conservative orthodoxy, in time its scholars and their works became almost indistinguishable from those of Deoband.[19] Nadwi served this theological school throughout his life in one or other capacity and undoubtedly must have helped in formatting and channelling his mindset. Besides his extensive study of religious sciences and Islamic history, Nadwi showed keen interest also in learning English which helped him to keep himself abreast of contemporary thought and events. Nevertheless, his thought reflects the influence of his *alma mater*, which he could not resist. As far as Mawlana Mawdudi is concerned he was a self-made person, although he was well instructed in traditional Islamic learning but he did not belong to any particular bent of mind. Accordingly to I.H. Qureshi, the seemingly bizarre pattern of his education soon become integrated under the motivation of his disciplined and well-directional mind and, instead of being a source of weakness, actually became an asset because his mind was free from the shackles of traditional modes of thinking. His thought could run into new channels instead of following the course set down by age-long grooves."[20] However, people belonging to Darul-Ulum's (Muslim

19. Aziz Ahmad, *Islamic Modernism in India and Pakistan*, Oxford University Press 1967, pp. 109, 112.

20. I. H. Qureshi, *Ullemain Politics*, p. 330.

theological centres) are not usually prepared to give credence and generally condescend to all those, who have not attained knowledge from such reputed centres. This psychological barrier together with the growing criticism against Mawlana Mawdudi and Jamaat-i-Islami, from the traditional *Ulama* circles also must have encouraged Mawlana Nadwi to abandon active role in Jamaat-i-Islami.

Mawlana Nadwi's open criticism to some ideas of Mawlana Mawdudi as well as Sayyid Qutub Shaheed ideologue of Ikhwan al-Muslimun (Egypt) first appeared in his Arabic book *Al-Nabuwwatu wal Ambiya fi Zu-al-Qur'an.*[21] In 1978 Nadwi wrote *Asr-i-hazir min din ki Tafhem aur Tashrih* (Eng. trs. *Appreciation and Interpretation of Religion in the Modern Age*) in which he vehemently inveighed against Mawlana Mawdudi's interpretations, particularly presented through his book *Qur'an ki Char Bunyadi Istilahen*: *Ilah, Rabb, Ibādat, Din* (*Four Basic Concepts* of *Qur'an*: *Illah, Rabb, Ibādat, Din*). Mawlana Mawdudi in this book suggests that the key concepts of the *Qur'an* are *illah, rabb, ibādat* and *al-din* on which revolves the whole axis of Islam.[22] He asserts that the *Qur'an* invites man to accept the creator or *rabb* as the sustainer and soverign and demands to harmonize his will with the will of Allah in all its aspects (*ibadah*) and to establish the will of Allah over the totality of life (*din*). The *Qur'an* presents a complete way of life — a code of conduct and a Scheme for organizing the total gamut of human life — belief, action and society. It does not divide itself into water-tight material and spiritual, political, religious, this wordly

21. Sec its English translation, Abul Hasan Ali Nadwi, *Islamic concept of Prophethood,* Lucknow, 1976. Originally Published in Arabic Urdu version available as, *Mansab Nubuwwat owr us kay 'ali Muqam Hamilin.*

22. Mawlana Mawdudi, *Qur'an Ki Char . . .*, p. 6.

and that wordly compartments. It creates only one supreme loyalty — to Allah and his Prophet; and tries to organize the whole fabric of human life on this basis. This is the path through which man can seek the fulfilment of his real nature. In principle, most of writings of Mawlana Nadwi seem to agree with these idea's but showed repugnance, and disagreed with the Mawdudi's interpretation of these terms and emphasis laid on them being the core and focal points of the real spirit and without which neither Islam can be strictly followed nor any invitation can be extended nor any work relating to establishment of Islam can be done. Nadwi argued that this led to new type of exegesis of the *Qur'an* and Islam which revolved round "Kingdom of God and Sovereignty of God" and purpose of the revelation of the *Qur'an* and Islam was reduced to establishment of the Kingdom of God.[23] He also disapproved the making of use of contemporary vocabulary like "Sovereignty of God," Islamic "Social order," movement, "state," "revolution" in a discourse on Islam. Accordingly, he claimed that, it is tantamount to the Politicization of true Islam and smacks of capitulation to the domination of Western thought and method of organizing life. Thus, Islam is redefined in terms of socio-political values instead of the eternal and goals like establishing the Islamic state become centred on this world rather than on securing Allah's pleasure in that world. According to Nadwi, "the real objective of life is attainment of pleasure of God, action in accordance with the Book and *Sunnat*, admission in paradise and salvation in the hereafter and that besides these every other endeavour in the way of religion, organization and leadership of parties and reformation of social and political systems and governmental rule, are mere means and methods, which are employed to

23. S. Abul Hasan Ali Nadwi, *Asr-i-hazir men Din ki Tafhim our Tashrih*, Darul-Arfat, Lucknow, 1980, p. 21.

attain this objective and the advancement and supremacy of Islam."[24]

Mawlana Nadwi in his rejoinder about writing this book (*Asr-i-hazir main din ki Tafhem aur Tashrih*) in response to Mawdudi's *Qur'an ki Char Bunyadi Istilahen*, which according to him had became *confessio fidei* of organization and intellectual core of Jamaat-i-Islami, and writes that he could not resist, therefore, went against personal *modus operandi* of writing in constructive, positive and uncontroversial manner. According to him, "he observed and fully realized that the literature, which Jamaat-i-Islami was bringing out was giving a new direction to the religious attitude and there was a great danger that a new meaning and interpretation of religion, and new set of values and new standards were likely to be evolved. There was a danger that the thinking and endeavour of the intelligent, educated, sincere, active and determined class were likely to leave the straight path of the book and the *Sunnat*, the way of the Prophet, concern for the hereafter, faith and accounting and therefore, were in danger of deflecting to the way of party organization (party politics) and to regain for the Muslims political power and governmental rule so much so that its return to the straight path may be difficult."[25] These apprehensions of Mawlana Nadwi about Jamaat-i-Islami seems exaggeration and jejune, because so far they have not astrayed and there is not a scintilla of such concerns. There seems over emphasis on certain things like politics in Jamaat's programme but it cannot be construed as deviation on their part.

However, Mawlana Nadwi criticized certain assertions of Mawlana Mawdudi present in his book *Qur'an ki Char*

24. Ibid., p. 7.

25. Ibid., pp. 23-24.

Buniyadi Istilahen, which are worth mentioning. For example: Mawlana Mawdudi seeks to prove that although the four Qur'anic terms. *Allah* (God) *rabb* (lord or Soverign) *Din* (faith) and *ibādat* (worship) were well-understood by the Arabs to whom the *Qur'an* was first revealed; their original meanings gradually lost their force and comprehensiveness to later generations.[26] With the result, writes Mawdudi, "through the mist that has come to surround the precise sense of the four terms in question, more than three-fourths of the teachings of the *Qur'an*, or rather, the real spirit thereof have become obscured and this is the main cause of the shortcomings that are to be seen in peoples' beliefs and despite the fact that they have not formally given up the faith of Islam but are still in its fold. Therefore, for the illustration of the central teachings and main focus of *Qur'an*, the complete exegesis of these terms is necessary."[27]

Such interpretations aroused irresistible attraction of certain Muslim scholars, who animadverted upon, especially Mawlana Nadwi who found it incongruous with the set principles. He cautioned, one whose acquaintance with Islam is limited and who is not aware of the fact that Almighty Allah Himself in *Qur'an* and *Hadith* promised to spare the *ummah* or Muslim community as a whole from ever-falling into error, might conclude from this that the true meaning of *Qur'an* was lost to a great majority of Muslims for centuries until at last the Mawlana Mawdudi was able to rediscover it and penetrate to its heart in the present age.[28] Furthermore Nadwi asserts that,

---

26. Mawdudi, *Char Buniyadi Islilahi*, pp. 5, 10.
27. Ibid., p. 10.
28. Nadwi, *Asr-i-hazir*, pp. 33-34.

> On a cursory look this conclusion may not appear very damaging and serious but its impact on mind and the way of thinking would be far-reaching for it raises doubts in the capabilities of the *ummat,* which is not only the bearer of the religions and the message but is responsible for its expansion over the world and its elucidation and Protection. It also casts doubts on the history of the reformers and religious doctors. For future also it will raise doubts about the authenticity of what is being said or understood today. It will also give strength to the philosophy of the "apparent and the hidden" and "the Kernel and the Shell" and make religious truths incomprehensible and obtrusive riddles, which was the way of different groups of Batimites (heretic) in different times.[29]

Mawdudi's statement, according to Mawlana Nadwi, is contrary to the basic characteristics and distinction of the *Qur'an,* which itself has repeatedly and emphatically stressed that it is a clear, lucid, explicit and a book easy to understand. They are the assertion of Allah, unassailable by any doubt or apprehension their real meaning cannot be twisted or distorted,[30] Nadwi emphasizes, and further writes: "Then how can it be believed that the book could not convey the real import and significance of the four basic terms round which, it is said, revolves the entire gamut of beliefs, action, exhortations and preachings."[31] Substantiating his rebuttal with the Qur'anic verses and exegesis of the prominent exegetes Nadwi negates the contention that many basic truths of the *Qur'an* remained concealed for a long time and remarked that this type of research conducted and style of description adopted by Mawlana Mawdudi would lead one to conclude

29. Nadwi, *Asr-i-hazir,* p. 34.
30. Ibid., pp. 35-39.
31. Ibid., p. 35.

that the *ummat* went through a long period of ignorance of the true import of the basic terms and their connotations and a mystery on which depended the soundness of their thinking and action. That would be tantamount to clear ignorance and negligence and even to perdition, which is contrary to established fact that Muslims are essentially immune to out right "ignorance" and this community would never fall in general and universal errors.[32]

Mawlana Nadwi has also quoted Allama Ismail al-Huzaibi (who was selected as the leader of Ikhwan-al-Muslimin, after the death of Imam Shahid Hasan al-Banna), to support his rebuttle of Mawlana Mawdudi's assertions. Allama Hasan Ismail al-Huzaibi in his book *Dawatun la Quzat* has commented on Mawdudi's book *Four Basic Qur'anic Terms* and has claimed that: "The assertion of the author (Mawlana Mawdudi) that in Muslim society the terms *Illah, Rabb, Din* and *Ibādat* were not understood as they were understood in pre-Islamic days at the time of descent of the *Qur'an,* is an unwarranted and untrue assertion and a baseless and fatuous accusation."[33] Mawlana Wahidudin Khan (Indian Muslim Scholar) came up with same accusations of deviation against Mawlana Mawdudi's interpretations.[34] It seems that here Mawlana Mawdudi's interpretations and remarks have been taken a miss and completely out of context. The above-mentioned scholars have gone too far in criticizing him, which actually he did not mean. As a matter of fact Mawlana Mawdudi was not averse to the arguments put forward by these scholars against his interpretations. He himself used these arguments

32. Ibid., p. 41.
33. Quoted by Nadwi, Ibid., pp. 43-47.
34. Mawlana Wahidudin Khan, *Din Ki Siyasi Tabeer* (Urdu), Maktaba Al-Risala, New Delhi, 1985, pp. 57, 61.

for underpinning his assertions at other places while responding to specific issues. Mawlana Nadwi has himself mentioned that, "on the same principle, the Mawdudi has based his arguments against Qadianinis in interpreting the words 'the last of the Prophets' which has been understood down the ages in only one sense and the community has been all along quoting the interpretation of its stalwarts and pilliars."[35] At other places Mawlana Mawdudi has mentioned that:

> It would be wrong to assume that Islam at any time was wholly routed and completely over-powered by this onslaught of "Ignorance." As a matter of fact, once a community accepted Islam, the lives of its people ever after bore in some degree that imprint of its reformative influence. It was all due to this imprint of Islam that great tyrants and absolute rulers shuddered, at times, with the fear of God, and were impelled to walk the path of truth and justice. It was all due to the teachings of Islam that in the dark periods of monarchy one comes across, here and there, upon personalities imbued with piety and high morals. Again, it was all due to the blessings of Islam that in the cradles of royal dynasties, which had acquired absolute rights to rule, were nurtured great many pious, just and God-fearing men, who, despite their royal rights, ruled, as far as they could, with a rare sense of duty and responsibility. . . . Then, despite the inroads made by Polytheistic culture, it continued exercising reformative and corrective influence on the beliefs, morals and social life of the common people. On this very account, the Muslim people all over the world have always been morally superior to non-Muslim communities.[36]

35. *Tafhimat* vol. III., p. 176, New Delhi edn. Quoted by Mawlana Nadwi, *Asr-i-hazir,* p. 43.

36. Mawlana Mawdudi, *A Short History of the Revivalist Movement in Islam,* Eng. tr. Al-Ash'Ari, M. M. Islami, Delhi, 1997, p. 34.

Thus, for that matter, it is unjust to doubt Mawlana Mawdudi's intentions and his remarks about the four basic Qur'anic terms, which according to him lost force and comprehensiveness to later generations,[37] This statement of Mawdudi should not necessary be construed to mean that, "*ummat* went through a long period of ignorance of the true import of the basic terms and their connotations and a mystery on which depends the soundness of their thinking and actions that would be tantamount to dispel ignorance and negligence and even to perdition,"[38] which Mawlana Nadwi and others tried to apprehend. The above-mentioned remarks of Mawdudi that, "Muslims are essentially immune to outright 'Ignorance' and never at any time was wholly routed and completely overpowered by this Onslaught of 'Ignorance'" and furthermore, as he mentioned that "Moreover, there have always been, in all ages, such people who followed Islam sincerely and firmly and endeavoured to order their as well as the lives of those under their influence, on the patter of Islam."[39] These statements of Mawdudi clearly obviates and itself refutes Mawlana Nadwi's contention that for the Mawdudi "the whole history of the *ummat* presents a spectre of unchecked decline and continuous decadence and the history of the middle period appears to him a barren desert and wilderness, which leads to unwarranted conclusion that Islamic record is dark and barren, that the Ummat-i-Muslimadiyya does not possess creative ability and nothing but darkness, deviation and apostasy prevailed in Islamic history, it will have to be inferred that the writer has jumped to fatuous conclusion, and his knowledge of the history of

37. Mawdudi, *Qur'an Ke Char . . .,* pp. 8-10.

38. Nadwi, *Asr-i-hazir me,* p. 41.

39. Mawdudi, *A Short History of the Revivalist,* pp. 34-35.

reform and renovation is woefully incomplete."[40] Mawlana Mawdudi would never have thought that such conclusions will be drawn from his assertions and his many writings are clear proof to nullify these accusations.

While commenting on the Mawlana Mawdudi's interpretation and explications of terms *illah*, *rabb*, *din*, and *ibādat*. Mawlana Nadwi points out that (Mawdudi) averred the "Sovereignty of Allah and *rabb*" is real goal and central point and *din* and *ibādat* both are ways and means designed to draw people to this Focal point.[41] As Mawdudi asserts "Essence of godhood is authority, whether it is conceived a sovereignty of a supernatural kind over the whole universe, or on the basis that man is bound by God's law in his wordly life and that of His injunctions are to be complied with because they emanate from him"[42] and "the Godhood and (political) authority are inextricably interconnected and are, in essence and significance, one and the same thing. He who has no authority can be no god, and he should not be so. And He who has all due authority, He alone can be, and ought to be, God. . . . Hence it is meaningless to regard anyone, who is without necessary power and authority as God (Allah), it is absolutely contrary to reason and reality, and it is quite absurd as well as useless to turn to these for help."[43] Dilating upon word *rabb* and *rabubiyat* he concludes that *Qur'an* uses them as exactly synonymous with supreme authority and sovereignty as well as difines the concept of *rabb* as absolute sovereign and undisputable lord and rules of universe.[44] Therefore, *ibādat*

40. Nadwi, *Asr-i-hazir*, pp. 47-49.

41. Ibid., p. 57.

42. Mawdudi, *Qur'an Ke Char . . .*, p. 20.

43. Ibid., pp. 26-27.

44. Ibid., pp. 80-81.

and servitude is obedience and loyalty to this Supreme Authority.[45] As far as the word *din* is concerned *Qur'an*, according to him, uses it as a comprehensive system and way of life. In the same sense, when a person accepts any one as Supreme Authority, submit and surrender before him and considers his orders as binding for obedience, and lives in accordance to ideals and practices, norms and values, rule, laws and regulations laid down by the same authority. Therefore, according to him in modern times concept of State to some extent could suffice meaning of *din* (religion).[46] Mawlana Mawdudi conceived state an important thing because compliance of rules and regulations other than the accepted supreme authority would be tantamount to disobedience. Furthermore he writes:

> All are different facts of a single, absolute authority and Sovereignty which is indivisible. If anyone regards the word of someone else to be deserving of obedience without any sanction from God, he is as much guilty of the offence of *Shirk* as the one who prays to or worships someone other than God. And if someone regards himself as the lord and master and absolute monarch of any part of earth in the political sense, this act too amounts as much to a claim to godhood as it would if he were to tell people that he was their helper and patron and guardian in the supernatural sense — godhood includes monarchy and rulership. And it is also stressed that *tawhid* necessarily requires that in this sense too no one should be believed to have any share with God.[47]

Mawlana Nadwi construed this interpretation as politicization of religion by adopting purely political language and

---

45. Ibid., pp. 91-92.
46. Ibid., pp. 108-09.
47. Ibid., pp. 28-29.

interpretation.[48] Similar views are expressed by Mawlana Wahidudin Khan in his book *Dīn ki Siyasi Ta'bir*. He blamed Mawdudi for presenting Islam in political idiom and equated his style with that of Karl Marx, who interpreted life only in Economic terms.[49] "In case of Mawdudi, politics achieved preponderance and central position in religion and around which whole of the religion revolves, to dominate religion politically became their real objective and purpose of being Muslim. With the result, all aspects of religion were translated in terms of politics and therefore, lost its import."[50]

Mawlana Nadwi not only blamed Mawlana Mawdudi for politicizing religion he also criticized Sayyid Qutb Shaheed for his adherence and advocation of same views. Both Qutb and Mawdudi derived similar conclusions from their assertion of the exclusive sovereignty (*hakimiyya*) of God. According to them, The principle of the unity of God altogether negates the concept of the legal and political sovereignty of human beings, individual or collective. God alone is the sovereign and his commandments are the law of Islam. Their emphasis on Islam as a comprehensive and transcendented world-view excludes the validity of all other systems and values as Pegitimate governing Principles of day to day life. Sayyid Qutb in his commentary, *Fi-Zilal al-Qur'an* on the verse "this is the eternal religion of Qur'an," in chapter Joseph says.

> This alone is the eternal religion. And so long as people do not follow God alone and recognize only his Sovereignty religion has no meaning nor the worship of God has any value. If in any matter they follow other than God their Subordination to God is imperfect and unreliable for the

48. Nadwi, *Asr-i-hazir*, p. 58.
49. Mawlana Wahidudin Khan, *Din ki Siyeas Ta'bir*, pp. 14, 22.
50. Ibid., pp. 24-25.

> unity of Divinity calls for unity of Providence *Rububiyat* and there are only two external manifestations of *Rububiyat*, viz, God's Sovereignty and his worship. In this way, both the words have the same connotation and are co-related. The worship that will distinguish a Muslim from a non-Muslim will be complete obedience and servility to the Sovereignty of God.[51]

Both Mawdudi as well as Qutb equates worship (*ibādat*) with the action of men to take men as their master and to follow the rules framed by them. For them to accept and follow any man-made law in any matter is to negate religion and to ascribe partners in sovereignty of God, which in the view of these gentlemen is nothing short of ascribing partners in divinity and providence. However, Qutb went a step further by linking this assertion to his concept of *Jahilliyya* (ignorance divine guidance) as a pervasive condition simultaneously straddling the Islamic and non-Islamic world. His definition of *jahilliyya* "as a psychological state, which rejects the guidance of God" lead him to advance a rigorous classification of all present-day societies.[52] He asserts:

> *Jahilliyya* has the same characteristics irrespective of time and place. Whenever peoples hearts are devoid of a divine

51. Sayyid Qutub, Fi-Zilal al-*Qur'an*, vol. 12, p. 200.
52. Sayyid Qutb's most radicalist Statements were published between 1960 and 1966. Four of his books, *Khasa'is al-Tasawwur al Islami*, [the characteristics of the Islamic conception and its foundation] (1960), *al Islam wa Mushkilat al-Hadara* [Islam and the problems of civilization], *Ma'alim fi al-Tariq* [Signposts along the road or Milestones] (1964). *Ma'rakat al-Islam wa al-Ra'smaliyya* [The Battle between Islam and capitalism and the revised edition of his exegesis, under the Auspices of the *Qur'an* (1958-66) have acted as the definitive Ideological articulation of contemporary "Islamic radicalism" and provided authoritative guidelines for a variety of Islamicist organizations.

> doctrine that governs their thought, and concomitant legal rules to regulate their lives, *jahilliyya* is bound to rear its head in one form or another. . . . The one in which contemporary societies wallow is not different in its nature from that of ancient Arabia before the rise of Islam.[53]

In his famous book *Ma'alim fial-Tariq* he writes:

> If we look at the sources and foundation of modern ways of living, it becomes clear that the whole world is steeped in *Jahilliyyah*, and all the marvellous material comforts and high-level inventions do not diminish this ignorance. This *jahilliyyah* is based on rebellion against God's sovereignty on earth. It transfers to man one of the greatest attributes of God, namely Sovereignty, and makes some men lords over others. It is now not that simple and primitive form of the ancient *jahilliyyah*, but takes the form of claiming that the right to create values, to legislate rules of collective behaviour, and to choose any way of life rests with men, without regard to what God has prescribed. The result of this rebellion against the authority of God is the oppression of His creatures.[54]

According to him contemporarily *jahilliyya* is, however, more sinister than the old one, the adherence of the latter were at least more polite with God, offering gifts to other deities in order to intercede on their behalf with Allah, the most sublime. Nowadays, other deities have been elevated above God, venerating what these deities prescribe, and rejecting out of hand what God had decreed.[55] He further states that, if any

53. Sayyid Qutub, *Pi zilal al-Qur'an*, rev. edn., vol. I, Dar al-shuruq. Beirut and Cairo, 1981, p. 510.

54. Sayyid Qutub, *Milestones* (Eng. tr. of *Ma'alim fi-al-Tariq*), A ARIF Pub., Bombay, 18 n.d.m, p. 12.

55. Sayyid Qutub, *Fi-Zilal al Qur'an*, vol. III, p. 1413.

one acknowledges the greatness of other than God and in any matter of life obeys him, he is neither a Muslim nor has he anything to do with religion. But one who believes in the Sovereignty of God and is not prepared to follow any creature of God, nor bows before him, he is a Muslim and in the fold of the religion.[56]

Both Mawlana Mawdudi and Sayyid Qutb considered ideology the engine of other developments in society. Thus, their idea of the oneness of God and of his exclusive transcendental sovereignty is meant to reinstate Islam as a political system. The decisive factor in performing the act of submission is not the mere belief in God's existence, rather, it is the admission of His exclusive authority in determining the moral; political and economic aspects of all societies. While commenting on this and Mawlana Mawdudi's assertion, that sovereignty and the authority are indivisible as he writes:

> If any one regards the word of someone else to be deserving of obedience without any sanction from God, he is as much guilty of the offence of *shirk* as the one who prays to or worships someone other than God. And if someone regards himself as the lord and master and absolute monarch of any part of the earth in the political sense, this act too amounts as much to a claim to godhood as it would if he were to tell people that he was their helper and patron and guardian in the supernatural sense.[57]

Mawlana Nadwi apprehends that this type of interpretation would be construed as equating *Ishirk fil Huqam* [Association (Polytheism) in the matter of order] with that of *Ishirk file al-Allahiyyah ya fil-Ibadah* [Association (Polytheism) in divinity or

56. Sayyid Qutub, *Ma'alim al-Fi-Tariq*, p. 200; *Milestone*, p. 97ff.

57. Mawdudi, *Qur'an ki Char . . .*, pp. 28-29.

worship].[58] He has pointed out that Mawlana Mawdudi has laid stress on and the central theme of his writings is the political subjugation, acceptance of anyone as supreme authority and to allow him the right of legislation and compliance of his orders. This would lead less educated person to consider polytheism in worship or consideration of anyone, in a supernatural sense, as capable of giving help or entitled to be beseeched, supplicated or to be venerated and prostrated before as lesser evils, as a custom of the ancient days when intellect of man was still in its infancy and when culture and civilization were at the elementary level and now that the world has progressed, to give attention to them, to contradict and confront them, is wasting time and energy and to be involved in a matter of lesser importance at the cost of the more important.[59] Which instead, according to Nadwi, is most important, primary, prior and has been the foremost call of all the Prophets and of their successors and heirs in all ages and climes and the main purpose of their lives. They forcefully countered the idolatry of their times expressing itself in the worship of idols, and of pious and venerated persons dead or alive.[60] He further asserts, "confrontation with Idolatry, its abolition and to rescue people from its clutches is the basic purpose of *Qur'an*" and the main objective of the Prophets, the reason for raising them, the foundation of their preachings, the end and main purpose of their efforts. That was the cultural theme of their preachings, the axis around which revolved all their activities, the base from which they proceeded forward and to which they always returned, the beginning and the

---

58. Nadwi, *Asr-i-hazir Ma*, p. 75.

59. Ibid., p. 57.

60. Ibid., pp. 56, 58.

end of their endeavour.[61] According to Mawlana Nadwi, "All the manifestations of paganism like servitude to other than God, acceptance of their power and laws contradictory to divine laws, submission and obsequiousness before such governments and acceptance of such laws and orders, which do not conform to vicegerency of God, they are subordinate to idolatry and polytheism and come next to them."[62] He called attention to that, "It would be tempering with religion if open polytheism is given lesser importance or is equated with political submission and rule or it is believed that polytheistic action and worship are a thing of the past or a relic of Pagan days. This would be against facts and observation. This polytheism and worship of other than God is present even today in all its ancient forms. . . . To consider them a thing of the past would be tantamount to have misgivings about the sacred efforts of the Prophets and their preachings and eternity of the *Qur'an*."[63]

There is no difference of opinion and who can deny this fact that *shirk* is the fundamental error at the root of all sin or transgression, which is the only sin that God cannot fogive, because it denies Himself, and prevents forgiveness.[64] *Shirk* is the fundamental state of being in revolt against God, irrespective of any professed belief in other gods. *Shirk* is the opposite of Surrender to God, which is acceptance and recognition of His reality: Knowledge or Islam. Mawlana

61. Ibid., p. 77.

62. Ibid., p. 84.

63. Ibid., p. 85.

64. *Al Qur'an*, God fogives not that aught should be with Him associated: less than that he forgives to whomsoever He will. Who so associates with the God anything, has gone astray into far error [4 : 116].

Mawdudi has written vehemently against it[65] and about his book *Qur'an ki Char Bunyadi Islalahat* (The four Basic Qur'anic terms) Maryam Jameelah writes that it bears a striking affinity to *Kitab al Tawhid* by Sheikh Mohammad Bin Abd al Wahab in its strong condemnation of reverence for saints and their tombs as tantamount to *shirk* (associating partners to God) and idolatry.[66] As a matter of fact Mawlana Mawdudi never contained the meaning and application of *shirk* to particular aspect only, he innocuously expanded it and tried to identify all other forms of *shirk* prevalent among societies. What he says is not new, nor he makes a departure from or repudiate the past. His views are not inconsistent with early Islamic era. In addition to the writings of contemporary scholars like Mawlana Mawdudi, Hassan al-Banna, Sayyid Qutb or of those in the recent past like Muhammad Ibn Abd al-Wahhab, Shah Waliullah, Shah Ismail Shaheed, one will find this is taken up equally forcefully in the early writings like those of al-Ghazzali, Ibn Taymiya, etc.[67] Furthermore, it does not seem that Mawdudi's explanation of *shirk* in any way lessens or diminish its value or importance, as queried by Mawlana Nadwi.[68] On the contrary, Mawlana Nadwi himself seems to have limited, the meaning and connotations of *shirk* and has tried to create distinction and gradation between open polytheism and

65. See Mawlana Mawdudi, *Tafim-ul-Qur'an*, vol. 'Jeem,' Lahore, p. 597-98 also quoted in-Sayyid Ahmad Qadri, Ahdi-E-Hazir Men Din Ki Tafhim Aur Tashrih Par ik Nazar, Markazi-Maktaba-Islami Delhi 1979, pp. 74-75.

66. Maryam Jameelah, *Aspects of Mawdudi's Thought*, Radiance 4-10 June 1989, p. 41.

67. Sayyid Ahmad Qadri, *Par ik Nazar*, pp. 58, 77 and also see. Sayyid Hamid Ali Qur'ani, *Istilahat aur Ullemai-Salaf wa Khalaf*, M. M. Islami, Delhi 1988.

68. See *Sayyid Ahmad Qadri Par ik-Nazar*, p. 54.

political submission,[69] which according to Mawdudi's explanation amounts to same thing.

Mawlana Mawdudi's emphasis on the sovereignty and ultimate authority of God and political submission came in the wake of modernist Ideological tendencies, where religion at its best is "ones personal affair." This attitude had become fossilized over the centuries and had come to be the accepted viewpoint the world over, even in the Muslim countries. In fact, no true religion ever confines itself to the spiritual aspect of human personality only to the exclusion of its intellectual and temporal aspects. All religions lay down rules for the spiritual as well as temporal guidance of men, as much in his relations to society as in his relations to his soul or to the ultimate reality. Religion deals with man as a whole and supervises all his activities — physical, intellectual or spiritual. In the early history of all great religions, this unity of man is observable. It was only later on when ease-loving persons found it difficult to maintain a coherence between their secular and sacred activities that a bifurcation came to be accepted between the two. Religion crystallized into lifeless dogma that could be safely entrusted to the clergy. The common worldly-wise man was left to do as be wished with little danger of interference from the other side. Religion and politics came to be segregated and the result in Allama Iqbal's words, was barbarism. This cleavage between religion and politics was more pronounced in Christianity, where the church was officially separated from the state some centuries back. Religion was no more a dynamic force in human society. It was just a personal affair of the individual. The hint was quickly picked up by all European nations and with the passage of time the

69. Ibid., p. 74.

attitude was accepted by the Muslim societies as well, when the latter came under European domination and influence. The result was evident-people lost sight of the true teachings of their religion and the slogan religion is a personal affair came to be accepted by all — Muslims and non-Muslims alike. This attitude was becoming more pronounced and dominant with success and advancement of West over the prostrate conditions of the Muslim world since nineteenth century onwards. Many in the Muslim world advocated the separation of religion and politics, and the establishment of modern nation — states modelled on the west. Mawlana Mawdudi's response was time-ously to revitalize Muslim political thought and to stop its further aggravation. Paradoxically, Mawlana Nadwi himself has glorified and advocated the same Mawdudi's ideas in his books *Sirati Sayyid Ahmad Shaheed* as well as *Madha Khasira al-Allama bi-Inhitat al-Muslimin.*[70]

In Mawlana Mawdudi's analysis, the whole modern civilization is based on three principles — secularism, nationalism and democracy. Secularism, or the idea of excluding the creator from "intervening" in people's social life, first emerged in the West as a reation against scholastic theology and its imposition by narrow-minded priests and obscurantists popes. It was, Mawlana Mawdudi explains, gradually transformed into "a separate world-view," and became "the cornerstone of their modern civilization. The relationship between man and God was deliberately sundered."[71] There is, Mawlana Mawdudi asserts, no separation between faith in God and adherence to His social, political and economic injunctions. Only an insane person

70. For further explanation see *Sayyid Ahmad Qadri Par ik Nazar,* pp. 55ff & 76ff.

71. Mawlana Mawdudi, *Our Message,* MM. Islami Delhi, 1981, p. 16ff.

would venture to think otherwise. To him the fundamentals of the doctrine of Islam and the tenets of its laws are one single whole. The latter is a practical translation of the former. It was only after centuries of "diabolic machinations" that the legislative exclusiveness (*hakimiyya*) of God became separated from the question of doctrine in the minds of Muslims and non-Muslims alike. Like atheism or immorality, secularism is a mere deviation, which prevents the normal course of human nature. With the exception of belief in the God of the *Qur'an* and his exclusive transcendental sovereignty, conforming as it does to the innate and instinctive inclinations of human beings, all other philosophical or ideological notions serve to erect barriers of artificial and imaginary solutions. Deviation and conspiracy, as the two most devastating scourges ever to afflict Islam. Both where the result of a long-term plan hatched by internal and external forces. Strangely enough, even Muslims often exhibit highly ambivalent and contradictory attitudes towards sovereignty of God. There were some [like Mustafa Kamal Ataturn (d. 1958)] who pronounced secularism and insisted on keeping religion out of politics. The rest, the overwhelming majority, firmly believing and ardently desired that Islam should be supreme in life, politics should not be separate from it. Yet paradoxically most of them confined religion to the spiritual sphere, denying thereby its validity as a socio-economic and political system. Sensing the dangers of this ideology,[72] in whatever form it may appear, now not only surviving but thriving, seems to have instigated Mawlana Mawdudi to emphasize the idea of ones of God and his exclusive transcendent sovereignty as means to reinstate Islam as a political system, and to counter adverse ideologies.

---

72. Ibid., p. 39.

Among other things Mawlana Nadwi queried the wisdom of Mawlana Mawdudi's interpretation of relationship between men and God as only of a servant and his lord, He writes "that the inference drawn out of the passages of the book Four Basic Qur'anic terms, in fact, from the whole of the book and numerous other writings of Mawdudi, that the only relation between God and Man, is that of lord and servant, a Sovereign and His subject and amongst hundreds of names and attributes of God, the real attributes are of sovereignty and authority to be obeyed."[73] In fact according to Mawlana Nadwi,

> It is true that belief in God and acceptance does entail belief in lordship of God and servitude of man, but it is only a fraction and not the totality of the attributes and essence of God; of His relationship with His creatures and that of His creatures with Him. In reality the relationship between the creator and the created; between the worshipped and the worshipper is far greater, wider, and deeper and far subtler and delicate than that of lord and servant, a king and his subject, a commander and the commanded.[74]

He asserts, that the demand of the names and attributes of God with which *Holy Qur'an* is replete with, are explicit, that one should love Him with all his heart and soul, leaves no endeavour in seeking Him and His pleasure, man is to fear Him, to beg and supplicate Him no doubt but he has also to fix his gaze on the wonder and beauty of His manifestations, to sacrifice everything in His way and to be constantly prepared to make even the ultimate sacrifice. This could be attained not only by fear, and limiting His attributes by

73. Nadwi, *Asr-i-hazir ma*, p., 68.

74. Ibid., p. 69.

recognizing Him only as Supreme Authority and Ruler but also as the real Beloved and the beginning and end of all beauty, grandeur, perfection and benevolence. This is for the reason that attachment and devotions, love and fascination cannot develop without knowledge and recognition of all attributes of, Allah, therefore, limiting His attributes may lead to error.[75]

This difference of opinion is also reflected in their interpretations and explanations of concept of *ibādat*. According to Mawlana Mawdudi, the meaning and essence of *ibādat* is obedience, servitude and loyalty to Allah.[76] In his book *Islami Ibadaat par Tehiqi Nazar* (A critical appraisal of the Islamic prayers) he gives the wide meanings of prayers as Islam understands them, which are far wider than the restricted meanings of worship. For him, Islamic prayers are not mere rituals, rites, the observance of which lead one to please the God. They have been made obligatory for the realization of the vast purpose of life, which is the enforcement in its entirety the Islamic way of life. To struggle relentlessly for it and to court and endure all hardships in its way that these Islamic prayers vouchsafe to a Muslim.[77] Accordingly, he writes that the concept of *ibādat* in Islam is that the man should spend whole of his life in obedience and servitude of Allah just like "full-time servant" even the single movement of his life should not remain without the worship (*ibādat*) of Allah. Whatever one does in this world should be in subservience to His *Shari'at*, [Islamic law].[78] In Mawdudie's

75. Ibid., p. 70ff.

76. Mawdudi, *Qur'an Ki Char*, p. 82ff.

77. Mawlana Mawdudi, *Islami 'ibadaat par eik tehuiqi Nazar*, Urdu Markazi, Maktabah Islami, Delhi, 2000, pp. 5, 17.

78. Ibid., pp. 9-10.

words: then only every action would be manifestation of faith and the sole purpose of all human endeavour in this worldly life would be to seek the good pleasure of God. Not only few moments but whole life is to worship. It is not that as understood by some to remain in isolation and worship but it is to become involved in day-to-day life and act according to dictates of Allah."[79] "The truth, justifiably is this," Mawdudi asserts, "whatever one does in his way, in subservience to his *Shari'at*, is *ibādat* (worship) and that covers his bargains, his domestic life, his social intercourse and his concentration in very thing wordly."[80] "This only is the way to 'Spiritual elevation' and to perceive Allah,' rather than to find him in forests, isolation and worldlessness."[81]

Mawlana Nadwi criticized Mawlana Mawdudi's this interpretation that meaning and essence of *ibādat* is obedience and loyalty. This he claim's is the outcome of Mawlana Mawdudi's particular explanation and understanding that the essence of *rububiyat* is authority, therefore, divinity and authority are inseparable and are one and the same thing in spirit and meaning and that the *Qur'an* treats *rububiyat* "Synonymous with Sovereignty." He was so much obsessed by this central point of divinity and providence, its speciality and single meaning and purpose writes Nadwi about Mawdudi's assertions, that the acts, manifestations and ways of worship, which are prescribed in the *Shari'ah* and required by the religion and were dear to the Prophet (SAAS) lost their importance in his view.[82] He blames Mawlana Mawdudi for giving devotional worship, His remembrance and excessive

79. Ibid., p. 11.
80. Ibid., p. 11 and also see his *Tafhimat*, vol. I, p. 55.
81. Ibid., pp. 13-14.
82. Nadwi, *Asr-i-hazir ma*, pp. 85-86.

involvement in prayers secondary place and treats involvement in them as ignorance of the essence of religion and relic of the days of decadence, thereby adopting a style of expression displaying belittling or ridicule of engagement in such acts.[83]

On the contrary Mawlana Nadwi, buttressing his argument by the verses of *Qur'an* and *Hadith*, emphasizes and stresses the importance of devotional worship and profusion of supererogatory prayers. He writes, "seeking forgiveness of God, his remembrance and involvement in prayers are so pleasing to God that the Prophet of Islam, the most exalted of men and through whose instructions we have received this blessing, stressed them times out of number."[84] While commenting upon the Mawdudi's interpretations he comes up with the apprehension and the psychological effect of such type of thinking and writing (the concept of God only as a sovereign and ultimate authority) would be that the attachment of people, whose understanding of Islam would be limited to this kind of interpretation, with God would be limited, dry, soulless and of a formal character bereft of inner emotions demanded of a believer.[85] Therefore, according to him if the purpose of apostleship is limited only to bringing about changes in this life, establishing culture on a sound basis and promoting reformative revolution and when the whole thing is so eulogized and over-emphasized it will overshadow the concept of love and approbation of God and expectations of final salvation. The whole train of thinking and effort, of struggle and action would get derailed from the rails of faith

83. Ibid., p. 86ff.

84. Ibid., pp. 90-91.

85. Ibid., pp. 91-90.

in the unseen, desire for the Hereafter, and longing for love and pleasure of God so assiduously advocated and stressed by the Prophet, would start running on the desire for prestige, supremacy and authority and materialism.[86]

Furthermore, Mawlana Nadwi, criticized and construed Mawlana Mawdudi's this statement "this is why *namaz*, fasting, *zakat* and *haj* have been made compulsory *ibādat* [*faraiz*], to call them *ibādat* does not mean that they alone are *ibādat*. On the contrary, it means that they prepare men for the real *ibādat* and serve as an unavoidable training course. . . . It lays the foundation of social setup without which human life will not transform into *Ibādat-i-illahi* (Complete worship of God). Without these four fundamentals there is no other way to achieve the real Goal,"[87] as giving the *ibādat* and the four pillars of Islam (prayer, fasting, *zakat* and *haj*) secondary importance and no more then means and methods and therefore suggests that the real objective is orderliness and subordination and establishment of the Kingdom of God.[88] On the contrary, Mawlana Nadwi asserts that the acts of worships, and the "pillars of religion" have the fundamental and pivotal position in the whole structure of the religion. The status of the prayers is not merely orderliness and subordination and establishment of the Kingdom of God but they are an end by themselves. And if, they are "means" of anything they are the means of attaining the pleasure of God and nearness to Him. They will be questioned and they will have to be accounted for it. The rest of the things like "establishment of the Kingdom of God and" evolution of a reformed human culture according to him

86. Ibid., p. 92.

87. Mawdudi, *Islami Ibādat per ek Nazar*, p. 16.

88. Nadwi, *Asr-i-hazir ma*, p. 94.

are no more than means and occupy secondary position.[89] While commenting on considering prayers only as means, what he implied from the writings of Mawlana Mawdudi, he apprehends the adverse effects of spiritlessness, and this type of understandings never generate attachment of the heart in prayers, any humility and submissiveness, meekness and penitence, contemplation and concentration, constant remembrance, sincerity, faith and self-assessment.[90] Instead according to him would finish the deep realization of its necessity and importance, longing and concern for progress and perfection, hence will perpetuate worldliness.

Mawlana Nadwi has referred only part of Mawlana Mawdudi's statement about the four pillars of Islam and inferred from that such an understanding. The another part of Mawdudi's statement which is "It lays the foundation of social set-up without this human life will not transform in to *ibādat-i-illahi* (Complete worship of God). Without these four fundamentals, there is no other way to achieve the real Goal, that is why they are called fundamentals of Islam, the pillars over the edifice of Islamic life stands and continues to stand,"[91] has been ignored by Mawlana Nadwi in his book *Asr-i-Hazir Men Din ki Tafhim Aur-Tashrih*. Here it seems that Mawlana Nadwi has quoted/took Mawlana Mawdudi's remarks completely out of context and therefore misinterpreted them. From this book *Islami Ibādat per ek Nazar* and many other books such as *Khutuba't* (Eng. trs. *The Fundamentals of Islam or Let us be Muslims*) and *Rasail-u-Masail*, etc, Mawlana Mawdudi has tried to emphasize the importance of these fundamentals of

89. Ibid., pp. 97-98.

90. Ibid., p. 98.

91. Mawdudi, *Islami Ibādat per ek*, pp. 16-17.

Islam time and again.[92] He never used pejorative terms for them, whatever he did was that he inveighed against the over-ritualization of Islam and despised to ignore political dimension of *sirah* and "ideological" consciousness. The question of politics has always been a grey area in the minds of contemporary Muslims. Mawlana Mawdudi made it a point to reinvigorate the diminishing political consciousness among Muslim. That is why, some people blamed him for politicizing religion and disparaging *ibādat* (Worship) which he actually never meant.

Difference of opinion is also found with regard to *tasawwuf*. Some of the writings of Mawlana Mawdudi were construed as against *tasawwuf*. Mawlana Nadwi writes about him that, "Mawlana Mawdudi has accepted, pretentiously that *tasawwuf* is yet another name for lethargy and inaction, escape from the realities of life, and not only retreat from the struggle between the truth and falsehood, but surrender and co-option. According to him, they are necessary corollaries and inseparable from one another."[93] Furthermore, he blamed Mawlana Mawdudi for making disparaging remarks about the revivalist endeavours of Mujadid Alf Sani, Shah Waliullah and his successors, who believed in and practised and taught *tasawwuf* to others. In his book, *A Short History of the Revivalist Movements in Islam*.[94] As a matter of fact, Mawlana Mawdudi glorified the role of these revivalists in this above-mentioned book.[95] And while analysing the causes of apparent failure

---

92. Also See, *Sayyid Ahmad Qadri Par ik Nazar*, pp. 86ff.
93. Nadwi, *Asr-i-hazir ma*, p. 100.
94. Ibid., pp. 99-100.
95. Mawdudi, *A Short History of the Revivalist*, pp. 88-89. Mawdudi writes that 'the great circle of the righteous and truth-loving *Ulama* trained and produced by Shah Waliullah and his sons and the enormous army of pious and God-fearing soliders raised by →

from "the worldly point of view"[96] in order to learn lessons from their trumphs and failure for future guidance, he comes up with certain causes, which kept them from establishing an Islamic state in India in spite of the humanly possible effort, they put in.[97] Accordingly, identifying the first cause he writes:

> The one weakness which in my opinion has always attended the work of our reformers ever since the time of Mujadid Alf-i-Thani till Shah Waliullah and his successors may be ascribed to their failure to form a correct view of the Muslim people's morbid attachment for *tasawwuf*. This was a malady, which might well have been cured by taking necessary precautions. But not only were the precautions not taken, the disease was aggravated by giving an overdose of the undesirable diet. True to God, I bear no personal grudge against the *tasawwuf* presented by these reformers in spirit it was indeed the real *tasawwuf* of Islam, nothing different from *ihsan*. But what I think should be carefully eschewed are the mystic allusions and metaphoric references, the mystic language, and the continuance of a peculiar mystic lore, customs and traditions. Obviously, the real Islamic *tasawwuf* does not stand in need of this particular mould. . . . After all what is the necessity of sticking and adhering to a form, which has been corrupted by un-Godly practices for long time. . . . A person may present the real

→ Sayyid Ahmad and Shah Shaheed have been a rare phenomenon in our recent history. When we read about them we feel as if we are reading the life-stories of the *Holy* Prophets companion and their followers living in the earlist period of Islam, ibid., p. 91 and while glorifying their role he writes."History bears evidence that the Soil of the subcontinent had neither witnessed the real Islamic *jihād* before them nor has ever seen such a phenomenon after them," p. 90.

96. Ibid., pp. 91-92.

97. Ibid., p. 92.

> teachings of Islam, but as soon as he adopts the traditional mystic lore and customs all the weaknesses and abuses associated with it through usage for centuries also return.[98]

Furthermore he writes,

> Just as a pure lawful thing like water is prohibited when it is deemed to be harmful to a patient, similarly the cult of *tasawwuf*, though allowable, needs to be eschewed and laid aside. For, through it the Muslims have become addicted to a kind of intoxication, which has lulled them to sleep and sapped them of life and reality for centuries. . . .[99]

Mawlana Nadwi in his book *Asr-e-Hazir men Din ki Tafhim aur Tashrih* mentioned only later lines from the whole topic, ignored the main purpose of Mawdudi's writings. Here it seems an unnecessary guibbling and hairsplitting on the part of Mawlana Nadwi. Thereby, he mistook him as totally against *tasawwuf* which is non sequitur and purpoted calumny against Mawdudi.

As far as Mawlana Mawdudi's views about *tasawwuf* are concerned he had already explained his position in an article published in *Tarjuman-ul Qur'an,* in its issue of February 1952. He write, "there is not one particularly defined form called *tasawwuf* several practices bear this little. The *tasawwuf* we believe and confirm is one, we reject and condemn is the other, we wish to reform and popularize is the third."[100] The Mawlana Mawdudi approved and supported the *tasawwuf,* "that prevailed in the early period of Islam," and was practiced by *Sūfīs* like Fadail bin Ayaz, Ibrahim bin Adham, Maruf Karkhi etc. During this period, Mawdudi writes

---

98. Ibid., pp. 92-93.

99. Ibid., p. 93.

100. *Tarjumanul Qur'an,* February, 1952, vol. 25, no. 3-4, pp. 407-08.

> *Tasawwuf* had no philosophy of its own, and had no separate or distinct way of life. Its conceptions and ideas, its rites and practices, were all derived from the *Qur'an* and *Sunnah*. It set the same object and ideal for life as had been set by Islam, namely devotion to and contemplation of Allah. Such Sufism is our ideal we wish to revive and popularize it.[101]

Accordingly to him, the other type of *tasawwuf* was that in which Greek and Stoic, Zoroastrian and Vedāntic philosophies had got mixed up. This type of *tasawwuf* incorporated monestic and yogic practices and customs and polytheistic ideas, which recognized the *Shari'ah* (Exoteric religion), *tariqah* (Esoteric religion) and *m'arifah* (Gnostic truth) as self-sustaining and independent but more often contradictory aspect of Belief, and which aimed at training man for purposes other than his duties as Allah's vicegerent on the earth. This type of *tasawwuf* had to be rejected and condemned.[102]

There was another type of *tasawwuf* says Mawdudi, 'which had in it and features of the *tasawwuf* of the first two types. The practices and ways of this type of *tasawwuf* were initiated and propounded by some very righteous and pious men, who were scholarly and noble-minded but not altogether immune from the evil effects of alien trends in *tasawwuf*. They tried their best to understand real *tasawwuf* of Islam and purge the prevailing *tasawwuf* of the un-Islamic elements. But in spite of that, their theories and practices could not remain wholly free from the effects of un-Islamic mysticism. Such *tasawwuf* had to be critically appraised so as to free it from un-Islamic practices.[103] In his book *Risalah Diniyat* (Eng. tr. *Towards Understanding Islam*) Mawlana Mawdudi writes about *tasawwuf*:

---

101. Ibid.

102. Ibid.

103. Ibid.

> *Fiqh* deals with observable conduct, the fulfilling of a duty to the letter. That concerning itself with the spirit of conduct is known as *tasawwuf*. For example, when we say our prayers, *fiqh* will judge us only by the fulfilment of the outward requirements such as ablution, facing towards the Kabah and the timing and the number of *raka'ahs*. *Tasawwuf* will judge our prayers by our concentration and devotion and their effect on our morals and manners. . . . But it is to the misfortune of the Muslims that as they sank in knowledge and character with the passage of time, they also succumbed to the misguided philosophies of nations, which were then dominant, partook of them and patched Islam with their perverted dogmas. They polluted the pure spring of Islamic *tasawwuf* with absurdities that could not be justified by any stretch of the imagination on the basis of the *Qur'an* and the *Hadith*. Gradully a section of Muslims appeared who thought and proclaimed themselves immune to and above the requirements of the *Shari'ah*. These people are totally ignorant of Islam, for Islam cannot admit of *tasawwuf* that takes liberties with the *Shari'ah*. No *Sūfi* has the right to transgress the limits of the *Shari'ah* or treat lightly primary obligations (*fara'id*) such as daily prayers, fasting, *zakah* and the *haj*. *Tasawwuf*, in the true sense, is an intense love of Allah and Muhammad (blessings of Allah and Peace be upon him) and such love requires a strict obedience to their commands as embodied in the Book of God and the *sunnats* of his Prophet. Anyone who deviates from the divine commands make a false claim of his love for Allah and His Apostle.[104]

In short, Mawlana Mawdudi differentiates Islamic *tasawwuf* from other kinds of *tasawwuf* and the *tasawwuf* he is not

---

104. Mawlana Mawdudi, *Towards Understanding Islam*, M.M. Islam Pub. New Delhi, 2002, p. 122.

comfortable with. His views about *tasawwuf* seems similar to that of Imam Ibn-i-Taymmiyyah, who inveighed against *Sūfi* practices, which were against the commands of *Shari'ah,* and were finding their way into the system of its discipline.[105] Shah Waliullah also thought it necessary to reform the Muslims and particularly those of the ignorant *sūfīs* whose actions were not in conformity with the laws of *Shari'ah,* he wrote a short treatise, *al-Balagh al-Mubin,* in which he discussed the history of idol-worship and polytheism (*shirk*), and then explained the true Islamic way, as is indicated by the *Hadiths* of the Prophet, in regard, for example, to visiting the graves of leading shaykhs etc. It may however be added that he was basically a *Sūfi,* in fact a practising *Sūfi,* as is clear from his references to their ideas and practices in his works.[106] Shah Waliullah through his works on *tasawwuf* and allied problems, wanted to create an atmosphere in which the genuine representatives of the *'Ulama* and the *masha'ikh* could work in harmony, but his efforts to achieve this objective did not meet with much success. However, since his time and through his successors a school

---

105. "The Mujaddidin who exerted profound influence upon the youthful Mawdudi's developing thought were Ibn Tajmmiyah (14th century) and above all, the Arabian Puritan, Sheikh Muhammad bin Abdul Wahhab (1703-87). Like both these predecessors, the Mawlana fully shared their unrelenting antagonism against Sufism into developed form in favour of rational exposition of the faith in contemporary idiom to attract the modern youth. These aspects of Mawlana's thought are most evident in his 'Towards Understanding Islam' (1932) and *khutbat* (1938)" Maryama Jameelah "Aspects of Mawdudi's thought." *Radiance,* 4-10 June 1989, p. 41.

106. Shah Waliullah has written several treatises in which he has discussed various aspects of *tasawwuf*. For instance, Fuyud al-Haramayn, Qawl al-Jamil, Anfas al-'Arifin, Altaf al-Quds ad Tafhimat, etc.

of the *'Ulama* has come into existence, who got themselves enrolled as disciples of eminent Shaykhs and sometimes could not resist deviationist tendencies. Mawlana Nadwi himself claiming Shah Waliullah as his *alma mater* expressed the same views about the deviationists in book *Tazkiyah wa Ahsan ya Tasawwuf wa salook*. He himself a practising *Sūfi*, adopted reconciliatory approach with regard towards *Sūfi* trends, which also is the hallmark of Imam Al-Gazali. He emphasized the need of *tasawwuf* and adduced several facts to support its necessity in the Muslim life, and called it *fiqh bataniyyah* (esotenic discipline or purification of the Esoteric self).[107] Mawlana Mawdudi on the other other hand not rejecting or minimizing the importance of Islamic *tasawwuf*, however, accentuates strict observance of *Shari'ah* in all its aspects including the purification of the Esoteric self.

Similarly, they adopted different approaches while interpreting and presentation of some aspects of Islamic history. Mawlana Mawdudi wrote *Khilāfat wa Malukiat.* In this book he tried to present lucid and objective picture of the historical events, which were responsible for the transformation of *khilāfat* into *malukiat*, without any ambiguity or attempt to hide behind a lot of unfathomable hocus-pocus. His approach slighted many, with the result he became the victim of a series of unjustified columnies. In his another book *Tajdid-i-Ihya-i-Din*, Mawlana Mawdudi presents in a brief but telling way the history of the Revivalist Movement in Islam from a critical angle renouncing usual unnecessary adulatory style of writing. He presented the hard facts of history with a view to learning lessons for future guidance. While highlighting the efforts and endeavours of these revered men,

---

107. Mawlana Nadwi, *Tazkiyah wa Ahsen ya tasawwuf wa Salook*, Majalis Takeekat-wa-Nashiryat Islami, Lucknow, 1989, pp. 13-31.

for revival of Islam he never shied away from stating boldly the causes of failure to attain the real objective, with a purpose to learn lesson from these failures and thereby may help us to shape our future destinies for the glory of Islam. In Mawdudi's words:

> . . . blind faith and careless estimation, however, can in no way help us in our efforts to revive and restore Islam. We shall have to understand fully the process of *tajdid*, and looking back upon our History determine to what extent and in what ways have the different leaders accomplished this work during the last centuries, how for we can benefit from their achievements, and how we can make up for any possible failings in their work.[108]

On the other hand, Mawlana Nadwi had a different approach, he wrote *Tarikh-e-Dawat-o-Azimat* (Arabic version entitled *Rijal-ul-Fikr wad-Da'wah fil Islam* and translated into English as *Saviours of Islamic Sprit*) exploring and glorifying the positive aspects of continuous efforts made during the past 1300 years for stimulating a spirit of re-awakening among the Muslims. Through this work he tried to bring into light contribution and endeavour of those eminent savants, who rose to the defense of Islam in order to arrest the onslaught of the evil forces, gave birth to various movements for upholding the Islamic morals and values. In the introduction to this book, he has categorically stated that in Islam there has been a continuity of reformative movement and there were no long interregnums of suspense or inaction. It seems that this work of Mawlana Nadwi is comprehensive and elaborated version of Mawlana Mawdudi's *Tajdid-i-Ihya-i-Din* but has been writing in uncritical, subjective rather than objective style. Himself, claims of having adopted from very beginning constructive, positive and

108. Mawdudi, *A Short History of the Revivalist*, p. 12.

uncontroversial way of penmanship and approach to compilation or writing and always avoiding controversial matters and verbal disputation.[109]

In the preface of his book *Saviours of Islamic Spirit* Mawlana Nadwi writes:

> In portraying the biographical sketches and character of the personalities mentioned, light has been shed on the intellectual, cultural and academic temperament of the time in order to make a correct assessment of the achievements of the personage concerned in its true perspective. It is necessary to cast a glance on the then prevailing situation before a place could be assigned to any individual in history. Assessment of any character, out of its own context of time and place, according to modern concepts and values might appear to be a work of critical study, but there can hardly be anything more unjust to the personality so evaluated. The success or failure of any individual can only be judged in the background of the conditions in which he has had an opportunity to strive for a cause, otherwise, the greatest and most eminent person can be depicted as a complete failure in the light of changed circumstances and according to the likes and dislikes of later histories. In fact, no historical figure, Islamic or otherwise, can claim a lasting recognition if it is viewed from a wrong angle.

Further he writes,

> The reader can easily discern from these pages the attitude of the author towards these because of moral and spiritual guidance and for this I need not apologies to those who would want me to be dryly objective.[110]

---

109. Nadwi, *Asr-i-Hazir Ma*, p. 23.

110. Nadwi, *Saviours of Islamic Spirit*, vol. I, Preface, p. XII.

In this and other works such as *Madha Khasir al-Alam bi-Inhitat al-Muslimin* and *Sirat Syed Ahmad Shaheed,* etc. Mawlana Nadwi has reviewed, recorded and interpreted history with a purpose to illuminate glorious and positive aspects of Muslim History. According to Sayyid Qutb who wrote Foreword to Mawlana Nadwi's book, *Madha Khasir al-Alam bi-Inhitat al-Muslimin* (Eng trs. *Islam and World*) the book is not only a representing example of religious and social research but of how history can be recorded and interpreted from the wider Islamic point of view and also he writes: "has offered suggestions to the Islamic world that are balanced and free from extravagancies and polemics. It is a remarkable example of how history should be recorded. It shows how a Muslim can take up his pen to record historical events and discuss their sequences without borrowing from European historians and copying their style which often lacks balances, historical veracity and adequate scholarship and research."[111] Mawlana Nadwi's style of writing history has been appreciated widely. It proved beneficial to explore positive aspects of continuous reformative endeavour savants of Islam. This type of work was wanting until Mawlana Nadwi filled the void.

Although there is common underline objective and interest to resuscitate Islam in the subcontinent and rise to the challenges posed by West and, more importantly, both shared a revivalist ideology and implicit a priori methodology, Mawlana Mawdudi and Mawlana Nadwi do not see eye-to-eye on some issues. They adopted different approaches and attitude, while interpreting certain issues leading to represent two paradigms of Islamic thought. Moreover, despite

111. Nadwi, *Islam and World,* Academy of Islamic Research and Pub., Lucknow, 1982 edn., pp. 5, 7.

distinctive differences in the blueprints for society both regarded Islam all-embracing ideology the union of religion and society, the relationship of Islam to all aspects of life, followed from the doctrine of unity of Allah (*tawhid*) and sovereignty over all creations embodied in the comprehensive nature of the *Shari'ah*; *Shari'ah* a complete scheme of life and all-embracing social order. We find common themes but a diversity of interpretations. While there is a unity of Islamic belief, there is also a variety of understanding both as to its implication and its implementation.

Conclusion

Qur'an and *Sunnah* forms the firm foundation, on which the whole edifice of Islamic thought has developed. From the early days of Islam revelation (*wahy*) was taken as the source of guidance and direction, and reason and *ijtihad* were used both as tools for understanding and interpreting, as well as for dealing with events and developing responses and policies. Throughout the history of Islam there is growth and development in Islamic thought. In spite of the fact that the *Qur'an* and the *Hadith* remain unchanged, as *ijtihad* proceeds, new opinions emerge. To address the new situations and changing circumstances according to the teachings of the *Qur'an* and the *Sunnah* and to adopt its primacy, the dynamic element of Islamic thought, *ijtihad*, played a vital role. Therefore, the *fiqh* (jurisprudence), *kalam* (theology), *falsafah* (philosophy), *tasawwuf* (mysticism) and other religious sciences are the manifestations of Islamic thought, which emerged as a result of evolution and development of Islamic thought itself as well as in response to new emerging situations. The growth and development of Islamic thought was inevitable, in order to face new situations in life and thought and to work out implications of the *Qur'an* and the *Sunnah*, that were not visible to the earlier people.

These branches of learning now appear to be independent of the *Qur'an*, but, as a matter of fact, they were direct and indirect outcome of the study of the *Holy* Book. These sciences grew over the ages as branches of that tree of knowledge, which has its roots in the Qur'anic revelations. Its major and minor parts are logically connected to it. Just as from seed of a tree emerge the roots, the trunk, the branches, the leaves and despite blossoming widely, every leaf is connected to its root.

Despite the demise of glorious *khilāfat* and consequent rift between political leadership and religious intellectual leadership, the religious scholars over the centuries continued to performed *ijtihad,* to understand the situation of the *ummah* as a whole, and to look objectively at problems and to apply the values and principles of Islam in society and organizations. These branches of knowledge are in fact, the cumulative endeavour of the righteous scholars of Islam, evolved in the course of centuries to make *Qur'an* and *Sunnah* applicable to new situations in life and thought. The historical methodology of Islamic thought used, as we know today is represented by the science of *usul-al-fiqh* (judicial source methodology) which, in turn, is represented in its general principles and axioms by the rational foundation and basic concepts of the Islamic mind. Therefore, Islam did never wink at the lapses of its followers. It was always on the alert, correcting, mending, admonishing; the *Qur'an* and the *Sunnah* were continually there intact and unpolluted — to guide and to judge on occasions of doubt and dispute. They kept alive the spirit of defiance against the libertinism of the ruling classes and against the other un-Islamic influences. The whole course of Islamic history is lighted up with the crusading endeavours of conscious determined, brave-hearted men who, like the true successors of the Prophet, faced the challenge of the time and restored, revived and kept on moving the *ummah* by resorting to *jihad* and *ijtihad.*

Medieval period of Islam produced a number of scholars and thinkers, who contributed to the development of Islamic thought considerably by using their *ijtihadi* capabilities. There were traditional scholars as well as the scholars, who had philosophical bent of mind and both these groups responded to the critical situations of their times. The prominent among them Imam al-Ghazali (1058-1111/450-505) and Ibn Taymiyyah (1263-1329/661-728), both, throughout their tenure, did their utmost to rebut the challenges confronting Muslim society and thought. Likewise, in the subcontinent religious doctors, Shaykh Abdul-Haq Muhaddith of Delhi (b. 1551), Shaykh Ahmad of Sarhind known as Mujaddid-i-alf-i-thani (971-1034/ 1564-1624), Shah Waliullah (1703-1763), Sayyid Ahmad Shaheed and Ismail Shaheed are scintillating personalities, who made remarkable contributions in reforming Muslim society and reinvigorate Islam in subcontinent in their respective times. So there has been a continuity of reform and revivalism throughout Islamic history.

In the recent past, when the Muslim world found itself face-to-face with modern Western culture and forced to taste the bitterness of defeat at its hands. For the first time, the *ummah* was confronted by a decidedly destructive enemy which threatened its entire civilization. Scholars produced number of responses to extricate itself from the crises and to institute reform to liberate itself from the challenges of Western influence. Mawlana Sayyid Abul A'Lā Mawdudi (1903-79) and Mawlana Sayyid Abul Hasan Nadwi (1914-99) are at the forefront among the radical responses. Through their writings, they provided an ideological foundation to the contemporary Islamic revivalism. They identified and responded to many of the concerns, which continue to trouble contemporary Muslim in executing Islam in day-to-day life. Their assiduous writings on Western culture, thought and ideologies and its incompatibility and emphasis on Islam as a comprehensible and transcendental world-view, obviated to a large extent the overwhelming influence of West.

Although there is common underlying objective and interest to resuscitate Islam in the subcontinent and rise to the challenges posed by west, more importantly, both shared a revivalist ideology an implicit a prior methodology. Mawlana Mawdudi and Mawlana Nadwi adopted different approaches and attitude while interpreting certain issues. However, Mawlana Mawdudi considered ideology, the engine of other developments in society. His idea of unity of Allah and of his exclusive transcendental sovereignty is meant to reinstate Islam as a political system. To him, the decisive factor in performing the act of submission is not the mere belief in God's existence; rather, it is the admission of His exclusive authority in determining the moral, political and economic aspects of all societies. The mere recognition of God's existence entails the belief in His sovereignty and rulership, there is Mawlana Mawdudi asserts, no separation between faith in Allah and adherence to His social, political and economic injunctions. The fundamentals of the doctrine of Islam and the tenets of its laws are one single whole; the latter is a practical translation of the former. It was only after centuries of "diabolic machinations" that the legislative exclusiveness (*hakimiyyah*) of Allah became separated from the question of doctrine in the minds of Muslim and non-Muslims alike, which is synonymous with the worship of idols or man-made images. According to Mawdudi, Islam is a well-defined systematic system of life, which has based on certain solid principles. Its major and minor parts are logically connected to its basic principles and a complete Islamic life emerges from its basic principles just as from the seed of a tree emerge the roots, the trunk, the branches, the leaves and despite blossoming widely, every leaf is connected to its root.[1] One of implications of the organic understanding of *Shariah* that is repeated over and over again in Mawdudi's writings, almost like a refrain, is that the *Shariah* does not recognize any division between religion and other aspects of life; and most specifically between religion and the state. There is, he insists, no area of man's activity and concern to which the *Shariah* does not address itself with specific divine guidance. Thus the cultivation of private piety, worship, and the ordering of the individual's relationship with God, the matters that are normally identified as "religion" in popular parlance, do not necessarily satisfy the demands of the shariah. True Islamic faith must issue into social action and attitude, must strive for the creation of an Islamic society as well as for personal righteousness.

Mawlana Mawdudi's major contribution and legacy was his systematic presentation of Islam, calling for restoration of Islam's primacy in personal as well as political lives. He attempted to provide a theoretical blueprint for the revival of Islam, or what he termed the process of Islamic revolution. In Mawdudi's words: "the thing which we wish to establish is called in Qur'anic terms *dīn-e-Haq*, the meaning of which may be anything to anyone but for us it means to accept Allah as the Real Ruler and to spend one's individual and collective life in His Servitude." The establishment of *dīn* (Allah's Sovereignty and Islamic system) in its entirety was the goal and aim of all his efforts and works, towards which he strove. He never ignores the importance of securing "Power," which, he believes, is *sine qua non* for the establishment of *dīn*. That is establishing and maintaining the sovereignty of God on earth

1. Mawlana Mawdudi, *Islam ka Nazariyyah-i-Siyasi*, Lahore, Islamic Publications, 1939. Eng. tr., *Political Theory of Islam* in Mawdudi, Islamic Law and Constitution.

or the way of life ordained by Him. He argues, that power and leadership in society are crucial and the decisive factors in human affairs; because human civilization travels along in the direction determined by the people, who control the centres of power, it can hardly resist. In a society, which is in the hands of those who have turned away from God, those desiring to travel towards God are in the precarious position of passengers in a train or individuals in a crowd, who desire to go in the opposite direction. Therefore, according to him, "only when power in society is in the hands of the Believers and the righteous, can the objectives of Islam be realized." It is therefore, the primary duty of all those, who aspire to please God to launch an organized struggle, sparing neither life nor property for this purpose. The importance of securing power for the righteous is so fundamental that neglecting this struggle, one has no means left to please God.[2] He further asserts that, it is not enough to preach sermons, nor merely the presence of large number of "good" individuals. What is needed is organized, collective struggle to bring God's earth under God's rule. He wrote extensively, besides other thing on the nature and character of an Islamic state as well as the primary requisite to establish it (*Islami hukumat kis tarah qaim hoti hai*) and through Jamaat-i-Islami which he founded in 1941, worked to implement politically the Islamic ideal. The struggle to achieve this God ordained purpose has been named by him as "Aqamat-e-Deen," "Shahadat-e-Haq" and "Tehreek-e-Islami."

On the other hand, for Mawlana Nadwi, the things like establishment of the kingdom of God and evolution of human

---

2. Mawlana Mawdudi, *The Islamic Movement: Dynamics of Values, Power and Change,* Eng. tr., by Khurram Murad, M.M. Islamic Pub., New Delhi, 2001, pp. 79-80.

culture, on the basis of goodness and betterment are no more than means and occupy secondary position.[3] According to him, "there is no difference of opinion, in my knowledge, amongst the *'Ulama* of Islam about the necessity of struggle for acquiring power and authority to enable enforcement of divine laws and authority in the society. Acquisition of this type of authority and power is the demand of the *Qur'an* and no negligence or lethargy in that regard is permissible. But all this only constitutes an important and unending means and is certainly not the whole of religion or the foremost objective.[4] For him it is only means to an end not end in itself, which is to seek the pleasure of Allah. He gave more importance to *ibadat* (worship) and the spiritual aspect of Islam as having fundamental and pivotal position in the whole structure of the religion and means of attaining the pleasure of Allah and his nearness. Mawlana Nadwi distinguished the term *iqamat-i-dīn* the establishment of religion (used in the *Qur'an* only at one place in the chapter Shura verse 13) as a comprehensive and having wider connotation than only, what some people think, the efforts for establishment of the "kingdom of God." It seems that Mawlana Nadwi often exhibit ambivalent and contradictory attitude towards power and politics. According to him, it is the whole of the religion and its teachings (belief, worship and daily business) and not only caliphate, government or acquisition of power and authority. He even disagreed with the use of contemporary vocabulary like "sovereignty of God," Islamic "social order" movement, revolution in a discourse on Islam and considered it tantamount to the politicisation of true Islam and smacks of capitulation

---

3. Mawlana Nadwi, *Asr-i-Hazir Main Din Ki Tafhim Aur Tashrih*, Academy of Islamic Research and Pub., Lucknow, 1982, p. 97.
4. Ibid., pp. 108, 110.

to the domination of Western thought and method of organizing life. Therefore, alleged those who intermingle faith with power (power politics) as redefining Islam in terms of socio-political values instead of the eternal, and goals, like establishing the Islamic state, becomes centred on this-world rather than on securing Allah's pleasure in that world.

Instead, Mawlana Nadwi emphasized the need of spiritual and esoteric training and its augmentation only through the abundance of acts of worship (*ibadat*). Following the traditional approach, he concurred with the programme of Mawlana Muhammad Alias and his Tabligi Jamaat, whose Islam is of narrowly traditional type — that is, based on prayer, fasting and so on, without much awareness of political and social issues. Mawlana Nadwi stressed the importance of reforming individuals and instead of establishing Islamic government (*Islami hukumat*) he accentuated the need of establishing Islamic society (*Islami m'ashirah*). According to him:

> Prophets used to transform men from inside, they emphasized the change in attitude and perspective of men rather than the changing of 'system' (*nizam*). System is always subordinate to attitude and outlook/frame of mind and if heart does not change, outlook never changes and nothing changes.[5]

In contrast to Mawlana Mawdudi's version of *akamat-i-dīn* (establishment of *dīn*), Mawlana Nadwi put forward the programme of Payam-i-Insaniyat' the message of humanity. He asserted that this "message of humanity" is more viable and has wider appeal, especially in the Indian context, which is inhabited by many nations and religions, more often in

5. Mawlana Nadwi, *Payam-i Insaniyat* (Urdu), 5 Lectures, Majlis-e-Tehqiqat wa Nashriyat-e-Islami, Lucknow, 1991, p. 17.

contention. Therefore, establishment of Islamic state in this situation seems improbable to him, in India, his original homeland, where he decided to remain after Partition, decision taken much in line with the many Deobandhi *'Ulama* and like millions of Indian Muslims. Through this programme he appealed to all irrespective of cast, creed or religion for the moral reformation and humanitarianism, based on the latent strength and competence of Islam, so as to give a fresh lease of life to the dying humanity, which has been brought to brink of social, moral and spiritual echoes by the materialism and individualism. Therefore, he attempted to invigorate fundamental aim and message of Islam to reform human society and bring humanity on the right path, by addressing the humanitarian issues, common to all religions and nationals living in India. Thereby, contemplating probable rather than impracticable.

However, it seems that the different methodology of interpretations, adopted by these scholars owe much to, taking into account the varying circumstances and situations, changing realities, needs and possibilities of their respective locations. Most probably Mawlana Nadwi in India (after Partition) perceived and related the situation and circumstances with the example of Prophets (SAAS) "Makkan period" (the initial phase during which an individual propagational style was used to spread Islam. This was a period in which the fundamentals of belief and the principles of change were suggested to society at large) while as Mawlana Mawdudi in Pakistan found himself in a situation similar to that of Prophets "Medinian Period" (when the Muslim state and society had gained absolute ascendancy over all its adversaries, was characterized by its completion of all detailed organisational and social arrangements for society ensuring its progress and protection). A comprehensive look at the progression of revelation and the prophetic mission will show the policies and the attempts used to deal with varying circumstances and situation, while maintaining the same basic principles stemming from a single divine source. The Makkan period, as it represents the stage of propagation and reform based on new and higher principles, and with generalizations. It is also for this reason that the prophet used to emphasize to his followers never to use confrontational methods or to return open hostility with hostility. Regardless of the price they had to pay in suffering, the early Muslim were never to turn away from the basic issues; the reform of society. While as, the "Medinian period" demanded establishment, socio-political order and active engagement.

Moreover, Mawlana Nadwi wrote extensively in Arabic language chose to address Arab's having key position in Islamic world for revival and resurgence of past glory of Muslims. His emphasis on the distinctive role of the Arabs in the fortunes of Islam and in his discussions of the unique function of the Arabis in renewing God's authentic religion, he clearly highlights "their nationalist formation" as being solely a product of Islam. Thence he did expect the Arab world, owing, among other things, to its glorious history, great achievements and strategic position, to shoulder the task of leading the entire Muslim world. Therefore, it seems that for Mawlana Nadwi, revival and reformation of Arab world is *sine qua non* for resurgence of Islam. Mawlana Mawdudi was completely silent on this particular issue. However, Sayyid Qutb, who was influenced by the writings both of there scholars, assigned the leadership of human kind to "the believers in the oneness of God," irrespective of their nationality or geographical location.

Although, Mawlana Mawdudi and Mawlana Nadwi appealed to the *Qur'an* and *Sunnah* in formulating responses to certain questions, their respective appeals issued in different results and interpretations. Common themes but a diversity of interpretations, while there is a unity in Islamic belief, there is also a variety of understanding — both as to its implications and its implementations. The study of these paradigms of thought bear witness to the divergence (*ikhtilaf*) of thought and action, essentially one of thought rather than of belief, one of method and not of meaning, and that the issue involved is one of means and not of ends. However, it should be clear that no one could possibly object to the value, principles, and beliefs, which form the foundation of Islam.

Appendix

Mawlana Sayyid Abu A'Lā Mawdudi at a Glance

1903	September: Born in Aurangabad (Daccan).
1906-1913	Education at home.
1914	Age 11, Joined Std, VIII in School (Madrasa Darul Ulum, Hyderabad).
1914.	Got degree of Maulvi from Madrasa Darul Ulum, Hyderabad.
1916	Age 13, Passed Maulvi Exam (equivalent to Matriculation) from Madrasa Fauqania Mashriqia Aurangabad.
1920	Age 17, Started his journalistic career in *Taj* daily and *Muslim.*
1926	Age 22, Got degree of "Ulum-e-Aqleea-w-Adbiya-w-Balaghat" and "Ulum-e-Asleeya-w-Farseea" from Mawlana Shareefullah Khan, Madrasa Darul Ulum, Fatehpuri, Delhi.
1927	Got degree in *Fiqh, Hadith* and Literature from Madrasa Aliya Arabia, Fetehpuri, Delhi.
1928	Passed the course in Jamai Tirmizi, and Motta Imam Malik from Madrasa Aliya Arabia Fetehpuri, Delhi.
1918-1928	Was editor of *Aljamiat*, Delhi for 10 years.
	Wrote *Al-Jihad Fil Islam* during this period.
	1 Book *Islam Ka Sarchashma-e-Quwwat*.
1933	Started Magazine *Tarjumanul Qur'an.*
1933-1938	Beginning of definite movement. Presenting Islamic principles for a State.
1935-1938	Wrote articles later republished in the form of book *Musalman Aur Maujuda Siyasi Kashmakash* (Part I).
1935-1938	Wrote *Masala-i-Qaumiyat.*

1938	Left Delhi and migrated to Punjab at the instance and invitation of Allama Iqbal.
1941	Founded the Jamaat-e-Islami in Lahore.
1942	Mawlana started writing *Tefheemul Qur'an.*
1943	Left Lahore and settled in Pathankot in "Darul Islam."
1947	After Partition, he had to leave Darul Islam. Settled in Lahore, Lahore became the centre of his Islamic movement.
1948	Demanded an Islamic Constitution from the Constituent Assembly.
1948	His demand was fulfilled in the form of "Resolution of Objections."
1949	Arrested on flimsy charges under "Punjab Safety Act."
1950	Released after 20 months.
1950	Protested and build public opinion against un-Islamic suggestions for the framing of the Constitution. The suggestions were withdrawn.
1951	January. Organized the preparation of a charter of 22 basic Islamic principles of an Islamic State and presented it to the government as a collective demand of Muslims. 33 *'Ulama*s representing all sections of Muslims were with him in preparing this Manifesto.
1951	Presented a new method of elections based on Islamic principles in the zonal elections of 1951.
1952-1953,	Led the movement for demanding an Islamic Constitution.
1953	28 March, Arrested.
1953	11 May, Sentenced to death for writing "Qadiani Masala". He refused to file a mercy petition and forbade his family and Jamaat to do the same. The sentence was converted into 14 years imprisonment after public and international protest.
1955	April, Released.
1956	Pressurized the new Constituent Assembly considerably to frame an Islamic Constitution.
	Wrote the *Tafheemul Qur'an.*
	More than 700 books.

1956 Attended "Motamar Islami Conference" in Damuscus, Syria, performed first *haj*.

1962 Read a paper "Islam me Adal-e-Ijtimai" in "Rabeta Alame Islami" which was founded in that very year.

He was selected as a member of the founding body of Rabeta Alam-i-Islami.

1962 Second *haj*.

1962 Was selected member of Advisory Council of Islamic University of Madina. Attended its meeting.

1963 Third *haj*. On 5, 6, 7 Zil Haj, Delivered lectures on the spot of Zam Zam. These lectures published under title of *Khutbat-e-Haram*.

Musalman Naujawano ke Faraiz Is Daur Me lecture in Masjid Dehlvi in Makkah after this *haj*.

1966 Fourth *haj*

Attended Annual conference of Rabeta Alam-i-Islami.

1959 Went to visit and observe the spots mentioned in *Qur'an*. Performed Umra too. Details of this trip published in *Safar Nama-i-Ardhul Qur'an*.

1961 Second Umra, and went to formulate syllabus of Madina University, to Saudi Arabia at the invitation of Shah Saud.

1962 II Umra

1962 III Umra

1966 IV Umra

1969 V Umara. Attended Rabeta Conference.

1970 6th September. Attempt to murder Mawlana Mawdudi failed when the would be assailant changed his mind after listening to Mawlana's discourses in the *Asr-i-Majlis*. The would be murderer became admirer.

1963 Despite the odds and despite refusal of permission to use loudspeakers an All-Pakistan Ijtemah of Jamaat-i-Islami Pakistan was held. Anti-social elements attacked the Ijtemah and a Jamaat worker Allah-Baksh was martyred. A ten-mile long memorandum with thousands of signatures, demanding Islamic system and fundamental rights was

	presented to the Assembly, after which the fundamental rights were included in the Pak Constitution.
1964	Jamaat declared unlawful. The Mawlana and his workers arrested. After 8 months, the Supreme Court declared the Government Order unlawful, lifted the ban on the Jamaat. Mawlana and his workers released.
1967	He was jailed for 2 months for talking on the subject of *Eidul Fitr*.
1968	A five-party front called the Democratic Movement of Pakistan was formed including the Jamaat-i-Islami for the restoration of democracy.
1970	31st May. Upon a call given by Mawlana Maududi, the "Shaukat-e-Islam Day" was celebrated with thumping success all over Pakistan.
1972	1st November After 31 years of struggle, Mawlana due to constant poor health, resigned as *Amir* of the Jamaat issuing a special appeal to the members. Two days later, he retired from practical political activity and devoted himself to purely literary and research work. Completed *Tafheemul Qur'an*.
1972 to 1979	Mawlana concentrated fully or writing work. During this period, he completed the basic work of writing the Prophet's life-history, of which two volumes have already appeared in public. Throughout this period, he guided the Jamaat-i-Islami politically.
1979	27th May. Left for America for treatment.
1979	22nd September. Expired in Buffalo in America. Buried in Lahore in Pakistan. (May Allah shower His choicests blessings upon him.)

Mawlana Syed Abul Hasan Ali Hasani Nadwi At a Glance

Born

6th Moharam-ul-Haram 1333 H (CE 1914) at Takia Kalan (Daira Shah Alamullah) Rae Bareli (UP, India)

Education

- His mother started his education with the *Holy Qur'an*, which was followed by regular Arabic and Urdu Education.
- His father Hakeem Syed Abdul Hai died in 1341 Hijri (CE 1923) when his age was a little more than 9 years. The responsibility of his upbringing and education fell on his mother and his elder brother Mawlana Hakim Dr. Syed Abdul Ali, who was himself studying at that time in a Medical college after completing his education at Darul Ulum Nadwatul-'Ulama and Darul Ulum Deoband
- Started learning Arabic From Allama Khaleel Arab Ansari Yamani, and in fact completed his education of Arabic language and literature under his guidance and supervision. In 1930 When Allama Taqiuddin Hilali (from Morraco) came to Nadwa Mawlana was particularly benefited by him.
- Participated with his elder brother Dr Syed Abdul Ali in the Nadwatul-'Ulama session held at Kanpur in 1926. The participants were greatly delighted by his Arabic-speaking power at such a young age. Some Arab-guests took him as their guide and interpreter. Dr Zakir Husain (The president of India afterwards) and Mawlana Abdullah Surti specially took him to their room and as a test asked him some questions.
- Took admission in Lucknow University in 1927. He was then the youngest student of the University. He secured the Degree of Fazil-e-Adab — with Gold Medal — from the University in 1929.
- Took lessons of Islamic Law (Al Fiqhul Islami) from Mawlana Shibli Jerajpuri in 1928.
- During his Arabic education Mawlana, Nadwi also studied classical Urdu books which helped him in the exposition and explanation of Islamic Faith and Thinking and in his mission (*Dawat wa Tabligh*) in a contemporary language.
- During 1928-30 he also paid special attention to the learning of English language. He utilized this in his literary works and call for ALLAH as well as during his travels to Europe and America afterwards. It also facilitated for him reading English references in the areas of history and Islamic studies.

- Was admitted to Darul Ulum Nadwatul-'Ulama in 1929 and attended *Dars-i-Hadis* (Lessons of *Hadith*) of Allama Muhaddis (Scholar of Traditions) Haider Hasan Khan, and literally read under him the whole of Sahihain (Baukhari & Muslim) Sunan-e-Abi Daud, and Sunan-e-Tirmidhi. Remained under his guidance for about two years and was greatly benefited by him in learning the art of Tradition.
- Took lessons of selected verses from Allama Khaleel Arab. And during his studentship at Nadwa 1929 Attended *Dars-i-Baidhawi* of Allama Haider Hasan Khan.
- In 1930, during his second journey to Lahore studied the initial portion of *sura-i-Baqra* from Allama Ahmad Ali Lahori.
- To Lahore studied *Hujjat-ullah-il-Baligha* from him and in the same year on his advice became the disciple of Hazrat Khalifa Ghulam Mohammad Bhawalpuri.
- In 1931, during his third journey.
- In 1932 (1351 *Hijri*) during his short-stay at Darul Ulum Deoband sought benefit (guidance) from Shaikh-ul-Islam Husain Ahamad Madani and attended his lessons in Sahih-ul-Bukhari and Sunan-i-Tirmidhi, and took lessons in Islamic Law (Juris-prudence) from Mawlana Eazaz Ali, and in Tajvid (Recitation of the *Holy Qur'an*), According to the traditions of Hafs from Qari Asghar Ali.
- In 1932, too during his fourth journey to Lahore, studied the complete commentary (*tafsir*) of the *Holy Qur'an* from Allama Lahori according to the course prescribed for *Fuzal-i-Madris-i-Arabia* (Graduates of Islamic schools).

His Life as a Scholar and Preacher

- Was appointed on the teaching staff of Darul Ulum Nadwatul-Ulama in July, 1934. Work primarily as a teacher of *Tafsir* (Commentary of the *Holy Qur'an*) *Hadith* (Traditions of the holy Porphet) and Arabic literature. Sometimes taught history and logic too. Went to Bombay in 1935 to invite the Dalit leader Dr. Ambedkar to embrace Islam.
- Undertook a journey in 1939 in order to acquaint himself with the religious and Islamic missionary centres, and was introduced to Shaikh Abdul Qadir Raipuri and eminent religious reformer Mawlana Mohammad Ilyas Kandhalwi. This contact continued with

the former's spiritual training and enlightenment and started missionary and reformation work in accordance with the latter's methods. Undertook many journeys in this connection and this continued — with as light difference of opinion in the method of working — till his mortal sickness in *Zilhijja* 1419 *Hijri* corresponding to March, 1999

Founded *Anjuman Talimat-i-Islam* in 1943 for imparting education of the *Holy Qur'an* and *Hadith*. This programme became very popular. The working class and the educated, specially attended these lessons in large numbers.

Was elected a member of the Managing Committee of Nadwa in 1948 and was appointed as Assistant (Deputy) Secretary Education of Nadwa in 1951 on the proposal of Allama Syed Sulaiman Nadwi, and was unanimously elected the secretary of Nadwatul-'Ulama following the death of Allama in 1954, and the Rector of Darul Ulum Nadwatul Ulama in 1961 following the demise of his elder brother Dr. Abdul Ali Hasani.

Became the General-Secretary of self-founded the movement of Payam-i-Insaniyat (The Massage of The Humanity) in 1951. Established the Academy of Islamic Research and Publications in 1959. Participated in the establishment of Dini Talimi Council (The council for Religious Education) in 1960, and Muslim Majlis-i-Mushawarat in 1964, and of Muslim Personal Law Board in 1972.

His Literary Works

- His First article in Arabic about "The Movement of Syed Ahmad Shaheed" was published in the magazine *Almanar* of Allama Syed Rasheed Radha Misri (Cairo, Egypt) in 1931. It was later brought out in a booklet form by the Allama Misri, the writer's age was then only 16 years.
- His first book in Urdu entitled *Sirat Syed Ahmad Shaheed* (Syed Ahmad Shaheed's Life and Mission) was published in 1938, and was warmly received by the religious circles of the united India. The writer was greatly encouraged and appreciated by the venerable personages and reformers of the time.
- Was invited by Aligarh Muslim University in 1938 to prepare a course on Islamic studies for B.A. His course was liked and approved by the University.

- Delivered a lecture in Jamia Millia Delhi at its invitation in 1942, which was later published as "Religion and civilization."
- Compiled *Mukhtarat Min Adab-il-Arab* (a selection from Arabic literature) in 1940, and completed the volumes of *Qasa-sun Nabiyyeen* (Stories of the Prophets) and *Al-Qiraat-ur-Rashida* (An Arabic Textbook for children also) from 1942 to 1944. The former two books are included in the course of a number of educational institutions and Arabic Language Centres of the Arab world.
- Compiled from 1944 to 1947 his famous Arabic work *Maza Khaseral Alamu Binhititil Muslimin* (The effect of the rise and fall of Muslims on the world, published in English with title *Islam and the World*). The Arabic Manuscript of the book was with him, when he went on his first *haj* pilgrimage in 1947, which was praised and admired by Arab scholars in Haramain Sharifain. And the Urdu translation of the book was already published in India.
- Was invited as visiting professor by Faculty of Shariah, Damascus in 1956. The lectures delivered on this occassion were later published in the first volume of *Rijalul fikre Waddawate Fil Islam = Tarikh-e-Dawat-wa-Azimat* (published in English with the Title : *Saviours of Islamic Spirit*).
- Wrote *Al Qadiani Wal qadyineia = Qadiyanyat-Tahlil-wa-Tajzia* (published in English with the title *Qadiyanism: A Cricitcal Study*) in 1958 at the order of his Spiritual guide Shaikh Abdul Qadir Raipuri, and *As Sirau Bainal Fikratil Islamiyyate Wal Fikratil Gharabiyya* (published in English with the title *Western Civilization Islam and Muslims*) in 1965, *Arkan-i-Arba* (published in English with the title *The Four Pillars of Islam*) in 1967, *Dastoor-i-Hayat* (published in English with the title *A guide Book for Muslims*) in 1980, *Islam ur Awwalin Musalmanon-ki-do-Mutzad Taswiren* (published in English with the title *Islam and the Earliest Muslims*) in 1984, Al Murtadhaa (The life of Caliph Ali) in 1988. From 1994 to 1999 penned seven volumes of his autobiography *Karwan-i-Zindagi.*
- Delivered lectures as a visiting Professor in Islamic University, Madina in 1963 (1383 *Hajri*) which were later published as *An Nubawwatu Wal Anbia Fi Dhauil Qura'ne Was Sunnaa* (published in English with the title *Islamic Concept of Prophethood*).
- Was invited as a visiting professor by "Umme Darman University Sudan" in 1966 and by "As-Syed Mohammad Bin Ali-Sannusi University Libya" in 1967 but could not undertake the journey.

- Went to Riyadh (S. Arabia) in 1968 at the invitation of Education Minister of Saudi Arabia for preparation of the course for the facility of *Shari'ah*. On this occasion delivered many lectures on education and training at Riyadh University (King Saud University) and Teachers training college, which were highly appreciated in the literary circles, and later formed part of his famous book *Nahwat Tarbeiatil Islamiyyatil Hurrah Fil Biladil Islamiyyah* (Towards a complete Islamic educational system).
- A number of his important books were written from 1964 to 1977 when he was incapable of reading and writing himself; because of cataract and glaucoma, and others read out books and news papers to him.
- The literary language of Mawlana is Arabic and Urdu. His important works are originally in Arabic, which have been translated in Urdu, whereas some books such as *Tarikh-i-Dawat-wa-Azimat* (*Saviours of Islamic Spirit*) from second to fifth volumes and *Karwan-i-Zindagi* (Autobiography) are originally in Urdu, which have been rendered into Arabic. Thus his important works are both in Arabic and Urdu.
- The number of his Urdu books and pamphlets is 290, and his Arabic books are 183, and his books published in English are about 60.
- His important books have been translated into French, Persian, Bengali, Turkish, Malaysian, Gujarati, Tamil, Malayalam and in other regional and international languages.

Mawlana's Contribution in Journalism

- Participated in the editing of *Al-Dhia*, an Arabic paper of Nadwatul Ulama in 1932, and of *An-Nadwa* an Urdu organ in 1940, started bringing out an Urdu paper *Tamir* in 1948 under the auspices of Anjuman Talimat-i-Islam.
- In 1958-59 took the responsibility of writing the editorials of *Al-Muslimun* published from Cairo. The first editorial of these was published under the caption "Riddatun Wala Ababakarin Laha" (published in English with the title *The New Menace and it's Answer*. Some articles were also published in *Al-Fatah*, a paper brought out by Muhibuddin Khateeb in Damascus.
- Was the patron of Urdu paper *Nida-i-Millat* which started its publication from Lucknow in 1963.

- Was also the chief patron of Arabic periodical, *Al Ba'asul-islami* since its inception in 1955, and Arabic paper *Ar-Raid* since its start in 1959 and Urdu fortnightly *Tameer-i-Hayat* since its publication in 1963, and the English organ *The Fragrance of The East*. All the four are brought out from Nadwa, and Monthly *Marif* the organ of Darul Musannefean (Shibli Academy) Azamgarh, and *Majallat-ul Adab-il-Islami* the Arabic organ of Universal League of Islamic Literature Riyadh and *Karwan-i-Adab*. The Urdu organ of Universal League of Islamic literature Lucknow.

Journies

- Undertook his first long journey to Lahore in 1929, where he met the *Ulama* and the elite. Also called on Allama Iqbal whose poem "Chand" (the Moon) he had earlier translated in Arabic.
- Went to Bombay in 1935 to invite the Dalit leader, Dr. Ambedkar to embrace Islam.
- Went on first *haj* pilgrimage in 1947 and stayed for some months in *Hejaz* (Mecca and Medina). This was his first foreign trip.
- Made his second journey to perform *haj* in 1951-52.
- His first visit to Egypt was in 1951. His book (*Islam and the World*) had already made a deep impression in literary circles there. That proved to be a good introduction for Mawlana Nadwi.
- During this journey also went to Palestine and visited Bait-ul-Maqdis and Masjid-e-Aqsa. On his return journey also met King Abdullah, the king of Jordan. Visited Jordan again in 1973, then 1984, 1998.
- On this occasion [1951] also went to Sudan and Syria. Its account was later published in Arabic titled *Mudhakkeratu Saih Fish Sharqil Ausat* (Urdu translation published in title *Sharqe Ausat Ki Dairy*.
- Visited Syria again — as a visiting professor — in 1956, and stayed there three months. On this occasion also went to Lebanon, and Tripoli, etc. On this occasion in 1956 also undertook his first journey to Turkey (its account was later published in Urdu titled *Do Haftay Turky Main* (Two Weeks in Turkey). Later undertook many other journeys to Turkey in 1964, then 1986, 1989, 1993, 1996 the later four visits were on the invitation of Universal League of Islamic Literature.
- Travelled to Burma in 1960.

- Visited Bangladesh in 1982, the lectures delivered in Bangladesh published in title *Tuhfai Mashriq*.
- Visited Sri Lanka in 1982, and Malaysia in 1987.
- 1964, then 1978, 1986, and last visit to Pakistan was in 1998. The lectures delivered in Pakistan published in title *Ahadeeth-i-Pakistan"* and *Tuhfai Pakistan*.
- Made several visits to Pakistan
- Undertook first journey to Kuwait in 1962, then visited Kuwait in 1968, 1983, and 1987. Undertook first visit to U.A.E. in 1974 at the invitation of H.H. Sultan Bin Mohammad Al Qasmi, then 1976, 1983, 1988, 1993, and the last visit to U.A.E. was in 1998.
- Visited Qatar in 1990, then in 1995.
- Some lectures delivered in Gulf Countries published in title *Ahadith Sareeha Ma'a Ikhwanenal Arabil Muslmeen*. Visited Jordan again (after the first visit in 1951) in 1973, then 1984, 1998.
- Visited Yaman in 1984. The lectures delivered in Jordan and Yaman in 1984 published in Arabic titled *Nafahatul Eeman Baina Sana'a Wa Amman*.
- Led a delegation of *Rabit-a-tul-Alam-il Islami* (Muslim World League) to Afghanistan, Iran, Iraq, Lebanon, Syria and Jordon in 1973 (its account was later published in Arabic titled *Min Nahre Kabul Ila Nahril Yarmook* and in Urdu titled *Daryai Kabuk Say Daryai Yarmook Tak*.
- Visited Mughrib-e-Aqsa (Morocco) in 1976. Then again in 1996, Its account was later published in Urdu titled *Doo Haftay Maghribe Aqsa Marakash Main* (Two Weeks in Morocco.)
- Went to Al Jazair (Algeria) in 1982, then again in 1986.
- Went on a tour of Europe in 1963. And visited Geneva, London, Paris, Cambridge, Oxford, etc. and some major cities of Spain. During this tour met many Arab scholars and delivered many lectures.
- Visited Europe again in 1964, then 1969, the lectures delivered in Europe published in title *Speaking Plainly to the West*.
- After this had to undertake several journeys to Europe particularly on the invitation of Oxford Centre for Islamic Studies in 1983.
- Went to America in 1977, then again in 1993, the lectures delivered in America published in title *From the Depth of the Heart in America*.

- Visited Belgium in 1985.
- Visited Taskhent and Samaraqand, and Bukhara in 1993.

Awards and Honours

During his second *haj* (Pilgrimage) in 1951-52 Shaikh Shaibi the key-bearer of *Holy* Kaba, Opened its door continuously for two days and allowed Mawlana Nadwi to take inside *Holy* Kaba whomsoever he Chose. So he invited in Shaikh Abdul Qadir Raipuri and many other persons.

Was elected correspondence member of *Maj-ma-ul-lughat-il-Arabia* (Academy of Arabic language) Damascus in 1956. Conducted the first session of the foundation and establishment of *Rabitatul Aalamil Islsmi* (Muslim world league) held in Mecca in 1962, in which His Majesty King Saud Bin Abdul Azeez and King Idrees Snnausi of Libya were also present the first meeting.

Was a member of the Advisory Committee (Board) of Islamic University in Madina, since its foundation and establishment in 1963 and continued in this capacity till a change in its administration was effected.

Elected a Member of Advisory Committee or Darul Ulum Deoband in 1382 AH (CE 1963). Had the honour of addressing the Pilgrims from the Musalla Shafa'i in Mecca Haram Shareef two days prior to *HUJ* in 1963.

Was a member of *Rabita-ul-Jamiat-il-Islamia* (league of the Islamic universities) Rabat, Morocco since the beginning.

- Was made a member of *Majma-ul-lughatil Arabia* (Academy of Arabic Language) of Jordan in 1980.
- Was honoured by King Faisal Prise in 1980 for his great services to Islam.
- Was awarded an honorary doctorate (Ph.D.) in Literature by the Kashmir University in 1981.
- Trustees of the Oxford Centre for Islamic studies since its establishment in 1983, and continued on this post till his death.
- Was the founding president of *Rabita-tul-Adab-il-Islami-Al-Alamiya* (Universal League of Islamic Literature) since its inception in 1984, and continued on this post till his death.

- Was elected President (Chairman) of All India Muslim Personal Law Board in 1985 and continued on this post till his death.
- A seminar was held in Turkey on his missionary and literary works on the occasion of the fourth general conference of the Universal League of Islamic literature held in Turkey in 1996.
- The present heir of the Shaibi family (the key-bearers of the *Holy* Kaaba) honoured Mawlana by placing the KEY at the door of KAABA and asking him to open it, on 8th Sha'ban 1417 *Hijri* (December, 1996) And Mawlana offered prayers supplicated inside Bait-ul-lah Shareef on the request of Prince Mish'Al Bin Mohammad Bin Saudbin Abdul Azeez A'Le Saud in which members and office, bearers of Muslim World league also participated. Was given the Eminent (Great) Islamic Personality Award of 1419 *Hijri* [1998] on the occasion of the Dubai world Recitation of the *Holy Qur'an* Competitions in Ramadhan 1419 *Hijri* (January 1999).
- Was given the Award of the 1998 Sultan Hassan-al-Bolkiah International Prize By Oxford Centre For Islamic Studies (OCIS) in recognition of his outstanding constitution to scholarship on biographical Studies of major figures in Islamic thought. The Award receiver by (his sister's son) Mawlana syed Mohammed Rabey Nadwi at a spacial Ceremony in Delhi (India) in July 1999, presented by H.E. Pehin Abdul Aziz Umar, Minister of Education of Brunei Darussalam, and Special Representative of H.M. Sultan Hasan-Al Bolkiah.
- In 22nd Ramadhan-ul-Mubarak 1420 *Hijri* (31st. December 1999) Prepared himself for Juma prayer, took bath and was reciting *Sura-e-Yasin* when the call came and he left for his heavenly abode.
- Mawlana Nadwi given shah Waliullah award by Islamic Objective Studies Delhi in Shaban AH 1421 According to the version of Dr. Manzoor Alam, director of IOS, the institute had decided to award Mawlana Nadwi during his life but he passed away before its formal announcement. This award was received by Mawlana Syed Mohammed Rabey Nadwi, the successor of Mawlana Nadwi, and his repheh (sister's son).
- Similarly, in the month of Shaban 1421 Hijri Mawlana Nadwi was awarded with a first grade medal of acknowledgement in reception of his valuable services in the field of Islamic & Arabic literature and culture by the Islamic Educational, Scientific &

Cultural Organization (of OIC.) Dr. Abdullah Abbas Nadwi — the Education Secretary of Nadwatul Ulama received this medal on behalf of Mawlana Nadwi's successor, Mawlana Syed Mohammed Rabey Nadwi the General Secretary of Nadwatul Ulama & the Rector of Darul Ulum Nadwatul Ulama, in a ceremony held in Rabat (Morocco).

Bibliography

In this bibliography I have included all those works, which have been mentioned in the Book. In addition, I have tried to provide basic references to those works, which deal with the major themes pursued in this study.

Works of Abul Aala Mawdudi

The following are the works of Mawlana Mawdudi which have been used in this Book.

Come let us change this world, Markazi Maktaba Islami, Delhi, 1991.

Dawat-i-Islami awr us Ke Mutalabat, Lahore, 1953.

Dawat-i-*Islami Kiya hay*, Haderabad Deccan, n.d.

Dawat-i Islami, Uskai Usul, Tariqa-i Kar Awr Muqtadiyyat, jt. ed. Amin Ahsan Islahi, Delhi: Markazi Maktaba-i Islami, 1978.

Din-i-Haqq, Markazi Maktaba. Islami, Delhi 1952; Eng. tr. *The Religion of Truth*, Markazi Maktaba Islami, Delhi 1984.

Hikmat-i Tabligh Lahore, n.d.

Hindustan men tahrik-i-Islami Ka Aindah laiha-i 'Amal Pathankot, 1947.

Human Rights in India, Leicester, 1976.

Islamic Economic System Principles and Objectives, Markazi Maktaba-i Islamic, Delhi. 1980.

Islam Ka Nizam-i Hayat, 24th edn., Lahore: Islamic Publications, 1986; Eng. tr., *The Islamic Way of Life*, Markazi Maktaba-i Islamic Pub., New Delhi, 1986.

Islam Asr-i Hadir men, Markazi Makataba Islamic, Delhi, 1990; Eng. tr. *Islam Today*, Cresent Pub. Co., Delhi, n.d.

Islami Hukumat Kis Tarah Qaim Hoti Hai?, 25th edn., Lahore: Islamic Publications, 1988; Eng. tr., *The Process of Islamic,* Revolution, Markazi Maktaba Islamic, Delhi, 1982.

Islam Ka Nazariya-i-Siyasi, Larore, 1939; Eng. tr., *Political Theory of Islam,* Markazi Maktaba Islamic, Delhi, 1989.

Islami Ibadat Par Aik Tahqiqi Nazar, 16th edn., Lahore: Islamic Publications, 1984.

Islam Ka Akhlaqi Nuqta-i-Nazar, Markazi Maktaba Islamic, Delhi, 1981; Eng. tr. *Ethincal Viewpoint of Islam,* Markazi Maktaba Islami, Delhi, 1979.

Islami Nizam Awr Maghribi La Dini Jamhuriyyat, 15th edn., Lahore, Islamic Publications, 1986.

Islami Law and Constitution, tr. and ed. Khurshid Ahmad, Lahore, 1955-1960.

Islami Nizam-i-Zindagi Awr Uski Bunyadi Tasawwurat, 13th edn., Lahore, Islamic Publications, 1984.

Islami Riyasat (Islamic State), Islamic Pub. Ltd., Lahore, 1981.

Islami Siyasat: *Musalman Awr Mawjudah Siyasi Kashmakash,* 4th edn., Delhi, Markazi Maktaba-i Islami, 1991.

Islami Tahdhib awr us Ke Usul-o-Mabadi, Lahore, 1955; Eng. tr., *Serialized in the Criterion,* Karachi, May-June, 1971, vol. 6, no 3 October 1973, vol. 8, no. 10.

Jamaat-i Islami us ka Maqsad, Tarikh, Awr Laih-i Amal, 19th edn., Lahore, Shuba-i Nashr-o Ishaat-i Jamaat-i-Islami, 1990.

Jamaat-i Islami Ke Dawat, Markazi Maktaba Islami, Delhi, 1989; Eng. tr., *Dur Maeeage,* Markazi Maktaba Islami, Delhi, 1981.

Al-Jihad Fil Islam, 5th edn., Delhi, Markazi Maktaba-i Islami, 1988.

Khilafat-o Mulukiyyat, 7th edn., Delhi, Markazi Maktaba-i Islami, 1988.

Khutbat, 40th edn., Lahore, Islamic Publications, 1989; Eng. tr., *Let Us Be Muslims,* Markazi Maktaba Islamic, Delhi, 2000.

Mas'ala-i Khilafat (The Question of Caliphate), Delhi, 1922.

Mas'ala-i Khilafat-i Zamin, Markazi Makataba-i-Islami, Delhi, 1993.

Mas'ala-i Qawmiyat, Markazi Makataba-i-Islami, Delhi, 1994.

Makatib-i-Sayyid Abu a'la Mawdudi, ed. Asim Numani, Lahore, vol. 1, 1970, vol. 11, 1972.

Mawlana Mawdudi Ke Interview, ed. Abu Taireq M.A., Markazi Maktaba Islami, Delhi, 1994.

Qur'an Fahmi Kai Bunyadi Usul, 2nd edn., Lahore, Idara-i Tarjumanul Qur'an, 1985.

Qur'an Ke Siyasi Taleem, Markazi Makataba Islami, Delhi, 1978.

Qur'an Ki Char Bunyadi Istalahain, Markazi Makataba Islami, Delhi, 1981.

Risala-i Diniyat, Hyderabad Deccan, 1932. Eng. tr., *Towards Understanding Islam*, Markazi Makataba Islami Pub., New Delhi, 2002.

Sahadat Haq Markazi Maktaba Islami, Delhi 1985, Eng. tr., *Witness to Mankind, The Purpose and Duty of the Muslim Ummah*, Markazi Maktaba Islami Pub., Delhi, 2000.

Sarwar-i Alam, 13th edn., Lahore, Islamic Publications., 1986.

Salam ati Ka Rastah, Lahore, 1940; Eng. tr., *The Road to Peace and Salvation*, Markazi Maktaba Islami Pub., New Delhi, 2000.

System of Government Under the Holy Prophet, Islami Publications Ltd., Lahore, 1978.

Tafhim al-Qur'an, Lahore, Islamic Publications, 6 vols., 1949-72.

Tafhimat, Lahore, Islamic Publications, 4 vols., 1940-75.

Tahrik Awr Karkun, ed. Khalil Ahmad Hamidi, Lahore, al-Manar Book Centre, 1986.

Tahrik-I Islam, ki Akhalaqi Bunyaden, Markazi-Makataba Islami, Delhi, 1954; Eng. tr. *The Islamic Movement: Dynamics of Values Power and Change*, ed. Khurram Murad, Markazi Makataba Islami Pub., Delhi, 2001.

Tahrik-i Azadi-i Hind Awr Musalman, Lahore, Islamic Publications, vol. I, 1987, 12th edn. and vol. II, 1987, 6th edn.

Tahrik-i-Islam: Kamyabi Ki Sharait; Eng. tr., *Islamic Movement Prerequisites for Success*, Markazi Makataba Islami, Delhi, 1973.

Tahrik-i Islami ka A inda La iha-i Amal, 14th edn., Lahore, Islamic Publications, 1989.

Ta'limat Eng. tr. *The Education,* Markazi Makataba Islami Pub., New Delhi, 2000.

Tajdid-o Ihya-i Din, 16th edn., Lahore, Islamic Publications, 1982, Eng. tr. *A Short History of the Revivalist Movement in Islam,* Markazi Makataba Islami, Delhi, 1997.

Tanqihat, 20th edn. Lahore, Islamic Publications, 1987, Eng. tr. *West Versus Islam,* Markazi Makataba Islami Pub., New Delhi, 2000.

The Message of Islam, Markazi Makataba Islami Publication., Delhi, 6, 1996.

The most comprehensive list of Mawlana Mawdudi's writings in Urdu, their translated versions in English, and writings about Mawlana Mawudidi, can be found in Khurshid Ahmad and Zafar Ishaq Ansari (eds.), *Islamic Perspectives: Studies in Honour of Sayyid Abul A'Lā Mawdudi,* London, 1979, pp. 3, 14.

Works of Abul Hasan Ali Nadwi

The following is not intended to be an exhaustive list of Mawlana Nadwi's works, though it represents a large part of his writings in Urdu. These are the works, which have been referred to in this Book.

A Misunderstood Reformer, Lucknow, Academy of Islamic Research and Pub., 1978-97.

Aik Ahamm Dini Dawat Ya Musalmanon Ki Amumi Talim-Tarbiyyat Ka Nizam, New Delhi, 1982.

Alam-i Arabi Ka Almiyya, 3rd edn., Lucknow, Majlis-i Tahqiqat-Wa Nashriyyat-i Islam, 1980.

Arkan-i Arba, 5th edn., Lucknow, Majlis-i Tahqiqat-Wa Nashriyyat-i Islam, 1981, Eng. tr. *The four Pilllars of Islam,* Academy of Islamic Research and Pub., Lucknow, 1976.

Asr-i Hadir Main Din Ki Tafhim-o Tashrih, 2nd edn., Lucknow, Dar-i, Arfat, 1980, Eng. tr. *Appreciation and interpretation of Religion in the Modern Age*, Academy of Islamic Research and Pub., Lucknow, 1982.

Darya-i Kabul Sai Darya-i Yarmuk Tak, tr. by Noor Azim Nadwi from the Arabic version *Min Nahr Kabul Ila Nahr al-Yarmuk*, Karachi, Majlis-i Nashriyyat-i Islam, n.d., written 1974.

Dawat-i Fikir Wa Amal, Majlis-i, Tahqiqat-Wa Nashriyyat-i Islam, Lucknow, 1999.

Hayat Abdul Hayy, 2nd edn., Pune, Urdu-Marathi Prakashan, 1988.

Fasadat Aur Hindustani Musalman, Majalis Tahqiqat Wa Nashriyyat-i Islam, Lucknow, 1991.

Hadrat Mawlana Muhammad Ilyas Awr Unki Dini Dawat, Lucknow, Majlis-i Tahqiqat-Wa Nashriyyat-i Islam, 1985, edn.

Hijaz Muqaddas Awr Jaziratul Arab, Lucknow, Majlis-i Tahqiqat, Wa Nashriyyat-i Islam, 1979.

Hindustani Musalman, Eng. tr. *Muslims in India*, Academy of Islamic Research and Pub., Lucknow, 1980.

Hindustani Musalman Aik Nazar Main, 4th edn., Lucknow, Majlis-i Tahqiqat-o Nashriyyat-i Islam, 1985.

Insani Dunya Par Musalmanon Kai Uruj-o Zawal Ka Athar, 5th edn., Lucknow, Majlis-i Tahqiqat-Wa Nashriyyat-i Islam, 1966. Eng. tr., *Islam and The World*, Academy of Islamic Research and Pub., Lucknow 1982.

Islam Mukamal Din Mustaqbal Tahzib, Majlis-i Tahqiqat-Wa Nashriyyat-i, Islam, Lucknow, 1992.

Islam Aur Magrib, Majlis-i, Tahqiqat Wa-Nashriyyat-i Islami, Lucknow, 1983.

Islam Aik Taghayyur Padhir Dunya Main, 2nd edn., Lucknow, Majlis-i Tahqiqat-o Nashriyyat-i Islam, 1985. Eng. tr., *Islam in a Changing World*, Academy of Islamic Research and Pub., Lucknow, 1977.

Karawan-i Medina, Karachi, Majlis-i Nashriyyat-i Islam, 1983.

Karawan-i Zindagi, Lucknow, Maktaba Islam, 6 vols., 1983-1991.

Maraka-i Iman-o Maddiyyat, Lucknow, Majlis-i Tahqiqat Wa-

Nashriyyat-i Islam, 1976. Eng. tr., *Faith versus Materialism,* Academy of Islamic Research and Pub., Lucknow, 1976.

Makatib Hadrat Mawlana Shah Muhammad Ilyas, 3rd edn., Delhi, Ajuman Taraqqi-i Urdu, 1972.

Mansab-i Nabuwwat Awr Uskai Ali Maqam Hamilin, Lucknow, Majlis-i Tahqiqat Wa Nashriyyat-i Islam, 1975. Eng. tr., *Islamic Concept of Prophethood,* Lucknow, Academy of Islamic Research and Pub., 1976.

Madhhab-o Tamaddun, Lucknow, Majlis-i Tahqiqat Wa-Nashriyyat-i Islam, 1979.

Al-Murtada, Lucknow, Majlis-i Tahqiqat-o Nashriyyat-i Islam, 1988.

Musalmanani Hind Sa saf saf Batiyia, Majlis-i Tahqiqat Wa-Nashriyyat-i Islam, Lucknow 1991.

Muslim Mumalik Main Islamiyyat-o Maghribiyyat ki Kashmakash, 3rd edn., Lucknow, Majlis-i Tahqiqat Wa Nashriyyat-i Islam, 1981, Eng. tr., *Western Civilization Islam and Muslims,* Academy of Islamic Research and Pub., Lucknow, 1969.

Mutala-i Qur'an Kai Usul-o Mabadi, Lucknow, Maktaba Islam, 1981.

Nai Dunya Amrica Main Saf Saf Batain, Lucknow, Majlis-i Tahqiqat Wa Nashriyyat-i Islam, 1977. Eng. tr., *From the Depth of the Heart in America,* Lucknow, Academy of Islamic Research and Pub., 1978.

Nabi-i Rahmat, 2nd edn., Lucknow, Majlis-i Tahqiqat-o Nashriyyat-i Islam, 2 vols., 1981.

Nishan-i Rah, 4th edn., Lucknow, Majlis-i Tahqiqat-Wa Nashriyyat-i Islam, 1980.

Nishan-I Manzil, sadarati Takrir Jamia Islamia Batkal, 8 November 1967, Jamia-Islamia Batkal, Mysor 1967.

Nuqush-i Iqbal, 4th edn., Lucknow, Majlis-i Tahqiqat Wa Nashriyyat-i Islam, 1975.

Paja Suragh-i Zindagi, 2nd edn., Lucknow, Majlis-i Tahqiqat-o Nashriyyat-i Islam, 1979.

Pandhrawin Sadi Hijri, Madi wa Hal Kai A inah Main, 2nd edn., Lucknow, Majlis-i Tahqiqat-o Nashriyyat-i Islam, 1980.

Purane Chiragh, Karachi, Majlis-i Nashriyyat-i Islam, vols. 1993 Payma-i-Insaniyat Panch Taqrira, Majlis-i Tahqiqat-Wa Nashriyyat-i, Islam, Lucknow, 1991.

Reconstruction of India Society What Muslims Can Do, Academy of Islamic Research and Publication, Lucknow n.d.

Sawanih Hadrat Mawlana Abdul Qadir Raipuri, 3rd edn., Lucknow, Maktaba Islam, 1995. 4th edn.

Sawanih Hadrat Shaykhul Hadith Mawlana Muhammad Zakariyya Sahib, Lucknow, Maktaba-i Islam, 1983.

Sharq-i Awsat Ki Dairi, 2nd edn. tr., Shamsul Haq Nadwi from the Arabic version *Mudhakkirat Sa ih fi al-Sharq al-Awsat,* Lucknow, Maktaba Firdos, 1984.

Speaking Plainly to the West, Academy of Islamic Research and Pub., Lucknow, 1973.

Sirat Sayyid Ahamd Shaheed, Lucknow, Majlis-i Tahqiqat-o Nashriyyat-i Islam, vol. I, 1986, 7th edn., and vol. II, 1977 (3rd edn.).

Ta mir-i Insaniyyat, Lucknow, Majlis-i Nashriyyat-I- Tahqiqat Wa Islam, n.d.

Tabligh-o Da wat Ka Mu jizana Uslub, Lucknow, Majlis-i Tahqiqat Nashriyyat-i Islam, 1981.

Tadhkira Hadrat Mawlana Fadl-i Rahman Ganj Muradabadi, 4th edn., Lucknow, Majlis-i Tahqiqat-o Nashriyyat-i Islam, 1957.

Tarikh-i Da wat-o Azimat, Lucknow, Majlis-i Tahqiqat-o Nashriyyat-i Islam, 5 vols., 1979-1984. Eng tr., *Saviours of Islamic Sprit,* Academy of Islamic Research and Pub., Lucknow, 4 vols, 1986.

Tazkiyya-o Ihsan Ya Tasawwuf-o Suluk, 3rd edn., Lucknow, Majlis-I Tahqiqat Wa Nashriyyat-i Islam, 1979.

Islamic Code of life and Uniform Civil Code, All India Muslim Personal Law Board Camp, Lucknow, 1992.

The New Menace and its Answer, Islamic Research and Publication, Lucknow n.d.

The Place of Knowledge and Its Responsibilities of those Who Acquire It, Academy of Islamic Research and Publications, Lucknow, 1981.

Presidential Address, All India Muslim Personal Law Board; held at Bombay on 15-16 December 1986; Kanpur 4-5 March 1989; Gujarat 7-8 October 1995; Jaipur, 9-10 October 1993; Calcutta 6-7 April 1985, Lucknow AIMPLB, n.d.

Dangerous Situation in Our Country and Responsibility of Patriots, Presidential Address Message of Humanity Conference at Hyderabad on 29 December 1988, Message of Humanity Forum, Lucknow, n.d.

Calamity of linguistic and Culture Chauvinism, Academy of Islamic Research and Publication, Lucknow. n.d.

Khutbah Sadarat Payami Insaniyat Conference at Lucknow 26-27 October 1980, Payami Insanyat Forum, Lucknow, n.d.

Presidential Address state Dini Talimi conference, Lucknow 4-5 June 1961; Aligrah 26-27 April 1998; Muradabad 14-15 June 1969; Allahabad 20-21 June 1964 .

Secondary Source References in Urdu

Ahmad, Khurshid (ed.), *Adabiyyat-i Mawdudi*, 3rd edn., Markazi Maktaba Islami Publications, 1985.

Al-Hasani, Muhammad, *Sirat Mawlana Muhammad Ali Mawngairi: Bani-i Nadwatul Ulamā'*, Karachi, Majlis-i Nashriyyat-i Islam.

Al-Tabag, *Ragab-Tarikar Afkar wa Alooom-i, Islami*, 2 vols., tr. Iftikhar Ahmeed Balkhi, Markazi Maktaba Islami, Delhi, 1983.

Akhtar Hakeem Muhammad (ed.), *Mawdudi sahib-Akabir ummat Ke Nazar ma*, Kutub Khana Insha-i Ahlum, Saharanpur, n.d.

Bahtah Muhammd Yousf (ed.), *Mawlana Mawdudi Apna Aur Dousru Ke Nazar ma*, Markazi Maktaba Islami, Delhi, 1990.

Islahi, Amin Ahsan, *Maqalat-i Islahi*, ed. Khalid Masud, Lahore Faran Foundation, vol. I, 1991.

Islahi, M. Yusuf, *Jama at-i Islami Ka Program Awr Tablighi Jamat Sai* Tawun, 2nd edn., Rampur, Maktaba Zikra, 1989.

Junaydi, A.H., *Urdu Adab Ki Tarikh*, 2nd edn., Aligarh, Educational Book House, 1991.

Khan, Shams Tabrez, *Tarikh Nadwatul Ulamā'*, Lucknow, Nadwatul Ulama, vol. II, 1984.

Khan, Wahiduddin, *Al Islam*, New Delhi, Matbuat-i Islami Markaz, 1985.

———, *Din i Kamil*, New Delhi, Matbuat-i Islami Markaz, 1985.

———, *Din Ki Siyasi Ta'bir*, Maktabah Al Risalah, New Delhi, 1990.

———, *Ihya i Islam*, New Delhi, Matbuat-i Islami Markaz, 1990.

———, *Fikr-e-Islami*, Makatab Al-Risalah, New Delhi, 1996.

———, *Madhhab Awr Jadid Chalenj*, New Delhi: Matbuat-i Islami Markaz, 1987.

———, *Rah i Amal*, New Delhi, Matbuat-i Islami Markaz, 1989.

———, *Ta bir ki Ghalati*, 2nd edn., New Delhi, Matbuat-i Islami Markaz, 1987.

———, *Tajdid i Din*, New Delhi, Matbuat-i Islami Markaz, 1990.

Murad, Khurram, *Mustaqbal Ki Hikmat-i Amali*, Lahore, Halqa-i Khawatin-i Pakistan, 1986.

Muzafar Beigh (ed.), *Azildar Park Mawlana Mawdudi Ke Asri Majalis*, Maktaba Zikra Rampur U.P, 1978.

Nadwi, Khwaja Iqbal A., *Badaltai Nasbul Ain: Mawlana Mawdudi, Mawlana Manzoor Nomani Awr Mawlana Ali Miyan kai Bahmi khtalafat Haqiqat Ki Roshni Main*, 2nd edn., Lahore, Hira Publications, 1990.

Nadwi, M.I.J., *Tarikh Nadwatul Ulama*, Lucknow, Nadwatul Ulama, vol. I, 1983.

Nadwi Muhasin Uthamani, *Din Ka Mutwazin Tasawoor, Ibadat Aur Kilafat Ke Jamiyat*, Qazi Pub & Distributors, New Delhi, 1997.

Nadwi, S. Sulayman, *Arab-o Hind Kai Ta alluqat*, Allahbad, 1930.

———, *Hayat-i Shibli*, Azamgadh, Matbaa Maarif, 1983.

———, *Sirat al-Nabi*, Azamgadh, Matbaa Maarif, vol. 7, 1980.

Nadwi, Mawlana Masood Alam, *Hindustan Ke Pahli Islami Tahreeq*, Markazi Maktaba Islami, Delhi, 1977.

Nizami, Khaliq A., *Shah Waliullah Dehlawi Kai Siyasi Maktubat*, Aligarh, 1950.

———, *Hadrat Sayyid Ahmad Shaheed Awr Unki Tahrik-i Islah-o Jihad*, Rae Bareli, Daira-i Shah Alamullah, 1991.

———, *Salatin-i Dehli Kai Madhhabi Rujhanat*, Delhi, Idara-i Adabiyyat, 1981.

———, Tarikh-i Masha ikh-i Chisht, Delhi Idara-i Adabiyyat, vol. I, 1980.

Nomani, Asim (ed.), *Tasawwuf Awr Tamir-i Sirat, Mawlana Mawdudi Ki Tahriron Ki Roshni Main*, 4th edn., Markazi Maktaba Islami, Delhi, 1990.

———, *Kuftar wa Afkar*, Markzi Maktaba Islami, Delhi, 1990.

Nomani, Manzoor (ed.), *Tasawwuf Kya Hai?*, 2nd edn. Lucknow, al-Furqan Book Depot, 1987.

———, *Malfuzat Hadrat Mawlana Muhammad Ilyas*, Lucknow, al-Furqan Book Depot, 1980 edn.

———, *Mawlana Mawdudi Kai Sath Mairi Rafaqat Ki Sarguzasht Awr Ab Maira Muwaqqaf*, Lucknow, al-Furqan Book Depot, n.d.

———, *Tabligi Jamaat. Jamaa, Ti Islami Aw Biralwi hazrat*, alfurqan Book Depat Laknow, 1989.

Qadiri, Hamid Hasan, *Dastan-i Tarikh-i Urdu*, Agra: Lakshmi Narain Aggarwal Publishers, 1957.

Qadiri, Alama Arshid, *Jamaat-i-Islami*, Makataba Jami Noor, Delhi. n.d.

Qasmi, Atiq Ahmad, *Fikr Ki Ghalati: Wahiduddin Khan Sahib Kai Afkar Ka Tanqidi Ja iza*, New Delhi, Makataba al-Irshad, 1990.

Qasmi, *Ibn Junayd, Mawlana Ali Miyan Awr Mawlana Mawdudi*, Delhi, Idara-i Shahadat-i Haq, 1981.

Siddiqi, Naeem, *Al Mawdudi*, Markazi Maktaba Islami, Delhi, 1995.

Uthmani, M. Taqi, *Hadrat Mu awiyya Awr Tarikhi Haqa iq*, Karachi, Idara al-Maarif, 1988.

———, *Islah-i Mu ashara*, Karachi, Maktaba Dar al-Ulum, 1980.

———, *Islam Awr Siyasat-i Hadira*, Karachi, Maktaba Dar al-Ulum, 1980.

———, *Nifadh-i Shari at Awr Uskai Masa il*, Karachi Maktaba Dar al-Ulum, 1980.

Yousuf, Mufti Muhammad, *Mawlana Mawdudi Par Ayatirazat Ka Almi Jayzizah*, Markazi Maktaba Islami Pub., New Delhi 1999.

Zakariyya, Muhammad, *Dehli Ki Tablighi Jamaat Par Chand Amumi-i taradat Awr Unkai Mufassal Jawabat*, Saharanpur, Yahyawi Kutub Khana, n.d.

———, *Fitna-i Mawdudiyyat Ya Jama at-i Islami: Aik Lamha-i Fikriyya*, 6th edn., Saharanpur, Kutub Khana Ishaat al-Ulum, 1983.

———, *Al-I tidal Fi Maratib al-Rijal Ya Islami Siyasat* , Saharanpur, Kutub Khana Ishaat al-Ulum, n.d.

Sayyid Hamid Ali, *Qur'ani Istitahat Awr Ulmayi salaf Wa Khalaf*, Markazi Maktaba Islami, Delhi, 1988.

Shah Ismail Shaheed, *Taqwiah, tul Iman*, Sa Lffiah Muslim Educational Trust, Srinagar, Kashmir.

Shami, Mujeebur Rehman, *Aik shakes karwan, sayyied Mawdudi Ka Mufasat Shakeis Mulala*, Markazi Maktaba Islami, Delhi.

Secondary Sources in English

Abdel-Malek, Anour (ed.), Contemporary Arab Political Thought tr. Michael Pallis, London, 1983.

Abbot, Freeland K., "Mawlana Mawdudi on Qur'anic Interpretation," *Muslim World*, 48 (1958), pp. 6-19.

———, "The Jama'at-I-Islami of Pakistan," *Middle East* 11.1 (winter 1957) : 37-51.

Abu, Sulayman Abdul Hamid, *A Crisis in the Muslim Mind*, Eng. tr. Yusuf Talal Delorenzo, International Islamic Pub., House Saudi Arabia, 1994.

Adams, Charles J., "The Ideology of Mawlana Mawdudi," in D.E. Smith (ed.), *South Asian Politics and Religion*, Princeton, 1966, pp. 371-97.

El-Affaendi, Abdelwahab, "The Long March from Lahore to Khartoum, Beyond the 'Muslim Reformation," *British Soceity for Middle Eastern Studies Bulletin*, 17, 2 (1990), pp. 137, 51.

Ahmad, Aziz, *Studies in Islamic Culture in the Indian Environment*, Oxford 1964.

———, *Islamic Modernism in India and Pakistan 1857-1964*, London, 1967.

———, *An Intellectual History of Islam in India*, Edinburgh, 1969.

———, and G.E. Von Grunebaum, *Muslim Self-Statement in India and Pakistan*, 1857-1968, (Wiesbaden, 1970).

———, "Mawdudi and Orthdox Fundamentatlism of Pakistan" *Middle East Journal* 21.3, (Summer 1967), 369-80.

Ahmad, Khurshid, and Zafar Ishaq Ansari (eds.), *Islamic Perspectives, Studies in Honour of Sayyid Abul A'Lā Mawdudi*, London, 1979.

Ahmad, Q., *The Wahabi Movement in India*, Calcutta, 1966.

Ahmad, Sayed Riaz, *Mawlana Mawdudi and the Islamic State*, Lahore, 1976.

Ajami, Fouad, *The Arab Predicament, Arab Political Thought and Practice Since* 1967, Cambridge, 1981.

Akhvi, Shahrukh, Religion and Politics in Contemporary Iran, Albany, 1980.

———, "Shariati's Social Thought" in N. Keddie, (ed.), *Religion and Politics in Iran*, London 1983.

Ali, Muhammad Mumtaz, "Education, An Islamic Perspective Mawdudi Philosophy," *Al HArmony*, Bangalore, April June 2000, pp. 49-57.

Ansari, M.A.H., *Sufism and Shari'ah, A Study of Shaykh Ahmad Sirhindi's Efforts to Reform Sufism*, London, 1986.

Antoun, R. & M.E. Hegland, *Religious Resurgence: Contemporary Cases in Islam, Christianity, and Judaism*, New York, 1987.

Arberry, A.J., *Sufism, An Account of the Mystics of Islam*, London, 1950.

Arjomand, S.A. (ed.), *From Nationalism to Revolutionary Islam*, London 1984.

———, *The Shadow of God and the Hidden Imam*, Chicago, 1984.

Arnold, T.W., *The Caliphate*, London, 1965.

Askari, Hasan, *Society and State in Islam, An Introduction,* New Delhi, 1978.

Aviad, Janet, *Return to Judaism, Religious Renewal in Israel,* Chicago, 1983.

Ayalon, Ami, *Language and Change in the Arab Middle East,* New York, 1987.

Ayoob, M. (ed.), *The Politics of Islamic Reassertion,* New York, 1981.

Al-Azmeh, Aziz, "Islamist Revivalism and Western Ideologies," *History Workshop Journal,* 32, 1991, pp. 44, 53.

Bahadur, Kalim, The *Jama'at-I-Islami of Pakistan,* New Delhi, 1977.

Baljon, John, *Modern Muslim Koran Interpretation,* Leiden, 1961.

———, *Religion and Thought of Shah Waliullah Dihlawi 1703-62,* Leiden 1986.

Bannerman, Patrick, *Islam in Perspective, A Guide to Islamic Society, Politics and Law,* London, 1988.

Barr, James, *Fundamentalism,* Philadelphia, 1978.

———, *Beyond Fundamentalism,* Philadelphia 1984.

Binder, Leonard, "al-Ghazali's Theory of Islamic Government," *The Muslim World,* 45, 3 (July 1955), pp. 229, 41.

———, *Religion and Politics in Pakistan,* Berkeley, 1961.

Bowler, Peter J., *Evolution, The History of an Idea,* Berkeley 1984.

Burke, E. & I.M. Lapidus (eds.), *Islam, Politics and Social Movements,* London 1988.

Canfield, R.L. (ed.), *Turko-Persia in Historical Perspective,* Cambridge, 1991.

Carr, E.H., *what is History?,* Penguin Books, 1964

Caplan, Lionel (ed.), *Studies in Religious Fundamentalism,* Albany, 1987.

Cassirer, Ernest, *The Myth of the State,* London, 1946.

Chadwick, Owen, *The Secularization of the European Mind in the Nineteenth Century,* Cambridge, 1975.

Cragg, Kenneth, "The Muslim Brotherhood and Jamaat-i Islami," Counsels in Contemporary Islam, Islamic Survey Series no. 3 (Edinburgh 1965), pp. 110, 24.

Dabashi, Hamid, "Ali Shariati's Islam, Revolutionary Uses of Faith in a Post-Traditional Society," *Islamic Quarterly*, 27, 4 (1983), pp. 203-22.

———, "Islamic Ideology, Perils and Promises of a Neologism" in H. Amirahmadi and M. Parvin (eds.), *Post-Revolutionary Iran*, New York, 1987.

Danner, Victor, "Western Evolutionism in the Muslim World," *The American Journal of Islamic Social Sciences*, 8, 1 (1991), pp. 67, 83.

Donohoe, J.J. & Esposito, J.L. (eds.), *Islam in Transition, Muslim Perspectives*, New York, 1982.

Enayat, Hamid, *Modern Islamic Political Thought*, Austin, 1982.

Esposito, J.L. (ed.), *Voices of Resurgent Islam*, (New York, 1983).

———, (ed.), *Islam in Asia : Religion, Politics, and Society*, Oxford, 1987.

———, *Islam, The Straight Path*, Oxford, 1988.

———, *The Islamic Theart : Myth or Reality*, Oxford, 1992.

———, (ed.), *The Iranian Revolution: Its Global Impact*, Miami, 1990.

Ezzati, Abul-Fazl, *The Revolutionary Islam and the Islamic Revolution*, Islamic Republic of Iran, 1981.

Faruqi, Burhan A., *The Mujaddidi's Concept of Tawhid*, Lahore, 1940.

Faruqi, M. Yusuf, "Early Fuqaha on the Significance and Role of the Khilafah", Hamdard Islamicus, 14, 1 (Spring 1991), pp. 5, 12.

Faruqi, Ziyaul Hasan, *The Deoband School and the Demand For Pakistan*, Bombay, 1963.

Fischer, Michael M.J., *Iran: From Religious Dispute to Revolution*, London, 1980.

Friedmann, Y., *Shaykh Ahmad Sirhindi: An Outline of His Thought and a Study of His Image in the Eyes of Posterity*, Montreal, 1971.

Gaborieau M., Popovic A., and Zarcone, T. (eds.), *Naqshbandis: Historical Development and Present Situation of a Muslim Order*, Istanbul, Paris, 1990.

Geertz, Clifford, *Islam Observed: Religious Development in Morocco and Indonesia*, London, 1968.

Gellner, E., *Nations and Nationalism*, Oxofrd, 1983.

Gibb, H.A.R. & H. Bowen (eds.), *Islamic Society and the West*. London, 1950.

Gibb, H.A.R., "Al-Mawardi's Theory of Khilafah," *Islamic Culture*, 11, 3 (July 1937), pp. 291, 302.

———, *Modern Trends in Islam*, Chicago, 1950.

———, "The Evolution of Government in Early Islam", *Studia Islamica*, 4 (1955), pp. 5, 17.

———, "*Studies on the Civilization of Islam*," ed. by S.J. Shaw and W.R. Polk, Islamic Book Service, Lahore, 1987.

———, "The Heritage of Islam in the Modern World", *International Journal of Middle East Studies*, I (1970), part I, pp. 3, 1 and part II, pp. 221, 37.

Gilani, Syed Asad, *Mawdudi Thought and Movement*, Islamic Pub. (Pvt) Ltd., Lahore, 1984.

Gilsenan, Michael, *Recognising Islam: Religion and Society in the Modern Arab World*, London, 1982.

Gopal, Sarvepalli (ed.), *Anatomy of A Confrontation: The Babri Masjid Ramjanmbhumi Issue*, New Delhi, 1991.

Grunebaum, G.E.V., *Medieval Islam: A Study in Cultural Orientation*, 2nd edn., Chicago, 1953.

———, *Islam: Essays in the Nature and Growth of a Cultural Tradition*, 2nd edn., London, 1961.

Haddad, Y.Y., *Contemporary Islam and the Challenge of History*, Albany, 1982.

———, "The Qur'anic Justification for an Islamic Revolution: The View of Sayyid Qutb," *The Middle East Journal*, (Winter 1983), pp. 14-29.

Haq, S. Moinul, *Islamic Thought and Movement in the Subcontinent (711-1947)*, Pakistan Historical Society, Karachi, 1979.

Haq, M. Anwarul, *The Faith Movement of Mawlana Muhammad Ilyas*, London, 1972.

Hasan, Masudul, *Sayyid Abul Aala Mawdudi And His Thought*, 2 vols., Lahore, 1984 & 1986.

Hashmi, Syed Masroor Ali Akthar, *Muslim Response to Western Education*, Commowealth Pub., New Delhi, 1989.

Hasan, Mushirul, *Nationalism and Communal Politics in India 1916-1928*, New Delhi, 1979.

Hodgson, M.G.S., *The Venture of Islam*, 3 vols., Chicago, 1974.

Hourani, Albert, *Arabic Thought in the Liberal Age 1798-1934*, Cambridge, 1983.

———, *A History of the Arab Peoples*, Cambridge, 1991.

———, "How Should We Write the History of the Middle East?," *International Journal of Middle East Studies*, 23 (1991), pp. 125, 36.

Hudaibi, H.I., *Dua La Quda: Abhath fi al- Aqida al-Islamiyya wa Manhaj al-Da wa Ilallah*, Cairo, Dar al-Tabaa wa al-Nashr al-Islamiyya, n.d.

Hussain, S. Ajaz, *A Brief History of Urdu Literature*, Delhi, 1964.

Ikram, S.M., *Muslim Civilization in India*, ed. A.T. Embree, London, 1964.

Iqbal, Muhammad, *The Reconstruction of Religious Thought in Islam*, London, 1934.

Izutsu, Toshihiko, *God and Man in the Koran: Semantics of the Koranic Weltanschauung*, Tokyo, 1964.

———, "Modern Ideas and Concepts in the Works of Mawlana Sayyid Abul A'La Mawdudi," *Islamic Studies* 42:2 (2003) pp. 247, 352.

Jameelah, Maryam, "An Appraisal of Some Aspects of Mawlana Sayyid A'Lā Maudoodi's Life and Thought," *Islamic Quarterly*, 31, 2 (2nd quarter, 1987), pp. 116, 30.

Jansen, J.G.J., *The Interpretation of the Koran in Modern Egypt*, Leiden, 1974.

———, *The Neglected Duty: The Creed of Sadat's Assassins and Islamic Resurgence in the Middle East*, London, 1986.

Jones, K.W., *Socio-Religious Reform Movements in British India*, The New Cambridge History of India, III.1, Cambridge, 1989.

Kamali, Muhammad Hashim, *Principles of Islamic Jurisprudence*, Pelanduk Publications, Malaysia 1989.

Keddie, N.R. (ed.), *Scholars, Saints and Sufis: Muslim Religious Institutions Since 1500*, Berkeley, 1972.

Kepel, Giles, *The Prophet and Pharaoh: Muslim Extremism in Egypt*, London, 1985.

Kerr, Malcolm, *Islamic Reform: The Political and Legal Theories of Muhammad Abduh and Rashid Rida*, Berkeley, 1966.

Khan, Qamruddin, *The Political Thought of Ibn Taymiyah*, Lahore, 1983.

Lambton, A.K.S., *State and Government in Medieval Islam*, Oxford, 1981.

———, "The Theory of Kingship in the Nishat ul-Muluk of Ghazali," *Islamic Quarterly*, 1, 1 (April 1954), pp. 47, 55.

Lapidus, Ira, *A History of Islamic Societies*, 2nd edn., Cambridge, 1989.

Lawrence, Bruce, *Defenders of God: The Fundamentalis Revolt Against the Modern Age*, London, 1990.

Levtzion, N. & J. Voll (eds.), *Eighteenth Century Renewal and Reform in Islam*, Syracuse, 1987.

Lewis, Bernard, *The Political Language of Islam*, London, 1988.

Lings, Martin, *What is Sufism?*, Berkeley, 1973.

———, *Muhammad*, New York, 1973.

Mahdi, M. and R. Lerner (eds.), *Medieval Political Philosophy*, Illinois, 1963.

Mahdi, Muhsin, "Islamic Philosophy in Contemporary Islamic Thought," in Charles Malik (ed.), *God and Man in Contemporary Islamic Thought*, Beirut, 1972.

Mallat, Chibli, *Shii Thought From the South of Lebanon*, Oxford, 1988.

Manzoor, S.P., "Islam as Politics: The Politics of an Alien Discourse," *Muslim World Book Review*, 9, 3 (1989), pp. 3-12.

———, *"Politics Without Truth, Metaphysics, or Epistemology," Muslim World Book Review*, 10, 4 (1990), pp. 3, 12.

———, "From Guidance to Governance: Discontents of an Ideological Self-Image of Islam," *Muslim World Book Review*, 11, 2 (1991), pp. 3, 14.

———, "The Future of Muslim Politics: Critique of the Fundamentalist' Theory of the Islamic State," *Futures* (April 1991), pp. 289-301.

Marty, Martin (ed.), *Fundamentalisms Observed*, Chicago, 1991.

Matthews, D.J., C. Shackle, and S. Hussain (eds.), *Urdu Literature*, London, 1985.

May, L.S., *The Evolution of Indo-Muslim Thought from 1857 the Present*, New Delhi, Uppal Pub. House, 1987.

McDonough, Sheila, *Muslim Ethics and Modernity: A Comparative Study of the Ethical Thought of Sayyid Ahmad Khan and Mawlana Mawdudi*, Ontario, 1984.

Metcalf, B.D., *Islamic Revival in British India: Deoband 1860-1900*, Princeton, 1982.

———, (ed.), *Moral Conduct and Authority: The Place of Adab in south Asian Islam*, Berkeley, 1984.

———, *Perfecting Women: Mawlana Ashraf Ali Thanwi's Bihishti Zewar*, Oxford, 1990.

Minault, Gail, *The Khilafat Movement: Religious Symbolism and Political Mobilization in India*, Delhi, 1982.

Mir, Mustansir, "Some Features of Mawdudis Tahfim Al-Qur'an," *American Journal of Islamic Social Science*, vol., 2, no. 2, December 1985.

Mitchell, R.P., *The Society of the Muslim Brothers*, London, 1969.

Moussalli, Ahmad, "Sayyid Qutb's View of Knowledge," *The American Journal of Social Sciences*, 7, 3 (1990), pp. 315-33.

Mujeeb, M., *The Indian Muslims*, New Delhi, 1985.

Mutahhari, Martyr Murtada, *Society and History,* Islamic Propagation Organization, International Relation Dept, Iran, 1985.

Nadwi, Abul Hasan Ali, *Life and Mission of Mawlana Mohammad Ilyas,* tr. Muhmmad Asif Kidwai, Lucknow, 1983.

Nadwi, Muzafferdin., *Muslim Thought and its Source,* idarah-i-Adabiyat-i Dellli, Delhi, 1983.

Nasr, S.H., *Traditional Islam in the Modern World,* London, 1987.

———, (ed.), *Islamic Spirituality: Foundations,* London, 1987.

———, (ed.), Islamic Spirituality: Manifestations, London, 1991.

Nasr, S.H., Dabashi, H., Nasr, S.V.R. (eds.), *Expectation of the Millennium: Shiism in History,* Albany, 1989.

Nasr, Sayyed Vali Reza, "Islamic opposition to the Islamic State: the *Jama'at-I-Islami,* 1977-1988," *International Journal of Middle East Studies* 24-4 (November 1992) : 261-283.

———, "Student, Islam, and Politics: Islami Jama'at Talaba in Pakistan," *Middle East Journal* 46.1 (Winter 1992) : 59-76.

———, *The Vanguard of the Islamic Revolution: the Jama'at-I-Islami of Pakistan,* [Berkely University of California Press, 1994].

Nasr, S. H. and Oliver Leaman (eds), *History of Islamic Philosophy,* Routledge, London & N. Y. 1996.

Nicholson, R.A., *The Mystics of Islam,* London, 1963.

Nizami, Farhan A., "Madrasahs, Scholars and Saints: Muslim Response to the British Presence in Delhi and Upper Doab 1803-57" (D. Phil. thesis, University of Oxford, 1983).

Nizami, Khaliq A., *Some Aspects of Religion and Politics in India During the Thirteenth Century,* Bombay, 1961.

———, *Studies in Medieval Indian History,* Allahabad, 1966.

———, "Early Indo-Muslim Mystics and Their Attitude Towards Muslims," *Islamic Culture,* 22, 4 (October 1948), pp. 387-98; 23, 1-2 (January-April 1949), pp. 13-21; 23, 3 (July 1949), pp. 162-70; 23, 4 (October 1949), pp. 312-21; 24, 1 (January 1950), pp. 60-71.

———, "Naqshbandi Influence on Mughal Rulers and Politics," *Islamic Culture,* 34, 1 (January 1965).

Page, David, *Prelude to Partition: The Indian Muslims and the Imperial system of Control 1920-32,* Delhi, 1982.

Philips, Abu Ameenah Bilal, *The Evolution of figh* (*Islamic Law & the madhabs* Tawheed Publications, Riyadh, 1990.

Piscatori, J. (ed.), *Islam in the Political Process,* Cambridge, 1981.

——, *Islam in a World of Nation-States,* Cambridge, 1986.

Pritchett, F.W., *Urdu Literature: A Bibliography of English Language Sources,* New Delhi, 1979.

al-Qaradawi, Y., *Islamic Awakening Between Rejection and Extremism,* Washington, D.C., 1981.

Quddus, Sayed Abdul, *Islamic Polity in Modern Times,* Feroz Sons (Pvt) Ltd., - Pakistan, 1987.

Qureshi, I.H., *The Administration of the Sultanate of Delhi,* 4th edn., Karachi, 1958.

———, *Ulama in Politics: A Study Relating to the Political Activities of the Ulama in the South Asian Sub-Continent From 1556-1947,* Karachi, 1974.

Qutb, Sayyid, *Ma alim fi al-Tariq,* Kuwait, 1978.

———, *Hadha al-Din,* Kuwait, 1978.

———, *Al-Khasa is al-Tasawwur al-Islami,* Kuwait, 1978.

———, *Al-Mustaqbal li Hadha al-Din,* Kuwait, 1978.

Rahman, Fazlur, "Muslim Modernism in the Indo-Pakistan Subcontinent," *Bulletin of the School of Oriental and African Studies* 21 (1958), pp. 82, 99.

———, *Islamic Methodology in History,* Karachi, 1965.

———, "Implementation of the Islamic Concept of State in Pakistani Milieu," *Islamic Studies,* 6, 3 (September 1967), pp. 205-24.

———, *Major Themes of the Qur'an,* Chicago, 1980.

———, *Islam and Modernity: Transformation of an Intellectual Tradition,* Chicago, 1982.

Rizvi, S.A.A., *Muslim Revivalist Movements in Northern India in the Sixteenth and Seventeenth Centuries,* Agra, 1965.

———, *A History of Sufism in India*, vols. I & II, New Delhi, 1975 and 1983.

———, *Shah Waliullah and His Times: A Study of 18th Century Islam, Politics and Society in India,* Canberra, 1980.

Robinson, Francis, *Separatism Among Indian Muslims: The Politics of the United Provinces' Muslims, 1860-1923,* Cambridge, 1974.

———, "Islam and Muslim Society in South Asia," *Contributions to Indian Sociology,* 17, 2 (1983), pp. 185-203.

———, "The Ulama of Farangi Mahall and Their Adab," in B.D. Metcalf, Moral *Conduct and Authority,* Berkeley, 1984, pp. 152, 83.

———, "Technology and Religious change: Islam and the Impact of Print," *Modern Asian Studies* (forthcoming).

Rosenthal, E.I.J., *Political Thought in Medieval Islam,* Cambridge, 1958.

———, *Islam in the Modern National State,* Cambridge, 1965.

Rumi, Jalaluddin, *The Mathnawi of Jalaluddin Rumi,* tr. and ed. R.A. Nicholson, London, 1925-40, 8 vols.

Sadiq, Muhammad, *Twentieth Century Urdu Literature,* Karachi, 1983.

———, *A History of Urdu Literature,* Delhi, 1984.

Sarkar, Sumit, *Modern India 1885-1947,* New Delhi, 1983.

Schacht, J. and C.E. Bosworth, *The Legacy of Islam,* 2nd edn., Oxford, 1974.

Schall, J.V., Reason, *Revelation, and the Foundations of Political Philosophy,* London, 1987.

Schimmel, A., *Mystical Dimensions of Islam,* Chapel Hill, North Carolina, 1975.

———, *Islam in the Indian Subcontinent,* Leiden, 1980.

Sharif, M.M., *Muslim Thought its Origin and Achievements,* Institute of Islamic Culture, Lahore, 1980.

Shariati, Ali, *Marxism and Other Western Fallacies,* tr. R. Campbell, Berkeley, 1980.

———, *On the Sociology of Islam,* tr. Hamid Algar, Berkeley, 1979.

Siddique, Sharon, "Conceptualizing Contemporary Islam: Religion or Ideology?," *Annual Review of the Social Sciences and Religion*, 5 (1981), pp. 203-23.

Sirriyeh, Elizabeth, "Modern Muslim Interpretations of Shirk," *Religion*, 20 (1990), pp. 139-59.

Sivan, E., *Radical Isıam Medieval Theology and Modern Politics*, London, 1985.

———, "Sunni Radicalism in the Middle East and the Iranian Revolution," *International Journal of Middle East Studies*, 21 (1989), pp. 1-30.

———, and M. Friedman (eds.), *Religious Radicalism and Politics in the Middle East*, New York, 1990.

Smith, W.C., *Modern Islam in India: A Social Analysis*, London, 1946.

———, *Islam in Modern History*, London, 1957.

———, *On Understanding Islam Select Studies*, Idarah-i Adabiyat Delhi, Delhi, 1995.

Stoddard, P.H., D.C. Cuthell, and M.W. Sullivan (eds.), *Change and the Muslim World*, New York, 1981.

Stowasser, Barbara (ed.), *The Islamic Impulse*, London, 1987.

Troll, C.W., *Sayyid Ahmad Khan: A Reinterpretation of Muslim Theology*, New Delhi, 1978.

———, Modern Islamic Trends in Indian Islamic Thought: The Recent Past" the paper submitted to the Conference at Sophia University, Tokyo, Japan, in July 1986.

Turner, B.S., Weber and Islam, London, 1974.

Voll, J.O., "The Sudanese Mahdi: Frontier Fundamentalist," *International Journal of Middle East Studies*, 10 (1979), pp. 145-66.

———, *Islam: Continuity and Change in the Modern World*, Boulder, Colorado, 1982.

Watt, W.M., *Muhammad at Mecca*, Oxford, 1953.

———, *Muhammad at Medina*, Oxford, 1956.

———, *Islamic Political Thought: The Basic Concepts*, Edinbourgh, 1968.

The Formative Period of Islamic Through, Edinburgh, 1973.

Welch, A.T. and P. Cachin (eds.), *Islam: Past Influences and Present Challenges*, Edinbourgh, 1979.

Wendell, C. (tr.), *Five Tracts of Hasan al-Banna (1906-1949): A Selection from Majmu at al-Rasail al-Imam al-Shaykh*, London, 1978.

Zubaida, Sami, *Islam, the People and the State*, London, 1988.

Reference Books

Abdullah Yusuf Ali, *The Holy Qur'an: Text, Translation and Commentary*, Saudi Arabia, n.d., first published in 1934.

Francis Robinson, *Atlas of the Islamic World Since 1500*, Oxford: Phaidon, 1982, pp. 118-29.

P.M. Holt, A.K.S. Lambton and B. Lewis (eds.), *Cambridge History of Islam*, Cambridge, 1970.

J.D. Pearson (comp.), *Index Islamicus*, Cambridge, 1958.

V.V. Tsybulsky, *Calendars of Middle East Countries: Conversion Tables and Explanatory Notes*, Moscow, "Nauka" Publishing House, 1979.

The Encyclopedia of Islam, 1st edn., Leiden: E.J. Brill, 3 vols., 1927-1936.

Shorter Encyclopedia of Islam, Leiden, E.J. Brill, 1953.

Dastur-i Jama at-i Islami-i Hind, 8th edn., Delhi, Markaz Jamaat-i Islami-i Hind, 1992.

Khalil Ahmed Hamidi, Naeem Siddiqi, Jameel Ahmed Rana Saleem Mansoor Khalid (eds), *Majllah-Tazkirah Sayyid Mawdudi*, Matabah ma'rif Islami, Lahore.

Jamaat-i Islami-i Hind: Aik Ta aruf, Delhi: Markazi Maktaba-i Islami, 1990.

The Constitution of the Jamaat-e Islami Hind: As Amended upto March 1990, Delhi, Markazi Maktaba Islami, 1991.

Periodicals

Bulletin of the School of Oriental and African Studies (London)

Der Islam (Berlin)

International Journal of Middle East Studies (Cambridge)

Islamic Culture (Heyderabad)

Islamic Quarterly (London)

Islamic Studies (Islamabdad)

Middle East Journal (Washington)

Middle Eastern Studies (London)

Muslim World (Hartford, CT, USA)

Muslim World Book Review (Leicester, U.K.)

Studia Islamica (Princeton)

Tamir-i Hayat (Urdu fortnightly, Lucknow)

Al-Ma'arif (Bilingual Urdu + English, Lohore)

Radiance (Delhi)

Zindagi-i-Nau (Urdu, Monthly, Delhi).

Index